SOCIAL CHANGE AND THE FAMILY IN TAIWAN

POPULATION AND DEVELOPMENT
A series edited by Richard A. Easterlin

PREVIOUSLY PUBLISHED
FERTILITY CHANGE IN CONTEMPORARY JAPAN
Robert W. Hodge and Naohiro Ogawa

SOCIAL CHANGE AND THE FAMILY IN TAIWAN

Arland Thornton and
Hui-Sheng Lin

with contributions by
Jui-Shan Chang
Ming-Cheng Chang
Deborah S. Freedman
Ronald Freedman
Thomas E. Fricke
Albert I. Hermalin
Mei-Lin Lee
Paul K. C. Liu
Te-Hsiung Sun
Maxine Weinstein
Li-Shou Yang

THE UNIVERSITY OF CHICAGO PRESS
CHICAGO AND LONDON

Arland Thornton is professor in the Department of Sociology,
research scientist at the Institute for Social Research, and
research associate at the Population Studies Center at the
University of Michigan. Hui-Sheng Lin is chief of the
Research and Planning Division of the Taiwan Provincial
Institute of Family Planning.

The University of Chicago Press, Chicago 60637
The University of Chicago Press, Ltd., London
© 1994 by The University of Chicago
All rights reserved. Published 1994
Printed in the United States of America

03 02 01 00 99 98 97 96 95 94   1 2 3 4 5

ISBN: 0-226-79858-5 (cloth)

Library of Congress Cataloging-in-Publication Data

Thornton, Arland.
    Social change and the family in Taiwan / Arland Thornton and Hui-
Sheng Lin ; with contributions by Jui-Shan Chang . . . [et al.].
        p.   cm. — (Population and development)
    Includes bibliographical references and index.
    1. Family—Taiwan. 2. Marriage—Taiwan. 3. Taiwan—Social
conditions—1988–   I. Lin, Hui-Sheng. II. Title. III. Series:
Population and development (Chicago, Ill.)
HQ686.T48   1994
306.85′095124′9—dc20   94-8973

CONTENTS

PREFACE

This book was designed as a collaborative project between the Taiwan Provincial Institute of Family Planning and the University of Michigan. This international collaboration with the Taiwan Institute has involved the University's Population Studies Center for more than three decades, under the leadership of Ronald Freedman and Albert Hermalin. The Family and Demography Program of the University's Survey Research Center, under the leadership of Arland Thornton, has been an active participant during the last thirteen years. During these three decades the collaboration has involved all phases of the research process, including study design, data collection, data analysis, and the preparation of research reports.

For this book the research team from the Taiwan Provincial Institute of Family Planning included its director, Ming-Cheng Chang, as well as Hui-Sheng Lin and Mei-Lin Lee, now of the National Chung-cheng University. Important collaboration was also provided by Te-Hsiung Sun (chairman of the Research, Development and Evaluation Commission of the Executive Yuan of the Republic of China), the Institute's former director, and Paul K. C. Liu of Academia Sinica. Hui-Sheng Lin coordinated the efforts of the Family Planning Institute.

The University of Michigan was represented by Ronald Freedman, the Michigan initiator of the original collaboration, Deborah Freedman, Thomas Fricke, Albert Hermalin, Li-Shou Yang, Arland Thornton, and Jui-Shan Chang, now of the University of Tasmania. Maxine Weinstein of Georgetown University also participated with the Michigan team. The efforts of the Michigan group were coordinated by Arland Thornton, who also provided overall leadership for the preparation of the book.

Financial support for the research provided in this book has also been collaborative. From the American side, research funds were provided by the National Institute of Child Health and Human Development. Chinese institutions providing financial support were the Chiang Ching-kuo Foundation for International Scholarly Exchange and the Republic of China Committee for Scientific and Scholarly Cooperation with the

United States, Academia Sinica. The Institute for Social Research, the Office of the Vice-President for Research, and the Population Studies Center of the University of Michigan provided financial support for the publication of the book itself.

The detailed research agenda and plans for the book were formulated at a workshop in Ann Arbor, Michigan, in August of 1988. The implementation of the research plan has involved extensive communication between the co-authors and several additional workshops in Taiwan and Michigan on issues of data, analysis strategies, and the texts of individual chapters.

The book was designed as an integrated volume that tells a unified story about family change in Taiwan. The chapters of the book address a set of interrelated issues and themes with a common voice. Those chapters were motivated by a common set of questions: What are the causal determinants of family structures and processes in Taiwan? How have family forms and relationships changed in Taiwan in recent decades? And what are the causal forces that have produced family change in Taiwan? Our research concerning these issues was organized around the life-course perspective and the modes of organization framework. These guiding questions and organizational frameworks are interwoven through the chapters of the book.

In addition to the close collaboration of the co-authors on their individual chapters, their numerous suggestions about chapters of which they were not primary authors strengthened the unity of the book. In addition to her role as a chapter co-author, Deborah Freedman edited many of the other chapters.

Many people other than the authors have made significant contributions to this volume. Judy Baughn has provided overall administrative support for the project. Linda Young-DeMarco made significant contributions in managing and processing data for the project. Kashif Sheikh helped with the organization of data and with the preparation of the manuscript and bibliography. Cindy Glovinsky prepared the index for the book and made numerous useful editorial suggestions for improving the quality of presentation. Additional valuable secretarial and computer assistance was given by Lois Groesbeck, Ingrid Naaman, and Cathy Sun. Additional assistance was provided by Jennifer Cancio, Annette Dentel, and Barbara Downs.

The book has benefited from comments and suggestions made by Richard Easterlin, editor of the series of which the book is a part.

We also appreciate the assistance of Geoffrey Huck, Karen Peterson, and Jennie Lightner of the University of Chicago Press, who have interacted with us with helpfulness and patience.

Finally, we express our appreciation to the Taiwanese men and women who provided the data that made this research possible. We especially acknowledge the thousands of individual Taiwanese who participated in the surveys that make up the bulk of the empirical evidence used in this book. We are also appreciative of the work of the staff of the Taiwan Provincial Institute of Family Planning, who conducted the high quality surveys used in the book.

Arland Thornton and Hui-Sheng Lin

One

Introduction

A. Thornton and H. S. Lin

Although social scientists have been studying family change for more than two centuries, the influence of large-scale social and economic transformations on family life remains one of today's controversial issues. Many of these debates center on the extent to which family relationships are modified by the social and economic forces of industrialization, urbanization, educational expansion, income growth, mortality decline, and intensive contact with other cultures. How do these transformations of social and economic organization change the ways in which marriages are formed and dissolved, the number and spacing of children, living arrangements, intergenerational relations, and extended family contacts? Which social and economic factor has the most influence on family change, and what aspects of family structure and relationships are the most susceptible to these forces? What are the causal mechanisms or forces that transmit the influence of such economic and social forces to trends in family and kinship relations?

This book contributes to an understanding of these issues through an intensive investigation of family change during the recent social and economic transformation of Taiwan. Our concern is with family change in Taiwan throughout the twentieth century, although we focus most intensively on the period following World War II. The research reported in this book was designed as a case study of social, economic, and family change in a single setting, with the central purpose of answering these questions for one society. However, at the same time that this is a case study of a single society, the hypotheses, conclusions, and explanations derived from the Taiwanese experience have relevance for understanding these same questions in other populations.

This opening chapter provides an introduction and overview of the book. We begin with a brief discussion of family life in the past in Taiwan and a summary of the social and economic transformations that have occurred in recent decades. The next part of the chapter introduces the reader to two conceptual frameworks used in the analysis—focusing on the life course perspective and the modes of organization framework.

We follow our discussion of conceptual frameworks with a presentation of our general methodological approaches to documenting and explaining family change.

Chinese migrants left their homes in southeastern China in the seventeenth and eighteenth centuries to settle in Taiwan. Although the rigors of the migration and living in a frontier society disrupted some aspects of social and economic life, these settlers brought the basic elements of historical Chinese culture with them to Taiwan, where they established a society that was overwhelmingly rural and primarily based on agriculture and fishing. Kinship was an essential feature of the Chinese culture these immigrants carried to Taiwan, and many of the activities of individual men, women, and children were conducted within family units. People relied heavily upon their kinspeople for means of subsistence, and information and skills were obtained largely from other family members. The central structures of authority for most Taiwanese were also based on kinship.

At the beginning of the twentieth century the structures of family processes and relationships in Taiwan were generally similar to those observed in Chinese families on the mainland (see chap. 2). Kinship was a central part of Chinese cosmology, with family relationships extending both to the ancestors of the past and to the future generations of unborn family members. Families were viewed as the primary societal units, and the interests of individuals were generally secondary to those of the larger family. Family elders were accorded great respect and exercised extensive authority over younger family members. The extended family was the ideal residential institution for Chinese women, men, and children, although high mortality precluded many from living in extended households. Marriages were early, universal, and arranged by the older generation, while childbearing levels were moderately high.

Taiwan became a colony of Japan in 1895 and continued so until Japan's defeat at the end of World War II. Taiwanese society experienced a number of changes during the Japanese period, including improvements in health, expanded educational opportunities, increased agricultural production, and improvements in transportation. Despite these important changes, the island emerged from Japanese colonization with a primarily rural and agricultural population with limited educational attainment (see chap. 3).

Social and economic change in Taiwan since World War II has been rapid (chap. 3). Taiwan has been transformed from an agricultural to an industrial society, utilizing the latest technology and the most efficient means of production, and is now an important international economic power with a rapidly expanding standard of living. It has also become an urban society: the major cities have been greatly expanded, and the rural areas have been incorporated into the urban system through impressive networks of transportation and communication. Educational opportunities have expanded manyfold, creating a current generation of very well educated men and women. The population is now integrated into the world system through numerous economic linkages, through the importation of news and information, and through the extensive travel of Taiwanese to other parts of the world.

If social scientists at the end of World War II had been able to foresee the future social and economic transformation of Taiwanese society, they would have confidently predicted that those changes would produce significant modifications in family life (Burgess and Locke 1953; Davis 1955; Notestein 1953). Their predictions would have been based upon nearly two centuries of social science literature reporting how the central features of family life in Western societies had been changed by industrialization, urbanization, and economic growth (Groves and Ogburn 1928; Durkheim 1984; Le Play 1982; Malthus 1986; Millar 1979; Westermarck 1894). This scholarly literature indicated that social and economic changes like those experienced in Taiwan after 1950 would lead to many family changes, including (1) a change from family-based social relationships to a life style with few obligatory family responsibilities and more allowance for individualistic interests; (2) a shift from extended to nuclear living arrangements and a contraction of kin networks; (3) shifts from young and universal marriage to older ages at marriage with many persons remaining single; (4) the transformation of marriage from an institution controlled by the older generation with little emphasis on sentiment to an arrangement among young people who regarded interpersonal attraction as an important component; and (5) the reduction of childbearing.

These ideas about the ways large-scale social and economic transformation modified family life had been refined by several generations of social scientists and had diffused beyond the boundaries of academia to become assimilated into the accepted wisdom of Western culture. This body of research and theory would have made it easy for scholars at mid-century to make confident predictions about how social and economic change would influence the nature of family life in Taiwan.

However, beginning in the 1960s and extending through the 1980s, the accepted wisdom about the effects of such transformations on family life was challenged by historical studies of family life in Western societies which demonstrated that many of the earlier conclusions about family life in the Western past had no basis in the historical record (Anderson 1986; Goode 1970; Hajnal 1965; Laslett 1974, 1978; Macfarlane 1979, 1986; Pollock 1985; Stone 1982; Watkins 1986a). These historical studies showed that the social and economic changes that had occurred in Western societies had not produced many of the family changes that several generations of earlier scholars had written about. In fact, the data showed that several key features of Western family life previously believed to have been the result of important social and economic changes were widespread in many Western societies before the other changes occurred. So revolutionary was this new historical research that many of the earlier conclusions have been labeled as myths in the recent literature (Goode 1970; Laslett 1987; Mount 1982; Ruggles 1987; Thornton 1991).

The story of family change in Western societies and the methodological and conceptual errors that produced the erroneous views have been discussed elsewhere and are beyond the scope of this book about Taiwan (Thornton 1991). For our purpose it is sufficient to note that the collapse of the knowledge and explanations of two centuries of family research transformed the well-accepted conclusions of the middle twentieth century into questions for today's research. It was no longer clear how family structures and processes in diverse societies are influenced by industrialization, urbanization, the expansion of education, declines in mortality, and expanded contacts with other societies. These discoveries also reopened old questions about the causal mechanisms connecting these societal transformations to changes in the various dimensions of family life. With the disintegration of the old knowledge, these questions have emerged again as central issues in family and demographic studies.

However, at the same time that research in Western societies was casting doubt on the extensiveness of historical trends in marriage, living arrangements, and intergenerational relations, studies of other populations were revealing important changes in these central family matters (Goode 1970). While a thorough review of this literature is beyond the scope of this book, we note that several recent studies have documented increases in age at marriage throughout large segments of Asia, declines in extended family living in several societies, and movement away from arranged marriages toward love matches in both Japan and mainland China (Atoh 1988, 1990; Barrett 1985; Cheung 1988, 1990; Feeney and Saito 1985; Kojima 1989; Kumagai forthcoming; Morgan and Hirosima 1983; Smith 1980; Tsuya 1991; United Nations 1989; Whyte 1988; Whyte and Parish 1984). All of these trends appear to be related to the social and economic changes occurring in these societies, but data limitations have prevented researchers from being able to specify precisely the causal forces responsible for the observed changes.

Several factors make Taiwan a valuable laboratory for addressing important unanswered questions concerning family change and economic and social transformation. As chapter 3 documents in detail, Taiwan has experienced unusually rapid social and economic changes in recent decades, which provide the opportunity to study the effects of such changes on family life without having to document centuries of history.

Taiwan, as appendix A details, also has extensive data resources which make possible the documentation of the changes that have occurred. These data resources include extensive vital statistics concerning marriage, divorce, childbearing, and mortality derived from a household registration system in existence since just after the turn of the century, as well as a sophisticated set of censuses covering most of the twentieth century. Taiwan also has been the locus of extensive ethnographic research qualitatively documenting structure and process in Chinese social life. Our research has also relied heavily on a series of island-wide surveys designed specifically for studying family and demographic change in Taiwan. These surveys were begun in the early 1960s and include repeated cross-sectional studies with a wide range of respondents. There also are panel studies of the same individuals over time. These data make it possible to document family trends during Taiwan's social and economic change from an agricultural to an industrial society. They also permit the evaluation of interrelationships among various family changes as well as the relationships between family change and trends in economic and social life. Thus, in Taiwan we can examine many dimensions of family change that are difficult to study in many other societies.

While the data available provide many opportunities for the study of family change in Taiwan, they also have their limitations. In many instances the time series we use are too short to document the beginnings of the important family changes of interest. The data also are limited in providing information about the complex and dynamic interrelationships among family members living in different households and communities. The data are also overwhelmingly quantitative, making it difficult to ascertain the insights about family change available from more qualitative approaches. Nevertheless, the breadth of the data that are available provides an opportunity to document and explain many important dimensions of family change in Taiwan.

Another advantage of conducting family research in Taiwan is that the population is relatively homogeneous. With the exception of a modest number of aboriginal people, the population is composed of Han Chinese who came to Taiwan in several waves of migration from the mainland. In addition, there has been little migration into or away from Taiwan during the past four decades.

Taiwan also is an excellent setting for the evaluation of theoretical ideas about family change because of the characteristics of the historical Chinese family system. As discussed earlier, the theoretical arguments offered by several generations of earlier social scientists to explain family change were formulated for societies with extended families, high parental authority, little individualism, arranged marriage, and young and universal marriage. Since many Western societies apparently did not have these family characteristics during the last several hundred years, it is difficult to use Western data to evaluate how different social and economic forces might influence such family characteristics. Since Taiwan had virtually all of these family attributes in its past, it is a particularly appropriate place to test those theoretical propositions.

Finally, Taiwan is a valuable laboratory for the study of family, social, and economic change because the historical structure of Chinese families shares many of its central features with numerous other family systems around the world. While each social system has its own unique family characteristics, many societies have historically had extended families, arranged marriages, high parental authority, low levels of individualism, and young and universal marriage. While we caution against applying our findings from Taiwan directly to other populations undergoing social and economic change, our conclusions should be valuable in generating useful ideas and hypotheses about family change in many other social settings. For all of these reasons, research focused on family change in Taiwan has a high potential for providing valuable scientific answers to central questions about family change.

Answers to the questions motivating this book require reliable basic descriptions of changes and continuities in Taiwanese economic, social, and family life. Chapter 2 utilizes both ethnographic and quantitative data collected in Chinese societies to document some of the central features of Chinese family life as they existed during the first half of the twentieth century and during the years immediately after World War II. While the bulk of this information is from Taiwan, some useful data from mainland China, the ancestral homeland of today's Taiwanese, are utilized for understanding Chinese family life in the past. Chapter 3 documents social and economic changes in Taiwan using information from a wide variety of vital statistics information, censuses, and population surveys. Beginning in chapter 5, we document recent family change in Taiwan and show how those trends are interrelated with ongoing social and economic changes.

Our investigation of family change focuses on the following dimensions of Taiwanese life: how families fit within the larger social organization of Chinese society; living arrangements; the linkages of the living with their ancestors; mate selection; the formation and dissolution of marital unions; and reproductive behavior. While some information is provided about family change in Taiwan before World War II, the primary emphasis of the book concerns family trends after the war.

While we believe that all of the aspects of family life covered in this book are important, we make no claims that they exhaust all familial dimensions worthy of study. In fact, we explicitly acknowledge that several important topics of family life in Taiwan receive insufficient coverage. Included among these are family relationships that extend beyond the household and the content of gender roles, particularly relationships between husbands and wives. In addition, while we address some issues of attitudes and values, we do not provide adequate coverage of the symbolic content of family life.

Conceptual Frameworks and Methodological Approaches

In the following sections of this chapter we provide a general introduction to two interrelated conceptual frameworks used in our analysis—the modes of social organization framework and the life course perspective. We consider these conceptual frameworks here because they provide overall direction to the specific theorization and analyses of the subsequent chapters. Following our discussion of the life course perspective we present our general methodological approaches to studying individual change across the life course, to investigating trends across historical time, and to separating individual aging effects from those of historical change. This discussion also describes our approach to estimation of the empirical factors that explain the observed historical trends.

While the following sections of this chapter provide a general conceptual framework, we reserve until chapter 4 a discussion of the specific ways we use these conceptual frameworks to theorize about family change in Taiwan. This division of labor between the two chapters is necessitated by the fact that theorization about family change in any society must explicitly consider both the structure of family life in that society's past and the nature of social and economic change in that society. Since our detailed discussion of historical patterns of Chinese family life comes in chapter 2 and our examination of social and economic trends occurs in chapter 3, we postpone discussion of specific theoretical ideas and expectations until chapter 4.

Modes of Social Organization

In our study of family changes in Taiwan and the ways they are interrelated with other social and economic forces we modify and expand the modes of social organization framework proposed by Thornton and Fricke (1987). The modes of social organization framework focuses on the social institutions which organize individual lives and interpersonal relationships. Particular attention is given to the extent to which individual lives are organized and experienced within family units rather than being directed and shaped by institutions based on nonfamilial relationships.

The modes of organization approach builds on the observations of many social scientists that the position of families in the larger social structure affects many dimensions of individual and family life (Durkheim 1978, 1984; Ogburn and Tibbitts 1933; Parsons and Bales 1955). Much of this literature focuses on the activities of individuals, particularly economic production (Caldwell 1976; Sahlins 1972; E. Wolf 1982). Other discussions have considered a broader range of activities, including education, reproduction, protection, and social and emotional support (Ogburn and Tibbitts 1933; Parsons and Bales 1955; Thornton and Fricke 1987).

This framework also focuses on the structure of authority, resources, information, associates, and beliefs about the cosmos. Thus, it examines the social organizations which have authority over the lives of individuals, the institutions which manage and coordinate individual activities, the social units where people spend their time, and the nature of the relationships between interacting individuals. The framework also considers the social units controlling scarce resources, including information, knowledge, skill, land, and the daily necessities of life. Also included in the framework is the organization of the cosmos and the way world views interrelate with human social institutions.

The central issue for the modes of organization framework is the extent to which authority, activities, resources, associates, and the cosmos are organized within kinship units rather than by nonfamilial institutions. This perspective asks how much time individuals spend within family groups performing tasks organized by familial authority as compared to activities managed and directed by schools, factories, or governmental agencies. It also compares the amount of information, skills, and other scarce resources obtained through relatives to that received from the mass media, the state, and schools. The distribution of authority between familial and nonfamilial units and the extent to which the cosmos is organized along familial rather than nonfamilial lines are also relevant to the modes of organization perspective.

The degree of familial organization can vary across individuals, over an individual's lifetime, across cultures, and across time within the same society. For these reasons it is useful to conceptualize modes of organization at both the micro- and the macrolevels.

While we believe that the degree of family organization should be considered separately for the various domains of human life, it is also useful to consider the extent to which the total set of human concerns is organized within families. To do this we formulate two distinct types that anchor the ends of a continuum of social organization. On one end is the family mode of organization in which all of the dimensions of life are organized within families. In this mode people experience all their activities, associates, information, means of subsistence, cosmology, and authority within a family frame of reference. Similarly, at the societal level one could imagine a familial mode of social organization in which all individuals have every aspect of their lives organized through kinship relationships. Thus, in a society with a familial mode of social organization, societal structure is undifferentiated, with all domains of human life organized within a matrix of kinship relations.

As noted elsewhere, the family mode of social organization is consistent with a wide range of social and economic settings (Thornton and Fricke 1987). While generally associated with rural societies, it can also exist in urban settings. The potential importance of family organization in urban settings is illustrated by Laslett (1984), who describes how economic enterprises were organized by families in London in the past.

In contrast to the family mode of organization is the nonfamilial mode of organization, in which no life domain is conducted within families. Since there are many nonfamilial institutions that can encompass the multiple domains of human life, there are also numerous ways in which individuals and societies can depart from a family mode of organization. For example, departures from family organization could take place through involvement with the institutions of school, factory, government, or the mass media. Consequently, this end of the organizational continuum is labeled simply as a nonfamilial mode of organization to emphasize the absence of the organizational characteristics found in the familial mode of organization at the opposite end of the continuum.

Departures from the relative uniformity of the family mode of organization toward the nonfamilial pole of the continuum are associated with a more complex or differentiated structure of social institutions.

Of course, the familial and nonfamilial modes of social organization are not descriptions of actual individuals or societies, but conceptual devices for categorizing and measuring social organization. Individuals and societies empirically similar to the familial end of the continuum are described as having familial modes of organizations, while situations empirically similar to the nonfamilial end are characterized as nonfamilial modes of organizations. Most individuals and societies, however, fall between the two polar types.

Although the family mode of organization has been conceptualized as an ideal type, there are numerous individual and social circumstances that come close to fitting the typology. Numerous scholars, including Millar (1979), Le Play (1982), Durkheim (1984), Parsons and Bales (1955), and Ogburn and Tibbitts (1933), have observed that in most historical societies the basic principle of social organization was the family. These societies were primarily family-based in that substantial fractions of individual experiences and activities were organized and managed by family units so that the range of individual activities was generally carried out within families. While recent research shows more extrafamilial organization of social life in past Western populations than previously recognized (Macfarlane 1979, 1986; Wilson and Dyson 1987), social organization in those societies was closer to the familial than to the nonfamilial end of the continuum (Demos 1970; Laslett 1984; Lesthaeghe 1980; Tilly and Scott 1978). This characterization becomes even clearer if the predominant familial organization of the past is compared with the more nonfamilial organization currently existing in Western societies.

The family mode of organization characterizes previous Chinese populations since many of the dimensions of life were conducted within kinship groups (Cohen 1970, 1976; Gallin 1966; Greenhalgh 1982b, 1985; Hsu 1971). The activities of individuals were largely conducted within family contexts, close associates were primarily family members, information and the means of subsistence were largely obtained through kinsmen, the universe included important family relationships, and family authority was very important in the lives of individuals (see chap. 2). Thus, family relationships were the dominant mode of social organization in Taiwan at the end of the nineteenth century.

While the Chinese mode of organization was primarily familial in the past, there also were important elements of nonfamilial organization. In the economic sphere there were many nonfamilial elements, including the rental of land from unrelated landlords, the employment of wage laborers who were not kinsmen, and involvement in an impersonal market of consumption and capital goods (Freedman 1964; Fried 1953; Greenhalgh 1990). Land in Taiwan was concentrated in the hands of landlords who rented it to tenant farmers. At the end of World War II many Taiwanese farm operators were landless and had to rent land at a high price from landlords, which involved negotiation and cash transfers outside of the family circle (see chap. 3).

Another important nonfamilial institution is the state, which has long had an important role in Chinese society (Freedman 1964; Fried 1953). Schools have also been important institutions in Chinese cultures for many years. However, even where other organizational levels played a role in Chinese society in the past, they were often modeled on existing family institutions. The very important nonfamilial institution of the imperial bureaucracy ratified commonly held norms of familial authority. The relatively high social mobility permitted by the civil exam system also emphasized family organization because the education needed to succeed on the exams was provided in lineage schools. At the same time, training in the Confucian classics emphasized familial norms, and the openness of this training to all strata ensured that these norms percolated through all social levels (see chap. 2). Many of the social relationships outside the kinship network also incorporated quasi-kin elements.

There are many reasons to believe that the social and economic transformation of Taiwan during the twentieth century would substantially modify the existing family mode of organization. As chapter 3 will document, many of the social and economic changes during the twentieth century have involved the proliferation and expansion of many nonfamilial social institutions, including the state, schools, factories, and the mass media. As a result of this differentiation of society, there could be declines in the amount of time spent with relatives and in the percentage of activities organized and directed by family institutions. There are also likely to be increases in the amount of information obtained outside the family and in the sharing of authority between families and other organizational entities. Numerous studies have shown that similar social and economic changes in other societies have shifted their populations from the familial to more nonfamilial modes of organization (Atoh 1988; Demos 1970; Laslett 1984; Ogburn and Tibbitts 1933; Thornton and Fricke 1987).

Since Chinese populations were historically very close to the familial end of the mode of organization continuum, the potential for change toward the nonfamilial pole was especially great. Chapter 5 provides empirical evidence concerning this issue, showing that the transformation of the mode of organization in Taiwan has been both substantial and rapid. That chapter also shows how this change has been guided by historical Chinese values and social structure so that important continuities are noted along with the significant changes.

The social and economic transformation of Taiwan and the resultant change in the family mode of organization have potentially important implications for many dimensions of individual and family behavior. The shift of many activities, associations, resources, and authority structures from familial to nonfamilial units has the potential for modifying significantly relationships within families and the interests and motivations of individuals. There are good reasons to believe that dramatic changes in the modes of organization in Taiwan have had important effects on marriage arrangements, marital timing, marital dissolution, childbearing, living arrangements, interactions with family members, and relationships with the ancestors. Of course, the direction and magnitude of the changes in family behavior and structure resulting from modification of the family mode of organization depend both upon the organization of family relationships and behavior in the past and the nature of the social and economic changes that occurred, topics that are addressed in chapters 2 and 3. For this reason we postpone until chapter 4 a discussion of the causal mechanisms that would translate the transformation of the family mode of organization into changes in other dimensions of family life. Chapter 4 also addresses the potential influence of other changes in Taiwanese history, such as the large influx of people from mainland China in the late 1940s, on family structure and behavior.

The Life Course Perspective

The life course perspective focuses on individual human beings and their journeys through life (Elder 1977, 1987). This framework takes a broad perspective on human life and considers many different forces influencing behavior and experience across the life span, including the biological, social, cultural, economic, and demographic (Elder 1977, 1987; Featherman and Lerner 1985; Hagestad and Neugarten 1985).

While the life course perspective explicitly recognizes the influences of internal biological forces in human behavior, it also embeds the lives of individual human beings within a complex web of social groups and relationships. Individuals are influenced by the many people around them, including those in small intimate groups, in the surrounding neighborhood and community, and in the larger society, as well as by the culture, economy, and political system of their community. An important feature of life course studies is analysis of the ways in which these familial, community, and societal forces influence individual behavior and relationships.

To understand social influences on individual behavior, we merge the life course perspective with the modes of social organization framework. As a result, we consider the activities of individuals, their patterns of authority, their sources of information and physical sustenance, and the people with whom they associate. As indicated earlier, a central issue in the modes of organization perspective is the organizational locus of these social dimensions of the life course, with particular emphasis upon whether these aspects of human life occur within the family or within other social groups or institutions.

A crucial dimension of the life course perspective is the web of interconnecting relationships with other people. The experiences of individuals intersect and overlap with many different people across the life course, each of whom can have a substantial influence on individual behavior and experience (Kahn and Antonucci 1981). In societies characterized by a family mode of organization, these associates are usually family members, but even in such societies one's associates may include unrelated neighbors, friends, and co-workers.

The life course perspective focuses on the roles that people occupy, including the familial roles of child, spouse, parent, grandparent, and mother-in-law as well as nonfamilial roles such as student, worker, and serviceman. Given the multiple roles people occupy and the many forces influencing their lives, events in one dimension of life can be very influential in other areas. Individuals also integrate and coordinate the various dimensions of their lives to keep the different aspects at least minimally consistent.

Individual change across the life span is a central issue in life course studies. The biogenetic forces influencing individuals cause important changes in physical stature, chemical makeup, and behavior across the span of life, while community forces change roles, relationships, and behaviors. These experiences and roles of individuals can also be influenced by the changes which occur in the lives of important others, such as the death of one's parents, the birth of a sibling, or the retirement of a spouse.

Many of life's changes involve role transitions, such as entering and leaving school, employment, and marriage. Other important transitions include the advent of parenthood, becoming a grandparent, and the decision to divide an extended household into two nuclear units. These transitions are particularly important in life course studies because they can involve central changes in roles, behavior, relationships, and responsibilities.

Age-related changes across the life course are frequently referred to as "aging effects." They represent the sum of the individual biological and social forces producing change within a person's life. Since these age-related changes are sometimes quite regular, some observers regard them as uniform sequences or stages. However, the life course perspective rejects the idea of uniformity in the aging process, noting many irregularities in the way different people experience life and the roles they occupy (O'Rand and Krecker 1990; Thornton 1991).

Another tenet of the life course perspective is that variations in one's early life experiences frequently affect subsequent behavior. For example, childhood experiences with parents and educational institutions could affect subsequent family formation and occupational experiences. Similarly, marriage and parenthood are often viewed as having implications for later economic and occupational activity.

Historical change is also an important element in the life course framework, since many external forces can produce substantial changes in the social, economic, and cultural environment in which individuals live. These changes can be the result of temporary forces such as wars and economic booms and depressions; they also can stem from longer-term changes associated with industrialization, urbanization, or the expansion of education and the mass media. Societal-level changes can, in turn, significantly influence the behavior of individuals and their families. Together, all of these historical changes in individual behavior are designated as historical effects in the life course framework.

In our model of the life course, economic and social changes carry no explicit scripts telling individuals how to change their family relationships, behaviors, and values. Instead, our perspective views historical family change as an adjustment process in which individuals and their kinsmen modify their historically existing family structures and processes to fit changed environments. As individuals and their families encounter new circumstances, they respond in terms of their accustomed values, relationships, and practices (Hareven 1982; Kung 1983). Such actors may modify and adjust their earlier family structures and processes either by inventing new ways of doing things or through the adoption of new structures and ideas from the outside. These modifications of old family forms can occur either through the adjustment of behavior and relationships within the lifetimes of individuals or through the incorporation of new generations of young people who pioneer new ways.

This view of social change suggests that preexisting central values, norms, and structures of a society will guide the ways in which adjustments are made to new environments. Furthermore, there is high potential for core cultural values and relationships to remain steady through long periods of social and economic change. Thus, it is necessary to focus upon family continuity as well as family change and to be alert to how old patterns continue even as modifications are made to meet the circumstances of a changing world.

Methodological Approaches

Historical changes can be conceptualized as taking two distinct forms: those associated with cohort and those linked with period. Period effects are defined as the results of societal change that influence all age and cohort groups similarly at one point in time, but with no persistent subsequent effects. Birth and marriage cohort effects, on the other hand, are defined as the results of societal change that affect only the individuals of one particular birth or marriage cohort, but with those effects persisting throughout the life of the cohort. Birth cohort effects generally posit that young people are particularly, and even uniquely, susceptible to some societal-level change that has long-lasting effects on those who experience it. Similarly, one can conceptualize marriage cohort effects that represent the persistent influence of social change on only one marriage cohort, usually those who are recently married. There can also be interactions between the various age, period, and cohort effects; however, these effects are complicated and beyond the scope of this chapter.

We use several approaches to document historical effects on the family experiences and values of individuals. One approach relies on repeated cross-sectional measurement to ascertain for multiple historical periods family behavior, attitudes, values, or organization at the time of observation. Such information is drawn from successive surveys, censuses, or vital statistics, being careful to maintain not only comparability of measures but also the population universe. The data collection time is the historical marker used in this approach. Because of the potential importance of age effects, it is necessary to ensure that the successive observations include the same age groups. To control for the possibility of changing age distributions across wide age ranges, we frequently estimate historical effects within relatively narrow age groups of the population, which permits examination of the extent to which historical effects vary across age groups.

A second approach to the documentation of historical family change relies on retrospective reports of events, experiences, or relationships in the past rather than reports about contemporary circumstances. Age is controlled in this approach by asking people to report experiences at the same general age or position in the life course—with childhood, adolescence, and marriage offering time frames frequently used in this approach. Individuals are categorized according to their birth or marriage cohort, with cohort being the historical marker used. Differences in experience or behavior across birth or marriage cohorts can then be attributed to historical change.

Surveys frequently include multiple cohorts of individuals, thus achieving the second approach with only one data collection. However, when the same questions are asked in multiple cross-sectional surveys, the coverage of cohorts is broadened and checks on data reliability are possible. The reliability of recall is particularly important in using this approach to measure historical change. Our several investigations of the similarity of reports for the same cohorts across multiple data collections document the reliability of such responses in Taiwan (Thornton, Chang, and Sun 1984).

While both of these approaches can separate historical effects from age effects, neither is able to further divide the historical change into period or cohort components, since both approaches control age, while combining cohort and period effects as indicators of historical change. While period is used as the historical marker in the first approach, each successive period is also associated with a different birth cohort, thereby confounding period and cohort. Similarly, in the second approach where cohort is used as the historical marker, each successive marriage or birth cohort is also associated with a different period, with period and cohort again confounded. As the age-period-cohort literature demonstrates, the identity of period and cohort when age is controlled makes the separation of the historical effect into its period and cohort components impossible without either additional substantive data or the imposition of very strong assumptions on the period-cohort data (Glenn 1976; Mason et al. 1973; Rodgers 1982, 1990).

Our approach to the explanation of observed historical trends involves the formulation and estimation of multivariate models of individual family behavior or values. We include the following predictors in these multivariate models: individual experience with important nonfamily activities such as school, employment, and dormitory living; the experiences of the individual's parents, namely their schooling and occupation; and residential experience in rural and urban areas. In estimating these multivariate models we have been sensitive to the appropriate causal ordering of variables and have tried to ensure that the predictor variables are temporally prior to the dependent variables.

Our estimation of multivariate equations has relied primarily on additive rather than interactive models. This decision was made primarily because we had no strong theoretical expectations concerning interactive models. In addition, preliminary analyses of models interacting substantive predictors with historical time revealed that most interaction effects were generally modest in size and added little to the simpler additive models.

The multivariate models include both the individual's experiences and one historical indicator—either period or cohort. The estimated effects of the experience variables represent the extent to which each of these experiences influences family attitudes or behavior. The estimated effects of the historical indicator in these equations reflect the magnitude of the historical trend that *cannot* be accounted for by the individual experience variables included in the equations. This part of the historical effect, therefore, is due to factors that have not been taken into account in the equations. These other factors could include unmeasured variables or errors in the measurement of the variables that are included in the equations.

More important for our purposes are the differences between the historical effects observed in the multivariate models—with personal experiences controlled—and the historical effects observed without controls for individual experiences. These differences reflect the part of the historical trend that *can* be accounted for by the individual experience variables included in the analysis. If there are large differences between the historical effects in the multivariate equations and the historical effects estimated without the controls, we know that historical changes in the predictor variables have played an important role in causing the trends in the family behavior in question. If the observed historical effect is totally eliminated in the multivariate models, the historical trend is entirely due to the individual experience variables included in the equation.

The multivariate models of individual-level family behavior and attitudes also provide useful insights for evaluating whether the observed historical trends are cohort or period effects. Methodologists have long suggested that the most appropriate way to separate these confounded effects is to conceptualize and measure the theoretical constructs that are believed to intervene between the respective historical effects and the dependent variable in question (Rodgers 1982, 1990). If one can account for the historical effects using predictor variables that are associated with cohort, the historical effects themselves can be interpreted as cohort effects. Similarly, the historical effects can be interpreted as period-related if the historical trends can be accounted for by variables associated with historical periods.

We are able to utilize this strategy because most of the individual experience variables used in our multivariate models, including education, paid employment, dormitory living, and urban residence before marriage, are associated with birth or marriage cohort rather than with period. This is true because they are measured early in life and are not changed by subsequent experiences across the life course. It is also plausible to argue that these determinants of family experience have their greatest influence during adolescence and the transition to adulthood, with the effects of these experiences extending far into adulthood. Since these variables are associated with birth or marriage cohort rather than with historical period, any trends in family behavior or attitudes that can be attributed to these variables can also be attributed to changes across cohorts rather than changes across periods. Of course, any historical effects remaining after controlling the cohort-related variables included in the multivariate equations could be the result of either cohort or period effects, and the separation of these remaining effects would require the introduction of additional variables, either cohort- or period-related.

Multivariate models using individual-level predictor variables associated with cohort also provide another approach to the identification of historical trends in family behavior or values. This approach relies on data from a one-time survey, but instead of using questions about family experiences at a particular time in the life course, this approach uses measures of family values or relationships at the time of the survey. Since all the measures of family variables in this approach refer to just one point in time—the survey date—all of the effects of that period are the same for all individuals participating in the study. As a result, none of the variance across individuals in this design can be attributed to historical period. Historical time can still enter the picture here, since the Taiwanese surveys represent multiple birth and marriage cohorts, which allow family attitudes or relationships at the time of the data collection to be compared across cohorts. However, unlike the approaches for studying historical trends discussed earlier, this procedure does not control for position in the life course. In fact, this strategy confounds age with birth cohort since each successive cohort is exactly one year younger at the time of the survey than the immediately preceding cohort. Consequently, it is not possible to straightforwardly interpret observed differences across birth cohorts as historical effects, since they could be the result of aging effects and have nothing to do with historical trends across cohorts.

Multivariate equations of the family variables using cohort-related individual experiences as predictor variables permit us to identify any historical effects that operate through these cohort-related experience measures. In so doing we use as predictor variables the same cohort-related measures discussed previously, including experiences in young adulthood with education, paid employment, dormitory living, and urban residence. Estimation of any historical effects operating through cohort-related variables in the multivariate equations is done by comparing the estimated effects of the cohort variable (which is also perfectly correlated with age) in the multivariate equations with the effects without the cohort-related predictor variables. The differences between the effects of cohort (age) in the multivariate equations and the effects estimated without the multivariate controls can be attributed to the historical effects that operate through the included cohort-related experiences. Of course, this procedure identifies as historical effects only the part of the relationship between cohort (age) and the family variable that operates through the cohort-related variables included in the multivariate equations. Any part of the correlation between cohort (age) and the family variable of interest that is not accounted for by the included cohort-related variables could be the result of either age or historical effects.

Organization of Book

As indicated earlier, we have prepared chapters 2–4 as historical and theoretical background for our research. Chapter 2 summarizes basic points about Chinese family life in the past. This knowledge of historical family structures and processes provides the baseline necessary for understanding subsequent family change. In chapter 3 we turn to the dramatic and widespread economic and social transformations that have occurred in Taiwan during the twentieth century. This account of social and economic trends provides understanding of the changing social organization that has modified the historical patterns of Taiwanese family life.

In chapter 4 we bring together the conceptual frameworks of chapter 1 with the realities of Chinese family life in the past and the twentieth-century transformation of Taiwan's social and economic structure. Chapter 4 considers the causal mechanisms that have operated in Taiwan to translate the observed social and economic changes into modifications of family structures and processes. We apply our conceptual and theoretical orientations to Taiwan's history to provide expectations of how the social and economic transformation of Taiwan has modified the historical patterns of Chinese family life. This theoretical discussion provides a framework for understanding and interpreting the empirical evidence about family change presented in subsequent chapters.

Chapter 5 marks the transition from historical and theoretical background to empirical analysis of changing family structures and processes. In chapter 5 we document the transformation of the modes of social organization in Taiwan from the familial end of the continuum toward a more differentiated structure. In doing so we discuss how the activities of the life course in Taiwan have shifted from a locus primarily within the family to include multiple activities conducted in other organizations.

In chapters 6 and 7 we shift our focus to marriage and the organization of the mate selection process. Chapter 6 documents changes in the ways in which spouses are selected and marriages arranged. It also traces trends in dating and premarital sex and pregnancy. Chapter 7 changes the emphasis from the documentation of marital trends to the investigation of causal forces influencing mate selection. Included in chapter 7 are analyses of both the determinants of individual marital arrangements and the extent to which trends over time in these individual determinants can explain the historical changes in the process of mate selection.

Chapters 8 and 9 form a second couplet on marriage, this one considering marital timing and extensiveness. In chapter 8 we discuss long-term trends in the prevalence and timing of marriage and speculate about the meaning of these trends for the future of marriage in Taiwan. Chapter 9 examines the determinants of marriage formation and considers explanations for both individual behavior and historical trends.

Chapter 10 shifts the focus from marriage formation to marital dissolution. The chapter's major goal is to understand trends in the overall rate of marital dissolution. We consider marital disruptions both from mortality and from the voluntary dissolution of marital unions through divorce.

In chapter 11 we examine the transition from high to low fertility in Taiwan. We investigate changes in both childbearing preferences and behavior. As part of this analysis, we also discuss the implementation and influence of Taiwan's family planning program.

Chapters 12 and 13 form a couplet focusing on extended family relationships. Chapter 12 considers co-residence of married children with their parents as well as intergenerational contacts between parents and children living in separate households. In chapter 13 we examine the determinants of parent-child co-residence and consider the extent to which trends in these determinants can account for historical changes in the amount of co-residence.

In chapter 14 we examine the Chinese family chain linking together the living with their ancestors and unborn children. A major issue in this chapter is the durability of this central dimension of Chinese cosmology and social organization in the face of recent economic and social changes. Our goal is to document any changes that have occurred in the ancestral chain as well as to isolate the central historical forces that explain those changes.

Finally, chapter 15 brings the book to a close by providing a summary and conclusions. In this chapter we highlight the major conclusions of our research and indicate some areas where future research is needed.

Two

Historical and Ethnographic Perspectives on the Chinese Family

T. Fricke, J. S. Chang, and L. S. Yang

In this chapter we explore the historical and ethnographic literature on the Chinese form of family organization in which the widest range of activities is organized by kinship. Although Chinese society has been characterized by a variety of social developments across time and although the political boundaries of the Chinese state encompass a wide regional diversity, a singular characteristic of the family system has been its remarkable unity and continuity.

Much of what we review in this chapter applies to the whole of Han China in the past, including Taiwan. Where appropriate, we will indicate when particular features are specifically Taiwanese in origin. Before reviewing the Chinese family, however, we shall place the following chapters in context by discussing the special features of Taiwanese history and describing the process by which Chinese family organization was transplanted to the island.

Taiwan: A Historical Overview

Taiwan, only about a hundred miles from the Chinese mainland, from which its highest mountains can be seen on a clear day, was settled in four major migrations, the first beginning some fifteen thousand years ago with the Taiwan Aborigines, a distinct population sharing cultural features with groups in the Philippines. The earliest permanent Chinese migrants arrived after 1500 (Meskill 1979),[1] although intensive waves of Chinese migration lasted from the early seventeenth through the nineteenth centuries. A third wave, by the Japanese, lasted the fifty years,

1. The earliest documentary references date from 589 to 618 when a military expedition was sent to "Liu-ch'iu" island, generally thought to be Taiwan.

from 1895 until 1945, with most Japanese leaving the island after World War II; the fourth major migration followed when the Nationalist party army and its supporters came to Taiwan.

Han settlement can be thought of as a continuation of the expansion of the Chinese population into the southern frontiers, driven largely by the quest for new land. By 1660 Taiwan's Chinese population had climbed to fifty thousand and the island was exporting rice and sugar to the mainland and beyond. Classically trained scholars came to the island as a part of the provincial government of Fukien Province in 1661. Thus, the settlement of Taiwan by the ancestors of its present majority population began at roughly the same time as the European settlement of the North American colonies.

Taiwan's re-creation of Chinese society is rooted in these processes of settlement. Early settlers were rugged pioneers attracted from land-poor Fukien by the possibility of opening small plots with their own and family labor. The key role in the opening of the Taiwan frontier was played by developers who received government grants of land, which they opened up to settler families from the mainland (Gates 1987; Meskill 1979). Such patents could be inherited, sold, or mortgaged; the organization of responsibilities could involve a series of landlords who acted as intermediaries between the patent holder and the actual tenant, who could, in some cases, acquire virtual ownership of the land (Meskill 1979: 47; Wickberg 1981: 212–13). This system of immigration tended to fragment lineage groups and force associations based on fictive kin links or regional origin. Furthermore, government restrictions prevented the immigration of entire mainland lineages or villages (Lamley 1981; Meskill 1979), leading to deemphasis of the strong lineages characteristic of the home regions. Where strong lineage organization was re-created in Taiwan (Pasternak 1972), it was the result of family development from a fresh start.

While the Fukienese (or Hoklo) majority constituted nearly all of the earlier waves of settlement and continued to arrive through the later period, the Hakka were represented almost entirely by later migrations mainly originating in eastern Kwangtung. Their later arrival is reflected in their concentration in the hilly and more mountainous parts of Taiwan, where extensive paddy agriculture and the tenancy system were not practiced.[2]

2. The Fukienese/Hakka distinction has played large in historical treatments of Taiwanese settlement and social process. An excellent summary of the migrations and the interethnic friction between these two groups is provided in Lamley (1981) and alluded

In 1885 Taiwan achieved provincial status in its own right and its capital was moved north to its current location at Taipei. Provincial status accelerated infrastructural improvement on the island: electricity was brought to the island; cables were laid for telegraph links to the world; the first railroad was developed. These early improvements were somewhat partial, however, and interrupted by hostility to the official policy of coexistence with the Aborigines. Nevertheless, by the time of the first census in 1893, Taiwan's Chinese population had risen to 2,546,000 and a thoroughly Chinese familial system had been transplanted from the mainland.

Continuities in Chinese Family Organization

Although our primary focus is Taiwan, it is necessary to examine the historical pattern on the island in terms of the larger Chinese family system. The known variation throughout China, as, for example across regions in the description of women's domestic positions in the north versus the south (Johnson 1983: 14–15) or in the family sizes of various social classes (Baker 1979; Lang 1968), is underlain by common principles of organization that have percolated through all levels of society (Cohen 1976).[3]

Antecedents of classic Chinese family organization must have existed well before the earliest documents extolling its ideals were written (Baker 1979: 11), but the systematic integration of state bureaucracy and family morality dates from the eleventh century (Gernet 1982: 344–46). Even the requirements of success in the civil examination system emphasized expertise in works such as the *Hsiao Ching* (*The Classic of Filial Piety*), in which family relationships were viewed as central to the organization of all society while the state itself ratified lines of family authority in law. The point is, of course, not that behav-

---

to in a number of other works (Gates 1987; Meskill 1979). While the Hakka have been described by some as maintaining greater lineage solidarity and organization than the Fukienese, Cohen (1976) stresses their overwhelmingly shared culture and social organization and suggests that differences resulted largely from migrations to different ecological regions.

3. Of the research into domestic organization in Taiwan alone, Arthur Wolf writes: "The discovery of a basic uniformity has occurred in the midst of a surge of evidence reporting unimagined diversity. What I take this to mean is that Chinese domestic institutions are extraordinarily flexible. A few basic ideas provide coherence and continuity without interfering with people's ability to adapt to a wide variety of situations" (1981b: 357).

ior and the legal codes necessarily coincided but that family ideology was so pervasive and unitary that the state took an explicit interest in buttressing it.

Also dating from an early period was the institutionalization of lineage and clan organizations (Gernet 1982: 319). Lineage organizations began to provide for the welfare of their members, establishing schools and ancestral shrines endowed by community land. Genealogical documents incorporating the governing rules of these organizations include elaborate essays on family themes, tributes to illustrious ancestors, and rules for including or excluding names from the genealogies themselves. Among the reasons for omitting names from the printed genealogies were disregarding one's ancestors, clan betrayal, and bringing dishonor to the clan (Liu 1959).

Central to the spread of ideology was the state examination system, a unique combination of family-organized educational institutions with state-organized exams which endured until this century. That system relied on standardized competition and the possibility that males from virtually any social group could participate and rise to the highest levels of the bureaucracy (Gernet 1982: 303–5). The openness of the system encouraged the development of lineage-supported and village schools which allowed children to live at home while attending them and made the primary limitation on educating children the economic needs of families for their sons' labor.

The openness of the civil exams assured the spread and homogenization of Confucian ideology ratifying Chinese family values through all levels of society (Ho 1962: 86; Meskill 1979: 257). Not only did lineages organize to aid the education of their male children, using family organization as a strategy for social mobility, but advancement itself was conceived as a way to honor one's family and ancestors.[4] Moreover, lineage schools ensured that even villages far from urban culture would have among them people who had studied those classics stressing family ideology.

---

4. Ho (1962: 90) quotes the advice of Ma Ch'un-shang to a scholar who must leave school to aid his sick parents: "After you return home you should consider practicing essays and passing examinations the best way to honor your parents. . . . Only by passing successive examinations and acquiring your *chu-jen* or *chin-shih* degree [intermediate and highest degrees offered in the civil examination system] can you instantaneously bring honor to your ancestors."

Levels of Organization and Family Ideology

Household and Family

In China, the explicit unit of organization for all society is the family,[5] spoken of with different terms for units corresponding roughly to English concepts of the domestic economic unit, the conjugal family, and the household. The Chinese terms for these basic levels of organization are relative. *Chia* may refer to the co-resident unit sharing a common hearth as well as to larger units encompassing more than a single household but with common ties to an estate.[6] Similarly, the Chinese term *fang* may refer to conjugal units within the *chia* as well as to larger collections of kin sharing both purse and property. It is convenient, however, to think of the *chia* as that group of kin who have rights in common property whether or not they technically co-reside under a single roof.[7] *Fang,* on the other hand, are defined on the basis of conjugal pairs, clearly recognized as the potential nuclei for new *chia* groups in Chinese culture (Cohen 1976: 57–59).

In general, an estate's division will be roughly equal between these *fang,* irrespective of the different number of children each has. This practice of equal inheritance among brothers has been reported to vary in some contexts, however (Diamond 1969; Watson 1985), especially those in which merchants attempt to keep together their estates by favoring their oldest sons.[8]

The literature suggests great variation in the size and composition of these groups, from the extended family compounds reported by Cohen (1976) to the predominantly nuclear households reported by others (cf. Fei 1939; Fried 1953), but all documents agree that common property is an essential characteristic of the *chia*. Here we use the term *chia* to

5. Research in the middle of this century concentrated on showing how the classic ideal of the co-residing five-generation family was an artifact of gentry society with little representation among the peasantry (Fei 1939; Freedman 1958; Lang 1968). Later research suggests a complex interaction between this ideal and the actual behavior of individuals resulting from strategic decisions of brothers, fertility, mortality, and other constraints (Cohen 1976). Also, see Sangren (1984) for a discussion of common features of Chinese organizations in general.

6. This should not appear strange to an English speaker, who generally uses the word "family" to mean the nuclear unit defined by husband, wife, and children or the larger kinship grouping including the husband's or wife's parents and siblings.

7. Such rights need not imply ownership, since tenancy rights might also be transferred across generations (Wickberg 1981). See the discussion on landlessness in chap. 3.

8. Baker (1979) mentions that the inheritance share was virtually equal in most cases; Cohen (1976) reports the same for a village in southern Taiwan; even Watson (1985), who focuses on inequality among brothers, suggests that unequal inheritance is anomalous.

refer specifically to that group holding all of its productive property in common. Households, on the other hand, refer only to the co-resident unit, which may or may not coincide with the *chia*.

Lineage and Clan

More important than normative statements about *chia* group composition are the common principles which structure individual relationships within and across *chia* groups, whatever their size and the specific kin links of their members. Although we shall discuss these principles in more detail later in this chapter, some become obvious at levels of organization that include multiple households and *chia*.

Much has been written about the patrilineal organization of Chinese society, particularly by anthropologists working in the southeast provinces of Fukien and Kwangtung, where corporate lineage groups dominated local society (Baker 1968; Freedman 1958, 1966). These lineages highlight the strongly agnatic (patrilineal) structure of society throughout China. Variation in the intensity of lineage organization also demonstrates the flexibility of family organization in China, where local forms reflect a variety of economic, political, and historical contingencies interacting with a common cultural system (Cohen 1985).[9] The corporate lineages of Southeast China were defined on the basis of all those males descended from a common ancestor and knowing their links to that ancestor, living together in a single settlement, and owning some (but not all) land in common. As with *chia* organization, lineage leadership was nominally vested in the male who was most senior in generation and age (Baker 1979: 49).

In practice, these corporate lineages used their common land to support ancestral halls and schools for their members. The key to this organization was common rights to the lineage trust. Although each individual *chia* owned its own property, all would benefit from patriline property and institutions. Corporate lineages did not simply expand in size with each new generation, however, but held within themselves the

---

9. The strong lineage organization in Southeast China has been variously attributed to rice cultivation, the need for extensive irrigation, and frontier conditions (Freedman 1966), to all of these plus the development of commerce (Potter 1968, 1970), and to all of these along with the historical pattern of initial settlement (Pasternak 1985). Whatever its origins, the strong lineage organization of Fukien and Kwangtung was not transferred to Taiwan even though most of Taiwan's population is descended from settlers from these areas. Cohen (1985) suggests that part of the reason is that these extensive corporate lineages require long periods of development. Fukien began to be effectively saturated with Chinese expansion from the north by about A.D. 1000, while the intensive settlement of Taiwan occurred in the eighteenth century (cf. Meskill 1979).

possibility of dissolving the more distant ancestral trust and establishing new corporate lineages based on more recent focal ancestors.

Even where lineage organization was less corporate, the strong identification of males descended from a known common ancestor conferred a special relationship. Ho (1962: 211–12) writes that wealthy kinsmen often acted on the neo-Confucian injunction to aid their poorer relatives by paying for their education or opening their private schools to them. Cooperative labor groups in agrarian society required help from nearby kinsmen, who would likely be members of common lineages.

The importance of the ideology of common descent to social cooperation extended to levels of organization beyond the lineage. Where *chia* and lineage can be thought of as units based at least partially on known kinship links, the clan is defined as a fictive kinship group based on common surname. Here again, the intensity of organization varied considerably. In the settlement of Taiwan, such common surname associations were extremely important since actual lineage groups could not usually survive the splintered migration from Fukien; the bonds uniting settlers were formed from quasi-kin groups defined by common surnames or regions of origin (Meskill 1979: 52). There is also evidence that the natural expansion of Taiwan's pioneer *chia* gave rise to localized lineage groups similar to those of Fukien. These stronger lineage groups are associated with the nucleated village settlements of southern Taiwan rather than the dispersed northern settlement patterns in which farmsteads were dispersed with their fields.

The important point here is the extent to which the Chinese have structured their relationships in terms of the family whether or not associated individuals in fact shared a known common ancestor.[10] Localized clusters of villages with different surname groups may be joined for festivals and ritual worship of deities that place them in a quasi-family relationship (Ahern 1981). Extremely close friendships were also transformed into fictive kin relationships by being ritually recognized (Jordan 1985). Even the Chinese state, in describing its officials as mothers and fathers to the local populace, used family metaphors (Baker 1979: 168). Thus, the family represented an overarching ideology and metaphor for all levels of Chinese society.

Generation, Age, and Gender

Whatever the form and cohesiveness of *chia* and lineages in China, the principles on which family authority was patterned emphasized the di-

10. But see Sangren (1984) for an approach which argues for antecedent principles underlying all Chinese organizations including families.

mensions of generation, age, and sex (Greenhalgh 1985). Distinctions based on these were built into kinship terminology, degrees of mourning for the deceased,[11] and the relationships between families united by marriage. They were further reflected in the activities of families, individual life course transitions, and access to education and employment. Within each *chia*, ultimate authority ideally resided with the oldest male; within lineages organized as they were in Southeast China, ultimate authority ideally lay with the oldest male representative of the earliest living generation. Of course, the locus varied with the conditions of a family. As individuals moved through their own life courses, their relationships with parents would alter, for example, and the tension inherent in authority relations between individuals would coalesce around the possibility of *chia* fission. Cohen (1976) suggests that the threat that a son might leave his *chia* with his inheritance share at marriage and take up residence in the Taiwanese village in which he worked made him a more equal partner in the domestic economy. Others write that such separation could only occur after a father's death (Freedman 1966) and that the father's authority endured throughout his life.

The Chinese word *hsiao*, translated as "filial piety" (inadequately according to Baker 1979), stresses the primacy of a child's relationships with its parents, a duty that transcended even what was owed to the state. Except for outright treason, for example, the state recognized the duty of children to their parents and did not require that they report the crimes of their parents (Baker 1979: 102). Filial piety centered on the relationship of a son to his father—one of absolute obedience (Hsu 1971). Its centrality to the processes of socialization and classical education (Ho 1962; M. Wolf 1972) stresses the extent to which the authority of seniors was a primary organizing principle of family activities. In the following pages, we will explore the ratification of this principle with attention to the respect shown to deceased ancestors and to the familial organization of individual activities.

In Chinese society of the past, family membership and economic cooperation, inheritance of property, and lines of authority were defined to an extraordinary extent through males. This orientation was reflected in kinship terminology which, for example, gave distinct kin terms to all male relatives out to third cousin but included a much narrower set of kin terms for maternal relatives. Similarly, male membership in the family and lineage was enduring across all stages of the life course while

---

11. Mourning grades refer to the customary mourning practices for degrees of kin relation. Most of the information for this discussion is taken from Baker (1979: 107–11) and Chao (1983).

daughters changed their membership at marriage. In fact, the transfer of a daughter's family membership extended to the expectation that she become involved in respectful activities directed to the ancestors in her marital home. Finally, although some portion of the marriage dowry was under the control of a new bride in her marital home, a daughter's inheritance share was far less than that of a son and never included land.

Age, as a principle of deference, was most important within generations. Thus, an oldest brother was expected to behave authoritatively with respect to his younger brothers. Sisters were ranked in a similar way. Although important, age was clearly secondary to gender, as exemplified by the principle which ranked in-marrying daughters-in-law in accordance with the relative ages of their husbands rather than their own relative ages. The wife of an eldest son required the deference of a younger son's wife even if the latter were chronologically older.

The Ancestors

Up to now we have discussed features of family organization and ideology pertaining to the living. An additional feature among the Chinese, for whom the afterlife is viewed as a duplicate of this world in which spirits are subject to the same needs as the living, is kin links extending beyond this life. Thus, the Chinese family "extends to the as yet unborn generations and to the long deceased ones" (Yang 1945) in ways that may be expected to affect the behavior of the living (Ahern 1971; Fei 1939; Hsu 1971; Wolf 1981b: 343). The corollary of a belief in a parallel world in which the dead require food, clothing, shelter, and money is that deceased ancestors require the support of the living. At the same time, good fortune (and bad) in this world is seen as deriving from the actions of the deceased. Both the living and the dead can suffer if proper respect is not paid to the ancestors.[12] Chinese ideology stresses the continuity of obligations unbroken by death. Genealogical connection does not by itself confer a position on a deceased ancestor, however; to receive unambiguous respect, the ancestor must first of all have provided an estate for the living (Ahern 1973). Thus did family obligations stretch in a timeless and unbroken chain in which the fortunes of the deceased

12. A great deal has been written about ancestor worship among the Chinese (Ahern 1971; Baker 1979: 71–106; Hsu 1971; Jordan 1972). The discussion here is extracted from all of these sources. Note that the Chinese word for worship, *bai*, can also be translated "to pay respects to" (Baker 1979: 99). Its connotation is much wider than the English concept, as is made clear by the three "reverences" that must be done at the marriage ritual—to heaven and earth, to the ancestors and to the husband's living parents, and the husband and wife to each other. All of these are described by the word *bai*.

and the unborn pivoted on the proper activities of the living (Baker 1979).

Ancestors are acknowledged in daily attention to the family's ancestral altar, where they reside in ancestral tablets. For those lineages with ancestral halls, tablets for the founding ancestors and for their most important descendants would be present in addition to the regular ancestral tablets in the individual *chia*. Daily attention to the ancestors is often no more than an offering of tea and incense provided by the married women of a household. More elaborate attention on special days is conventionally performed by the male household head. Ancestors may be acknowledged for special blessings to the family such as an unusually good harvest, as well as for special life course events for living family members such as marriages and births. These ceremonies imply that ancestors continue to take part in family life, and daily attention to them reinforces lines of authority favoring senior members of the family while conferring responsibility for maintaining the stability of family relationships on younger members (cf. M. Freedman 1970b). Ancestors are present on the altar much as the living family members are present within the domestic circle.[13]

For obvious reasons, there are limits to the number of tablets that can fit on a family altar. Tablets were removed in a process analogous to the segmenting of lineages or the partition of households. Thus, as ancestors became more distant, their ritual importance also declined. In practice the number of generations represented was roughly the same as that in the ideal five-generation family and enumerated in the mourning grades. While in the special circumstances of a particularly illustrious ancestor tablets from remote generations might continue to be kept on the family altar, the usual practice was to attend only to the tablets of those with whom living members of the family had personal contact and, thus, with whom the continuity of relationships was most concrete.

Family and Household Processes

In this section we begin to examine the activities centrally performed or organized by familial groups as a whole, turning in the next section to

13. So important was the need for descendants to provide for the ancestors that mechanisms existed for even unmarried sons to have "descendants" who would care for them. Hsu (1971) mentions that an unmarried male who died might have a son given to him by his brother so that he could be revered as an ancestor and have his tablet represented on the altar. An unmarried daughter who died could not be similarly represented with descendants although a "husband" could be arranged for her to perform mourning rituals.

the life courses of individuals within the family. We have mentioned above that the *chia* was defined primarily in terms of the economically cooperative, property-owning group and that common residence was not a necessary condition of *chia* membership. In practice, however, the common identity of household and *chia* groups is the most common pattern mentioned in the ethnographies (Fei 1939; Gallin 1966; Gates 1987; Harrell 1982), with exceptions in the form of expansion into compounds or households of brothers and parents in close proximity to one another (Cohen 1976). The size and composition of *chia* groups is partly contingent on prevailing demographic conditions and on each one's particular trajectory of growth and expansion from a conjugal pair.[14] In spite of the classical encouragement of the greatest possible extension of coresiding agnatic kin, the greater likelihood was for sons to live with their fathers for a time after marriage, after which they could continue to live patrilocally or decide to set up a separate household with their own wife and children. A variety of factors could affect the decision. The record is full of reports of tension between mothers-in-law and daughters-in-law. Such tension could be the nominal instigation for household fission. Or another brother might bring in a wife, and simple matters of space might encourage fission. When the identity of interests remained strong and household tensions remained modest, the Chinese pattern was for married brothers, their wives, and their children to live together in a single household with their parents.

When the composition of the *chia* overlapped that of the household, nearly all activities within it were organized in tight conformity with the principles of kinship organization discussed earlier. Ideally, the oldest male within this corporate property-owning group had final authority over decisions affecting the use of the labor and resources available to it. Allowing for variation in day-to-day management, the overwhelming picture is one of direct paternal control over the activities of the household *chia* and of a high degree of paternal decision-making power within the dispersed household *chia* group where that pattern existed.

The coordination of activities was based on the understanding that production benefited the group as a whole. This common orientation meant that the *chia*'s production above that paid out for taxes or rent went to support its members. Similarly, the proceeds of any surplus sold on the market went into a common fund and decisions about where to invest these proceeds necessarily affected the family. When *chia* members

14. See Cohen (1976) for a discussion of the growth and fission of *chia* and the variant patterns that may characterize different circumstances.

diversified into productive activities outside of agriculture, they did not go into them as individuals. Rather, functioning very much as a corporation, decision-making members of the *chia* decided as a group whether members should diversify.[15] Thus did familial organization of production flourish in a variety of economic circumstances from the strictly agrarian to more mixed and urban (Cohen 1976: 95; Gates 1987).

Chia units were tightly integrated. Their productive resources were common. Their ritual activities were common for the most part, taking place at family altars within individual households or within *chia* compounds. If units were sufficiently large, they could conceivably be independent in terms of labor, too. Nevertheless, *chia* groups found it necessary to go beyond their boundaries from time to time to act in cooperation with members of other similarly organized groups. In agrarian settings, cooperation was needed especially at harvest time. Generally, the units of cooperation were found close by, however, and the members of nearby economic units were likely to be patrilineally related, almost by definition in single lineage villages.

In the multiple lineage villages more common in Taiwan, cooperative groups outside the *chia* or small lineage group are more flexibly organized. Gallin (1966) demonstrates that in circumstances such as these, ties created through marriage may become important to the organization of labor exchange even though these affinal connections were not generally used in this fashion. Thus, while Chinese society of the past emphasized the primacy of agnatic kin, who would usually be found in proximity to each other, Gallin and Gallin (1985: 101) write that connections between families become important when interests extend beyond the village and land-based economy. Similarly, on the mainland, where such interests have become important in commerce and politics, affinal relationships between families (but not lineages) would be stressed (Watson 1985).

Consistent with the strong familial organization of Chinese society was the almost complete socialization of children within the *chia* environment. The births of children, especially sons, clinched a woman's place in her marital family and began the process by which her husband's attention and orientation began to shift from fulfilling the wishes of his parents to the potential for establishing his own domestic unit based on his own *fang*. Margery Wolf (1972) suggests that a woman's interests

15. Indeed, the early settlement of Taiwan may have been hastened by such *chia* diversification of their productive economy. During the early settlement phase, males moving to Taiwan intended to stay for a limited time, earning money and returning to their *chia* on the mainland (Lamley 1981; Wickberg 1981).

were themselves bound up in retaining the allegiances of her children through the formation of her own "uterine family," and it is not surprising that stress was placed on inculcating the virtues of obedience and loyalty.

Unfortunately, no data exist for the time allocation of boys' and girls' activities before the introduction of schools, but evidence from the latter part of this century suggests that youth began to receive differential socialization at an early age. Wolf (1972) and Gates (1987) both indicate that daughters were involved quite directly in household tasks at an age when sons were still left to range free and play. Surrounded by the totalizing family environment and encouraged to behave in conformity with ideals embodied in *hsiao,* a daughter's education in the family begins with early participation in the whole range of family activities. For all children, the contact with mothers was greatest in the early years up to about age 10, but fathers always had final authority (Cohen 1976: 88; Hsu 1971: 225). Children were socialized in the active context of family work and were directed in these activities as they became productive by their fathers or, if in a joint household, by the more senior males.

Engagement and Marriage

Few life course transitions reverberated through the family, affecting the relationships between individuals and the organization of domestic groups, to the extent that marriage did.[16] The marriage of a son created a new *fang,* which could form the seed of a new domestic unit and the possibility of *chia* fission; the marriage of a daughter typically took a productive family member from the natal *chia* group. A mother's relationship with her son could be threatened by her new daughter-in-law whereas a daughter entered an unknown environment in which she was uncertain of her reception. The tensions between wives and their husbands' mothers have, in fact, been enshrined in casual talk as the reason for the division of households (Cohen 1976; Wolf 1972). Moreover, marriage opened the *chia* and the lineage up to the judgment of outsiders. Indeed, a daughter's earlier and more strict supervision in her natal home was related to her expected departure. An unfilial daughter, unschooled in domestic tasks or disobedient to her new mother-in-law, reflected on the quality of her natal kin and had repercussions for the marriage

16. As with other aspects of the Chinese family, an extensive literature exists for marriage. Most of this discussion is based on the work of M. Wolf (1972), A. Wolf and Huang (1980), Cohen (1976), and Gallin (1966) with supplementary material from other sources.

chances of her younger siblings. Similarly, a tyrannical mother-in-law would occasion comment and make it more difficult for a good marriage to be arranged for her remaining sons (Wolf 1972). With so much at stake, it is not surprising that the longstanding Chinese ideal was to leave events leading up to marriage nearly entirely in parental hands. Nor is it surprising that marriages were instituted through an intricate series of negotiations designed to protect the interests of the families involved.[17]

In many societies marriages create important alliance and cooperative relationships among the families involved. Past Chinese behavior, however, was organized to create patriline insularity and the connections between lineages united by marriage appears to have been minimal. This is most true of areas and families organized for agrarian production in the strong lineage areas. Yet it is also true that marriage links created potential networks that were mobilized for political and commercial reasons in the past (Baker 1979).

"Major marriage." In the dominant Chinese marriage pattern, spouses were expected at the minimum to come from outside that group which defined the mourning grades. It was also desirable that they come from outside the same surname group, although this was a less stringent requirement. Wolf (1972) reports a general feeling in village Taiwan that spouses should be from different villages as well, a pattern with obvious implications for the isolation of the new bride, who must leave her natal home for the *chia* of virtual strangers, and also one with implications for the relations between families joined by marriage. Careful orchestration of the marriage was essential with many opportunities to break off the process without loss of face.

The process began with parental negotiations and research into available prospects, a process initiated traditionally by the groom's rather than the bride's family. Parents were interested in bringing in a daughter-in-law of roughly the same social background as their son, since too great a difference in origins might lead to problems. A too wealthy background might mean a daughter-in-law unaccustomed to work, while too poor a background might result in the undesirable baggage of affines asking for loans. Initial inquiries and characterizations of families were made through an intermediary or go-between, who was usually a woman. Go-betweens enticed the parents of potential wives with detailed summaries of the economy of a groom's household. If no objections

17. Margery Wolf puts it well: "The main difference between marriages arranged by parents and those arranged by children is that a girl will choose a man to marry whereas her parents will choose a family" (1972: 103).

were raised, a formal meeting would be arranged in which, in the past, a mother and her son and a few relatives would visit the home of the prospective bride, perhaps catching a glimpse of her as she served tea to the visitors.

Ancestors were explicitly involved in the process. Two families finding no impediments in the first inquiries would "exchange the eight characters"—the year, month, day, and hour of birth for both the boy and the girl. Placed in red envelopes, these characters would sit on the family altar for three days awaiting the opinion of the ancestors. Any misfortune within this period would be interpreted as a negative response, and negotiations would be broken off with no loss of face for either party. Here, as Margery Wolf writes, the simple dropping of a rice bowl could terminate the process.

Beyond this point, however, negotiations would begin in earnest. Bride-price needed to be set; the reputations of both families and a girl's position in her new family were in part contingent on these negotiations. Half a year's income could easily be spent in acquiring a bride, while the bride's family would busily acquire the dowry that would be transported to their daughter's new home in a public display that reflected on their own honor and formed the core of their daughter's inheritance share. This dowry would become an important supplement to their daughter's economic position when her husband finally divided his own property from his father's estate (Chen 1985).

The ritual elaboration of "major marriage" underscores its importance to family processes. Early negotiations were tentative and exploratory, with increasing elaboration and public display until the transfer of the bride to her husband's home. Little was left up to the bride or groom in these marriages, since family standing and processes were at stake. The primary importance of marriage was its fulfillment of obligations to the ancestors by ensuring the continuance of the family. Marriage marked the start of a new generation in the family continuum, and the most feared outcome of a new marriage was that a new daughter-in-law would be barren (Wolf 1972: 108). At the same time, new daughters-in-law represented new potentials for divisiveness within the family and these threats were contained through the extreme family control exerted throughout the marriage process over both sexes. Even after the arrival of the new bride, in order to keep husband and wife from forming new interests in conflict with those of the senior generations within the household, the couple were sometimes discouraged from speaking to each other or showing open affection.

While the interests of parents in controlling their children's marital options are clear, we might wonder what interests were served for the children. Wolf reports, for example, that in spite of the traumatic break with their natal home for a life with strangers, love marriages were not attractive to daughters in the northern Taiwanese village of her field-work. Part of the answer for this lies in the familial context of the entire system of activities within which people lived their lives. Few nonfamilial institutions existed to present alternative support networks for individuals whereas the opportunities for independent living in the largely agrarian structure of society were minimal. As daunting as marriage to strangers might be, a woman's natal family always presented a refuge in bad times in a normal marriage. A love marriage could cause a daughter's natal family to lose face in society and disincline them to aid her if things went wrong later. At the same time, in an agrarian economy her husband's future is bound up in the land he will receive from his father and the cooperative relations he maintains with his agnatic kin. If the risks that come with a daughter-in-law are great under normal circumstances, the threats she poses for alienating a son's affections in a love marriage are even greater and she is likely to be resented for "stealing" a son. In those circumstances, most daughters were content to leave the arrangements of marriage up to their parents (Wolf 1972: 102–5).

"Minor marriage." While a major cultural emphasis within marriage included satisfying the ancestors' demand for descendants, alternative forms of marriage demonstrated the flexibility of the Chinese for simultaneous attention to more earthly concerns. We have shown that marriage was always a high risk proposition from the point of view of *chia* stability. In Taiwan and parts of South China such as southern Fukien, where the majority of Taiwan's Fukienese originated (A. Wolf and Huang 1980; M. Wolf 1972), *sim-pua,* or "minor" marriages, represented an important strategy for reducing the monetary costs of bringing in a daughter-in-law as well as the risks of alienating a son's affections. Minor marriages were contracted through the expedient of "adopting" a daughter-in-law at an early age, raising her with one's own family, and marrying her to a son when she came of age.

The advantages of *sim-pua* marriages were several. A daughter-in-law could be groomed for the needs of her marital home; her relationship with the mother-in-law would be more dutiful than that of a son's wife brought in at a later age as a stranger to the household; she would be unlikely to threaten the uterine family bonds between a mother and her son. Moreover, the costs of raising a child, particularly when a woman contributed to the *chia* domestic economy as she was raised, were far less than the expense of bride-price and the marriage feasts of major marriages. Her character was known, and the uncertainties of going through a go-between were done away with. Even better for the marital household, if the adopted daughter-in-law showed signs of being incompatible with the family, she could simply be married out and the process of arranging a major marriage for the targeted son could be initiated.

In spite of the advantages, there were also problems with this marriage form. Arthur Wolf suggests that fertility was much reduced in these minor marriages—it was 25% less than that of major marriages (A. Wolf and Huang 1980; A. Wolf 1985b). The possibilities of divorce were also much higher. In marriage records for a northern Taiwanese district, only 1.2% of the major marriages ended in divorce compared to 24.2% of the *sim-pua*. Margery Wolf also mentions evidence in the form of village gossip that these minor marriages were more likely than major marriages to involve women in extramarital affairs (1972: 182). Nevertheless, before 1925 over half the marriages in the Taipei Basin itself were *sim-pua* marriages.

Who was most likely to enter into these alternative marriages? Because the risks and costs associated with major marriage might be expected to vary in their impact across social classes, poorer families being the least likely to afford the expense of a proper wedding, we might expect poor *chia* groups to be more likely to arrange these sorts of marriages for their sons. In an upper-, middle-, and lower-class comparison of the frequencies for this form, Sophie Sa (cited in A. Wolf 1985a) found that percentages of minor marriages increased from 11% for upper-class women to 19% for middle-class to 23% for lower-class. But Arthur Wolf suggests that the rationale is more complex and is in part related to regional traditions, with 40% of the marriages in northern Taiwan in the early twentieth century being of this type compared to not more than 10% in the south (1985a).

Whatever the reason for entering into this type of marriage, its frequency suffered a drastic decline after 1930, and it disappeared almost completely during the later Japanese period. Wolf (M. Wolf 1972: 180) gives this disappearance as an early example of the effects of wage labor on intergenerational relations. She speculates that sons did not like this form of marriage and that the economic power afforded by Japanese jobs in the north allowed them to avoid these arrangements, but only to the extent that they accepted parental arrangements for major marriages!

Uxorilocal marriages. Marriage typically removed a daughter from her natal home to begin a new life with her husband's family. Both major and minor marriages involved variations on this theme, the important differences having to do with the timing and the ceremonial complexity surrounding the transfer of residence. Another variant of marriage style occurred in cases in which a family was without sons of its own and unable to adopt a son to fill the breach. In these marriages, called uxorilocal by anthropologists, a son-in-law would be brought into the household to live with his wife's kin.[18]

In China, this was an option of last resort. It reflected poorly on the man agreeing to it, since by definition only an unfilial son would forsake his own parents and ancestors to provide for and produce descendants for others. Likely male candidates for this marriage form, moreover, were often from poor households without a compelling inheritance share in their own natal families. Ideally they would be induced to change their surnames to those of the wife's parents, they would renounce a claim on their children as descendants of their own patrilineal ancestors, and they would agree to act as sons within their wives' natal families (M. Wolf 1972: 192). The undesirability of these conditions left room for negotiation, and in some variations uxorilocal sons-in-law would agree to assign their wives' surname to alternating children or to the first son only. In Taiwan, these marriages are reported for the pool of men with unusual breaks from the normal life course: orphans, the poor, Mainlanders separated from their families and sources of inheritance by movement to Taiwan after World War II.

Undesirable though uxorilocal marriage may have been, Barclay (1954) has demonstrated that it was a fairly frequent form in the early part of this century in Taiwan. Using the Japanese records so important to historical demographic research in Taiwan, he reports that 22% of all registered marriages in 1906 were uxorilocal. Moreover, there is evidence of a steady decline in this sort of marriage throughout the first part of this century. In 1930, only 16% of the registered marriages were so reported, and by 1943 the percentage had further declined to 6%. Barclay himself attributes this decline to the undesirability of these mar-

---

18. Adoption in China was a strategy for resolving several crises in the family's responsibility for providing descendants for the ancestors. A woman whose children died or who was barren could adopt children, preferably from closely related agnates of her husband. But the option of adopting sons was somewhat restricted both because of the reluctance of families to release their own sons and because of the consequent expense of procuring an adopted son versus a daughter. For the childless woman, a daughter could be adopted to "lead in a son" in an uxorilocal marriage. Even families with daughters of their own might turn to this strategy because uxorilocal marriages were regarded as of somewhat lesser status than a normal marriage. The stigma would then be visited on an adopted daughter rather than their own (M. Wolf 1972: 172).

riages in the Chinese scheme, suggesting that when economic necessity did not force these unions, Taiwanese males were increasingly unlikely to enter into them.

Age at marriage. Among the responsibilities of parents to their children was the provision of a good marriage (Baker 1979; M. Wolf 1972). The historical evidence suggests that most Chinese parents adroitly performed this task, at least to the extent of finding a spouse, in spite of the risks to which marriage exposed their *chia.* Barclay (1954) reports, for example, that marriage was early and close to universal for most Taiwanese in the Japanese era. Percentages of ever-married women 35 years old and above were consistently above 99% for every census from 1905 to 1935.[19] For men, the percentages of those ever married in this group were consistently over 95%. Some evidence of the early nature of these marriages is seen by looking at the 20- to 24-year-old age group, in which 92% of all women reported ever having been married in the 1905 census. At the same time, we begin to find evidence of a trend when we look at the percentages of ever-married women across censuses for this age group. Subsequent percentages drop to 87% in 1915 and reach a low of 83% in the 1935 census. Evidence also suggests that the mean age at marriage for women in the Japanese period rose slightly from 18 in the 1905 census to 20 by the 1935 census; the mean ages for men actually dropped from 25 in the 1915 census to 23 in the 1935 (Casterline 1980). Village studies indicate that brides in minor marriages were younger on the average than brides in other forms of marriage, but that in uxorilocal and major marriages brides tended to be about the same age. Not surprisingly, given the undesirable nature of uxorilocal marriage, males entering into these unions tended to marry later than others while minor marriages were again contracted at the youngest ages.[20]

Family building and marriage. The strong emphasis on producing descendants for the ancestors and the relatively early ages at which marriages took place imply high fertility rates in the Chinese past. Once

19. These Japanese censuses were conducted in Taiwan in 1905, 1915, and every subsequent five-year period. Barclay presents grouped figures for both formal and informal marriages, that is, those legally registered and those unregistered.

20. Wolf and Huang (1980: 135) present evidence that median ages for minor marriage were consistently around 17 for all five-year cohorts of women born between 1891 and 1920. For major and uxorilocal marriages, the median ages at marriage for these cohorts tend to be around 19. For males born between 1886 and 1915, the median age for minor marriage is around 21 for all five-year cohorts. Medians for major marriage are between 23 and 24 and for uxorilocal marriage between 24 and 27, but generally always the highest in any given cohort.

again, the excellent records on Taiwan available to us from the Japanese era have allowed scholars to study fertility in some detail (Barclay 1954; Pasternak 1983; Wolf and Huang 1980). A host of village studies report that a woman's position in her new household was cemented by the birth of a child, especially a son. Even when the first birth was a daughter, the catastrophic fear of having arranged a marriage with an infecund daughter-in-law was relieved and subsequent male births could be anticipated (M. Wolf 1972).

Using Japanese registration data, Barclay reports crude birthrates ranging between 40 and 46 births per thousand for the five-year periods between 1906 and 1940 (1954: 241). These estimates may be biased, however, due to omitted registrations in addition to the well-known effects of changing age composition on crude rates. A more dependable estimate based on the number of women in the fecund years between 15 and 49 and taken from the more reliable census data cited above suggests general fertility ratios in the neighborhood of 200 births per thousand women with trends across time indicating an increase in the number of births from 1930 to 1935.

Looking at village statistics from the Japanese period, Pasternak (1983) and Wolf and Huang (1980) have examined total marital fertility rates (TMFRs) by type of marriage. In general, their findings indicate lower marital fertility for minor marriages in three village areas for which they have data. Thus, while TMFRs for both major and uxorilocal unions are above 7.5 for all three areas, minor marriage fertility is considerably lower, 4.9 and 5.7 for the two villages examined.[21]

Widowhood and divorce. In the Chinese system as we have described it, one might expect marriages arranged by parents to endure throughout the lives of spouses. The great care taken by parents to ensure compatibility between spouses' backgrounds, the injunctions of filial piety, and the very expense of marriage all seem to argue for highly stable marriages. These marriages can end in two ways, each with its own implications.

The death of a spouse had different implications for men and women. Chinese men were very likely to remarry and, indeed, were encouraged to do so as a way of enlarging their pool of descendants. Pasternak (1983: 70) shows that the probabilities of widower remarriage declined

---

21. The association of minor marriage with lower fertility, especially puzzling given the earlier marriage ages for these unions, has sparked a lively literature concerning the causes for this pattern. For our purposes here, however, we will only note the pattern and suggest that the reason is tied to the lack of sexual attraction between spouses in minor marriages (Wolf 1966, 1970) and the higher divorce rates associated with these marriages.

considerably with age, as we would expect in a world where older widowers were more likely to have large numbers of descendants. An older widower with sons who were themselves already married would only be hastening *chia* fission by bringing in a new wife and threatening his sons with the possibility of having to divide their property with another co-heir. They might feel it better to cut their losses by dividing the property early and receiving a larger share as a result.

Wives, on the other hand, were expected to remain faithful to their deceased spouses and to avoid remarriage. Legal codes from the past included statutes designed to buttress a widow's loyalty to her deceased husband by penalizing her economically if she remarried (Spence 1978).[22] The negative effect of these statutes, however, was to encourage her husband's parents or brothers to enlist in her remarriage so that they would get access to the property. In fact, although widows remarried less often than widowers, they often *did* remarry, with rates varying considerably between locales. Pasternak shows that the rates of remarriage within five years of a husband's death dropped off considerably for women 30 years old and above, by which time they would be well established with their own uterine families and potentially enjoying considerable power within the *chia* on their own (1983). Indeed, other village evidence suggests that those widows remarrying at later ages are also more likely to take an uxorilocally resident husband into the *chia* established by her former husband (A. Wolf 1975). We can imagine that such cases of uxorilocal remarriage were cases in which the Ch'ing legal code would not apply—either because the deceased husband's agnates were few and unlikely to press the point or because the woman's sons were grown and in control of the *chia*.

If widow remarriage was discouraged by prevailing social norms and legal sanction, divorce appears to have been even more frowned upon. Freedman (1958; see also Yang 1945) suggests that divorce was extremely rare in Fukien and Kwangtung while acknowledging Taiwan as exceptional for its frequency of marriage failure. Again, Barclay presents striking figures for Taiwan's Japanese occupation era indicating a high level of divorce that, like the rates for uxorilocal and minor marriages, declined through the first third of the century. Before 1920, the percentage of Taiwanese marriages dissolved within the first five years was at least 10%, and nearly 15% if only first marriages were counted (Barclay

22. "If a widow remarries, her husband's property, as well as the dowry she originally brought with her, shall become the property of her former husband's family" (cited in Spence 1978).

1954: 221). This figure declined to 4% of those marriages registered in 1939.

Ethnographic and historical reconstruction suggests some reasons for the high incidence of divorce in Taiwan as well as for its decline throughout the Japanese period. Margery Wolf (1972) has pointed out that uxorilocal and minor marriages were among the most brittle of unions, and these declined during the Japanese era. For uxorilocal unions, the reasons for instability lay in the extent to which they countered the entire thrust of Chinese normative patrilineal orientation. Wolf and Huang (1980) suggest that minor marriages, on the other hand, created a brittle union because of the close association between the spouses in their years of socialization. Arthur Wolf provides village evidence that the rates of divorce for major, uxorilocal, and minor marriages were 7%, 18%, and 18%, respectively, for women born between 1881 and 1915 (1975: 105). The same general pattern obtained elsewhere (Pasternak 1983: 81).

Non-normative Patterns

Our discussion of marriage and divorce opens a consideration of behaviors that do not seem to fit the normative Chinese pattern in the past. These behaviors stand as a caution against oversimplifying and idealizing the integration of the Chinese family and social system. Ethnographers report, for example, the relatively strict separation of the sexes in the past. Yang (1945: 63) writes of a mainland village that unrelated boys and girls were kept apart as much as possible after the age of 12 until marriage; sexual relations unsanctioned by marriage were forbidden, and the consequences of adultery included loss of clan status for males if it occurred with a woman married into their clan. The old women of a Taiwanese village similarly recall the days of obsessive sexual segregation and continue to be uncomfortable with the thought of their unmarried daughters at work in factories (M. Wolf 1972: 96–97).

In spite of these apparent normative restrictions, the evidence for the existence of prostitution, adultery, and rather high rates of bastardy and premarital conception in the past is unimpeachable. An early Jesuit visitor to China, Matteo Ricci, noted the prevalence of prostitutes in seventeenth-century Chinese society (Spence 1984), and one finds mention of the institution in more recent ethnography (M. Wolf 1972). In the past, these women were all very likely to marry, often uxorilocally, or to become concubines for wealthy men. The conditions that would cause daughters to go into prostitution, at least temporarily, were in fact often the same as those that would lead to uxorilocal marriage: an absence of brothers in the *chia* combined with relative poverty and a filial need to support one's parents.

Somewhat related was the practice in China's past of taking concubines. Concubinage was also related to polygyny in that it represented a less formal, but recognized, possibility of union in Chinese society. In order to forgo the expense of marriage to another wife, a man might take a concubine in response to the infertility of his first wife. Baker (1979) reports that the children of concubines had the same rights to inheritance as the children of regular unions, and Barrett (1980: 297) reports that the Japanese in Taiwan recognized concubinage as a form of quasi-marriage in which children would have a right to inheritance. On the other hand, Barrett suggests that the paternity of a concubine's children was not, in all cases, acknowledged, which suggests that there was some leeway in the extent to which these inheritance claims were acknowledged.

Both prostitutes and concubines, when paternity for their children remained unacknowledged, account for some of the high rates of child-bearing outside marriage found in Taiwan's recent past (Barrett 1980). The need for financial and emotional security and the familial context in which this was provided made it imperative that even prostitutes take steps to build their own uterine families (M. Wolf 1972). At the same time, the rates for illegitimate births in the past were too high to be entirely due to the paternally unclaimed children of concubines and the independent efforts of prostitutes. Barrett presents evidence to show that illegitimacy rose throughout the early years of this century until 1935, when over 4% of all births involved unclaimed paternity. These figures are exclusive of births to concubines in which paternity was officially claimed. He suggests, moreover, that the explanation for these high rates must take account of the high incidence of illegitimate births among divorced and widowed women. Wolf and Huang (1980) also suggest that widowed women were not entirely celibate in one village, where the percentage of those bearing illegitimate children is well over 35% for those widowed below age 35. They suggest that widowed women, unless they had sons available to help them, bartered their sexuality to bring a man's help to their domestic economy. They further argue that these women chose to remain unmarried since they had nothing to gain by placing themselves under a male's dominance in marriage. Certainly, they had much to lose by remarriage if the dictates of the Ch'ing legal codes mentioned above were adhered to.

Births to never-married women apparently accounted for a smaller number of illegitimate children. The strictures against contact between the sexes may have been sufficiently strong to inhibit premarital sex in most cases, but even here premarital conceptions in one Chinese village may have been as high as 12% of all first births (Pasternak 1983). These rates tended to be highest for uxorilocal marriages. While we can only speculate here about the causes for higher rates of premarital conception, Pasternak suggests that the reason lies in the nature of uxorilocal marriage, the need to recruit male labor into the *chia*. The premarital conceptions may have resulted from the greater freedom accorded women without brothers, who would inevitably be less supervised in their day-to-day field work. Further, the compatibility of the incoming son-in-law may have been tested with his living with the family for a time before marriage. In cases where marriages were called off when problems developed during this testing period, the consequent birth would contribute to rates of illegitimacy.

Historical Changes from the Past Century

Japanese Occupation: 1895–1945

The Japanese occupation of Taiwan separated the island from the turmoil occurring on the mainland during the decline of the last Chinese dynasty and had important implications for changes in the island's infrastructure. Meskill (1979: 271) suggests that an important impact of the Japanese occupation resulted from attributes of their bureaucratic and non-family-based administration of the island. An effective police system bringing order to a region considered the most difficult to govern of all China's provinces was introduced (cf. Lamley 1981). More important perhaps was the development of an infrastructure for that administration: regular land surveys were conducted, transportation links improved, and health and education institutions developed. Although Taiwan was run as a gigantic sugar plantation by the Japanese, with business profits going to Japan, much of the tax collected went directly into local improvements of harbors, railroads, and other communication links (Gates 1987: 39–40) and the interethnic tension characterizing earlier periods largely disappeared.

Perhaps the most dramatic Japanese intervention in Taiwan's family life was the creation of an island-wide schooling system. Originating in an elementary course of instruction known as the common school, the system of education on Taiwan had as its original goals the dissemination of the Japanese language and the teaching of ethics and practical knowledge useful to efficient administration of the colony. The six-year common school course was instituted for students aged 8 to 14 in 1898 and expanded to include 7- to 16-year-olds in 1904. Although the Japanese were intent on teaching history, science, and arithmetic and ending what they regarded as Chinese superstition, they nevertheless retained in the early years of the occupation a number of features of the Chinese private school system. Students learned Chinese from such texts as the *Classic of Filial Piety* in the first grade and continued with the classics in this fashion until the fifth and sixth grades, when the style of teaching was in the Japanese fashion (Tsurumi 1977: 20).

Japanese efforts to build schools and encourage attendance were remarkably successful. In 1898, 26 schools were established; by 1906, there were 180 schools and about thirty-two thousand Taiwanese students attending. To be sure, this was a small percentage of the total population, but the trend throughout the Japanese period was one of increasing and more regular attendance for all school-age children. Tsurumi (1977: 148) provides figures for the growth in percentages of school-aged children enrolled in elementary school from 1907 to 1944. Where in 1907 only 4% were enrolled, the percentage had grown to 13% in 1917, 29% in 1927, and 47% in 1937. Growth in attendance even continued through the war years until by 1944, 71% of all school-aged children were enrolled in elementary schools.

Furthermore, although enrollment rates for boys were greater than those for girls throughout the period, the gap steadily declined. Indeed, Japanese policy explicitly encouraged the schooling of Taiwanese girls as a way of disseminating Japanese values in the population (Tsurumi 1977: 26–30, 62–63). In 1920, 39% of the school-aged boys were enrolled compared to 9% of the girls. By 1944, the comparable figures were 81% for boys and 61% for girls. Attendance and completion rates expanded apace with the overall increase in enrollment. In 1907, daily attendance levels for enrolled students were reported as 70% and by 1918, 92%.[23] Completion rates for the same period rose from 69% to 88% for boys and 49% to 82% for girls.

In spite of these changes, the Japanese allowed and even encouraged the continuity of many features of Taiwanese family organization. Landlord-tenant relations, largely unchanged, were adapted to the needs of Japanese production only insofar as a new layer was added to the direction of revenues (Lamley 1970). Other aspects of society such as inheritance practices, most marriage and adoption customs, and religious prac-

---

23. Tsurumi (1977: 62) suggests these official figures may overestimate attendance; they nevertheless indicate the general trend.

tices were relatively untouched (Cohen 1976; Gates 1987), especially in the rural areas. Some changes were introduced in the form of prohibitions of foot-binding and the beginnings of open primary education for women. Public education on a different model than the civil examination system, although made generally more available, was nevertheless quite restricted, and it was only after 1922 that Japanese-speaking Taiwanese children were allowed into Japanese schools, from which they could proceed to Japan for further training. This affected primarily the children of urban families while the Taiwanese were generally channeled into teaching and medicine if they pursued education at all (Gates 1987).

Twentieth-Century Social Movements

Although Taiwan was largely insulated from mainland political and social changes during the Japanese period, the impact of outside ideas on the family at the turn of the century is worth mentioning here. While the stability of the Chinese family system was threatened in rural areas by increasing population and the diminishing land base on which the ordered continuity of ancestors and descendants depended (Stacey 1983), urban intellectual movements also directly confronted the old Chinese family values. Although their immediate impact was limited to a small circle of the urban elite, the issues raised demonstrate the widely held Chinese belief in the complete integration of family and society.

The first influences of Western education were felt in the cities during the later nineteenth century. In 1862 an interpreters' college was established in Peking and soon after in Shanghai and Canton, while under missionary influence boys began to be sent to study in the United States, France, and England in the 1870s. At the same time, missionary schools were established in China itself, particularly in Taiwan and the southeast, and were an important source of Euro-American ideas.

With the events of the later nineteenth century, including the dismemberment of China and the end of the civil examination system in 1905, the Confucian system that mutually reinforced state and family ideology was severely weakened on the mainland. Intellectuals, in keeping with Chinese tradition, identified the crises within society as having to do with the family and campaigned for radical transformations of the system. Their attacks went to the core. They demanded an end to arranged marriages and even the whole concept of filial piety, demands that became explicit during the 1911 revolution overthrowing the last Chinese dynasty. Although Taiwan was somewhat insulated from these currents because of the Japanese occupation, a number of these proposals made their way into the Nationalist party (KMT) as reform platforms intended primarily to raise the status of urban women. Stacey (1983: 77–78) writes that these reforms found their way into the Family, Kinship and Succession Books of the 1931 KMT succession code as a compromise between Western values and the old Confucian authoritarianism. While the succession code attempted to bring greater equality to women in the civil code, it nevertheless reaffirmed the rights of males in matters of family authority. In a later development known as the New Life Movement, the KMT retreated somewhat from the earlier criticisms of the Confucian system and stressed again historical values in support of an orderly society.

Thus, Taiwan entered the twentieth century and the postwar era with most of the older values of the Chinese family system unaltered. Its insulation from the mainland and the Japanese policy of noninterference in local organization and the KMT retention of earlier values make the changes since World War II a laboratory for the effects of economic change, industrialization, urbanization, and the introduction of nonindigenous values on an intact family system.

Three

The Social and Economic Transformation
of Taiwan

A. Hermalin, P. K. C. Liu, and D. Freedman

Introduction

The social and economic conditions surrounding individuals and families, both locally and on a national level, are important influences on their behavior. The socioeconomic structure and demographic parameters define the opportunity space to a great extent, pointing up expanding and contracting possibilities and providing key inputs into the context within which options are weighed and decisions made.

This chapter describes the rapid transformation which has occurred in many spheres of social and economic life in Taiwan during the twentieth century, with particular emphasis on the post–World War II period. Given the vast amount of potentially relevant data, the strategy chosen is as follows: The introductory section presents a long-term view of Taiwan on a few selected dimensions, to establish the trends and patterns of change and the key turning points. This is followed by a detailed examination of several key historical periods, defined by major political or economic shifts. A common set of social, economic, and demographic factors will be reviewed in each period, but the amount of detail per factor will vary with its saliency for the period.

The Major Socioeconomic and Demographic Trends

During the twentieth century, Taiwan both completed its demographic transition, involving the move from high to low levels of mortality and fertility, and transformed itself from a rural, agricultural society to one that is highly urbanized and industrial. This change was accompanied by a tenfold increase in per capita income, in constant dollars. Much of this transformation occurred in a period of less than forty years—from the late 1940s to the mid-1980s—a remarkable compression which had ramifications for many facets of Taiwanese life, yet left many other aspects of traditional Chinese family values and practices intact, as demonstrated throughout this volume. Table 3.1 presents a broad range of social and economic indicators from 1949–88; Table 3.2 presents a reduced set of indicators from the prewar period. These tables and tables 3.3–3.11, which expand on each topic for the 1949–88 period, will be referred to throughout the chapter.

Figures 3.1–3.4 present the broad sweep of a few key demographic and economic indicators since 1906, shortly after the start of the Japanese colonial period. Figures 3.1 and 3.2 present data on key indicators of fertility and mortality levels, the total fertility rate and the life expectancy at birth, respectively. Total fertility displays a curvilinear pattern, rising gradually from a little under six children per woman to a peak near seven children in the early 1930s and remaining at that high level throughout the decade. The sharp decline associated with World War II was followed by a postwar baby boom which restored fertility to prewar levels in the early 1950s. But from the mid-1950s a sharp decline set in which brought total fertility to replacement levels by the mid-1980s. The rate of decline was particularly marked from the mid-1960s, which coincides with the introduction of an intensive family planning program, along with rapid socioeconomic development. The United Nations review of regional fertility trends from the mid-1950s through the mid-1980s indicates that the sharpest declines occurred among the nations of East Asia, and among these, Taiwan's was one of the most rapid (United Nations 1989, table 12).

In contrast to fertility, mortality conditions improved much more gradually and continuously throughout the twentieth century. As shown in figure 3.2, life expectancy at birth, around thirty years in 1906, advanced to forty-eight years in 1941, a gain of about one-half year for each elapsed calendar year. Little additional change occurred until the late 1940s, due to the war and postwar dislocations, but life expectancy advanced rapidly thereafter—particularly through the late 1960s. Between 1948 and 1968 expectation of life advanced by twenty years, from forty-eight to sixty-nine years, and another five years was added between 1969 and 1988.

Figure 3.3 presents one measure of urbanization, the proportion of the population in cities of fifty thousand or more. This measure also displays a gradually increasing pattern over the century, with acceleration after World War II. In 1906, the proportion urban was about 11% and this ratio grew slowly, reaching only 22% in 1941. Table 3.3, which traces the postwar period, shows that by 1961 the proportion urban was 41% and increased to 65% by 1979; since then the rate of growth in

TABLE 3.1 Indicators of Social and Economic Development, Taiwan, 1949–88

	1949	1952	1955	1958	1961	1964	1967	1970	1973	1976	1979	1982	1985	1988
Economic indicators														
GNP (B. NT$ at 1986 prices)	—	163	211	253	308	421	551	741	1,059	1,257	1,674	1,942	2,523	3,543
GNP index	—	100.0	129.3	155.3	188.5	257.7	337.7	454.1	648.9	770.2	1,026.1	1,190.4	1,546.0	2,171.4
Per capita income (1,000 NT$ at 1986 prices)	—	18	21	23	25	32	38	48	64	72	90	97	120	164
Per capita income index	—	100.0	116.4	126.9	138.4	172.7	208.6	259.9	350.4	390.0	488.2	528.2	651.5	894.8
Net savings as % of nat. inc.	—	15.3	14.6	15.3	18.4	20.3	23.1	25.6	34.4	32.3	33.4	29.7	32.6	34.9
Agri. prod. index (1952 = 100)	—	100.0	118.7	144.7	158.8	182.4	215.8	245.5	282.4	312.7	357.0	362.3	400.5	437.7
Indust. prod. index (1952 = 100)	—	100.0	149.7	189.4	279.9	400.0	627.8	1,105.9	1,924.9	2,481.1	3,664.5	4,017.8	5,197.0	6,829.0
% labor force in agriculture	—	56.1	53.6	51.1	49.9	49.5	42.5	36.7	30.5	29.0	21.5	18.9	17.5	13.7
Education indicators														
Junior high school enrollment	16.0	17.1	26.3	36.9	39.9	43.5	51.0	66.8	77.3	76.2	86.0	89.4	90.1	90.6
Senior high school enrollment	—	7.7	10.1	15.6	21.9	23.9	28.0	41.6	47.9	59.1	52.8	63.7	68.4	76.0
Communication and transportation														
Newspaper or magazines/1,000 pop.	—	—	—	—	—	37.4	—	53.1	76.2	90.4	141.3	164.4	194.8	199.1
TV sets per 1,000 households	—	—	—	—	—	14.3	—	371.0	738.0	931.1	1,007.6	1,028.7	1,054.5	1,100.0
Telephone subscribers (thousands)	17	25	34	46	65	88	135	249	487	986	1,861	3,230	4,228	5,322
Highway passenger-kms. (millions)	—	1,010	2,037	2,668	3,420	4,322	5,603	7,004	9,636	13,642	19,281	20,832	20,495	16,940
No. of passenger cars (thousands)	2.8	2.6	4.8	6.7	9.0	12.4	25.1	49.5	95.1	171.0	340.7	592.2	915.6	1,579.1
Household amenities														
Electricity														
% households served	—	—	—	—	74.7	82.6	92.4	96.3	97.8	99.6	99.7	99.7	99.7	99.7
Per capita annual consump. (kwh)	—	23	27	35	46	63	100	163	227	310	405	458	563	740
Piped water														
% population served	—	28.8	27.5	28.7	30.8	37.3	39.1	39.0	46.3	53.7	63.8	72.4	77.9	81.7
Health indicators														
Life expectancy at birth	51.0	58.6	62.5	64.2	65.0	66.5	67.0	68.2	69.0	70.0	71.9	72.4	73.3	73.6
Calories per person per day	—	2,078	2,247	2,359	2,430	2,364	2,504	2,658	2,574	2,771	2,845	2,749	2,874	3,017
Reproductive variables														
Total fertility rate	5,900	6,615	6,530	5,990	5,535	5,100	4,220	4,000	3,210	3,080	2,660	2,320	1,885	1,850

Sources: GNP, total and per capita, indexes; savings: Directorate-General of Budgets, Accounts and Statistics, Executive Yuan, 1990. Agricultural production index, industrial production index, % labor force in agriculture: Directorate-General of Budgets, Accounts and Statistics, Executive Yuan, 1989b. Education: see table 3.5. Communication and transportation: see table 3.10. Household amenities: Council for Economic Planning and Development, Manpower Planning Department, Executive Yuan, 1989. Life expectancy at birth: Lu, Gary L. T., 1978; Directorate-General of Budgets, Accounts and Statistics, Executive Yuan, 1989b, table 14. Calories: Council for Economic Planning and Development, Manpower Planning Department, Executive Yuan, 1989. Total fertility rate: Ministry of the Interior 1974a; Ministry of the Interior 1982; Ministry of the Interior 1989.

TABLE 3.2 Selected Demographic and Socioeconomic Indicators, 1905–40

	Total Population (in 1,000s) (1)	% of School-Age Pop. in Elem. School (2)	Expenditures on Public Health (per million NT$) (3)	Expenditures on Transportation (per million NT$) (4)
1905	3,123	4.7	11.8	108.6
1910	3,299	5.8	14.8	123.7
1915	3,570	9.6	21.7	192.2
1920	3,758	25.1	26.1	223.7
1925	4,147	29.5	67.2	191.6
1930	4,679	33.1	109.9	358.4
1935	5,316	41.5	102.0	416.8
1940	6,077	57.6	90.8	623.0

Agricultural Indicators

	Total Agricultural Population (in 1,000s) (1)	Number of Farms (in 1,000s) (2)	Cultivated Area (1,000 ha) (3)	Crop Area (1,000 ha) (4)	Percent of Cultivators Who Are Owners (5)
1905	1,962	360	625	686	—
1910	2,087	364*	674	731	33.7
1915	2,253	—	700	812	31.3**
1920	2,262	423	749	830	31.8
1925	2,340	394	775	925	29.9
1930	2,534	411	812	976	29.3
1935	2,790	420	831	1,090	31.6
1940	2,984	430	860	1,117	31.1

*Pertains to 1909. **Pertains to 1916. —Not available.

Sources:

Top: Col. 1: Provincial Government of Taiwan 1946; table 50, pp. 80–83.
           Col. 2: Data for 1905 come from Tsurumi 1977; table 1, p. 19.
                   Data for 1910–40 come from Tsurumi 1977; table 13, p. 148.
           Col. 3: Ho, Yhi-min, 1966; table E-4, p. 159.
           Col. 4: Ho, Yhi-min, 1966; table E-3, p. 157.

Middle: Col. 1: Data for 1915 and 1920 come from Ho, Yhi-min, 1966; table 9, p. 39. (The figure for 1915 is the average of 1914 and 1916; the 1920 figure is the average of 1919 and 1921.)
                   Data for 1905–40 except 1915 and 1920 come from Provincial Government of Taiwan 1946; table 194, p. 513.
           Col. 2: T. H. Lee et al. 1972; table III-2, p. 4.
           Col. 3: Provincial Government of Taiwan 1946; table 176, p. 516.
           Col. 4: Ho, Yhi-min, 1966; table 17, p. 50.
           Col. 5: Provincial Government of Taiwan 1946; table 194, p. 514.

TABLE 3.2 continued

	AVERAGE PER FARM			PERSONS PER	
	Household Members (1)	Farm Workers (2)	Cultivated Land (3)	Cultivated Hectare (4)	Crop Hectare (5)
1905	5.4	3.0	1.7	3.1	2.9
1910	5.7*	3.2*	1.8*	3.1	2.9
1915	5.6**	3.0**	1.8**	3.2	2.8
1920	5.3	2.7	1.8	3.0	2.7
1925	5.9	3.0	2.0	3.0	2.5
1930	6.2	2.9	2.0	3.1	2.6
1935	6.6	3.1	2.0	3.4	2.6
1940	6.9	3.2	2.0	3.5	2.7

Data per Farm and per Hectare

*Pertains to 1909. **Estimated.

Sources: Col. 1: Average household members = total agricultural population/number of farms.
Col. 2: Average farm workers per farm = gainfully occupied population in agriculture/number of farms.
Data of gainfully occupied population in agriculture come from Ho, Yhi-min, 1966; table 11, p. 43.
Col. 3: T. H. Lee et al. 1972; table III-2, p. 4.
Col. 4: Persons per cultivated hectare = total agricultural population/cultivated area.
Col. 5: Persons per crop hectare = total agricultural population/crop area.

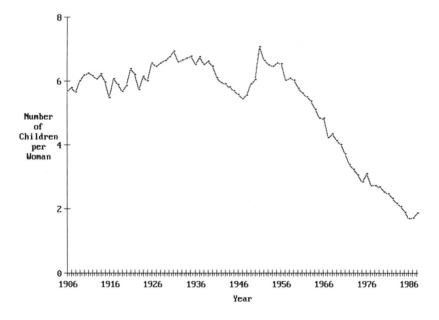

Figure 3.1 Total fertility rate.

Figure 3.2   Life expectancy at birth.

the proportion urbanized has slowed, with the proportion advancing to 73% in 1988.

These patterns of change in demographic characteristics can be contrasted in figure 3.4 with an important economic indicator—per capita income. Here the estimated data are difficult to capture in a single curve. Rather, two different patterns are indicated. Between 1906 and 1942, per capita income grew gradually, advancing less than 500 Taiwanese dollars a year (at 1981 prices). Between 1942 and 1948, the war and its aftermath cut per capita income in half, wiping out the gains occurring since 1906. From that point on, however, per capita income grew rapidly, at an average of 6% a year from 1948 to 1988. Still, not until 1964 did per capita income regain the level of the late 1930s. (Alternate estimates of pre- and postwar per capita income point to a more rapid recovery; see Hsing 1971, 152–53). At this point, however, the demographic and socioeconomic fabric was quite different on many dimensions from its prewar counterpart, and the country was embarked on a very different course, which will be revealed in our closer examination of these periods. Before that we take a broad overview of the postwar

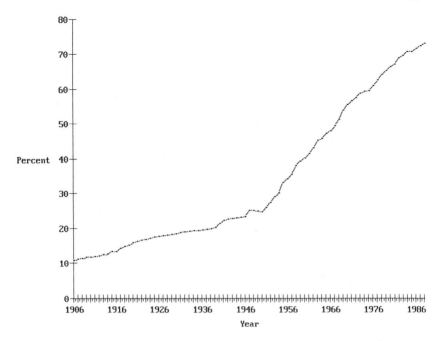

Figure 3.3 Percentage urban.

period by examining in table 3.1 a series of social and economic indicators.

The economic indicators shown in table 3.1 reflect the rapid rise in per capita income previously discussed, as well as the exceedingly rapid industrialization of the country. The index of industrial production rose by a factor of 68 between 1952 and 1988, while the agricultural production index rose only fourfold, and the proportion of the labor force engaged in agriculture and fishing declined from more than one-half to less than one-seventh.

The postwar period was also marked by a rapid transformation of the educational system in Taiwan. As shown in table 3.1, in the mid-1950s only about a quarter of those aged 12–14 were in junior high school and about a tenth of those 15–17 were in senior high; by 1988, enrollment in junior high was almost universal and three-quarters of those 15–17 were in senior high. As discussed in detail below, enrollment in college also advanced dramatically over this period.

Associated with higher incomes and education has been a mushrooming in the consumption of mass media and a wide variety of household and durable goods. As indicated in table 3.1, newspaper circulation

TABLE 3.3 Demographic Indicators, Selected Years, 1949–88

	Population (1,000)	Households (1,000)	Average Household Size	Age Distribution, Percent of Population			Birthrate per 1,000	Death Rate per 1,000	Rate of Natural Increase per 1,000	% of Pop. in Cities of 50,000 or More
				0–14	15–64	65 or Over				
Period I										
1949	7,397	1,332	5.55	41.1	56.4	2.5	42.4	13.1	29.2	24.9
1952	8,128	1,492	5.45	42.4	55.1	2.5	46.6	9.9	36.7	27.4
1955	9,078	1,629	5.57	43.4	54.1	2.5	45.3	8.6	36.7	33.2
1958	10,039	1,804	5.56	44.6	52.9	2.5	41.7	7.6	34.1	37.9
1961	11,149	2,002	5.57	45.9	51.6	2.5	38.3	6.7	31.6	41.4
Period II										
1961	11,149	2,002	5.57	45.9	51.6	2.5	38.3	6.7	31.6	41.4
1964	12,257	2,188	5.60	45.5	51.9	2.6	34.5	5.7	28.8	45.7
1967	13,297	2,388	5.57	43.3	53.9	2.8	28.5	5.5	23.0	49.3
1970	14,676	2,620	5.60	39.6	57.4	3.0	27.2	4.9	22.3	55.5
1973	15,565	2,865	5.43	37.1	59.7	3.2	23.8	4.8	19.0	58.8
Period III										
1973	15,565	2,865	5.43	37.1	59.7	3.2	23.8	4.8	19.0	58.8
1976	16,508	3,183	5.19	34.7	61.7	3.6	25.9	4.7	21.2	60.9
1979	17,479	3,593	4.86	32.7	63.2	4.1	24.4	4.7	19.7	65.2
1982	18,458	4,032	4.58	31.2	64.2	4.6	22.1	4.8	17.3	68.8
1985	19,258	4,361	4.42	29.6	65.3	5.1	18.0	4.8	13.2	70.6
1988	19,904	4,808	4.14	27.9	66.4	5.7	17.3	5.2	12.1	72.9

Note: Population, households, and age distribution based on year-end data. Birthrates, death rates, and rate of natural increase based on mid-year population. Households include ordinary households, business households, and single households. Starting in 1969, population figures include armed forces living on military bases and inmates of institutions.

Sources: Population: 1949–88, Ministry of the Interior 1989, table 88, p. 1054. Households: 1949, Taiwan Provincial Government, Department of Civil Affairs, 1959, p. 52; 1952–58, Directorate-General of Budgets, Accounts and Statistics, Executive Yuan, 1961, table 7, pp. 28–29; 1961–64, Directorate-General of Budgets, Accounts and Statistics, Executive Yuan, 1966, table 18, pp. 54–55; 1967, Taiwan Provincial Government, Department of Civil Affairs, 1968, table 1, p. 1; 1970, Taiwan Provincial Government, Department of Civil Affairs, 1971, table 1, p. 540; 1973, Ministry of the Interior, Republic of China, 1974a, table 1, p. 473; 1976–88, Ministry of the Interior, *Taiwan-Fukien Demographic Fact Book, Republic of China,* for the years 1977, 1980b, 1983, 1986, and 1989. Age distribution: 1949, Directorate-General of Budgets, Accounts and Statistics, Executive Yuan, 1975, table S-1, pp. 8–9; 1952–88, Council for International Economic Cooperation and Development, 1988, table 2-7a. Birthrate, death rate, rate of natural increase: 1949–88, Ministry of the Interior, 1989, table 88, p. 1054. Percent of population in cities and towns of 50,000 or more: Urban and Regional Development Statistics, compiled by Urban and Housing Development Department, Council for Economic Planning and Development, Executive Yuan, for various years from 1965 to 1988.

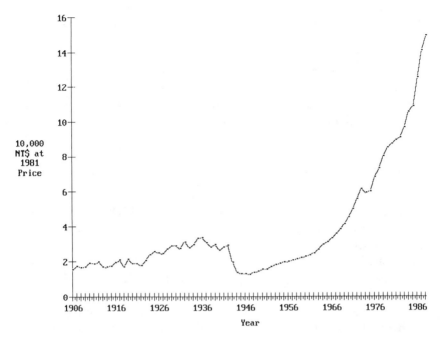

Figure 3.4 Per capita income.

and the ownership of telephones have advanced very rapidly, particularly since 1970. The number of passenger cars in operation grew by a factor of 8 between 1976 and 1988; electrification was widespread by the early 1960s and facilitated the rapid development of a variety of appliances.

With this general picture as a backdrop, we turn to a more detailed examination of specific periods. The rest of the chapter is structured for the most part as an examination of discrete periods. The periods to be reviewed are the precolonial period, before 1895; the colonial period and its immediate aftermath, 1895–1949; and the postwar period, 1949–88. Analysts tend to subdivide the postwar period into segments according to major governmental policies or key aspects of the economic structure. As an example, Speare, Liu, and Tsay (1988), who follow Rostow's model of economic development, demarcate the period into the takeoff phase, the labor intensive phase, and the industrial upgrading phase. While we hold a more agnostic view with regard to any inherent sequence of developmental stages, we do examine three distinct postwar periods: 1949–61, 1961–73, and 1973–88, which closely parallel the subdivision used by Speare, Liu, and Tsay (1988). Except for the precolonial and colonial periods, we will review a common set of social, economic, and demographic trends for each of these periods, but vary the degree of emphasis as appropriate to the period. As an aid to the exposition, these postwar periods are demarcated in tables 3.3 to 3.10, and a common set of measures is shown for selected years in each period. To avoid undue repetition, not every table will be discussed for each period; rather, a given topic may be treated in detail in one period while in another it will merit much briefer attention.

Precolonial Period

The Chinese had already begun to settle in Taiwan before the Dutch occupation, which lasted from 1624 to 1662 (Ho 1978, 9). Additional numbers came when Ming loyalist Cheng Ch'eng-Kung (Koxinga) arrived with his army in 1662 (Ho 1978, 9). The pace of immigration accelerated when the Manchu (Ch'ing) dynasty took over Taiwan as part of China in 1682. During the years of the Manchu reign, the government showed little interest in investing in Taiwan, although at the end of the nineteenth century some officials in China did appoint a new governor with ambitious plans to construct a north-south railway, lay a cable line to Fukien, dredge harbors, and establish a shipping company and coal industry. Most of these plans came to naught, in part because of minimal mainland support and disinterest and hostility among the local population (Ho 1978, 23).

During the Ch'ing period, there was a slow but steady increase in population, cultivated land, and agricultural output. The economy was based on traditional agriculture and was not highly commercialized. Contacts with the outside world were few, limited to treaty ports, with the result that Taiwan remained a closed, self-sufficient economy at the end of the nineteenth century (Ho 1978, 10–24). The Ch'ing government rule ended in 1895 when they had to cede Taiwan to Japan after their defeat in the first Sino-Japanese war.

The Colonial Period

Taiwan's marked economic growth, which eventually transformed it from a labor-intensive agricultural economy to a prosperous, high-technology society, began in 1895 with the Japanese occupation. Japan's colonial policy in Taiwan had two principal economic objectives: (1) to promote the production and export of sugar and rice and (2) to keep economic power in Japanese hands (Ho 1978, 32). To this end, the

Japanese instituted a variety of programs designed to increase agricultural yields, while maintaining political and economic control.

To achieve their goal, the Japanese colonizers made sizable investments in a number of areas, including industrial and agricultural infrastructure, agricultural productivity, public health, and basic education. Capital formation during the colonial period amounted, on average, to about 40% of the colonial government's total current expenditures (Ho 1978, 35). Almost 60% of these fixed capital investments were allocated to transport and communication, both of which were strategically important to the modernization and commercialization of agriculture. As shown in table 3.2, actual expenditures on transportation increased from 109 million NT$ in 1905 to 623 million NT$ in 1940. When the Japanese took over Taiwan, there were almost no roads or railroads; by 1940 Taiwan had 907 kilometers of railroads and 12,076 kilometers of roads (Ho 1978, 35).

The Japanese also invested heavily in agriculture. At least one-third of the government's developmental expenditures, or 10% of current total government expenditures, was spent in promoting agriculture through research, extension work, and subsidies (Ho 1978, 35). From 1900 to 1944, 165 million yen was invested in irrigation facilities, 58% of which were financed by the Japanese. This led to an increase, between 1905 and 1940, of the area under irrigation from 195,000 to 530,000 hectares, while the proportion of cultivated land under irrigation increased from 31 to 62% (Lee, Liu, and Tsai 1972, table II.7). These changes also led to an expansion of the total area under cultivation and, through double cropping, to an even more rapid expansion of the crop area, defined as the total acreage on which any crops are grown during the year. Table 3.2 shows that the cultivated area grew by 24% between 1905 and 1925 and another 11% between 1925 and 1940, for an overall growth of 38%; over the same two periods crop area grew by 35 and 21%, respectively, for an overall increase of 63%. Facilities for marketing, credit, research, and agricultural extension were established; the food processing industry was upgraded; land tenure was simplified; and taxes were stabilized. The Japanese created a widespread agricultural extension network which introduced new seed strains, new cropping techniques, and increases in both natural and chemical fertilizers. The distribution of inputs into agriculture shows an increase in the value of working capital from 8% in 1905 to 17% in 1940 (Lee, Liu, and Tsai 1972, table II.8). Farmers' associations formed the core of the agricultural extension network for spreading high-yielding seed strains and new cultivation techniques, agricultural cooperatives distributed fertilizer and provided credit, and irrigation associations financed and maintained waterworks; all these organizations penetrated to local levels. By 1928 farmers associations and agricultural cooperatives employed approximately forty thousand persons, including thirteen thousand extension workers. On a per farm basis, this amounted to one extension worker per thirty-two farm households (Ho 1968, 329–32). Substantial investments also were made in improving human capital. Mortality was reduced by public health measures which controlled the spread of cholera and plague, thus eliminating major epidemics. General health services were improved by the gradual substitution of modern medical doctors for the predominant Chinese herb doctors (Liu and Tsay 1982, 357). Government expenditures for public health services amounted to 12 million NT$ in 1905, rose to over 100 million NT$ in 1930 and 1935, and slowed somewhat in 1940 as World War II approached (table 3.2). Crude death rates declined from thirty-one to eighteen deaths per thousand between 1906 and 1943 while the birthrate hovered around forty over much of the period (Ho 1978, 26). The net result was an acceleration in the growth rate of the total population, and, to a lesser extent, of the agricultural population, at the end of the prewar period. The average annual growth rate of the total population doubled from 1.3% per year for the 1905–15 period to 2.6% per year for 1935–40 (see table 3.2). From 1905 to 1940, the growth rate of the agricultural population was generally more erratic and increased at a slower pace than the total population, though it still increased by over 600,000 between 1925 and 1940, for an annual growth rate of 1.6% per year.

This growth, coupled with the patterns of growth in number of farms and cultivated land, led to increased pressure on land beginning about 1925. While the amount of cultivated land per farm remained fixed during 1925–40, the third part of table 3.2 shows that the average number of people and, to a lesser extent, of workers per farm increased steadily as did the number of persons per cultivated or crop hectare. The index of agricultural production increased about 50% between 1925 and 1940, postponing the diminishing returns to labor that otherwise might have occurred (Ho 1978, 27).

Despite the considerable inputs into agriculture, farm work became more, rather than less, labor intensive, due to irrigation works, multiple cropping of rice, and the adoption of new seed strains, without significant improvements in tools or machinery. Living standards improved somewhat, but remained at or near subsistence levels (Hermalin and Lavely 1979, 206). Even in agriculture, many farm accounting and managerial functions were handled by landowners. There was not much change in the income distribution of farm families or in the size of farm holdings during this period. Table 3.2 shows that about a third of Taiwanese farmers owned the land they cultivated. This proportion changed little between 1905 and 1940. In addition, some farmers were part owners of the land they cultivated. However, the distribution of land ownership was very unequal. A 1920 survey showed that the lowest 43% of owners held only 6% of the land while the upper 12% held 62% of the land (Ho 1978, 42). The small industrial sector provided only limited participation to the Taiwanese, partly because of restrictive regulations regarding capital ownership and partly because the Taiwanese lacked investment capital. The proportion of Taiwan's labor force in agriculture and fishing was approximately 75% when the Japanese arrived in 1895; in 1940 the proportion was 70% (Hermalin and Lavely 1979). In short, the changes put in place were accomplished with minimal impact on either the labor force structure or the economic and social life of farmers.

Most Taiwanese were effectively barred from postprimary education, but the Japanese did gradually extend elementary education to all Taiwanese males. In 1905 less than 5% of the Taiwanese school age population was enrolled in elementary school, which increased to 25% in 1920 (40% of males and 9% of females) and to 71% in 1944 (81% of males and 61% of females) (table 3.2 and Tsurumi 1977, 148). Despite the high enrollment in elementary schools and the rise in literacy, from 1% in 1905 to 17% in 1940 (with literacy defined as the ability to read and write Japanese), by 1940 only twelve thousand Taiwanese had more than an elementary education (Directorate-General of Budgets, Accounts and Statistics 1978, 432).

Thus, in the first forty years of the twentieth century, Taiwan could be characterized as undergoing highly selective social change. Notable changes occurred in infrastructure, in the conduct of agriculture, in public health, and in the provision of elementary education. At the same time, little changed in the rhythm and horizons of daily life: a high proportion of the population remained on the farm, little opportunity existed for advanced education or nonfarm employment, choices and the sense of improvement were circumscribed to the technical aspects of agricultural production, and only limited increments occurred in the standard of living.

The Onset of Economic Expansion, 1949–61

World War II inflicted serious damage on Taiwan's industry, agriculture, and general infrastructure as a combined result of Allied bombings and neglect of the irrigation network and industrial plants. According to Hsing (1971, 149),

> It was reported that, on VJ Day in 1945 when Taiwan was retroceded to the Republic of China, about three-fourths of industrial productive capacity and two-thirds of power-generating capacity were destroyed, over one-half of the existing rails, bridges, station facilities, and rolling stock were incapacitated, and only one-fourth of the highways remained serviceable for motor vehicles, while harbors were largely ruined and blocked by sunken ships. As a result, agricultural output dropped to 45 per cent and industrial output to less than one-third of their respective pre-war peaks.

Further exacerbating Taiwan's problems following its retrocession to the Republic of China was the exodus of the Japanese, who constituted the bulk of the technical and administrative personnel and skilled laborers, and a rampant inflation that reached 3,500% in 1949. In addition, the Nationalist government preoccupied with the war against the Communists, provided only limited assistance.

However, relative to other less developed countries, Taiwan had many assets which augured well for its economic prospects. Its infrastructure, though seriously damaged, was still extensive; its agricultural sector remained productive; there was considerable institutional development in such services as health, farmers associations, and banking facilities, a fairly literate population, and a stable society (Ho 1978, 103–4). Thus, despite many ongoing problems, clear signs of recovery are evident in the immediate postwar period. By 1949, rice production approached 90% of its prewar peak and sweet potatoes surpassed their earlier peak; among a number of key manufactured products there was similar recovery to the levels reached prior to the war (Hsing 1971, 150–51).

Several subsequent external events affected Taiwan's economic prospects. From 1946 to 1950, more than a million mainland government and army personnel arrived in Taiwan (Ho 1978, 105). The influx of a sizable core of managers, technicians, and entrepreneurs filled the managerial void created by the withdrawal of the Japanese; they also brought with them a sizable amount of industrial capital (Fei, Ranis, and Kuo 1979, 26, 51). Since these decision makers were not affiliated with local interest groups, they were more free to promote long-term interests for the economy as a whole. The large infusion of U.S. economic and military aid from 1949 to 1967 was critically important to Taiwan's economic restructuring; this aid helped Taiwan control their inflation, provided needed foreign exchange, and made possible a high level of capital formation (Jacoby 1966). Total U.S. assistance over the period 1949–67 amounted to U.S. $4.2 billion, of which $1.8 billion was economic aid and $2.4 billion was military expenditures (Ho 1978, 110).

The Nationalist government, after some early inept political strategies, which generated considerable ill will among the Taiwanese population, moved quickly to institute a program which would first take care of basic needs and then proceed to a faster industrial development. These steps were essential if Taiwan was to provide food and employment for its rapidly growing indigenous population, absorb the Mainlanders, and support a sizable military establishment. The first imperative was to stabilize the monetary system. The revaluation of the basic currency, governmental sequestering of all foreign exchange earnings, and the introduction of savings deposits tied to the price index helped bring inflation under control.

The initial strategy involved a sizable investment in agriculture to provide food for the growing population. First, the government instituted an extensive land reform program in 1949: rents were reduced, landlord holdings and corporately held lands were compulsorily purchased by the government in return for bonds and shares in government-owned industries, and the land was resold to tenant farmers. The tenant price, which remained fixed at two and one-half times the annual yield of the land, assessed as of 1948, was payable in twenty semiannual installments, plus 4% interest. Laws were enacted to prevent speculation or accumulation of land, to safeguard the rights of tenants, and to eliminate absentee landlords. This "land-to-the-tiller" program curtailed, but did not entirely eliminate, rural tenancy and significantly improved both the absolute and the relative income position of former tenants. Table 3.4 shows that, between 1949 and 1961, the number of farms increased by 29% and the proportion of cultivators who fully owned their land grew from 36% in 1949 to 65% in 1961. This contrasts with the slow pace of change on these indicators between 1930 and 1940 (table 3.2).

Land reform also changed the rural power structure by transferring authority from landlords and lineage organizations to the individual farmer. This led to the democratization of rural political roles wherein elected village heads, rather than landlords, formed the basic link between farm households and the central government, and all rural fees and assessments were paid directly to the government. The shift in the rural authority structure and the security of farm tenure undoubtedly increased the farmers' commitment to entrepreneurship and investment.

Agricultural production increased by 59% between 1952 and 1961 (table 3.1). The postwar agricultural growth was accomplished with little

TABLE 3.4 Agricultural Development in Postwar Period

	Total Agricultural Population (in 1,000s)	No. of Farms (in 1,000s)	No. of Workers (1,000)	Cultivated Area (1,000 ha)	Crop Area (1,000 ha)	% of Cultivators Who Are Full Owners	% of Farm Inc. Earned off Farm
Period I							
1949	3,880	621	—	865	1,438	36	—
1952	4,257	680	1,642	876	1,521	39	—
1955	4,603	733	1,667	873	1,508	59	—
1958	4,881	770	1,707	883	1,588	61	—
1961	5,467	801	1,747	872	1,613	65	—
Period II							
1961	5,467	801	1,747	872	1,613	65	35
1964	5,649	835	1,810	882	1,673	67	—
1967	5,949	869	1,723	902	1,696	67	—
1970	5,991	880	1,680	905	1,656	77	51
1973	5,868	877	1,624	896	1,567	78	54
Period III							
1973	5,868	877	1,624	896	1,567	78	54
1976	5,563	871	1,641	920	1,606	82	61
1979	5,639	898	1,380	915	1,494	85	74
1982	4,876	814	1,284	891	1,380	85	72
1985	4,146	772	1,297	888	1,257	83	75
1988	3,781	732	1,113	895	1,216	86	76

<table>
<thead>
<tr><th></th><th colspan="3">Per Farm</th><th colspan="3">Per Hectare</th></tr>
<tr><th></th><th>Household Members</th><th>Farm Workers</th><th>Cultiv. Land (hectare)</th><th>Persons per Cultiv. Hectare</th><th>Persons per Crop Hectare</th><th>Workers per Crop Hectare</th></tr>
</thead>
<tbody>
<tr><td>Period I</td><td></td><td></td><td></td><td></td><td></td><td></td></tr>
<tr><td>1949</td><td>6.25</td><td>—</td><td>1.39</td><td>4.49</td><td>2.70</td><td>—</td></tr>
<tr><td>1952</td><td>6.26</td><td>2.41</td><td>1.29</td><td>4.86</td><td>2.80</td><td>1.08</td></tr>
<tr><td>1955</td><td>6.28</td><td>2.27</td><td>1.19</td><td>5.27</td><td>3.05</td><td>1.11</td></tr>
<tr><td>1958</td><td>6.34</td><td>2.22</td><td>1.15</td><td>5.53</td><td>3.07</td><td>1.08</td></tr>
<tr><td>1961</td><td>6.83</td><td>2.18</td><td>1.09</td><td>6.27</td><td>3.39</td><td>1.08</td></tr>
<tr><td>Period II</td><td></td><td></td><td></td><td></td><td></td><td></td></tr>
<tr><td>1961</td><td>6.83</td><td>2.18</td><td>1.09</td><td>6.27</td><td>3.39</td><td>1.08</td></tr>
<tr><td>1964</td><td>6.77</td><td>2.17</td><td>1.06</td><td>6.40</td><td>3.38</td><td>1.08</td></tr>
<tr><td>1967</td><td>6.85</td><td>1.98</td><td>1.04</td><td>6.60</td><td>3.51</td><td>1.02</td></tr>
<tr><td>1970</td><td>6.81</td><td>1.91</td><td>1.03</td><td>6.62</td><td>3.62</td><td>1.01</td></tr>
<tr><td>1973</td><td>6.69</td><td>1.85</td><td>1.02</td><td>6.55</td><td>3.74</td><td>1.04</td></tr>
<tr><td>Period III</td><td></td><td></td><td></td><td></td><td></td><td></td></tr>
<tr><td>1973</td><td>6.69</td><td>1.85</td><td>1.02</td><td>6.55</td><td>3.74</td><td>1.04</td></tr>
<tr><td>1976</td><td>6.39</td><td>1.88</td><td>1.06</td><td>6.05</td><td>3.46</td><td>1.02</td></tr>
<tr><td>1979</td><td>6.28</td><td>1.54</td><td>1.02</td><td>6.16</td><td>3.77</td><td>.92</td></tr>
<tr><td>1982</td><td>5.99</td><td>1.58</td><td>1.09</td><td>5.47</td><td>3.53</td><td>.93</td></tr>
<tr><td>1985</td><td>5.37</td><td>1.68</td><td>1.15</td><td>4.67</td><td>3.30</td><td>1.03</td></tr>
<tr><td>1988</td><td>5.16</td><td>1.52</td><td>1.22</td><td>4.22</td><td>3.11</td><td>.92</td></tr>
</tbody>
</table>

Sources: Total agricultural population, number of farms, full owners, cultivated area: 1949–58, Joint Commission on Rural Reconstruction, Rural Economics Division, 1966. 1961–73, Joint Commission on Rural Reconstruction, Rural Economics Division, 1977. Agricultural workers: 1952–85, Council for International Economic Cooperation and Development, 1981, table 4.4. Agricultural population, farms, cultivated area, crop area: 1976–85, Council for International Economic Cooperation and Development, 1987, tables 4.2 and 4.4. Crop area: 1949–73, Provincial Government of Taiwan, Department of Agriculture & Forestry, 1978, table 5, p. 20. Owner-cultivators: 1976–88, Directorate-General of Budgets, Accounts and Statistics, Executive Yuan, 1989b, table 164, p. 276. Farm income earned off farms: Directorate-General of Budgets, Accounts and Statistics, Executive Yuan, 1989c, table 6. 1988 data on population, farms, workers, area: Council for International Economic Cooperation and Development, 1989, pp. 64, 66.

or no expansion of cultivated area, since most of the economically viable agricultural land was already under cultivation. Instead, enhanced productivity came through the increased use of fertilizers and more intensive use of arable land via new cropping patterns and intercropping. While the amount of cultivated land remained almost fixed between 1949 and 1961, the crop area increased by 12% (table 3.4). Although agricultural fixed capital increased during the postwar period, the most dramatic increase was in working capital, particularly in chemicals and commercial feeds (Ho 1978, 150 and 353). Between 1949 and 1961 working capital more than doubled, accounting for 35% of the increase in agricultural growth (Ho 1978, table 9.2 and p. 155). The government also invested heavily in support services for farmers. Agricultural research institutions played an important innovating role in the adoption of pesticides, the development of mushroom cultivation, and the introduction of improved farm tools and machinery. The colonial extension service was revived and reorganized under different auspices as the Joint Council on Rural Reconstruction (JCRR), and its influence became more pervasive due to increasing rural literacy. Government-sponsored farm credit facilities were reinstituted, providing 57% of the farm loans by 1960. There was also a considerable investment in public works in rural areas between 1952 and 1959, as shown by surveys in eighteen townships done by JCRR in each of these years (Kirby 1960). Total investments in public works in these areas totaled 43 million NT$, of which about 32% went to transport and communication, while almost as much was invested in school construction.

Fertility rates were high throughout this period. The total fertility rate, which was around 6.0 in 1949 and 1950, was in the neighborhood of 6.5 or higher through 1956 before declining to 5.6 by 1961 (see fig. 3.1). The high fertility rates, coupled with rising educational aspirations, began to exert considerable pressure on school facilities. As table 3.3 indicates, the population was growing by well in excess of 3% a year during the 1950s while, in addition, the proportion under age 15 was steadily increasing. The government invested heavily in education, both to accommodate the growing number of schoolchildren and to improve labor quality. Between 1952 and 1961 the proportion of total government expenditures devoted to education increased from 7 to 13% (Council for Economic Planning and Development 1988, 24). Despite these increases in funding, most schools had to run several shifts each day to accommodate the ever-growing number of children in primary school. Primary attendance was compulsory for both boys and girls.

The increasing birthrates exacerbated the pressure on farm families; it was difficult to support large families on the small acreage allotted to families under land reform, although double cropping utilized some additional labor. The amount of land owned by the average farm household decreased from 2 hectares in 1940 to slightly more than 1 hectare in 1961 (tables 3.2 and 3.4), while the size of the average farm household remained very large. It was difficult to obtain additional land by purchase or rental, and small plots could not be further subdivided by inheritance and still remain economically viable. Most farm families were likely to have some members who were either unemployed or underemployed. Although the unemployment rate, in standard labor force terms, was under 3% during the 1950s (table 3.7), the underemployment rate was much higher (Liu 1988, fig. 1). This pressure created interest in limiting family size, in educating the young to compete for better jobs in the industrial sector, and in creating new nonfarm positions in and around the rural areas.

On the educational side, these pressures are manifest in the increasing proportion of school age children at each level of education. As table 3.5 indicates, by 1961 attendance at primary school was almost universal; about two-fifths of those 12–14 were in junior high, and about one-fifth of those 15–17 in senior high. In each case, the proportion of males attending was higher than females, but between 1949 and 1961 female attendance rose faster than male attendance at each schooling level. At the college level, less than 1% were enrolled in 1949, while almost 5% of those 18 to 21 were enrolled by 1961. These increases in enrollment served to meet the growing aspirations of families and also mitigated the growth in labor force and the number of nonagricultural jobs that had to be created.

The ability of farm families to earn income away from their own holdings was a key factor in reducing the level of migration to urban places and also served to consolidate family income and savings, thus enhancing the demand for nonagricultural production. The increasing density of persons per farm and per hectare is clear from table 3.4, but the number of workers per hectare remained relatively stable. This meant that increasing numbers had to be provided for in other ways. As noted, increased school enrollment took up part of the slack, and migration to the cities from rural areas also reduced some of the pressure on farm families. Between 1949 and 1961, the proportion of the population in cities of fifty thousand and over increased from 25% to 41% (table 3.3). Much of the migration was to smaller places, since the proportion of

TABLE 3.5 School Attendance Rates by Level of Schooling and Sex, Selected Years, 1949–88

	Primary School (Ages 6–11)			Junior High School (Ages 12–14)			Senior High School (Ages 15–17)			College (Ages 18–21)		
	Males	Females	Total	Males	Females	Total	Males	Females	Total	Males	Females	Total
Period I												
1949	—	—	79.1	—	—	—	—	—	—	—	—	—
1952	93.1	74.1	84.0	23.5	10.3	17.1	11.7	3.6	7.7	2.1	0.3	1.5
1955	96.4	87.9	92.3	35.4	16.7	26.3	14.6	5.6	10.1	4.4	0.8	2.6
1958	97.4	92.2	94.8	47.7	25.3	36.9	21.8	8.9	15.6	5.5	1.5	3.6
1961	97.5	94.3	96.0	49.2	30.1	39.9	29.0	14.3	21.9	7.0	2.3	4.7
Period II												
1961	97.5	94.3	96.0	49.2	30.1	39.9	29.0	14.3	21.9	7.0	2.3	4.7
1964	97.9	95.7	96.8	52.5	33.9	43.5	29.4	17.6	23.7	11.3	4.8	8.1
1967	98.1	96.9	97.5	60.2	41.2	51.0	33.4	22.3	28.0	14.8	8.1	11.0
1970	98.3	97.7	98.0	74.4	58.8	66.8	47.8	35.1	41.6	21.5	16.3	19.0
1973	98.2	98.0	98.1	83.4	71.0	77.3	53.4	42.1	47.9	24.3	18.2	21.3
Period III												
1973	98.2	98.0	98.1	83.4	71.0	77.3	53.4	42.1	47.9	24.3	18.2	21.3
1976	99.5	99.4	99.4	79.9	72.3	76.2	63.1	54.9	59.1	22.1	19.0	20.6
1979	99.7	99.7	99.7	88.4	83.6	86.0	53.8	51.7	52.8	24.1	23.6	23.9
1982	99.8	99.8	99.8	89.7	89.1	89.4	63.8	63.5	63.7	23.8	25.3	24.5
1985	99.8	99.9	99.9	90.0	90.2	90.1	67.6	69.2	68.4	26.0	28.4	27.2
1988	99.9	99.9	99.9	90.7	90.4	90.6	72.5	79.7	76.0	29.2	32.7	30.9

Note: School attendance rates represent the number of students at each level divided by the population in the age group specified, expressed as a percentage. Years refer to the school year starting with the year specified (e.g., 1970 = school year 1970–71). The data for 1949–67 may not be fully comparable to those from 1970–88 since the two series come from different sources, which employ somewhat different definitions.

Sources: 1970–88: School attendance rates by sex: Council for Economic Planning and Development, Manpower Planning Department, Executive Yuan, 1989, table 1-5, p. 25. School attendance rates, total: primary school: Council for International Economic Cooperation and Development, 1989, p. 290; junior high, senior high, college: totals are weighted averages of the rates by sex, with the weights based on the number of males and females in each age group, as provided by the annual *Taiwan-Fukien Demographic Fact Books* (Ministry of the Interior). For 1970, the weights of .51 for males and .49 for females are used.

1951–67: Primary school attendance rates by sex and total: Ministry of Education, 1988, table 8, p. 28. Junior high attendance rates by sex, and total calculated from number of students by sex: Directorate-General of Budgets, Accounts and Statistics, Executive Yuan, 1971, p. 843; and total students from Ministry of Education 1968, pp. 18–19; and school age population, by sex, Taiwan Population Studies Center 1965, vol. 1, p. 244. Senior high and college: rates by sex and total, data provided by Council for Economic Planning and Development.

1949: Primary school: Provincial Government of Taiwan, Bureau of Accounting and Statistics, 1965, p. 368.

the population in cities of one hundred thousand or more increased only four percentage points to 29% over the same period.

The potential migration flow was held in check by the continued expansion of rural industrialization and by the feasibility of doing seasonal work on other farms (Speare, Liu, and Tsay 1988, 88–90). Rural industrialization can be traced back to the Japanese period, through the erection of sugar refining and other agrobusiness. Rural industrialization was also aided by Japanese investment in roads and rural electrification and other aspects of the infrastructure described above. After 1949, governmental policy and action encouraged further rural industrial growth. Another important contribution was an increased demand by farmers for nonfood consumption, such as building materials, that could be met by local industry.

Detailed figures of the proportion of farm income obtained off the farm are not available for the 1949–61 period. By 1964, the Survey of Personal Income Distribution shows this percentage to be 35% and rising rapidly (table 3.4). Sample surveys of farm families in 1952 and 1957 provide additional indicators of changes in farm incomes and its sources (Tsui 1959). These surveys show that while farm income increased 17% in constant dollars between 1952 and 1957, the percentage of receipts from nonfarm sources increased from 13 to 22% over this period. The proportion of farm income received in cash increased from 44% in 1952 to almost 63% in 1957 (Tsui 1959, 23 and 25).

Since agriculture could not reasonably support the growing population, the government, in the early 1950s, began an industrialization program which focused on import substitution. Government measures to promote import substitution included tariffs, import controls and multiple exchange rates, prohibition or control of nonessential consumer imports, and preference for imports which would facilitate manufacturing in Taiwan. To finance industry, the government used various means to divert a share of agricultural earnings to the industrial sector. Farmers were required to sell a considerable quantity of rice to the government at an official price pegged below wholesale; farmers also had to buy their fertilizer from the government, the sole supplier, at a monopoly price substantially above the cost of production (Ho 78, 180–81).

Several factors contributed to the success of the import substitution program: (1) although the agricultural sector was taxed to provide capital for the industrialization program, governmental support for agriculture, through measures previously described, nurtured the vigorous growth of agricultural productivity, which held food prices down and minimized the pressure on industrial wages as long as the rural labor surplus existed; (2) the nature of the land reform program ensured a relatively wide participation of former landlords in private industrial activity; (3) the rise in agricultural incomes provided a market for consumer goods (Ranis 1979).

The results of these policies were substantial. Between 1949 and 1954, manufacturing production increased at an average rate of 22% per year (Ho 1978, table 10.1, 187). Table 3.6 shows that gross domestic product grew by 91% in constant prices between 1952 and 1961 and manufacturing increased its share from 13% to 19% over this period. While rehabilitation of war-torn industries, particularly in food processing, contributed to the rapid growth rate, import substitution accounted for a large share of that expansion.

The rise in incomes, particularly in the agricultural sector, provided a ready market for the locally produced manufactured goods. A significant portion of the increase in income was used for improving dwellings and purchases of various consumer goods. This is revealed by data on consumption trends among village residents in eighteen townships from surveys in 1952 and 1959 which interviewed 1,350 households, three-fourths of which were rural (Kirby 1960, 58–59). A 1962 survey in Taichung, the provincial capital, at the end of the import substitution period documents a fairly wide ownership of consumer durables in an urban setting. Most households owned a bicycle and a timepiece, while a majority owned a sewing machine, an electric fan, an iron, and/or a radio (Freedman 1967, 61).

The changes in agriculture and manufacturing did not immediately translate into major shifts in labor force trends. As table 3.7 shows, the labor force participation rate edged downward between 1952 and 1961 for both men and women, due in part to the increasing educational opportunities for young people previously noted. As expected, the distribution of employed persons by industry shifted from agriculture toward the industrial and service sectors, but the changes were modest. Similarly, there were small declines in own account workers and unpaid family workers and an increase in the proportion of paid employed persons. Since these statistics derive in part from household registration data, they probably mask the degree of change, since individuals frequently fail to promptly update occupation on their registration records.

The rapid expansion of import substitution industries during the early 1950s slowed as the limited domestic market became saturated. Import substitution was achieved quickly in industries where technology was fairly simple; local production of cotton textiles, bicycles, and flour supplied the market demand within four years. After 1954, import substitu-

TABLE 3.6 Gross Domestic Product and Percentage Share by Activity, Selected Years, 1952–88

	PRODUCT[a]		Index 1952 = 100 (1981 prices)	PERCENTAGE COMPOSITION OF GDP BY SECTOR			
					Industrial:		Service & Other[d]
	Current Prices	1981 Prices		Agriculture[b]	Total[c]	Manuf.	
Period I							
1949	—	—	—	—	—	—	—
1952	17,251	146,557	100.0	32.2	19.7	12.9	48.1
1955	29,981	189,747	129.5	29.1	23.2	15.6	47.7
1958	44,966	229,348	156.5	26.8	24.8	16.8	48.5
1961	70,043	280,524	191.4	27.4	24.2	18.9	48.6
Period II							
1961	70,043	280,524	191.4	27.4	24.2	18.9	48.6
1964	101,966	371,391	253.4	24.5	26.4	22.9	49.2
1967	145,817	497,681	339.6	21.0	29.2	24.9	49.7
1970	226,805	659,251	449.8	16.6	35.0	29.2	48.5
1973	410,405	951,606	649.3	12.2	39.9	36.8	47.9
Period III							
1973	410,405	951,606	649.3	12.2	39.9	36.8	47.9
1976	707,710	1,150,116	784.8	10.7	41.8	33.8	47.4
1979	1,195,838	1,557,255	1,062.6	8.4	43.9	35.9	47.7
1982	1,886,915	1,824,624	1,245.8	7.2	44.7	35.1	48.1
1985	2,393,024	2,249,563	1,534.9	6.1	45.8	37.1	48.1
1988	3,335,234	2,985,374	2,037.0	4.7	46.7	38.4	48.6

Sources: Council for International Economic Cooperation and Development, 1989, table 3-1a; Directorate-General of Budgets, Accounts and Statistics, Executive Yuan, 1988b, tables II-5, III-2.

[a] In millions of NT dollars.

[b] Includes hunting, forestry, and fishing.

[c] Total includes mining, manufacturing, electricity, gas and water, and construction.

[d] Includes wholesale and retail trade, transportation and communication, finance and insurance, personal service, government and other services.

TABLE 3.7 Labor Force Participation Rates by Sex, Unemployment Rates, and Distribution of Employed Persons by Industry and Class of Worker, Selected Years, 1949–88

	Civilian Labor Force Participation Rate[a]			Unemployment Rate[b]	Distribution of Employed Persons by Industry			Distribution of Employed Persons by Class of Worker			
	Male	Female	Total		Agriculture[c]	Industrial[d]	Service[e]	Employers	Own-Account Workers	Unpaid Family Workers	Paid Employees
Period I											
1949	—	—	—	—	—	—	—	—	—	—	—
1952	89	41	66	2.9	56.1	16.9	27.0	2.2	34.3	28.5	34.9
1955	88	39	64	2.5	53.6	18.0	28.4	2.2	33.0	27.7	37.1
1958	88	37	63	2.4	51.1	19.7	29.2	2.2	31.8	26.8	39.2
1961	86	36	62	2.5	49.8	20.9	29.3	2.1	30.8	26.5	40.6
Period II											
1961	86	36	62	2.5	49.8	20.9	29.3	2.1	30.8	26.5	40.6
1964	84	34	59	4.3	49.5	21.3	29.2	2.2	29.8	26.3	41.7
1967	81	34	57	2.3	42.5	24.6	32.9	2.3	27.6	23.7	46.4
1970	79	35	57	1.7	36.7	27.9	35.3	2.9	26.2	20.1	50.9
1973	77	42	59	1.3	30.5	33.7	35.8	2.7	25.1	16.2	56.1
Period III											
1973	77	42	59	1.3	30.5	33.7	35.8	2.7	25.1	16.2	56.1
1976	77	38	57	1.8	29.0	36.4	34.6	2.5	23.9	14.5	59.1
1979	78	39	59	1.3	21.5	41.8	36.7	4.1	21.0	11.2	63.7
1982	76	39	58	2.1	18.9	41.2	39.9	4.3	21.1	10.5	64.1
1985	75	43	59	2.9	17.4	42.2	40.1	4.3	20.8	10.8	64.1
1988	75	46	60	1.7	13.7	42.6	43.7	4.5	18.9	9.5	67.1

Sources: 1952–61: Directorate-General of Budgets, Accounts and Statistics, Executive Yuan, 1984. 1964–88: Directorate-General of Budgets, Accounts and Statistics, Executive Yuan, 1989a.

[a] Defined as those 15 or older employed or seeking civilian employment divided by the sex-specific population 15 or older.

[b] Defined as the proportion of the labor force unemployed.

[c] Includes hunting, forestry, and fishing.

[d] Includes manufacturing, mining, electricity, gas and water, and construction.

[e] Includes commerce, transportation, and communication; finance; insurance and real estate; public administration; and personal service.

tion became less effective when it expanded to more sophisticated industries; for example, efforts to substitute domestic chemical fertilizers for imports succeeded only in the early 1960s. As a consequence, the rate of growth of manufacturing declined from an average annual rate of 22% between 1949 and 1954 to 11% annually in the 1955–62 period (Ho 1978, 187, 189).

Contributing to this problem were the inefficiencies of many new businesses, most of them family enterprises. Government policies had fostered this situation by protecting industries both from foreign competition, through import controls, and from domestic competition, by limiting the establishment of new enterprises. Given these problems and the inability of import substitution to generate the foreign exchange needed to import capital and employ the growing labor force, a new industrial strategy was designed. Between 1958 and 1963 the Taiwan government opted for an export-led industrialization strategy rather than moving into secondary import substitution (Liu 1988, 8). Several reforms and new programs encouraged private enterprises to raise their productivity and to attract investments from both local and foreign hosts for the development of new export industries. The multiple exchange rate was abolished and replaced with an effectively devalued unitary rate, and a rational tariff system was introduced. Policies were instituted to encourage industrial investments locally and abroad. Export promotion schemes were adopted, including lower loan rates for export industries and various preferential tax incentives to lower production costs (Liu 1988, 8–9) (Ranis 1979, 219–20).

By 1961, although per capita income in Taiwan was just returning to pre–World War II levels, the socioeconomic climate, and undoubtedly the mood and expectations of the population, was radically different. Many of the features associated with future social and economic change began to emerge quite clearly during the 1949–61 period. Ownership of land and agricultural production were greatly increased, providing a strong prop for the economy, a source of savings, and a demand for local industrial production. The challenge of absorbing the rapidly growing surplus of farm labor was met via the rapid expansion of both educational opportunities and manufacturing capability. The decentralization of many of the new factories into rural areas mitigated the pace of urbanization and reduced the pressures on the larger cities. At the same time, these factories served as a source of diffusion of new ideas and outlooks through the many commuters who returned to their farm families each night or weekend. Communication and exchange were also fostered by improvements in transportation and the spread of radio ownership. Although there were some problems as the import substitution strategy encountered limitations, the government's willingness to adjust and innovate in pursuit of an improved standard of living, a balanced economy, human resource enhancement, and other social and economic goals augured well for future development.

The Labor-Intensive Period, 1961–73

The policies initiated in the late 1950s paid off handsomely during the 1960s and overcame potentially serious demographic trends. Per capita income rose about 8% a year on average during the period, doubling the rate of growth in the previous period. The index of industrial production advanced an average of 16% per year, surpassing the very strong growth of the 1950s (table 3.1), as Taiwan transformed itself into an export economy.

Between 1962 and 1972, exports grew from 13 to 43% of GDP and the share of industrial products in exports, primarily nondurable consumer goods, increased from 50 to 83% of all exports (Ranis 1979, 221). As table 3.6 demonstrates, gross domestic product in constant prices more than tripled between 1961 and 1973, and the proportion accounted for by manufacturing doubled over this period.

These remarkable results were achieved despite the rapid growth in the labor force, which exerted great pressure on Taiwan's job creation capabilities. Conversely, the ability to absorb these new entrants at relatively low wages into labor-intensive industries helped fuel the rapid rise in exports and the overall growth of industrial production. Between 1961 and 1973 the population aged 15–24 increased 80% as the large birth cohorts of the early 1950s came of age. In addition, the rate of exodus of labor from rural areas rose rapidly from 0.9% per year between 1952 and 1965 to 2.1% between 1965 and 1974 (Liu 1989, 10). Urbanization was most rapid during this period; the proportion of the population living in cities of fifty thousand or more rose from 41 to 59% from 1961 to 1973 (see table 3.3), and the percentage in cities of one hundred thousand or more grew rapidly as well (data not shown). As a consequence, the unemployment rate advanced sharply in the early 1960s, though it remained low in absolute terms (table 3.7). Nonetheless, the growth in export industries and their concentration in labor-intensive industries increased manufacturing employment 10% annually during the 1960s so that the labor surplus was dissipated by the early 1970s

(Liu 1989, 9). As table 3.7 indicates, the proportion of employed persons in the industrial sector grew rapidly during this period while unemployment declined rapidly from 1964 to a low point in 1973.

Several features of the previous period were also evident during 1961–73. Agricultural production grew during the 1960s by over 4% per year (table 3.1), less than in the previous decade, but still contributing to the new industrial program by keeping food prices relatively stable (Liu 1988).

The government's placement of industrial developments near rural areas contributed to its export strategy by making it possible for many rural residents to work in industry without changing their residence, thus mitigating the pace of urbanization. The proportion of industrial establishments in the five largest cities was only 34% in 1951 and remained stable through 1971 (Ranis 1979, 222–26). The government also provided an effective infrastructure, including good transportation and communication networks, universal electrification, and efficient public administration. This made it possible for many rural residents to work in nearby industrial plants while continuing to live at home, where they could still do part-time agricultural work (Liu 1988). Most farm households maintained some farm pursuits while earning nonfarm income from those household members who commuted to work in nearby industrial enterprises. The proportion of farm household income earned in nonagricultural pursuits increased from 35% in 1964 to 54% in 1973 (table 3.4).

The implications of these changes for household income and savings are shown in table 3.8. Disposable income per household in constant prices increased an average of 5% per year between 1964 and 1973, with growing disparity between the average income of farm and nonfarm households. The rapidly rising incomes facilitated a high savings rate, which varied between 8 and 15% annually over this period, as determined by the Survey of Income and Expenditures. (Measures of income distribution and the changing pattern of expenditures are discussed below.)

The government's educational system was redesigned to facilitate industrial development. Originally, there were two types of junior high schools—one with an academic curriculum, the other with a primarily vocational curriculum. By 1968, junior highs became solely academic because the shift to more technical industries required a longer period of academic training as the basis for more advanced vocational training. The government fostered vocational and technical education, both in

TABLE 3.8 Income, Consumption, and Savings

| | DISPOSABLE INCOME PER HOUSEHOLD | | | | INCOME DISTRIBUTION | | |
| | | | Ratio | | Shares to: | | |
	Current Prices (1,000 NT$) (1)	1986 Prices (1,000 NT$) (2)	Farm to Nonfarm Household (3)	% Saved (4)	Lowest Fifth (5)	Highest Fifth (6)	GINI Coefficient (7)
Period I							
1949	—	—	—	—	—	—	—
1953	—	—	—	—	—	—	.56
1955	—	—	—	—	—	—	—
1958	—	—	—	—	—	—	—
1960	—	—	—	—	—	—	.44
Period II							
1960	—	—	—	—	—	—	.44
1964	29	120	96.6	11.2	7.7	41.1	.32
1968	39	144	71.2	8.9	7.8	41.4	.33
1970	44	152	67.1	8.0	8.4	38.7	.29
1973	71	191	76.9	15.1	—	—	—
Period III							
1973	71	191	76.9	15.1	—	—	—
1976	116	225	82.1	17.9	8.9	37.3	.28
1979	188	304	79.7	22.0	8.6	37.5	.28
1982	275	337	81.0	23.8	8.7	37.3	.28
1985	320	387	81.5	23.5	8.4	37.6	.29
1988	410	478	80.8	26.4	7.9	38.3	.30

Sources: Directorate-General of Budgets, Accounts and Statistics, Executive Yuan, 1989c: Cols. 1 and 2: table 1, p. 10. Col. 3: table 5, p. 13. Col. 4: table 9, p. 18. Cols. 5–6 and 7, 1964–88: table 4, p. 13; Col. 7, 1953 and 1960: Liu 1988, p. 21.

vocational high schools and in five-year junior colleges. (The five-year vocational college began in 1949 and expanded in the 1960s; the first three years are considered high school and the last two, college.) At each level of schooling, students must pass an exam to enter the next level. The strong emphasis on fairly high-level vocational training provided manpower for the shift to more complex technologies. Teacher training also underwent continual upgrading.

School enrollment rates increased markedly throughout this period, along with government investments in education. Primary education was almost universal at the start of this period, while enrollment at the secondary and tertiary levels increased rapidly throughout (table 3.5). Enrollment at the junior high level increased from 40% of those 12 to 14 in 1961 to 77% in 1973; for senior high the advance was from 22% to 48% of those 15 to 17; and at the college level, enrollment advanced from under 5% of those 18 to 21 in 1961 to 21% in 1973. The sharp increase at the junior high level was aided by the initiation in 1968 of nine years of compulsory schooling. At every level of schooling the rate of increase in enrollments was more rapid for females than for males, so that by 1973 differentials by sex had greatly diminished (table 3.5).

The sharp increase in the education of women was prompted both by the desire of families to enhance a daughter's marriage prospects, given the rapid rise in male education, and by the expansion of jobs for young educated women, since unmarried daughters usually contribute a significant portion of their earnings to their parents. One result of the rapid rise in educational attainment and the tendency to delay marriage until the completion of schooling was an increase in the average age at marriage. In 1962, 12% of women 15–19 and 60% of women 20–24 were married; by 1973, these figures had dropped to 6% and 45%, respectively.

During this period there were also a number of new initiatives that had significant economic and demographic consequences. In a move to attract more foreign investment, the government initiated the first of its Export Processing Zones (EPZ), in Kaoshiung in 1965. As Li (1988, 92) notes, behind the immediate goals of reducing red tape and enhancing foreign investments were the larger goals of promoting employment and earning foreign exchange. Li (1988, 93) defines an EPZ as an expansion of the free trade area zone concept: "It is innovative in two ways: it has an integrated, simplified administration, and it puts primary stress on production for export (rather than any processing being merely an extension of an essentially transshipping activity)." The success of the first EPZ led to the construction of two more, which opened in 1971.

Another important innovation was the initiation of an island-wide family planning program in 1964. In the late 1950s and early 1960s, concerns were voiced about the high rate of population growth. A successful experiment in the city of Taichung in 1962–63, which demonstrated both interest in limiting family size and acceptance of the intrauterine device, led to an island-wide family planning program in 1964 (Freedman and Takeshita 1969). The program was very successful; its first five-year target was for six hundred thousand acceptors and was exceeded by about 5% (Sun 1987, p. 7 and table 1). Succeeding targets were also matched closely by performance, and through 1985 the program could point to more than 6 million acceptors of intrauterine devices, pills, condoms, and sterilization. Although fertility showed some decline in the late 1950s, the trend of decline accelerated after the introduction of the program, and multivariate analyses indicate that program inputs had an independent effect on fertility beyond the social and economic factors that were also impinging on fertility decisions (Hermalin 1978).

Industrial Upgrading Period, 1973 to Present

Taiwan's economic expansion was interrupted in the 1970s by a series of economic problems, including international monetary disorders, two oil shocks, and a worldwide economic recession. Taiwan's dependence on the export of labor-intensive manufactured goods to industrialized countries made it especially vulnerable to the recession which followed the first oil shock of 1973. Businesses found it difficult to sustain high export levels of textiles, apparels, and other labor-intensive goods as the costs of energy and other imported goods rose; wages were kept high by the labor shortage; and businesses were confronted by rising protectionism in the Western industrial countries and increasing competition from other developing countries (Liu 1988, 11–12).

A multipronged attack on these problems was launched. Taiwan's fixed exchange rate relative to the U.S. dollar helped alleviate the monetary crises of the early 1970s so that the NT dollar appreciated only minimally against the U.S. dollar. (A partially floating exchange rate system was then introduced, but the exchange rate fluctuated in a narrow range through 1986.) To address the inflationary trend generated by the oil shocks of 1973 and 1979, the government allowed one-time increases in the prices of key commodities and services. This allowed prices to adjust to costs to counter the increases in oil prices, but also curbed inflationary expectations. The consumer price index advanced 55% between 1973 and 1975 and 30% over 1978–80, but prices stabilized at 3–5% increases in most of the remaining years (Directorate-General of Budgets, Accounts and Statistics 1989b, table 74, p. 150; Liu 1988, 11).

In formulating an industrial strategy to meet the twin problems of increasing competition and increasing protectionism, the government faced several hurdles. One was insufficient investment. The many small-scale family enterprises which dominated the labor-intensive phase were not able to expand their enterprises or to diversify through investments in more capital and technological-intensive industries and were neither able nor motivated to invest in the infrastructure needed to support such new enterprises. Taiwanese factories in 1980, 85% of which were still fairly small scale with less than fifty workers, were hard pressed to find investment funds since private internal investment had become very sluggish (Liu 1988, 12–13).

Another factor in determining industrial policy was the change in the size and character of the labor force. The falling birthrates in the 1960s led to appreciably slower growth in the age group 15–24, from 5% per year in 1961–73 to only 1.2% per year between 1973–85, thus exacerbating labor shortages (Ministry of the Interior 1989). The growth in the total labor force also declined somewhat from 3.8% per year between 1961 and 1973 to 2.9% between 1973 and 1985 (Council for Economic Planning and Development, Manpower Planning Department 1986, 138). The character of the labor force also changed as school attendance increased substantially between 1973 and 1986 at all levels. While the lower birthrates made it imperative to redirect efforts away from labor-intensive pursuits, the significantly higher levels of schooling provided the manpower to staff more knowledge-intensive industries.

The government's strategies to redirect their industrial policies were implemented first in the 1970s and then into the 1980s. After the first oil shock (1973), the government instituted projects to sustain growth and redirect industry by launching the Ten Major Development Projects, which included such heavy industrial facilities as a steel mill and a shipbuilding and petrochemical plant, as well as sizable investments in infrastructure, namely nuclear power stations and transportation facilities. This program, over the years 1973–79, accounted for 30% of the nation's total fixed capital formation (Liu 1988, 12).

During the 1980s, after the second oil crisis, the investment strategy shifted from heavy industry toward more high-tech industries. The 1979 second oil crisis had revealed the vulnerability of the heavy industry strategy, since high energy costs were associated with many of these endeavors. Growing environmental concerns also played a role in redirecting efforts to technology-intensive industries rather than capital-intensive ones (Speare, Liu, and Tsay 1988, 8).

The government's new strategy to promote high technology was two-pronged: its purposes were to assist high-technology industries and to upgrade education. First, the government instituted several new programs to assist the development of high-technology industries. A Science and Technology Development Program was initiated in 1979, which devoted a substantial sum to research and development spending. Another program targeted strategic industries—for example, machinery manufacturing, information, and electronics—which became eligible for tax holidays, low-interest loans, and subsidies from the government. The government also established a science-based industrial park in 1981, which by 1985 included forty-nine companies, with a total investment capital of U.S. $46.8 million. About half of the park employees hold university and higher-level degrees. It also supported technology transfer, channeled through imported capital, foreign investment, and technical cooperation (Liu 1988, 11–12). Additionally, twelve large-scale projects were inaugurated after the 1979 oil shock, six in infrastructure, five in transportation, and one in nuclear power, to combat the world economic downturn as well as to build infrastructure for industry.

The other facet of the government's strategy for industrial upgrading was to further improve Taiwan's educational levels by devoting more resources to education. The government almost tripled per capita expenditures on education (in constant NT$) between 1971 and 1987, partially by reallocating funds from declining primary school enrollments to higher education (Council for Economic Planning and Development, Manpower Planning Department 1988, 7). Senior high school enrollment increased from 48 to 64% between 1973 and 1982 and to 76% in 1988, with a larger increase for females so that their high school matriculation equaled that of males by the early 1980s. College education increased among both sexes, with a faster pace among females; by 1988, 31% of persons aged 18–21 attended college (table 3.5).

While the prospective declines in population growth made it imperative to expand into less labor-intensive pursuits, the changing size and character of the labor force made it feasible to redirect efforts from labor-intensive to knowledge-intensive pursuits, as the increasing enrollments in secondary schools and colleges provided the skills to manage the new jobs.

Economic growth slowed somewhat during the 1970s and early 1980s, but remained high relative to most other countries. Between 1973 and 1985, agriculture production increased almost 3% per year on average and industrial production increased over 8% per year, somewhat less than the 4 and 18% in the previous period, while real GNP grew over 7% per year (table 3.1).

The labor needed for the post-1970 shift toward new industrial pursuits came from two sources. There was a continuing exodus to industry from the farm. Table 3.7 shows that the percentage of employed persons working in agriculture decreased from 31 in 1973, to 14 in 1988. The rapid increase in the use of farm machinery after 1960 made it possible for farm families to maintain their farm income while earning extra income from nonfarm jobs held by some family members, a strategy more feasible because of the placement of factories in rural areas. The percentage of farm income earned off the farm increased from 54 to 76% between 1973 and 1988 (table 3.4). Between 1970 and 1986, agricultural employment decreased from 6 million to 4.2 million (Council for International Economic Cooperation and Development 1989, 66).

Table 3.7 shows a steady decline in the proportion of employed persons in agriculture from 1973 to 1988, with increases occurring in the industrial and service sectors. It also shows that the increase in female labor force participation, from 35% in 1970 to 46% in 1988, provided a second source of labor for industrial expansion. Some of this increase is attributable to the rising age at marriage, giving women more years to work before assuming marital responsibilities. Many young women who formerly had been unpaid family workers could now work for wages in nearby factories while still living at home or could work away from home, sometimes living in a facility provided by the enterprise. Table 3.7 shows sharp declines in own account workers and unpaid family workers over the period. By 1978, 33% of all employed persons were women, increasing to 38% in 1987. Women constituted 41% of the manufacturing work force in 1978 and 44% in 1987 (Directorate-General of Budgets, Accounts and Statistics 1989d, 39).

In the post-1973 period Taiwan was able to maintain economic momentum by shifting its orientation from labor-intensive to knowledge-intensive industries, taking advantage of its continuing strong investment in education and using resources to develop appropriate infrastructure and to smooth out fluctuations in the level of private investment.

Income Distribution and Life-Style

To conclude this review of Taiwan's broad economic changes, we focus on two aspects which have implications for the social welfare of Taiwanese families—the degree of income equity among households and the change in life-styles, such as the acquisition of consumer durables.

Taiwan is fairly unique among developing countries, having enjoyed a long period of economic expansion while maintaining a remarkable degree of income equity. Comparing income quintiles in 1987, income in Taiwan for the highest fifth was 4.7 times that of lowest income group, 4.3 in Japan, 5.0 in West Germany, 7.5 in the United States, 8.0 in Korea, 10.1 in the Philippines, and 33.3 in Brazil. The Taiwan ratio may be an overstatement, since the larger incomes of its highest quintile reflect its greater household size and larger numbers of employed persons. Eliminating the household size differential, Taiwan's ratio narrows to 2.5 (Directorate-General of Budgets, Accounts and Statistics 1988c, 2–3). Some reasons for Taiwan's relative equality of incomes may be

(1) the successful family planning program, which decreased fertility among all population strata and thus prevented the inequality effects of large differences in family size due to uneven diffusion; (2) the decentralization of industries, which alleviated dislocations and minimized urbanization costs; and (3) the successful implementation of land reform, which laid the foundation for an equitable distribution of both land ownership and industrial capital. Government efforts to encourage small- to medium-size family enterprises via the development of labor-intensive industries, and particularly the provision of low-cost educational opportunities at all levels, paved the way for an equal sharing of the fruits of economic growth (Liu 1988, 21). The Gini coefficients in table 3.8 confirm the improvement in income equality from 1964 to the early 1980s, based on figures from the Survey of Personal Income Distribution, which began in 1964. Estimates for years before 1964 indicate a higher Gini coefficient in the 1950s, suggesting a downward trend through most of the post–World War II period. Improvements in equity as reflected in the Gini coefficient slowed in the late 1970s, and since the early 1980s the coefficient has increased (table 3.8). Though Taiwan's income distribution still is extremely equal compared to other countries, there is some concern about this drift toward inequality.

The spectacular growth of the Taiwan economy and its relatively equitable distribution of income have allowed the Taiwanese to enjoy rapid and extensive changes in life-styles: acquisitions of new consumer durables, more widespread and extensive education, and new recreational activities, many of which are pursued outside the family. These new and more sophisticated activities can affect traditional familial arrangements and values, including decisions about family size and living arrangements.

As Taiwan's per capita income increased rapidly, the pattern of consumer expenditures changed dramatically. Table 3.9 presents the percentage distribution of expenditures. Since 1964 the figures are from the Survey of Income and Expenditures; those before 1964 are taken from the National Income Account to provide longer-term trends. The data indicate a sharp decline in the proportion spent for food (including beverages and tobacco) from about 60% in the 1950s and early 1960s, to 35% by 1988. Categories showing noticeable increases, particularly since 1964, include housing and household equipment (from a combined total of 21% to 28%); transportation and communication (from 2 to 8%); and recreation and entertainment (from less than 1% to over 6%).

These shifts reflect a society with growing contacts with one another and the rest of the world, and increased discretion on how to allocate

TABLE 3.9 Percentage Distribution of Expenditures

	Food, Bev, Tobacco	Clothing, Footwear	Rent, Fuel, Power	Furniture, Household Equipmt.	Medical Care	Transp., Commut.	Recreation, Entertainmt.	Education, Culture	Misc.
Period I									
1949	—	—	—	—	—	—	—	—	—
1952	61.8	5.5	16.2	—	2.6	1.8		5.7	6.5
1955	59.7	6.5	16.8	—	2.9	1.6		5.5	6.9
1958	59.0	5.7	18.3	—	2.8	2.0		5.4	6.7
1961	58.8	5.2	15.4	2.6	4.2	1.7		5.4	6.6
Period II									
1961	58.8	5.2	15.4	2.6	4.2	1.7		5.4	6.6
1964N	56.1	5.7	15.1	3.1	4.5	2.6		5.6	7.4
1964P	59.7	6.3	17.2	3.4	5.3	2.0	0.8	4.1	2.6
1967	—	—	—	—	—	—		—	—
1970	52.5	5.8	18.2	4.0	6.0	3.0	2.3	4.9	4.3
1973	—	—	—	—	—	—	—	—	—
Period III									
1973	—	—	—	—	—	—	—	—	—
1976	46.4	6.8	21.4	3.9	4.6	5.0	2.6	4.6	4.7
1979	41.0	7.4	22.9	4.6	4.6	6.1	4.2	4.4	4.8
1982	38.7	6.6	24.3	4.4	5.1	6.9	4.5	5.0	4.6
1985	38.2	5.9	23.5	4.1	5.3	8.3	5.0	5.1	4.5
1988	35.0	6.1	23.2	4.7	5.2	8.4	6.5	6.0	4.9

Note: Data for 1952–61 are available only from National Income Accounts and represent distribution of *private* expenditures. Data from 1964 on are from the Survey of Personal Income and Expenditures. For the year 1964, data are shown on both bases to allow calibration of the differences. Recreation and entertainment from 1964 on includes restaurant meals. Education and culture includes newspaper expenditures.

Sources: 1949–64: Directorate-General of Budgets, Accounts and Statistics, Executive Yuan, 1990, table 7, p. 18. 1964–88: Directorate-General of Budgets, Accounts and Statistics, Executive Yuan, 1989c, table 11, p. 20. Data on recreation and education from special tabulation.

improved family incomes. Further evidence of the rapid changes in lifestyle are presented in tables 3.10 and 3.11. Table 3.10 shows the substantial upsurge in various measures of communication and transportation, ranging from newspapers and magazines, television, telephones, and visitors to Taiwan, to automobiles and other travel. While these data suggest that Taiwanese families were being exposed to many new ideas and people, the improved transportation and communication infrastructure also served to maintain family cohesiveness as individual family members migrated to cities or abroad for educational and occupational opportunities.

Ownership of most consumer durables was limited in the 1960s, but the pace of acquisition increased rapidly in the 1970s. Between 1964 and 1972, ownership of a refrigerator increased from 2 to 39% and for motorcycles from 3 to 30% (table 3.11). By 1979, almost all households owned a refrigerator; over half owned a color TV, a washing machine, and/or a motorcycle; and two-fifths owned a telephone and radio/recorder. (Black and white televisions had been owned by most households in the 1970s but subsequently were displaced by the advent of color TV.)

By 1988, refrigerators and color televisions were found in almost all households, and telephones and washing machines were owned by more than 80% of the households, with motorcycles following close behind. New items, such as air conditioners and cars, were steadily gaining ground.

There also appears to have been a steady increase in both attendance and expenditures on recreational activities, although the data are limited. Questions from four surveys of families with a woman of childbearing age, from 1970 through 1986, asked the wives how often, during the past year, they had gone to the movies, eaten in a restaurant, or taken a vacation trip involving an overnight stay. Movie attendance declined substantially during 1970–86, probably because of competition from television, while in 1973–86 visits to restaurants doubled and overnight recreational travel increased tenfold. In recent years foreign travel has become an important new form of recreation, as well as an opportunity to maintain family contacts. In 1988, 1.6 million Taiwanese (8% of the total population) traveled abroad, an increase of 50% over the previous years. A substantial part of this increase stemmed from the recent approval of visits to relatives on the mainland (*Free China Journal* 1989, 3). Table 3.9 shows that the proportion of expenditures on recreation and entertainment increased sevenfold between 1964 and 1988.

TABLE 3.10 Communication and Transportation Indicators in Selected Years, 1949–88

	Newspapers or Magazines (1,000 pop.)	TV Sets per 1,000 Households	TELEPHONES Number of Subscribers (thousands)	TELEPHONES Per 1,000 Households	Number of Students Studying Abroad	Number of Visitors to Taiwan	PASSENGER TRAFFIC IN MILLIONS OF PASSENGER KMS Railways	PASSENGER TRAFFIC Highways	MOTOR VEHICLES Passenger Cars (thousands)	MOTOR VEHICLES Commercial Vehicles (thousands)
Period I										
1949	—	—	17	13	—	—	—	—	2.8	4.1
1952	—	—	25	17	377	—	1,934	1,010	2.6	5.6
1955	—	—	34	21	760	—	2,550	2,037	4.8	7.1
1958	—	—	46	25	674	16,709	3,703	2,668	6.7	8.6
1961	—	—	65	32	978	42,205	3,763	3,420	9.0	11.5
Period II										
1961	—	—	65	32	978	42,205	3,763	3,420	9.0	11.5
1964	37.4	14.3	88	40	2,514	95,481	4,027	4,322	12.4	14.8
1967	—	—	135	57	2,472	253,248	5,112	5,603	25.1	24.5
1970	53.1	371.0	249	95	2,056	472,452	6,212	7,004	49.5	49.0
1973	76.2	738.0	487	170	1,966	824,393	8,018	9,636	95.1	78.5
Period III										
1973	76.2	738.0	487	170	1,966	824,393	8,018	9,636	95.1	78.5
1976	90.4	931.1	986	310	3,641	1,008,126	8,479	13,642	171.0	143.6
1979	141.3	1,007.6	1,861	518	5,801	1,340,382	7,327	19,281	340.7	217.6
1982	164.4	1,028.7	3,230	801	5,925	1,419,178	8,204	20,832	592.2	333.7
1985	194.8	1,054.5	4,228	970	5,979	1,451,659	8,309	20,495	915.6	429.4
1988	199.1	1,100.0	5,322	1,105	7,122	1,935,134	8,233	16,940	1,579.1	524.1

Sources: Newspapers or magazines, TV sets: 1964–88, Council for Economic Planning and Development, Manpower Planning Department, Executive Yuan, 1989, p. 14. Telephone subscribers: 1949, Directorate-General of Budgets, Accounts and Statistics, Executive Yuan, 1964, no. 24, table 129; 1952–88, Council for International Economic Cooperation and Development, 1989, table 7-22. Students abroad: 1952–55, Directorate-General of Budgets, Accounts and Statistics, Executive Yuan, 1961, table 142; 1958–88, Council for International Economic Cooperation and Development, 1989, table 14-12a. Number of visitors to Taiwan: 1952–88, Council for International Economic Cooperation and Development, 1989, table 7-15, p. 135. Passenger traffic: 1952–88, Council for International Economic Cooperation and Development, 1989, table 7-6a, p. 122. Motor vehicles: 1949, Directorate-General of Budgets, Accounts and Statistics, Executive Yuan, 1975, table 147; 1952–88, Council for International Economic Cooperation and Development, 1989, table 7-4.

TABLE 3.11 Percentages of Taiwanese Households with Household Equipment and Appliances, 1964–87

	Color TV	Refrigerator	Telephone	Air Conditioner	Videotape Recorder/ Player	Radio and Recorder	Washing Machine	Sedan Vehicle	Motor- cycle	Personal Computer
Period I										
1949	—	—	—	—	—	—	—	—	—	—
1952	—	—	—	—	—	—	—	—	—	—
1955	—	—	—	—	—	—	—	—	—	—
1958	—	—	—	—	—	—	—	—	—	—
1961	—	—	—	—	—	—	—	—	—	—
Period II										
1961	—	—	—	—	—	—	—	—	—	—
1964	—	1.7	1.5	—	—	—	—	—	2.9	—
1966	—	4.5	1.7	—	—	—	0.4	—	5.6	—
1968	—	10.4	2.4	0.5	—	—	1.7	0.1	11.2	—
1970	—	22.8	4.4	—	—	—	7.0	—	19.2	—
1972	—	38.7	8.7	—	—	—	16.7	—	29.6	—
Period III										
1972	—	38.7	8.7	—	—	—	16.7	—	29.6	—
1976	12.9	74.2	22.1	3.6	—	—	38.6	1.5	44.6	—
1979	58.6	89.6	41.1	11.6	1.1	40.2	60.1	4.1	58.8	—
1982	83.1	94.3	67.6	17.2	5.8	47.9	70.5	7.2	68.5	—
1985	92.3	96.7	82.1	24.0	20.7	56.1	77.8	11.9	71.9	2.3
1988	97.3	98.0	89.1	34.3	51.0	65.2	84.0	19.2	75.2	4.0

Source: Directorate-General of Budgets, Accounts and Statistics, Executive Yuan, 1989c, table 18, p. 27.

Conclusion

This chapter has traced some of the major economic, social, and demographic trends for Taiwan in the twentieth century, with particular attention to the post–World War II period. By almost any measure this period was one of dramatic and successful change. Taiwan transformed itself from a high-fertility, agricultural society with a small proportion of highly trained people to an urban economy with advanced industries and infrastructure, a highly skilled work force, and a comfortable and rapidly growing level of income. Fertility dropped sharply from the late 1950s to the late 1980s, while expectation of life and other measures of health continued to improve. National social and economic policy proved very adept at addressing a series of formidable issues ranging from land reform, job creation, and labor shortages to a volatile international economic environment. The successes and improvements reviewed here also brought forth many of the problems associated with rapid industrial and social change: deterioration in the quality of the environment; increases in crime; higher divorce rates; speculations in real estate and stock; traffic gridlock in many cities; and the neglect of public areas and streets in towns and cities (Hsueh 1989; Ping-lun and Shen 1989).

How these massive changes impinged on individuals and families as they sought to maintain norms and values and yet adapt to and take advantage of the new elements in society is the focus of the remaining chapters.

Four

Theoretical Mechanisms of Family Change

A. Thornton, T. Fricke, L. S. Yang, and J. S. Chang

Introduction

Our theorization concerning the influence of social and economic change on family structures and relationships in Taiwan begins with the central observation of chapter 1—that Taiwanese society in the past was primarily organized within family units. While land was frequently rented from landlords, the activities and energies of individuals were generally mobilized, organized, and directed by the family units to produce the necessities and luxuries of life. The family also provided its members the basic socialization, information, and training necessary to live in the community in which the individual was embedded. Large percentages of the interactions with others involved kinspeople, and the family exercised considerable authority over its members. Furthermore, the central feature of the Chinese cosmos was the family chain of relationships that extended back to ancestors and forward to unborn generations.

In Chinese society the kinship groups conducting the central activities of life generally pooled resources and responsibilities and participated in specialization and division of labor among family members. These features required coordination among the activities and goals of individual family members as well as the integration of individual life courses with the events occurring in the family group. Kinship relations were also vital linkages binding individual family groups into larger communities. The stability of family systems from one generation to the next was maintained through complex relationships unifying production, distribution, consumption, reproduction, socialization, and the transmission of property within and across kinship groups. Although there was plenty of room for family conflict and divergence of interests in this family-organized system, there were still numerous points of convergence of family and individual goals and well-being. Furthermore, this convergence of individual and family interests was generally reinforced by cultural norms emphasizing family loyalty and commitment.

As documented in the previous chapter, Taiwan has experienced numerous large-scale social and economic transformations during the past four decades. Of central importance for a study of Taiwanese families are the transformations from an agricultural to an industrial economy, a rural to an urban society, an economically poor society to a society with a strong and expanding economy, a relatively uneducated population to an increasingly well educated populace, a society with relatively little contact with the outside world to a society enmeshed in numerous international networks, and a high-mortality to a low-mortality society. As the next chapter will show, these social and economic changes modified the family mode of organization through the proliferation of social structures outside the family that came to organize many of the dimensions of life formerly managed within family units. The loci of many fundamental individual activities have been shifted from familial settings to other social institutions, such as factories, schools, dormitories, governmental bureaucracies, and the mass media. Activities that were commonly performed previously by households in the familial mode of organization were increasingly performed by other groups. Taiwanese now spend smaller fractions of their time in family activities with people who are relatives, receive smaller fractions of their information and ideas from family members, and experience the authority of family leaders alongside that of organizations outside the family.

A main plank in our theoretical framework is the idea that this transformation of social organization from a system where the individual life course is conducted primarily within kinship units to a system where individual experience is carried out within a broad range of social institutions has substantial implications for the structure of personal interrelationships and processes. Of central importance is the introduction of many new elements and opportunities into the system by the expansion of multiple nonfamilial social institutions. The family's control over information and the training of children declines. There are increasing opportunities for individuals to obtain the necessities and luxuries of life outside the family, and individuals begin to engage in the economic system on their own. At the ideational level, there are new belief and value systems. The rearrangement of activities and the availability of new ideas present many opportunities for the divergence of the interests of individuals and their families, for the decline in the authority of family leaders, and for conflict between the ideas of individual family members. These changes, in turn, present numerous opportunities to adjust individual behavior and relationships.

The rest of this chapter is devoted to identifying the relevant elements of the transformation of the family mode of organization and specifying how changes in them are likely to influence specific dimensions of the historical Chinese family system. This discussion focuses on educational expansion, the shift from a labor-pooling to a wage-pooling family economy, the migration from rural to urban areas, the expansion of nonfamilial living arrangements, the growth of income and consumption aspirations, the expansion of the mass media, the introduction of new ideas, and the secularization of beliefs. We also consider the potential influence of several unique features of recent Taiwanese history, including the influx of immigrants from the mainland after World War II and the institution of universal military service for young men. We focus on the specific processes of family change associated with each of these factors, although recognizing that joint occurrences of these changes can produce adjustments in individual behavior and relationships well beyond the additive effects of single factors. Attention is also given to the ways these adjustments to the new mode of organization are guided by preexisting cultural values, relationships, and social structures. Despite our strong belief that recent Chinese family history reflects an interesting combination of change and continuity, this discussion primarily focuses on change.

Educational Expansion

In chapter 2 we discussed the importance of China's historical education system for supporting the family system and disseminating its values throughout society. Here we discuss the influence of a qualitatively different form of schooling on family organization. China's civil examination system differed from the present system in a number of ways. While education previously was confined to males in families who could afford to free sons from familial production activities, education is now universal and mandatory for all children. In the past schools were private and organized by families and lineage groups, although sometimes including children from other families as pupils; today schools are organized by the state and financed largely with public funds. Finally, historical education in China steeped pupils in the classics with a strong normative tradition ratifying overlapping state and family values. Today, the primary content of education includes technical preparation and knowledge designed to enhance the individual's ability to compete in a complex world economy. While the normative stress placed on education as the means to success is continuous with the past, in what follows we refer to the contemporary system of education and its influence.

School enrollment and educational attainment have multiple and diverse effects on family structure, relationships, and attitudes. Most immediately and perhaps most importantly in a society like Taiwan, school enrollment can substantially reduce the amount of time parents and other family members spend with children. Instead of spending most of their maturing years with family members as in the past, children enter school at very young ages and spend large amounts of time outside the family environment. Educational commitments in Taiwan also extend considerably beyond the classroom. Given the tremendous pressure for high performance on formal examinations, which is a prerequisite for admission to a prestigious school at the next level, Taiwanese young people spend considerable amounts of time studying, and many attend special tutoring sessions during the evenings. Given the documented historical importance of mothers in the socialization of children during the early years, the introduction of primary schools may have its strongest effects on the formation of mother-child bonds, while school attendance beyond age 12 would be more likely to affect the relationships between fathers and sons who previously worked together on family farms (see chap. 2).

The shifting of substantial fractions of young people's time from the parental home to educational institutions can substantially modify the authority of parents over their children. School attendance shifts the locus of control and supervision from parents and family to a public institution for large portions of the day. At a minimum, this change in the locus of children's activities removes them from direct observation and supervision by their parents, thereby enhancing children's room for maneuverability vis-à-vis their parents. It also creates the potential for schools to impart values and attitudes to children that might be at variance with those of their parents. Of course, in the Taiwanese school system the potential for schools to modify preexisting patterns is limited to a certain extent by the strict discipline in schools and by the schools' commitment to historical Chinese values.

Rapid increases in educational attainment also create an educational generation gap. Children acquire more access than their parents to ideas and skills valued beyond the local context—both directly through the schools and indirectly through literacy and access to the information network transcending their parents' more limited world (Ogburn and Nimkoff 1955). The children's higher levels of education and access to new ideas can increase their ability and willingness to challenge parental authority while making parents less confident in enforcing their own wishes (Caldwell 1982; Chekki 1974; Hull and Hull 1977).

Education also is an investment in human capital and, as such, enhances the opportunities of young adults in the new labor market and increases their potential wages. This may result in more autonomy from parents because children have more money to spend on their own or because they contribute more to the household economy. Although education expands the resources available for children's autonomy, the increased investments by parents in their children's educations may enhance the subsequent need, ability, and commitment of children to provide resources to their parents (Greenhalgh 1985). This may be particularly important for daughters, who historically left their natal families at marriage to live with their husbands' families (Greenhalgh 1985).

Extended schooling, which provides a new set of activities and roles for young people, takes time and can postpone the assumption of adult roles. One adult role that could be delayed in this way is marriage—a potential that is very large in a population where age at marriage was generally quite young in the past. Of course, since young people did not begin to marry until well into their teenage years, elementary school attendance could become quite widespread without directly delaying entrance into marriage. Junior and senior high school would have more direct effects on the postponement of marriage.

School attendance also can delay entrance into the work force, thus substantially decreasing young people's ability to contribute to the family economy. If school attendance continues well into the teenage years when the productive potential of a child could be substantial, the opportunity costs become significant. Schooling also increases the direct costs of rearing children due to the additional expenses of tuition, books, and special clothing. There can be little doubt, at least during the school years, that school attendance causes a dramatic shift from children making contributions to the family economy to their being substantial net consumers.

Of course, the lifetime influence of school attendance on children's contributions to the family economy is less clear. One important question is whether there is a net positive economic return on the investment in schooling, with later earnings exceeding the costs invested in education. If this is so, then school attendance might be seen merely as a rearrangement of the flows of the economic costs and benefits of children over the life course rather than a redirection of the overall flows.

This calculus also depends upon the disposal of children's earnings after they complete their schooling and enter the work force. If children have extensive work careers and continue to contribute to the parental family economy, the investments in children's education might increase the overall economic value of children and possibly exert an upward pressure on the demand for children. On the other hand, if children's work careers are short or if their adult earnings are not integrated into the parental family economy, their contributions to the parental family may be less than their educational costs, resulting in important financial flows from the parental generation to children. In that case, the expansion of schooling opportunities would increase the costs of children relative to their financial contributions, which might reduce the number of children desired. Of course, one unknown key element is the perception of parents about the expected contributions of children.

The benefits of children's educational accomplishments are not limited to financial contributions to the parents. The educational achievements of children also bring honor and prestige to the family. They also enhance the well-being of both the children and the larger family chain.

Given the patrilocal and patrilineal nature of the Chinese kinship system, the influence of schooling on the functioning of the family economy is likely to be different for sons than for daughters. In the historical Chinese marriage pattern a woman married at a fairly young age and joined her husband's family's household and economic unit, thus limiting her ability to contribute to her natal family. This historical cultural system might tend to limit the amount of education that parents would be willing to provide for their daughters. On the other hand, the historical Chinese pattern of desiring compatible spouses for sons and their families—seeking "matching doors"—would motivate parents to provide their daughters with educations roughly equivalent to the schooling provided to sons.[1] The extension of education for daughters also might increase female age at marriage so that daughters would have a longer time to contribute to the parental family.

Parents of a daughter who has strong earning capabilities might be motivated to postpone her marriage in order to retain her earnings for the natal family. A daughter may also voluntarily postpone her marriage, because she feels indebted to her parents for their investment in her education and wants to reciprocate their assistance to some extent before marriage. Thus, the combination of increased educational expenses and higher earning capacity of young women could exert substantial upward pressure on age at marriage in Taiwan.

The expansion of parental investment in a daughter's education may

1. Such a pattern has been documented in South India, where educated husbands demand at least minimally educated wives in keeping with their own educated status. Education itself is seen as a value that enhances a daughter's marriage prospects, the links that may be created through marriage, and the status of the daughter's family (Caldwell, Reddy, and Caldwell 1983; Fricke, Syed, and Smith 1986).

also increase her earning capacity after marriage, which could rationalize or legitimize the daughter's long-term financial commitment to her natal family. The allocation of family resources to a daughter's education increases her prestige and potential income, which is acknowledged by both parents and parents-in-law and is perceived as an important part of her dowry (Tsui 1987, 19). As parents allocate more family resources for a daughter's education, their bargaining power in marriage negotiations probably increases, giving them a stronger basis for asking for their daughter's commitment to her natal family after marriage. Parents of an educated daughter may be particularly motivated to follow this strategy when the potential bride has several younger siblings. Even if parents do not think about an educated daughter's utilitarian value and ask her postmarital assistance, the greater earning capacity of a well-educated woman gives her more capability to assist her parents if the need arises. Therefore, a better-educated daughter can be an alternative source for old age security, since she is able to make a greater long-term economic contribution to her natal family.

Finally, school attendance provides young people with access to new ideas and values (Caldwell 1982; Inkeles and Smith 1974; Schak 1975). These new ways of looking at the world can come from the schooling process itself, as new ideas and attitudes are portrayed in the educational curriculum. They can also be gained from new access to the mass media, including television, newspapers, magazines, and movies.

The new ideas brought by education and literacy can originate from either that society's own elite or from abroad. As we will argue in a later section, new values and attitudes originating from Europe and the United States are potentially very powerful in Taiwan because they portray such dramatically different images of individual behavior and family relationships. They also carry the high prestige historically associated with the economic, political, and military power of Western societies. These new values and ideas learned in school and through the mass media can not only immediately influence parent-child relationships and interactions with peers but also carry over into adult relationships.

From a Labor-Pooling to a Wage-Pooling Family Economy

As discussed in chapter 2, the family in the Chinese past organized, directed, and managed its internal sources of labor to produce its means of existence. The difficulties of labor-intensive production required all members of most families to contribute to the household economy, with specific activities generally allocated along gender and age lines. Women and children, as well as men, were generally involved in family production, and under most circumstances all made important contributions to the family's production of necessary goods and services. Thus, the Chinese family was very much a labor-pooling economic system similar to the pattern described for historical England and France by Tilly and Scott (1978).

An important element of the historical Chinese family was the control of the senior generation, particularly males, over the means and output of production, a control that was particularly important in an environment of scarce economic alternatives. The older generation maintained control over the household economy well into the children's adulthood; consequently, the younger generation could not become truly independent economically before the older generation transferred the economic unit to them. The disparity in status, wealth, and power between parents and children made the transfer of rights to the means of production an important juncture in the life course, both for the older and for the younger generations. Furthermore, the authority of young daughters-in-law was generally constrained by both age and gender, and their influence in the family economy was extremely limited for many years of their lives. Although many of these features of the Chinese labor-pooling family economy were present elsewhere around the world, the historical Chinese system probably emphasized and enforced the authority of the elders and the responsibility of the younger to the older generation to an extent unequaled by many other historical family systems.

A major characteristic of large-scale industrialization around the world has been the transformation of the labor-pooling family economy into a wage-pooling family economy in which many people work outside their household boundaries but pool their wages into a common family fund (Thornton and Fricke 1987; Tilly and Scott 1978). Although systematic information about people's ideas and motivations during the early years of industrialization is limited, it appears that all family members continue to view the economic activities of individuals as family contributions (Dublin 1979; Early 1982; Hareven 1982; Tilly and Scott 1978). Although the demands of childrearing and the performance of household tasks initially limit the participation of wives in the formal wage economy, unmarried women and men are typically involved more heavily in the wage economy (Davis 1984).

In many respects the wage labor activities of children are seen as simple extensions of the family economy, as responses to family rather than individual needs, and as obligatory family contributions. In fact, Dublin (1979) reports that payroll records from industrializing Lowell,

Massachusetts, during the 1850s and 1860s "provide repeated instances in which fathers signed for and probably picked up their children's pay envelopes, [and] these children, then did not even receive their wages which went directly into the family till." Current ethnographic work in Chinese populations suggests strong parallels in the tendency to send children to work for wages as a contribution to the family economy (Greenhalgh 1985; Huang 1984; Kung 1983; Salaff 1981). A major theme of Kung's (1983) study of single female Taiwanese factory workers, for example, is their perceived obligations to contribute money to their families (also, see Cohen 1976).

Despite the evidence that families initially regard wage labor employment as a straightforward extension of the historical family economy, the transformation of the family economy from labor pooling to wage pooling potentially has numerous widespread effects. Of crucial importance here is that while individuals may actually contribute their wages to the family economy, they still participate in the formal economy as individuals rather than as family members (Goode 1982). Whereas family heads maintain control over resources and consumption in the family mode of production, individuals gain considerable control over the earnings from their production in the wage labor economy. Thus, in a wage labor economy children have considerable capacity to decide whether to contribute their incomes to the family economy or to establish a separate economy on their own—a source of autonomy that was very difficult to attain when family elders controlled the means of production (Goode 1970, 1982).

The control of individuals over their earnings has expanded steadily in the West (Tilly and Scott 1978), and today there is little expectation that children will contribute substantially to their parents, even when they are living at home (Bachman 1983). Although we expect that the strong Chinese historical tradition of family commitment and filial piety will exercise a significant brake on the separation of young people from the family economy in Taiwan, the new wage economy exerts a powerful force in this direction. It is likely that the wage-pooling economy of the parental family will become increasingly fragmented, with the younger generation increasingly maintaining control over their earnings and more frequently establishing their own separate economic units.

We accept the observation of numerous social observers that the transformation of the family labor-pooling economy into a wage-pooling economy, with individuals controlling their own output, significantly increases the independence of individuals within the family. As Goode (1982, 175–91) has argued persuasively, the result is that family and household heads have diminished ability to command allegiance and exercise control over individual family members. Within the existing system of family relations the immediate effect would be to enhance the possibilities for negotiating family decisions made by members of the senior generation, particularly when they impinge on the interests of juniors. Since family heads cannot ensure that individual family members will do better under their leadership than on their own, the economic necessity of maintaining family bonds is significantly reduced, and individuals and couples often find it more feasible and attractive to follow individualistic solutions rather than family elders.

The reduced economic control of the family head is probably manifest in numerous dimensions of parent-child relationships. As young people mature and make the transition to adulthood, they probably have more say about their economic activities, their living arrangements, and their choice of a spouse. The autonomy of the younger generation probably extends to postmarital decisions as well, such as whether to live with parents and how many children to have. The increasing separation of first- and second-generation economies can also result in the younger generation providing less psychological and economic support for their parents as the older generation retires from the labor force and faces a period of reduced financial and physical capacity. Finally, if young people become more economically independent from their parents and increasingly maintain separate financial units, they may also have less motivation to maintain their reliance on and support of their ancestors. That is, an increased economic emphasis on the individual and the nuclear family might lessen the importance of more remote ancestors in the lives of autonomous Chinese individuals and couples.

A related issue is the separation of economic production from land. While many Taiwanese families in the past owned no land, those who did viewed their land as an important gift from the ancestors. This ancestral gift helped to bind together the living and the dead and was seen as a guarantee of the living remaining filial to the ancestors. While land reform reduced the number of landless farmers and many people with wage jobs in the cities retained ownership of land, the increased importance of industrial employment and human capital resulted in a relative decline in the economic importance of land to individual and family well-being. As land has become relatively less important to the young, we might expect a reduction in the role played by the ancestors in the daily lives of their descendants.

As with school enrollment, nonfamily employment shifts the locus of many primary economic activities out of the household. Such a change reduces the time spent in the family and increases interactions with peers in nonfamilial settings (Tilly and Scott 1978). This can be particularly important for employed children whose parents are unable to observe, supervise, and control their children, making it easier for children to be influenced by others. Factories, like schools, also become primary socialization agents where children are exposed to many ideas and influences unavailable in the family home—forces that can cause a redefinition of values and appropriate behaviors. There is also some evidence that factory employment is seen by some as a route to obtaining the financial resources for obtaining higher levels of education (Huang 1984) and, as argued earlier, increased education can modify individual and familial relationships.

Of course, both schools and nonfamily employment can significantly modify relationships with peers. As young people spend more time in settings removed from parental control and supervision, and often with peers whose families may not know each other well, they experience a basis for new nonfamilial primary groups. If educational systems and work places include both young women and young men, the pattern of interactions between the sexes can be modified. The potential for unsupervised interactions between young women and young men increases dramatically, with important implications for mate selection. We expect the expansion of school enrollment and paid employment to be associated with greater social contact among young men and women, more involvement of young people in the mate selection process, more young people meeting their future spouses at school and work, and greater personal and sexual intimacy before marriage. These changes are probably also reflected in greater levels of intimacy between husbands and wives after marriage (Rindfuss and Morgan 1983).

There are also good reasons to believe that paid employment influences the formation and dissolution of marital unions. On the one hand, one would expect that the income associated with wage jobs would enhance the ability of couples to marry and establish their own households. Given the historical marriage customs and division of labor in Taiwan, paid employment might influence women's marriages most by accelerating the accumulation of a sizable dowry. Paid employment before marriage might also allow women to contribute more economically to their families after marriage as well; however, this effect would probably be smaller for women than for men, who spend considerably more time in paid employment after marriage. Furthermore, many of the paid jobs held by young women in Taiwan are not particularly pleasant—a fact which may motivate some to accelerate their marriages in order to terminate such employment. But this mechanism would be most likely among young women who were independent enough to arrange their own marriages. The income from paid employment could also alleviate the frictions associated with marriage and limit the likelihood of divorce.

On the other hand, there are also causal forces associated with paid employment that would result in lower rates of marriage and higher incidence of divorce—with these effects being most relevant to the experiences of women. Of central importance for Taiwan is the possibility that parents might want to postpone for a period of time the marriages of their employed daughters in order to extend the length of time those daughters would be contributing economically to their natal families. Paid employment might also provide young women independent sources of income that would make them want to postpone marriage or to forgo it entirely. Both of these effects on marriage would probably be greatest for those with the best employment opportunities. Since parents have historically had such great authority over the marriages and economic contributions of their daughters, it is likely that the negative effects of paid employment on the rate of marriage would outweigh the positive influences posited in the previous paragraph. Divorce could also be facilitated by paid employment if unhappily married women were able to make enough from their own employment to permit them to live independently.

Urbanization, Migration, and Nonfamily Living Arrangements

The special requirements of capital-intensive industry include large-scale organization and worker concentration. Industrialization is often accompanied by urbanization, including the establishment of new cities and the expansion of old ones. This frequently leads to considerable geographic mobility and extensive rural migration to cities. This has been true in Taiwan, although the extent of urbanization there has been lessened through conscious efforts at rural industrialization and by the provision of good transportation and communication networks, which have enabled some rural residents to work in nearby enterprises and others to commute to cities for employment (see chap. 3).

In some cases entire families move from agricultural areas of family production to urban areas and wage economies. In many cases, though, only part of the family moves, the younger people often being the ones who migrate to the cities to take advantage of new employment opportunities. This youthful migration consists of young couples who migrate to cities while leaving their parents to maintain their original economic unit and residence, as well as numerous single women and men who leave rural areas to seek their fortunes (and, often, the larger family's fortune) in the city (Huang 1984).

The migration of young people, many of whom are unmarried, from rural to urban areas has provided an interesting living arrangement dilemma for virtually all rapidly urbanizing societies, a problem exacerbated within Chinese culture, where there has been little tradition of nonfamily living arrangements as there was in the West (Barclay et al. 1976; Hajnal 1982). Some of these young people could live with their urban relatives, but for others this was impossible, either because they had no relatives living in cities or because of insufficient housing. In Western societies, where there was a long historical tradition of young people living and working in the households of nonrelatives (Kussmaul 1981), the solution frequently involved living with unrelated people as boarders or lodgers. In fact, in the late nineteenth century between 15 and 20% of all urban households in the United States included lodgers (Modell and Hareven 1973). Another alternative in the West was provided by companies that built dormitories to house single workers during the early years of industrialization (Dublin 1979; Hareven 1982; Tilly and Scott 1978). The latter strategy has been replicated in other societies, including Japan and Nepal (Taeuber 1958; Thornton and Fricke 1987), while previous research establishes the existence of work-related dormitories in Taiwan (Arrigo 1980; Diamond 1979; Kung 1983).

Parents and other people concerned about the health and morals of young people often believe that work-related dormitory living constitutes a significant break from historical family living arrangements. In the United States there was concern that dormitory residents would have less supervision and more freedom than was healthy (Dublin 1979; Hanlan 1981), a fear that has been noted more recently for Taiwan (Kung 1983). Efforts were made in both settings to ensure that dormitory living was as similar to familial arrangements as possible, with supervisors assigned to guide the behavior of the young residents and to enforce rules concerning appropriate behavior. Although Kung (1983) reports that these mechanisms were able to severely restrict the independence of residents in the Taiwanese dormitories she studied, the small number of supervisors were unable to provide the supervision that would replicate the control and knowledge of activities obtained by parents in the home environment. Consequently, dormitory living is likely to increase the autonomy of children relative to their parents, intensify the interactions of young people with their peers, increase the involvement of children in mate selection, and lead to greater intimacy in courtship and marriage.

The change from rural child to urban industrial worker can be a difficult transition. Many migrant workers report considerable homesickness in the city, an adjustment problem which sometimes results in a return back to the parental home (Huang 1984). The sharp differences in styles of living experienced by young people as they migrate to cities as well as the strong cultural attachments between parents and children in Chinese society probably exacerbate these adjustment problems.

Some factors would ameliorate the effects of the separation of young migrants and their families. One is the continuing integration of the separated households within the family economy and family network (Gallin 1978; Huang 1984; Kessinger 1974). This possibility is particularly likely in Taiwan, which has a long history of continuing economic interdependence of family members across different households, resulting in a diversified and dispersed family economic unit (Greenhalgh 1985).

Another factor ameliorating the effects of rural-to-urban migration is that in Taiwan, as elsewhere, many of these moves encompassed a relatively short distance, permitting frequent trips from the city to visit relatives in the home village. In addition, there undoubtedly has been extensive circulatory migration, with young urban migrants returning to their homes when they were needed there (Huang 1984). While frequent visits and circulatory migration retarded the city's influence on the young rural migrants there, it also probably accelerated the process of "rurbanization"—the transformation of the countryside by urban influences—as young people undoubtedly brought ideas and ways of living they had learned in the cities back to the countryside with them (see Goldstein 1985).

Urbanization and the restructuring of economic opportunities can also influence residential patterns after marriage. Chinese families have historically displayed a strong tendency toward village exogamy, with newlyweds living with or near the husband's parents. With the new geographical distribution of jobs, a young couple might be motivated to live with or close to the wife's parents if their geographical location provided proximity to better employment opportunities, an outcome noted in another patrilineal society (Klass 1978). Similarly, the distribution of employment opportunities may motivate young couples to live independently. Actually, because of the size of cities and the opportunities for contacts among young people in urban settings, brides and grooms will probably be more likely now than in the past to have lived in the same geographical location before marriage, making for less isolation of the bride from her natal home after marriage.

The migration of young people to the city may also have an influence on the lives of the older generation. If all the children of a rural couple migrate to the city, the parents will be faced with a difficult dilemma as they reach their older years. In order to stay in the countryside with their friends and familiar surroundings, they must forsake the possibility of living with their children in old age, since that would require them to migrate to the city as well.

The phenomenon of boarding and lodging in the United States almost disappeared during the twentieth century, as living standards increased, the population became more urbanized, and rural-urban migration decreased (Modell and Hareven 1973). In recent years, however, single persons have taken the initially discouraged step toward residential independence and are now increasingly maintaining their own private households, either living alone or with housemates (Kobrin 1976; Michael, Fuchs, and Scott 1980; Thornton and Freedman 1983). There may be future increases in independent living in Taiwan as well, although the lack of a historical tradition there for children living apart from their parents may prevent this from occurring. If this new pattern of independent living occurs in Taiwan, it will reflect greater independence of children from their parents and could be the impetus for yet more autonomy of young people.

Since rural to urban migration decreases the number of people who are able to share households with their relatives, we expect extended family living to decline during urbanization. This, however, does not necessarily mean that extended family living will be lower in cities than in rural areas. In fact, there are several reasons to expect the opposite— with urban areas having higher, not lower, prevalence of extended households. People in rural areas may live in nuclear households because their relatives have migrated to cities, while rural-to-urban migrants may find it useful to share living quarters with their relatives—both relatives who have always lived in the city and those who have recently moved there. Furthermore, elderly parents who had stayed in the rural areas when their children migrated to the cities may later decide that they want to move to the city to live with their children. At the same time, young people who grow up in cities may have less motivation than their rural peers to migrate away from their parents because they can locate jobs in their own communities. Because of these migration dynamics, it is not surprising to find that urban households are more extended than rural ones in Taiwan (Lavely 1982; Shu and Lin 1989), a finding also observed in nineteenth-century England (Anderson 1971, 1972).

Urban living also changes patterns of association with others in the community. Whereas interpersonal ties within rural areas are frequently general, multipurpose, and familiar, relationships in cities are often segmented, specialized, and unfamiliar (Wirth 1938). The proliferation of institutions in cities frequently results in people interacting with each other in terms of their specialized institutional roles rather than as complete individuals. As specialized relationships become predominant over general ones, individuals are less dependent upon particular persons and less constrained by the personal and emotional controls of intimate groups. Consequently urban dwellers have many more alternatives than those living in rural areas. Of course, while the city proliferates contacts with strangers, interrelationships with people in specialized roles, activities away from the family, and increased privacy, such specialization and freedom does not necessarily reduce the importance and frequency of associations with family members (Fischer 1976).

Cities are also centers of transportation and communication networks (Hawley 1971). Consequently, city dwellers have access to more information than those living elsewhere. This includes information generated within the society as well as news from the international community. The additional information can be both the source of new innovations and a reinforcement for changes that have already been initiated. Furthermore, the close integration of urban and rural areas in Taiwan ensures the rapid dissemination of information from the cities to the more peripheral areas.

The Growth of Income and Consumption Aspirations

A key feature of Taiwan's social and economic transformation has been the rapid growth in income and economic well-being. As chapter 3 documents, the economic growth rate in Taiwan has been among the highest in the world during the last four decades, and that expansion has been translated into a rising personal standard of living.

Economists tell us that as long as tastes and relative prices remain constant, the primary effect of income growth is the loosening of the budget constraint, allowing individuals to buy more of whatever it is they value. So one would expect the purchase of more food, consumer durables, education, medical services, and trips abroad, all of which have occurred in recent Taiwanese history (chap. 3). If one believes that budget constraints historically placed some limits on marriage, childbearing, and extended family living, one might expect that income growth would lead to younger marriage, higher fertility, and more extended family living.

Of course, tastes in family matters may shift across time, and the additional economic resources could be used to finance the newly acquired tastes. Independent living is one new family goal that could be achieved with additional resources as young married couples might be able to afford their own apartment, making it possible for them to live independently from their parents. Similarly, an easing of the budget constraint among older adults might make it possible for married couples and their parents to live separately and thus to enjoy added privacy. Further, if parental incomes rise enough so that parents no longer needed economic assistance from children, economic flows from children to parents might diminish. These changes have accompanied rising incomes in the West (Kobrin 1976; Smith 1981), and it would not be surprising to see such arrangements emerge in Taiwan as well, even though there is more historical emphasis on communal living in Chinese culture.

Numerous social observers have noted that industrialization and economic growth expand material aspirations by creating new products and improving old ones (Alison 1840; Malthus 1986; *Nation* 1868). With more consumer goods available and more money with which to purchase them, consumption aspirations apparently expand along with economic resources, preventing income from outpacing consumption aspirations. The expansion of educational aspirations along with income growth also is likely, especially given the historical Chinese emphasis on education.

Aspirations for consumer goods may also increase faster than either income or the things essential for family life. In the nineteenth century increasing consumption aspirations were offered as an explanation for what was believed to be declining marriage rates in the West (Alison 1840; Malthus 1986; *Nation* 1868), and more recently the idea has been used to help explain declines in childbearing (Easterlin 1980). It is possible that rising aspirations may lead to later marriage and fewer children in Taiwan as well.

Mass Media and New Ideas

Just as the organization of individual activities has been transformed by the expansion of institutions outside the family, so has the structure of access to ideas and beliefs. Previously, individual access to beliefs, values, and views about the world were determined largely by the individual's local environment, the family being an important component of that milieu. The values and attitudes of individuals were for the most part structured and determined during childhood by the family of socialization. Across the subsequent years of the life course, the individual's access to alternative ideas was greatly limited by the restriction of contacts with individuals and information outside the circle of kinspeople. New ideas and alternative ways of viewing the world were both received and evaluated within the context of the family.

The family's near monopoly over the flow of information and ideas to individual family members has been shattered in many ways during the past century. Beginning well in the past and accelerating rapidly in recent years, Taiwan has developed an impressive national system of transportation and communication. As discussed in chapter 3, an efficient railroad system was created early in this century, and the island now has an effective system of highways and secondary roads. A telephone system was created and has now spread island-wide. The number of newspapers and magazines multiplied dramatically, as did total circulation. Radio and television met with quick success and rapidly saturated the island, while movies became widespread and popular. The result of this transformation of transportation and communication was that individuals were connected directly with a national network of information and ideas that could be controlled and directed only partially by family leaders.

Of course, this breaking of the near monopoly of families over individual communication was a two-pronged change. On the one hand, it required the creation of the system of railroads, highways, telephones, television networks, radio stations, magazine publishers, and movie production and distribution. On the other hand, it required changes in the tastes and ideas of the population to produce an appreciation and market demand for the new and expanding products. The expansion of schooling helped produce a population with the literary skills and interest to understand and appreciate the new information sources. Industrial employment helped expand the need for new sources of information, and the accompanying rising standard of living provided additional resources for the consumption of communication and transportation goods such as cars, motorcycles, telephones, televisions, and radios, as well as the purchase of magazines and movie tickets. Also, urban living helped to bring individuals within easy range of a greater number and wider variety of communication outlets.

At the same time that Taiwanese individuals were being brought into direct interaction with a national mass media network of information and ideas, the society was being integrated into an international network of new cultural values and ideals. Historically, the island has had considerable experience interacting with people from foreign countries. The influence of Japan was particularly important, since Taiwan was a Japanese colony from 1895 to 1945. Thus, the entire population of Taiwan born before 1945 was in contact with Japanese culture, many having been educated in Japanese schools with values and ways of thinking different from their Chinese ancestors.

Although some observers have noted that the Japanese colonial government made no explicit efforts to modify family life in Taiwan (Barclay 1954), at least two colonial policies had direct relevance for family relations. One was the introduction of schooling for both boys and girls, with large fractions of young children attending school at the end of the colonial period. As we argued earlier, there are many ways in which the spread of education can change the nature of family relations across and within generations.

A second important intervention of the Japanese government centered on footbinding, which was very widespread at the beginning of the colonial period. At the time of the first colonial census in 1905, more than 70% of all Taiwanese women over age 20 were footbound (Barrett 1989). The Japanese government forbade footbinding, and by the 1915 census the number of children and teenagers who were footbound had been nearly eliminated (Barrett 1989). Since footbinding significantly impaired the mobility of girls and women to move and work beyond the local setting, its restriction by the colonial administration removed one important physical limitation to the opportunities for females in Taiwanese society. It also had the potential to modify relationships between girls and their parents and between wives and husbands.

Barrett (1989) has also argued that the penetration of the colonial administration to the village level affected the structure of power within families. He suggests that the Japanese police sometimes intervened in family disputes, which probably limited to some extent the power of the family hierarchy.

After World War II, Taiwan became a part of China again. To diminish the Japanese historical influence on Taiwan, the government prohibited importation of Japanese movies. However, the implementation of a free trade policy, the increase of foreign travel, and historical Japanese ties have made Japanese cultural influence important once again in present-day Taiwan. The contact with Japanese culture has probably helped to demonstrate to Taiwanese the pluralistic nature of the world and the existence of multiple world views and ways of doing things.

Both mainland China and Taiwan have had considerable contact with Western societies for hundreds of years, including contact with travelers, missionaries, and traders. Taiwan also experienced a brief period of

Western colonization in the seventeenth century, and the mainland underwent an extensive period of Western domination in the nineteenth century. The years of Western domination convinced many Chinese that China needed to undergo extensive change to restore the country's respected position in the world.

Western domination also convinced many Chinese of the superiority of Western technology, social organization, and ways of life. These people believed that Western society represented the apex of societal development and offered a prototype on which the Chinese could model their own social and economic reforms. Many dimensions of Western culture were included in the package that many Chinese tried to emulate. These included not only the technology, knowledge, and economic organization of Western countries but also political systems and many dimensions of personal and family life. This made many Chinese not only open to the influence of the West but also actively desirous of adopting many of the features of Western social organization so that they could reach the level of social development they perceived in the West.

Contacts with the West, particularly with the United States, accelerated after World War II. Beginning in 1951 there was a substantial American military presence in Taiwan (Liu 1979), and business and commercial contacts increased. A steady and wide stream of magazines, television programs, and movies were imported directly from the United States, and American formats and themes were adopted in Chinese programs. There has also been a rapidly accelerating flow of Taiwanese visitors to foreign countries. The result is that in recent years individual Taiwanese have been brought into direct, extensive, and intensive contact with Western cultures, with many values different from those predominant in Chinese society in the past. Given the continuing view of the West as a model to be emulated, Taiwanese society has been particularly open to the adoption of a wide range of Western cultural patterns.

What are the major new ideas and values that the Taiwanese found as they came into contact with Americans and Western Europeans? Crucially important is the Western European and American mate selection system, with its emphasis upon the autonomy of young people in choosing their spouses (Macfarlane 1986). There also is the associated complex of dating, courtship, emotional intimacy, and sexual involvement. The Chinese mass media not only has distributed numerous Western shows and articles, with their often exaggerated emphasis on autonomy, sentiment, and sex in dating and courtship, but also has focused upon mate selection, love, and intergenerational conflict in its own productions

(Schak 1975). In a frequent plot in Chinese movies, a young couple fall in love only to have their romance squelched by parents exercising their prerogatives of choosing their children's mates. This is not to say that similar stories have been absent in historical Chinese art and literature. Earlier Chinese poetry, for example, incorporated romantic themes similar to those appearing in cinema and on television today. What is different today is the portrayal of these conflicts between filial piety and individual interest by the mass media to all strata of society and, perhaps more important, the real possibility in the contemporary setting of evaluating and acting on one's own desires.

Also important is the Western nuclear household, which emphasizes independence and privacy (Laslett 1974). In Chinese media programs multigenerational households are often portrayed as creating considerable intergenerational conflict. A solution to the dilemma of privacy versus filial piety sometimes suggested is for the two generations to maintain separate but geographically proximate households.

Another message from the internationalized mass media says that success depends on individual rather than familial accomplishments. Media images portrayed from the West focus much more intensely on individuals and their private interests as compared to the historical Chinese emphasis upon the family collective, including the family chain.

A related theme of interest focuses on equal opportunity, access, and authority. Here the important idea is the illegitimacy of status and authority differentials based upon age and gender.

Small families are another new message portrayed by the mass media in Taiwan. Low fertility and small families are key features of twentieth-century families in the West and are portrayed as such in the media. The small family ideal has also been officially endorsed as a priority policy by the government, with the mass media vigorously used to persuade young Chinese women and men to limit their childbearing.

Finally, there is the idea of political democracy. De Tocqueville's (1955) theme that the organization and emotional tenor of relationships in family and civil society parallel each other reverberates throughout China's own Confucian ideology. It is not surprising that Chinese political reformers of the early twentieth century linked the equalization of family relationships to widespread social reform (see chap. 2). As de Tocqueville (1955) has suggested, political democracy is potentially related to democracy in family relationships, even to the point of increasing intimacy and attention between former hierarchical relations.

While it is appropriate to emphasize how the world seen in movies, on television, and in the written word differs from the historical Chinese family system and family relationships, the Taiwanese mass media is not totally awash in Western images and messages. The media continues to emphasize historical Chinese values such as filial piety, and historical images of women and men and gender-based behavior and roles are still frequent. In fact, popular movements, such as the Chinese Cultural Renaissance Movement, have resulted in governmental policies and programs to further historical Chinese values in late-twentieth-century Taiwan. The result has been the incorporation of historical values explicitly in the national school curriculum and also in certain media programs.

Although an emphasis upon historical Chinese values and patterns of family life continues to be an important—and perhaps still dominant—element of the mass media in Taiwan, those historical values now share time and space with family ideas and structures not previously emphasized in Taiwan. The existence of a set of alternative images and messages in the media provides a new set of models for behavior, some of which can be directly adopted. One example of the diffusion of a Western family trait to Taiwan was the introduction of the white wedding gown prior to World War II. In more recent years the white wedding gown has become extremely popular in Taiwan and the historical red Chinese wedding dress is now worn less frequently.

The possibility that these new ideas become elements in the numerous interactions and negotiations occurring regularly within Taiwanese families is even more likely. They probably validate the behavior of young people as they date, form intimate relationships with their partners, and make their own decisions about marriage. They also help legitimate the younger generation as they make independent decisions about employment and living accommodations which are opposed by their elders. They probably help validate the behavior of those who give individual interests more weight than the interests of the family collective. Also, as individuals contemplate adopting contraceptives to limit family size, the images and support provided by the media, including advertisements for family planning, can help tip the weight in favor of the adoption of contraception. In short, as efficient communication and transportation systems have made new ideas and images of the family from the West accessible to the general population, these new values and messages can directly change the thinking of individuals and provide external support for new ideas generated by individual Chinese women, men, and children.

The expected effects of the changes of the message, changes in the medium, and availability of the mass media in Taiwan are consistent with those we would expect from the structural shifts in education, paid employment, nonfamilial living arrangements, and urban living. Consequently, the structural and ideational shifts probably have operated in reinforcing ways, changes in one dimension serving to buttress the effects of the others. This system of mutually reinforcing and interacting influences has probably enhanced both the speed and magnitude of the family changes observed in Taiwan.

Secularization

Several societies have experienced a secularization of beliefs and world views as science has removed more and more of personal experience from the supernatural and otherworldly to the earthly here and now. While religion continues to play a significant role in the lives of many individuals and their families in the West, reliance on religion as a solution to the problems of life, belief in the authority of religious leaders, and faith in the intervention of the supernatural in the lives of individual women and men has declined (Alwin 1988; Glenn 1987; Roof and McKinney 1987; Thornton 1989). We expect that similar processes have been operating in Taiwan and that the role of the supernatural has receded, while at the same time continuing to be important.

The decline of religion as a source of support for historical family norms and behavior has been offered as an explanation of historical family change in the West, particularly the role of reduced religious authority in permitting the adoption of contraception and the increase in divorce. More recently, religious change has been linked with trends in premarital sex, nonmarital cohabitation, marriage, divorce, and childlessness (Lesthaeghe and Surkyn 1988; Lesthaeghe and Wilson 1986; Thornton 1985, 1989).

One would expect that any secularization of Chinese society would also influence family relationships, norms, and behavior, although, given the fundamentally different spiritual worlds, the shape of the effects could be quite different in Taiwan than in the West. Since the ancestors are a central part of the Chinese spiritual world, any diminution of the importance of the supernatural in Taiwan would probably weaken the historical family chain linking the living with the ancestors and future descendants. The living might place less reliance on their relationships with their ancestors and be less diligent in looking after their welfare. They might also be less concerned about how their own children might care for them after death.

A likely important fallout of any reduction in the centrality of the ancestors would be less commitment to filial piety, since the eternal strength of the family chain would be weakened. This could reduce both the authority of the elders in the family and the commitment of the generations to each other. A reduction in emphasis on the family chain could also place more emphasis on the here and now in Chinese family relationships, with the nuclear family growing in importance at the expense of more extended relationships.

Taiwan's Unique Recent History

The Communist victory on the mainland and the subsequent transfer of the Nationalist government to Taiwan is a unique feature of Chinese history which could influence family life. The large influx of Mainlanders to Taiwan in the late 1940s included several diverse groups, including government officials, business leaders, and a large number of military personnel. While the business and government leaders were well educated and frequently came with other family members, the migrating army was heavily weighted toward young single men with limited educational credentials.

The large influx of young single men undoubtedly had a major influence on the basic demographic character of Taiwanese society. Perhaps most important was the distortion of the sex ratio at the young adult ages. This would significantly alter the Taiwanese marriage market by dramatically increasing the ratio of men to women in the prime marrying years. The result would be a substantial marriage squeeze, enhancing the prospects of marriage for women and detracting from the alternatives for men.

The migration of Mainlanders to Taiwan probably influenced the marriage prospects of the migrants more than those of the native Taiwanese. The marriage market in Taiwan during the years immediately after the migration was largely segregated into two parts—the migrant Mainlanders and the native Taiwanese. The likely result is that many Mainlanders postponed marriage and some may have never married. Over time, however, many of them probably married native Taiwanese women, most of whom would have been considerably younger than their husbands. This extensive age gap would also probably increase the likelihood of widowhood for the women who married these soldiers.

In 1951 the government instituted, and has since maintained, a policy of universal military service for young men (Chang 1981). This policy has a potentially great influence on family processes and behavior, with the expected effect on marital timing being particularly great. Since military service interrupts the normal life course, it is likely that the marriages of men would be postponed. Women's ages at marriage could also be delayed since their potential marriage partners were spending time in the military.

The universal military experience also provided all Taiwanese men extensive nonfamily experiences. They were pulled out of family economies and households and from the control of parents and placed in barracks under military authority. Although the soldiers were tightly controlled and had relatively few opportunities for recreation and leisure, even limited amounts of off-duty time in cities provided those from rural areas numerous opportunities for access to new ideas and styles of behavior. They also had the opportunity to mix with soldiers recruited from all walks of life. This undoubtedly led to a broadening of the circle of contacts as well as access to many ideas unavailable in rural areas. Also, military service probably extended the marriage market geographically by providing opportunities for young men to meet women outside their customary milieu.

Two aspects of the timing of military service make it a particularly important potential source of family change in Taiwan. The first important temporal aspect is the timing in the individual life course. Past research has demonstrated the importance of the young adult years in the socialization process. Those are years when many young people are solidifying their views and approaches to life, and events and experiences during these years seem to be especially persistent in the memory (Schuman and Scott 1989). Following this idea, it is likely that the military experience, and the associated new exposure to nonfamily environments, activities, authority, and information, would have particular influence on the many men serving in the military.

The second important temporal aspect is the timing of this policy in Taiwan's history. The universal military service policy was adopted when Taiwan was still largely agricultural, rural, and limited in educational opportunities. Consequently, there were probably millions of Taiwanese men for whom the military experience was the first extensive nonfamily experience other than attendance at elementary school. Thus, the universal military service policy, which exposed men to an intensive period of nonfamily experience at an impressionable period in the life course, may have played an important role in the changes occurring in Taiwan—a role that may not have been sufficiently appreciated in earlier work.

The Role of Structural Opportunities

In this chapter we have suggested ways in which schooling, paid employment, urban living, residence in dormitories, increased income, military service, increased access to the mass media, secularization, and contact with new ideas can lead to changes in family structure and relationships. Although we have couched our discussion in terms of the consequences of these organizational and ideational changes for the individuals and families they directly affect, the consequences are not merely for those who become educated, work and live outside the family, live in cities, serve in the military, or are immersed in new ideas through the mass media. The behavior and ideas of those who have such experiences and exposure can also be observed and copied by those not directly experiencing them. Similarly, those whose ideas and values are altered by these experiences can communicate them directly to others. Because of the preexisting communication networks among kinspeople, the family is a particularly effective institution for informally spreading new ideas. Also, the availability of schools, paid employment, nonfamily living, cities, and increased incomes can alter the relationships among family members even if none of those individuals participate directly in these new experiences. Furthermore, as new patterns of behavior become more available and frequent in the population, norms and expectations can shift and influence the behavior and relationships of nearly everyone in the population. Consequently, new family structure, behavior, and values can spread even more rapidly than the structural and ideational forces driving them.

An example of this kind of effect is provided by Wolf and Huang's (1980) analysis of marriage change in Taiwan early in this century. Many marriages in Taiwan in the early part of this century were arranged very early in childhood under total parental control, the future daughter-in-law being adopted into the home of the husband's family, where she lived until marriage. Today this pattern has disappeared, and Wolf and Huang attribute this change to the increasing independence of young people, caused by a relatively small but still significant increase in employment opportunities outside the family context during the first few decades of this century. They argue that the changes in marriage could occur because of the increased opportunities even though very few people actually participated in the new paid employment.

An important determinant of the availability of new opportunities is geography, particularly one's position in the rural-urban hierarchy. As previously noted, schools, paid employment, dormitory living, and access to the news media were generally available in Taiwanese cities before they spread to the countryside. Also, although basic educational facilities and the mass media eventually became widespread in the Taiwanese countryside, colleges and employment in large industries continue to be more accessible in the cities.

Despite Taiwan's emphasis on rural industrial development, schooling and employment opportunities are still unevenly distributed, which could create a significant dilemma for many rural Chinese families. Whereas Taiwanese urbanites can generally take advantage of virtually the entire range of educational and employment opportunities in the society while living at home, rural residents must migrate to the cities to take advantage of many of these same opportunities. Rural children who remain in the country during their growing-up years miss the opportunities available in the cities but have the experience of growing up within the context of the family mode of organization. Those rural children who migrate to the cities for schooling or employment not only have much greater exposure to nonfamilial environments and experiences than their country cousins who remain in their home village but may even have more nonfamily experiences than urban Taiwanese, who can take advantage of most of the same opportunities while living in their parental home. That is, young people from rural areas who must migrate to the cities may be subject to more influences outside the family than are city-raised people who are attending the same schools and working in the same jobs.

Because of the great importance of age and genealogical position in determining the roles, statuses, responsibilities, and attitudes of individuals, position in the life course at the time of historical modifications in the social and economic environment has major ramifications for the ways in which individuals are influenced by and view those changes. That is, there is often no uniform influence upon individual lives independent of life course position but, rather, an important interaction of the effect of historical change with individual and family time.

This point is of sufficient importance to merit some examples of particular relevance for our study. As in most societies, the Chinese have historically organized life so that socialization and learning are compressed into the early years of life, while responsibility for economic production increases across at least the first four or five decades of the life course. Consequently, as schools are introduced, children who generally lack major economic responsibility are the ones who obtain educational training, while their parents must continue their commitment to economic production. Similarly, when it comes time for a family member to leave the farm to obtain employment in the city, the migrant probably will be a younger person, since young people can usually do as well in the city as older people and have considerably less experience and expertise on the family farm. And, of course, changes in attitudes toward marriage and childbearing cannot influence the marriage and childbearing behavior of those who have already gone through the first decades of the life course, but can have considerable influence on young people who are making decisions about marriage and childbearing.

Five

The Changing Organization
of Individual Activities

T. Fricke, P. K. C. Liu, A. Thornton,
D. Freedman, and L. S. Yang

Ethnographic and historical accounts of Chinese society highlight the overwhelming extent to which families organized individual activities and the flow of information. Work, the distribution of resources, and the comportment of leisure time activities were all accomplished within or organized through the *chia*. Buttressed by familial norms and by the state-sanctioned Confucian system, this same group also dominated contexts of socialization and residence. And even as the bureaucratic and administrative structures of the Chinese state disseminated Confucian family values throughout society, their personnel were recruited through an examination system dependent on family-organized private schools.

The model of family and social change presented in chapter 4 suggests that the forces of change in Taiwan—urbanization, industrialization, and the expansion of nonfamilial institutions and ideologies—affect the environment within which people organize their activities, alter the range of options available to individuals, and change the structure of authority in Chinese families. Increasing public education, for example, may tip the balance of skills and knowledge toward young people rather than their parents, and this may affect their relationships. The material foundations of these same relationships may be simultaneously altered by young people's increased participation in the wage labor economy by deemphasis of agricultural production. Thus, changes in the organization of activities historically performed within families are critical to our understanding of subsequent individual transitions and the family mediation of larger social changes.

This chapter documents changes in the family organization of individual activities. We focus on shifts in the activities of socialization and education, production and income redistribution, and living arrangements in the last fifty years. Where in the past the Chinese family stood as a totalizing institution, the massive transformations occurring throughout the twentieth century have led to an increasingly extrafamilial organization of education and production. While it is also true that contemporary Taiwanese society shows great continuity with the past, this chapter documents considerable change in virtually every aspect of individual life for which we have measures. These changes, moreover, are all predicted by the theoretical model developed in the previous chapter.

Data and Methods

To get a sense of the individual changes in key activities in Taiwan, we use a series of questions from the island-wide surveys administered to samples of ever-married women since 1965. For women, these questions relate to education, work experience, and living arrangements. Questions allow us to examine not only participation in these activities but also the extent to which work is organized by families and the nature of family control over wages. Parallel information exists for the husbands of these women for all but the living arrangement and income flow variables.[1] Supplementary data for this chapter include the recent ethnographic explorations of Taiwanese village and urban life which have increasingly turned to explicit examinations of social change (Gates 1987; Greenhalgh 1988; Hu 1984; Kung 1983).

Our general approach is to examine trends in activities by the marriage cohorts of respondents to the 1986 island-wide survey. We choose to emphasize marriage cohorts in the presentation of trends since the sample available to us is based on the population of ever-married women in Taiwan. Trends presented by birth cohort from this sample are dampened from their true levels because of truncation biases. The marriage cohorts are a better reflection of change across time, although the true population trends for Taiwan probably lie between the levels estimated separately for birth and marriage cohorts. See appendix B for a full discussion and examples of the relevant truncation bias issues in these analyses.

Our strategy is to explore the organization of activities within both a woman's natal and her marital families, the two contexts historically dominating a woman's life course. Ethnographies often describe marriage as a watershed event in women's lives which, even when they have

---

1. Because the island-wide Taiwan surveys sampled married women, the truncation biases for husbands' data make their information less representative of trends for all males. These issues are discussed in appendix B. We will make less use of husbands' data for these reasons, using them as supplementary material for fleshing out the more general trends.

been involved in nonfamily organized activities in their natal homes, redirects them toward increasingly domestic-centered pursuits (Kung 1983; M. Wolf 1972).[2] Our data allow us to explore the family organization of production in the postmarital environment both before and after the birth of a child. We are thus able to explore familial organization of women's activities both before and after marriage and before and after childbirth, historically one of the most important markers of status change within the marital home.

Finally, our model of change suggests that individual background and experiences early in the life course will affect the family organization of later activities. We will therefore explore changes in some of the experiences shown to be powerful causes of later behavior, especially education (Thornton et al. 1984), as well as contexts of early socialization such as rural, town, and urban living. These last explorations will be pursued by documenting marriage cohort trends within these natal family context and educational attainment groups.

Persistence and Change

Before launching into a discussion of the transformation of individual-level participation in family productive activities, we need to discuss the unique character of Taiwanese industrialization. We will explore trends in which individuals participate increasingly in production outside their own natal and marital families. While this is an important trend, we need also to realize that the quite dramatic transformations of experience in Taiwan are shaped by continuities of organizational style (Hamilton and Kao 1988; Sangren 1984).

Family firms. One area of paradox is that the businesses and factories in which the majority of people work are themselves organized as family firms. A 1983 survey[3] of business groups which have led Taiwan's industrialization indicates that sixty-three out of ninety-six are owned and controlled outright by single individuals or closely related family members, while an additional thirty-one are owned and controlled by people who can be considered as related in ways parallel to the fictive kin groups that have been so important to Taiwan's settlement. Susan Greenhalgh

2. Outside Taiwan, marriage has been shown to have similarly powerful implications for women's participation in nonfamily activities, especially wage labor (Davis 1984; Fricke et al. 1990).

3. Information from the 1983 China Credit Information Service (Zhonghua Zhengxinso) survey of ninety-six largest business groups in Taiwan cited in Hamilton and Kao (1988).

estimates that close to 97% of "all Chinese business firms on Taiwan are family firms" (1988: 239).[4] Indeed, family organization of these firms may be seen as evidence of the continuity of the family mode of organization and its flexibility in a variety of economic contexts, including industrialization.[5] Thus, where in the past Chinese society was defined by a close integration of family and state ideologies and organization, Taiwan's industrialization and the transformation of the productive activities of individuals relative to their own *chia* groups are occurring within a larger organizational context that continues to parallel family modes of authority and relationships. One important result of this unique form of technological and economic change is that the models of success for the Taiwanese continue to be models based on past Chinese patterns of familial organization. While individual experiences are less likely to be organized by their own families, particularly in the area of work, they are nevertheless carried out within another family environment; familial organization is a constant. Thus, the successful adaptation of Chinese familial patterns to industrialized and market activities underscores the multiple ways in which changes in the content and location of activities can be consistent with earlier patterns of authority and relationships between family members.[6]

Material life and leisure. These continuities and changes are illustrated, too, by the changing material contexts of family life on Taiwan at levels beyond the individual. Thus, in chapter 3 we saw that where in 1967 only 11% of Taiwan's people reported the presence of a television in their households, less than twenty years later, in 1986, fully 97% reported the presence of *color* televisions (see table 3.11). Other items such as refrigerators, rice-cookers, and telephones reveal similar patterns of rapid expansion and saturation in a short period.

From the point of view of mode of organization, changes in ownership of these goods imply far more than mere increases in family disposable

4. Greenhalgh bases her estimate on China Credit Information Service figures, which indicate that 62% of firms employing fifty or more workers are family organized, and on an assumption based on ethnographic work that all firms with less than fifty workers are family run. The 97% and 62% figures may thus be taken as the range for all firms.

5. Greenhalgh points out that where family members occupy key positions within these firms, they do so in a manner that parallels their age, sex, and generation position within the family itself. Moreover, the marshaling of assets and individual control over them parallels the historical inheritance structures of Chinese families (1988: 231–34).

6. See, for example, the comparative literature on Chinese family firms in a variety of other settings such as Singapore (Yao 1987), the Philippines (Omohundro 1981), and Hong Kong (Ward 1972). See also Hamilton and Kao (1988), Salaff (1988), and the volume by Winckler and Greenhalgh (1988) for more detailed discussion of the familial organization of firms in Taiwan.

income. Television, for example, is a powerful source of nonfamilial ideas and alternative family images. Programming in Taiwan has been an important avenue for importing Western ideas of family life regardless of whether or not these are viewed positively. Meanwhile, other consumer durables such as refrigerators, rice-cookers, and washing machines reduce the necessary time spent in domestic tasks and can free women for production outside the family context. Telephones, automobiles, and motorbikes, on the other hand, enhance and widen the potential for establishing and maintaining links of communication. The ownership of all these items has increased substantially.

That the Chinese of Taiwan are taking advantage of the free time offered by these items is indicated by the reports on pleasure trips and eating outside the household. In 1969, 82% of the respondents to an island-wide survey reported that they had not eaten in a restaurant in the past twelve months. In 1986, that percentage had dropped to 63% while the percentage of respondents who had eaten out five or more times went from 3% to 12% in the same period. Similarly, the percentage of respondents reporting overnight pleasure trips nearly doubled from 19% to 37% in those two surveys.

By themselves, of course, these indicators of change cannot be implicated in either increasing or decreasing the extent of integration and interaction in activities among family members. Indeed, the enhanced communication possibilities afforded by telephones and transportation may help to sustain links between parents and children as they become less likely to co-reside after marriage (see chap. 12). Leisure time, too, even when used in new kinds of activities outside the household, can still be organized as family activities.

Individual Activities within the Natal Family

Chapter 3 documented patterns of urbanization and industrialization characterizing Taiwan's recent history. Here we examine some of these transformations in terms of their impact on individuals and their families. Table 5.1 presents evidence of striking cohort trends for a range of activities historically organized within families. Not only has the organization of these activities changed but the first panels reaffirm the changes which have occurred in the natal family background of our respondents.[7]

7. For table 5.1, we have constructed a supplement (printed at end of chapter) which replicates these trends by birth cohort, since readers may wish to examine premarital events in this format. A comparison of levels through time for panels presented by birth and marriage cohorts, however, indicates that the birth cohort presentation flattens trends where they exist. Our discussion is based on trends for ever-married women born between

Contexts of socialization. Women are increasingly likely to be socialized within urban contexts, as shown by the percentage of women who grew up in cities. Where 16% of the 1955–59 marriage cohort grew up in a city environment, 28% of the latest marrying cohort of women grew up in cities. For the same cohorts of women, growing up in rural areas declined from 68% to 51%. These slight changes are amplified when we consider the revolution in transportation links to cities mentioned earlier, to say nothing of the industrialization of the countryside itself. Finally, these environments are those of early socialization while environments of adult residence have been shown to be increasingly urban themselves (chap. 3; Hu 1984).

The transformation from agrarian to urban life in Taiwan is also indicated by the percentage of fathers whose primary occupation was farm work. Among the represented marriage cohorts, the percentage of women from farm backgrounds smoothly declines from 66% in the 1955–59 group to 41% of those married in 1980–84. This is paralleled by changes in the organization of parental work. Fathers of these women are increasingly likely to be employed outside their families through time. For the 1955–59 cohort of women, 22% of their fathers worked in jobs organized outside their own families; among the women married in 1980–84, this percentage increased to 35%.

Although changes in the experience of women's parents are impressive, they are not expected to be as dramatic as those for the different cohorts of women themselves, since most of these parents had moved through the critical early phases of their life courses before or at the onset of the most dramatic post–World War II changes. These include the land reforms of the 1950s and the rapid industrialization beginning in the early 1960s; during this later period widespread participation in wage labor occupations began to affect even rural areas (Gallin 1966). We therefore expect the impact of these changes to be registered most obviously in our respondents' lives rather than in those of their parents.

Education. Formal public schooling is especially important for later changes in family relationships. At the very least, schooling takes children out of the domestic unit for significant periods, reducing their contact with family members. Such formal schooling is often the first experience of nonfamily socialization for individuals, and its effects, even apart from the content of educational curricula, may be expected to have implications throughout the rest of the life course.

1935 and 1964, a period covering the most dramatic years of change in Taiwan's recent history.

TABLE 5.1 The Organization of Premarital Activities by Marriage Cohort, 1986 Survey

	MARRIAGE COHORT						
	1955–59	1960–64	1965–69	1970–74	1975–79	1980–84	Total
Number of Respondents[a]	236	538	647	773	964	978	4,290
I. Contexts of socialization							
Type of area in which wife grew up							
Country	68	60	63	63	53	51	58
Town	15	22	20	19	21	21	20
City	16	18	17	18	26	28	22
Total	99	100	100	100	100	100	100
Wife's father's occupation							
Farm	66	61	57	58	46	41	52
Nonfarm	34	39	43	42	54	59	48
Total	100	100	100	100	100	100	100
For whom wife's father worked							
Self/family/relative	78	76	72	74	68	65	71
Other	22	24	28	26	32	35	29
Total	100	100	100	100	100	100	100
II. Educational attainment							
Wife's education							
Illiterate/no formal	50	32	18	10	4	1	13
Primary level	44	54	63	62	45	26	47
Jr. high level	4	7	10	12	20	27	16
Sr. high level	1	4	6	12	25	35	19
College/university	1	2	2	5	6	10	6
Total	100	100	100	100	100	100	100
Husband's education							
Illiterate/no formal	18	12	8	3	2	0	5
Primary level	54	54	53	47	35	19	39
Jr. high level	12	12	14	18	19	24	18
Sr. high level	8	14	17	19	27	35	24
College/university	7	9	8	13	18	22	15
Total	100	100	100	100	100	100	100
III. Employment before marriage[b]							
Wife's work pattern before marriage							
No work	18	14	12	8	4	2	8
Worked at home, no wages	47	41	35	21	8	3	19
Worked at home for wages	6	5	5	5	3	3	4
Worked outside the home	30	40	48	67	86	92	69
Total	100	100	100	100	100	100	100
Women's employer at first job							
No work for pay	66	55	47	29	12	6	27
Self/family/relative	5	3	5	5	4	4	4
Other	30	41	48	66	84	90	68
Total	100	100	100	100	100	100	100
Women's employer at first job— workers for pay only							
Self/family/relative	14	8	10	7	5	4	6
Other	86	92	90	93	95	96	94
Total	100	100	100	100	100	100	100

TABLE 5.1 continued

	MARRIAGE COHORT						
	1955–59	1960–64	1965–69	1970–74	1975–79	1980–84	Total
IV. Living arrangements[c]							
Women's living arrangements while working							
No nonhome work	71	60	52	33	14	8	31
Home/relative	22	29	33	35	48	50	40
Dormitory	4	7	12	25	32	37	24
Other	4	4	4	7	6	5	5
Total	100	100	100	100	100	100	100
Women's living arrangements while working—nonhome workers only							
Home/relative	74	73	68	53	56	54	58
Dormitory	14	17	24	37	38	40	35
Other	12	10	8	10	6	6	8
Total	100	100	100	100	100	100	100
V. Income flows before marriage[d]							
Women's use of earnings							
No earnings	66	55	47	29	12	6	27
Mostly to parents	28	37	44	55	67	69	56
Not mostly to parents	7	8	9	16	22	26	17
Total	100	100	100	100	100	100	100
Women's use of earnings—workers for pay only							
Mostly to parents	81	83	83	78	76	73	76
Not mostly to parents	19	17	17	22	24	27	24
Total	100	100	100	100	100	100	100

[a] The number of respondents is based on total respondents by marriage cohort. The total includes cases within cohorts not reported in the table because of their small samples. Individual cells have slightly different bases because of missing data.

[b] For these panels we have used information from a series of questions. The English translations of question wording are:

"Did you work for money outside the home before you were [first] married? For how long?"

"Did you work for money at home before you were [first] married? For how long?"

"Did you help in a family business or farm but not for money before you were [first] married? For how long?"

[c] For these panels we have used information from a series of questions. The English translations of question wording are:

"Did you live at home while you were working?"

"Did you live in a dormitory while you were working?"

"Did you live with relatives while you were working?"

"Did you live in places other than your home, dormitory, or with relatives while you were working?"

A hierarchical form of coding was used for this panel; if the answer to all questions was yes, the respondent was placed in the "other" category.

[d] The English translation of this question's wording is, "Besides room and board, what did you mostly do with the money you earned when you were working and living away from home before marriage?"

The implications of schooling both for domestic labor and for socialization are, of course, tied to the number of years attended and the level of attainment. Those with no formal schooling remain primarily within the orbit of family in their childhood years. Those attending only primary levels are removed from the household for brief periods when, especially for males, their economic contributions for the domestic economy are minimal. Moreover, the values taught, apart from those which instill loyalty to the nation, are the family-oriented ones of "obedience, propriety, perseverance and respect for seniors" (M. Wolf 1972: 80). Attending junior high school and above increases the potential impact on a family's economy while simultaneously expanding the role of extrafamily socialization. It is also at these levels that education on subjects beyond the mechanics of reading, writing, and basic math skills increases. At the same time, the decision to send children through any noncompulsory level is itself a strategic decision based on parental calculations of a child's potential long-term contribution to the family. The substantial fees for junior high were only abandoned around 1980 (Gates 1987: 206) so investment in a child's education was not taken lightly by parents.

Formal education has been widely available in Taiwan for virtually all males since the Japanese era whereas the Taiwanese government encouraged at least primary education, beginning at age 7, for all children throughout the island in the 1950s. Grades 1 through 6 were the first to become compulsory while education through grade 9 became compulsory in 1969. This is reflected in the cohort trends for men and women in table 5.1. For men married to the women in the 1970–74 marriage cohort, school attendance was virtually universal and for women of that cohort, only 10% did not attend school at all. This is especially meaningful given an earlier pattern in which daughters contributed to the family at a very early age "while boys were still playing freely or in school" (Gates 1987: 106; M. Wolf 1972).

These trends tell us that Taiwan moved rapidly in the first postwar decade from a society where a large percentage of women and a modest percentage of men spent most of their socialization years within the family to a society in which no person escapes extensive contact with nonfamily institutions in his or her childhood. Furthermore, these trends were well under way during the Japanese period. We might also look at the picture in terms of individuals removed from making contributions to the family during years when their domestic labor is least essential. Attending primary school removes children, especially boys, from the household at a time when they contribute only minor help to the family. Besides, with the increase in labor-saving devices documented in chapter 3 and mentioned in the ethnographic literature (Cohen 1976), the kinds of tasks that even girls might be involved in (Gates 1987: 106) are less time consuming and make the impact of early schooling on household labor demands less dramatic.

Trends in the percentage attending primary school or less, presented in table 5.1, demonstrate that the majority of both males and females born in the earliest cohorts were not separated from the family at ages when their contribution to the household would begin to be more important. Seventy-two percent of the husbands of women married in 1955–59 had either primary or no schooling; even for those husbands of women married in 1970–74 this is true of 50%. Of women, a substantial majority within the earliest cohorts were in this category, for which the effect of schooling on family production was minimal. Ninety-four percent of those women married in 1955–59 were in this group while of those married in 1975–79 a still large minority of 49% were so categorized. The tendency for women to be less involved than men in activities that would remove them from the domestic orbit during these early years is also consistent with the strong Chinese tradition stressing the investment in education for sons over daughters as a way of enhancing the potential for future contribution to the family. Daughters, being expected to leave the home in any case at marriage, are best used in their early years to make a contribution to the natal home while sons can be invested in to increase the future value of their contribution.

Given this context, the rapid rise in percentages of women attaining high school or higher levels of schooling is all the more extraordinary. Of those women married in 1955–59, only 2% reached these levels. Of the 1965–69 marriage cohort, 8% reported high school or above levels. Finally, by the most recent marriage cohort of 1980–84, the percentage of women receiving these levels of schooling rises to 45%. Comparable figures for their husbands—15%, 25%, and 57%—indicate a steadily declining proportional difference in educational levels for men and women and affirm the general increase in education levels for the whole population.

Nonfamily employment. Throughout the postwar period, nearly all Taiwanese women have worked at either family enterprises or outside the home before marriage. Our data in table 5.1 indicate that the minority of women with no experience of this kind has steadily declined from the 18% of women married in 1955–59 who reported no work for family or extrafamily enterprises while living with their natal families. More important for showing how families organized individual productive activities is the high percentage of women in the early cohorts who worked for their families. Of those women married in 1955–59, for example, 47% reported working for their families without wages. A further 6% of these women worked for their families or relatives and received some form of remuneration—we might speculate that they worked for relatives outside the *chia* since, as mentioned earlier, the potential network of paternal relatives includes all of those descended through males from a common great-great grandfather. It is conceivable that payment was made for work outside the *chia* but within the lineage or village. Other cases in this category may also refer to piecework—for example, with textiles—that could be performed at home. The historical literature for European family transformation indicates the prevalence of such cottage industry (Tilly and Scott 1978) although it appears not to have been a major pattern for Taiwan.

Family work without pay smoothly declines across cohorts, and the decline accelerates after the 1970–74 marriage cohort. For the most recent marriage cohort, only 3% report that they worked without pay for their families. The complementary trend in the changing organization of work has been the massive increase in nonfamily employment of women from 30% for the earliest cohort to 92% for the most recent.

Confirmation of this pattern comes from the information on women's employer at first job before marriage. Coupled with the increasing likelihood of women working for pay since the earlier period is the great increase in occupations which take women outside their natal families. The next cells in table 5.1 show, moreover, that while working for pay has always been highly associated with nonfamily work, this association has strengthened through time. Thus, of those women married in 1955–59 who worked for pay, 86% were working for employers outside their families; that percentage has increased to 96% for the most recent marriage cohort.

Living arrangements. We have seen that nonfamily experiences in schooling and work have become an increasingly important part of men's and women's life courses in Taiwan since the war. In the history of European and North American families, these transformations are associated with greater relative autonomy for members of younger generations. Yet we know from the ethnographic material reviewed earlier that deference to elders embodied in the principle of *hsiao,* or "filial piety," established rigid lines of authority within the family. Children's activities were expected to be controlled by and enacted for the good of the family, whose interests were defined by older males within the *chia* (Baker 1979). Here, we ask ourselves how the exposure to nonfamily institutions in employment was constrained and what effect they had on family production. Lydia Kung's (1983) ethnography of Chinese women in factory work, for example, stresses the continuity of these new forms of employment with prior family organization, pointing out that the production of daughters working in factories is thought of as a part of their natal *chia* production.[8]

The island-wide survey data allow us to assess this continuity by asking women about their living arrangements while working outside the family. In the past, a typical Chinese woman would live her entire life until marriage within her natal home, after which she would enter a new *chia* within which her actions would again be closely supervised, this time by her mother-in-law (M. Wolf 1972). Looking at the living arrangements in table 5.1 and assuming that women who did not work outside the household lived at home, we can see that of the 1955–59 marriage cohort 93% of the respondents reported living only at home. This percentage declines steadily through the succeeding years. Even though a majority (58%) of the 1980–84 marriage cohort still report living only at home, the dramatic increase in residence outside the home before marriage from 8% to 42% is especially striking in a setting where control over children, particularly daughters, was so fundamental to family organization in the past.

By far, the majority of women not living in a kin environment while working lived in supervised dormitories where the fears of parents regarding their daughters' (and their own) honor could be assuaged.[9] Looking at the trends for dormitory living for working daughters by themselves in table 5.1 we see a tremendous increase from 14% for the 1955–59 marriage cohort to 40% for the 1980–84 cohort. The practice of living neither with kin nor in a dormitory while working has always been a small part of the picture for Taiwan, and there are no clear trends. Kung (1983: 69) found in her study of factory women that company dormitories provided acceptable substitutes for home living to the extent that "dormitory regulations, curfews, bed-checks and the like convey an impression of order that allays the worries of parents." Moreover, the

8. Cohen makes the same case for both men and women in a village context (1976).

9. This replication of a supervised quasi-family environment is the strategy used by textile factory owners in New England to reassure the rural parents of daughters employed in their mills (Hareven 1982).

organization of dormitory living is consistent with the Chinese pattern of creating quasi-kinship organizations in any situation in which real kin structure was lacking (Baker 1979: 162–74).[10]

Nevertheless, the quality of supervision within the dormitories is far less stringent than that possible within the family. Standard midnight curfews might be far more generous than those allowed at home; identification with nonfamily peers and exposure to a range of ideas from outside the local context are surely more likely with dormitory living. Even Kung's informants admitted that, while the reluctance to send daughters to factories had subsided, they still felt that young people in dormitories were more susceptible to bad influence and the dangers of becoming less filial.

Income flows. A final measure of continuity in family organization comes from questions about the flow of earnings by these women. The position of daughters in their natal homes has always been ambiguous. On one hand, they were involved in helping with family work at an earlier age than their brothers. On the other, they were lost to family production at an early age when they moved into the households of their husbands. In addition, they required a dowry of a size that would reflect favorably on the honor of their natal families. With increases in women's participation in nonfamily wage earning we might ask whether their earnings are put into personal savings, an indication of increasing autonomy, or are given to their parents. Ethnographers are clear on this point. Chen (1985), for example, reports that the earnings from these more common factory jobs are expected to be put into the common family fund in a rural area of southern Taiwan. On the other hand, he also mentions that, although daughters contribute their wages to the family economy, there is an underlying expectation that their dowries will be correspondingly larger.

Evidence from the island-wide survey presented in table 5.1 supports the picture of a continuing filial flow of income. Where only 28% of the women married in 1955–59 provided earnings for their parents, 69% of those married in 1980–84 did so. It is clear that daughters are making a greater monetary contribution to their families than in the past. The implications of this new level of contribution include potentially greater participation in decision making both for family decisions and for individual life course decisions. This increase in daughters' contribution to

10. Thus, visits to dormitories in 1989 indicated that supervisors were often referred to by kinship terms such as "big sister" and "mother" and were even invited to the weddings of their charges. (Thornton's unpublished fieldnotes from visits to factory dormitories.)

their natal families through time is, however, largely a result of the general increase in daughters working at wage labor. This is made clear in the last panel of table 5.1, which presents data for only those women working for pay before marriage. Among these women we find that the percentage giving most of their earnings to their parents has declined from 81% in the 1955–59 marriage cohort to 73% in the 1980–84 cohort. Thus, although women are generally more likely to be making monetary contributions to their families than in the past, there is also evidence for increased autonomy and individuation of interests in the growing percentage of working daughters who do not turn over most of their earnings to their parents.

Family Organization and Work in Early Marriage

Marriage has historically been the most significant watershed in a woman's life, taking her from the familiar environment of her natal home into the home of strangers. As discussed in chapter 2, the new bride was expected to act dutifully in her new home: to satisfy the domestic labor demands of in-laws and to provide descendants for the ancestors. In this new setting, supervision of the new daughter-in-law was, if anything, more onerous than the normal supervision of daughters in their natal homes. Daughters-in-law freed others from daily tasks by, for example, taking over the day-to-day care of the ancestral tablets and the chores of the family (M. Wolf 1972; Ahern 1973). As in other societies in which women were expected to join their husbands' families after marriage, a working daughter was a more trusted potential contributor to the family's common fund than a working daughter-in-law, whose interests were always somewhat suspect.

Table 5.2 gives evidence of very dramatic trends in the propensity for daughters-in-law to work in other than household tasks between marriage and first birth. Women married in 1955–59 were unlikely to be involved in such activities—84% of them reported no work between marriage and first birth.[11] The 16% of this cohort reporting work in this early marital period steadily and dramatically increases with successive cohorts until the 1980–84 marriage cohort, when a majority, 58%, do so. When we look at where these women are working, the story is as dramatic. Of the early cohort just 8% report working outside the marital home; this percentage increases to 46% for women married in

11. See question wording at bottom of table. Since a category of response for the question included "worked, but not paid," we interpret the "no work" category as no non*domestic* work.

TABLE 5.2 The Organization of Marital Productive Activities before Birth of First Child by Marriage Cohort, 1986 Survey

	MARRIAGE COHORT						
	1955–59	1960–64	1965–69	1970–74	1975–79	1980–84	Total
Number of Respondents[a]	236	535	644	768	948	899	4,111
Marital workplace							
No work	84	76	74	68	56	43	62
In home	8	10	9	8	10	12	10
Outside home	8	14	17	24	33	46	28
Total	100	100	100	100	100	100	100
Woman's employer							
No work	84	76	74	68	56	43	62
Self/husband/relative	9	9	8	8	10	9	9
Others	7	15	18	24	34	48	29
Total	100	100	100	100	100	100	100
Marital workplace—workers only							
In home	50	43	35	25	24	20	26
Outside home	50	57	65	75	76	80	74
Total	100	100	100	100	100	100	100
Woman's employer—workers only							
Self/husband/relative	55	38	32	25	22	16	24
Others	45	62	68	75	78	84	76
Total	100	100	100	100	100	100	100
Women's use of earnings							
No work	84	76	74	68	56	43	62
No payment for work	6	7	5	4	5	3	4
Family expenses	10	14	15	20	26	32	22
Savings/personal	0	3	6	7	11	20	10
Other uses	0	0	0	1	2	4	2
Total	100	100	100	100	100	100	100
Women's use of earnings— workers for pay only							
Family expenses	96	80	71	70	67	58	66
Savings/personal	4	18	27	25	27	35	29
Other uses	0	2	2	5	6	7	5
Total	100	100	100	100	100	100	100

Note: For these panels we have used information from a series of questions. The English translations of question wording are:

"Did you work for money during the time after your marriage and before your first live birth? At home or outside of home?"

"Were you employed by your family or by others?"

"What did you do with the money you earned?"

[a] The number of respondents for work experience in marital home is based on the number of women in each cohort who had at least one live birth. The total includes cases within cohorts not reported in the table because of their small samples. Individual cells have slightly different bases because of missing data.

1980–84.[12] Furthermore, the next panels in the table tell us that these women who work outside the home are likely to be working for other than family members, suggesting that such work represents a real change in the extent of supervision by a husband's family members after marriage. Looking at trends for workers alone, we see an increase in the percentage working outside the home from 50% of those married in 1955–59 to 80% of those married in 1980–84. Work for other than family members increases from 45% of these working wives married in 1955–59 to 84% of those married in 1980–84.

Finally, women's contributions to marital family expenses have also increased across cohorts, as can be seen from the last two panels of the table. From a low of 10% for the group of women married in 1955–59 to a high of 32% of those married most recently, women are contributing to the domestic economy in ways that might be expected to increase their role in the management of *chia* affairs. At the same time, the percentage of all women contributing most of their earnings to savings or personal ends has also increased. Virtually no women married in 1955–59 put their earnings into personal uses or savings compared to 20% of those married in 1980–84. Finally, of those women working for pay, the likelihood of them putting their earnings to personal uses increases from 4% to 35% across the represented cohorts. If the ethnographic literature is correct in suggesting that daughters-in-law are highly motivated to form independent domestic units with their husbands, we might speculate that these savings are directed toward that end.

Changes in the propensity for new daughters-in-law to work outside their marital homes through time may produce changes in the balance of authority in those settings. Daughters-in-law who work outside have the potential to contribute to the *chia* economy monetarily; in doing so, they may gain a say in decisions much as sons do when they work outside (Cohen 1976). They are also in a position, in union with their husbands, to prepare for a joint strategy of eventual independence, and this may contribute to the process of emotional nucleation that Caldwell has raised as one of the key components of family and demographic transi-

12. One argument about marriage and work in patrilineally organized societies is that marriage takes women out of the workplace and puts them into the domestic environment (Fricke, Thornton, and Dahal 1990; cf. Davis 1984). Comparing the figures for women who worked outside their marital home for all cohorts with the figures for women who worked outside their natal homes in the same cohorts supports that contention. Thus, where 8% of the 1955–59 marriage cohort worked outside their marital homes before first birth, 30% of that same cohort worked outside their natal homes before marrying. Further, the differentials increase through time, as a comparison of the cells in tables 5.1 and 5.2 indicates.

tion elsewhere (1982). Moreover, when the workplace for these women is outside the marital home, they are less subject to the direct supervision of their mothers-in-law; such supervision was a key, and worrisome, element of their lives in the marital home in the past. Thus, the nature of marriage itself could be changed by the ability to work outside their new home.

Family Organization of Work after Childbirth

Kung (1983: 143) mentions that, in spite of the general availability of work to married women who desire it, the sentiment against working after marriage is quite strong and grows even stronger after the birth of a child. Kung's informants stressed that a woman needed to have time for her children, that the family should come first in her life. In table 5.3 we extend our exploration of the family organization of productive activities to the period after a woman's first childbirth. This suggests that even here we find large historical changes.

The percentage of women performing no nondomestic work between the births of their first and second children is 74%. This compares to 62% who did no such work between marriage and childbirth and only 27% not working before marriage. Differential percentages for those whose worksites were outside their homes are equally dramatic, 16% between the birth of their first and second children, 28% during the period after marriage but before childbirth, and 69% before marriage. Nevertheless, the propensity to work outside the family after the first birth transition, while not so rapidly increasing as the propensity to work between marriage and childbirth, is on the rise. Where only 6% of the 1955–59 marriage cohort of woman worked outside the family between their first and second births, the percentages steadily increase until 26% of the most recently married cohort did so. Furthermore, the next panel demonstrates that the tendency for employers to be unrelated closely tracks these changes in the location of work—from 4% to 28% across these marriage cohorts.

Considering only those women who worked after childbirth, the data show changes in both the location of work and the relationship of employer. Where half of those working mothers married in 1955–59 worked in the home, only 29% of those married in 1980–84 did so. Moreover, where 68% of the working mothers in the earliest marriage cohort were either self-employed or worked for relatives, only a quarter of those in the latest marriage group did so.

As we might expect, increasing propensity to work is followed by a

TABLE 5.3   The Organization of Marital Productive Activities between Birth of First and Second Children by Marriage Cohort, 1986 Survey

| | MARRIAGE COHORT | | | | | | |
	1955– 59	1960– 64	1965– 69	1970– 74	1975– 79	1980– 84	Total
Number of Respondents[a]	233	527	632	740	895	515	3,570
Marital workplace							
No work	88	81	78	77	69	62	74
In home	6	9	9	8	10	11	9
Outside home	6	10	13	14	21	26	16
Total	100	100	100	100	100	100	100
Woman's employer							
No work	88	81	78	77	69	62	74
Self/husband/relative	8	9	8	8	9	10	9
Others	4	10	14	15	22	28	17
Total	100	100	100	100	100	100	100
Marital workplace—workers only							
In home	50	48	41	37	34	29	36
Outside home	50	52	59	63	66	71	64
Total	100	100	100	100	100	100	100
Woman's employer—workers only							
Self/husband/relative	68	45	38	36	30	25	34
Others	32	55	62	64	70	75	66
Total	100	100	100	100	100	100	100
Women's use of earnings							
No work	88	82	78	77	68	62	74
No payment for work	5	6	5	4	4	5	5
Family expenses	6	10	13	14	19	23	15
Savings/personal	0	2	3	5	7	8	5
Other uses	0	0	1	1	2	2	1
Total	100	100	100	100	100	100	100
Women's use of earnings— workers for pay only							
Family expenses	94	80	78	72	69	69	72
Savings/personal	6	16	18	24	25	25	23
Other uses	0	4	4	4	6	7	5
Total	100	100	100	100	100	100	100

Note: For these panels we have used information from a series of questions. The English translations of question wording are:

"Did you work for money during the time after your first live birth and before your second live birth? At home or outside of home?"

"Were you employed by your family or by others?"

"What did you do with the money you earned?"

[a] The number of respondents for work experience in marital home is based on the number of women in each cohort who had at least two live births. The total includes cases within cohorts not reported in the table because of their small samples. Individual cells have slightly different bases because of missing data.

general increase in the percentages of women who contribute to family expenses after the birth of a child. Where only 6% of the 1955–59 marriage cohort contributed monetarily to their families after having children, the percentage doubled for the 1965–69 group and almost doubled again to 23% for the most recently married group. The same trend toward increased personal, rather than family, use of wages characterizes working mothers as characterizes those who worked for pay during other life course periods. Here, the percentage increases from 6% of working mothers married in 1955–59 to 25% of those married in 1980–84.

Trend Variations by Area, Family Background, and Education

Our discussion has thus far focused on overall trends for all of Taiwan. We have encountered striking evidence of change and continuity in key components of social organization since the Japanese era. Nonfamily institutions have enlarged their share of the socialization process in the form of schooling. Children's involvement in the wage economy has increased dramatically with the consequence that they spend more time in nonfamily environments. This is reflected in the increasing propensity of daughters to work outside the home before marriage. In addition, these work opportunities have necessitated that daughters' living arrangements before marriage be increasingly outside the home. While the tendency has been to transfer the supervised living arrangements of home to the dormitory arrangements that have become so important a part of a daughter's premarital experience, the literature suggests that the quality of supervision is far less encompassing than that of the home. Indeed, these schools, jobs, and dormitories expose children to nonfamilial influences to an extent and at a scale inconceivable in the China of the past. We have seen also that the nonfamilial context in which children spend increasing portions of their growing-up years continues beyond marriage.

While these general trends are pervasive and dramatic throughout Taiwan, the theoretical discussion of the previous chapter suggests that many of the transformations in social organization are correlated with the spread of education and urban living. Since in Taiwan senior *chia* members are primary decision makers and individual activities are regarded as parts of integrated family strategies, we might expect that the organization of the family economy as reflected in a father's working status would influence decisions about whether to send a child to school beyond the required levels or to use the child to make a direct contribution to the family. School attendance beyond the primary grades forces trade-offs between the deferred benefits of education and immediate labor and monetary contributions for the combined *chia* economy. In tables 5.4 through 5.7 we explore some of these effects for the overall trends in natal family activities just discussed. Table 5.8 extends this discussion to activities in the marital home. We will look at selected variables by the type of area (country, town, city) in which a person grew up and by the work status of fathers (self or family employed, nonfamilially employed). In addition, because education occurs at a theoretically powerful point in the life course and is the first exposure to new ideas and technical skills in a nonfamily environment, we will explore nonfamilial employment, living arrangements before marriage, and income flows by schooling levels. For our discussion of marital work experience, we use husband's familial work status as an indicator of the overall marital family economy in much the same way we use father's work status to define the natal home economy.

Education. Table 5.4 portrays trends in the education of women in terms of its intersection with family responsibilities. Attendance at levels less than junior high indicates the least conflict with the immediate needs of the *chia* economy. Attendance beyond junior high, on the other hand, indicates the need for conscious decisions to be made on the part of the senior generation to forgo substantial immediate economic contributions for other perceived benefits of educating children. The pattern of education for women again indicates striking changes across time for all strata while also demonstrating that women raised in rural areas have always been more likely than their town and city sisters to receive less than junior high school education. Nevertheless, the percentage of women receiving low levels or no education has declined considerably in rural areas, from 97% for the earliest marriage cohort to just 34% for those married in 1980–84.

Corresponding to the decrease in low levels of education is a steadily increasing percentage of women receiving high school or greater levels of schooling. For women of all strata, the percentage going on to high school or greater levels of schooling increases spectacularly across the represented cohorts. No rural women from the 1955–59 marriage cohort achieved these levels of education; 33% of rural women in the 1980–84 marriage cohort have done so. The same cohorts of women raised in towns show increases from 3% to 50%, of women raised in urban areas from 5% to 66%.

TABLE 5.4   Percentage of Respondents Attaining Indicated Schooling Levels by Area of Early Socialization and Organization of Father's Work by Marriage Cohort, 1986 Survey

| | MARRIAGE COHORT | | | | | | |
	1955–59	1960–64	1965–69	1970–74	1975–79	1980–84	Total
A. Less than junior high							
Type of area grew up in							
Country	97	92	90	81	56	34	69
Town	89	84	77	65	46	26	55
City	87	69	58	48	36	16	39
For whom father worked							
Self/family/relative	93	90	85	77	51	29	63
Worked for others	96	74	73	57	43	24	48
B. Junior high							
Type of area grew up in							
Country	2	3	7	9	21	32	15
Town	8	9	14	12	17	24	16
City	8	17	17	19	19	18	18
For whom father worked							
Self/family/relative	5	6	9	11	22	29	16
Worked for others	4	12	12	14	16	20	15
C. More than junior high							
Type of area grew up in							
Country	0	5	3	10	22	33	16
Town	3	6	8	23	38	50	28
City	5	14	24	33	45	66	43
For whom father worked							
Self/family/relative	2	4	6	12	27	42	20
Worked for others	0	13	15	31	41	55	36

Note: For this and all subsequent tables the cell entries indicate the percentage of people in each particular strata-cohort who had the characteristic of interest. See table 5.1 for number of respondents.

While important differentials by the area in which they were raised characterize the educational experience of women, there is strong convergence in the percentages of women receiving education at the junior high level and beyond by the employment status of their fathers. The earliest cohorts support a picture in which daughters were kept out of school in part to aid in the domestic economy if we assume that those fathers who worked for themselves or family members were more likely to require the aid of their children in family enterprises. Of the 1955–59 marriage cohort, only 7% of women whose fathers were self or family employed received junior high or greater levels of education. By the 1980–84 cohort, 29% of these women from family enterprise environments received a junior level education and 42% received greater levels, a striking increase. For those whose fathers worked for others the percentage stopping at junior high school increased from 4% to 20%. The percentage of these daughters of nonfamilially employed fathers receiving high school and higher levels increases from 0% to 55% across the same cohorts.

These trends demonstrate that the educational revolution is pervasive for all areas of origin on Taiwan but that they appear to interact with the needs of the domestic economy for the immediate labor of children. Urban areas show high levels of schooling across all cohorts for reasons that are at least partly related to the nonagrarian nature of the urban setting as well as the earlier and greater availability of schools at all levels. Once again, the tendency to minimize the impact of schooling on family activities is most prevalent across all cohorts in the rural areas, where we would expect agrarian activities would require more help from children. It is also in these areas that we might expect greater adherence to old patterns of separation between daughters and their natal homes at marriage. This would make it more important to realize the immediate contribution of a daughter than to anticipate future support.

Nonfamilial employment. Table 5.5 demonstrates that, as with schooling, rural-urban and family environment differentials occur in the likelihood of involvement in nonfamily employment. Even more striking than the trends for schooling across cohorts, however, is the extent to which the percentage of women working for nonfamily members has converged across every category. From the large differentials characterizing the cohort of women married in 1960–64 in which 31%, 47%, and 64% of country, town, and city-raised women worked outside before marriage there has been a rapid increase and convergence so that between 87% and 94% of the 1980–84 cohort were doing so in all residential strata.

A similar convergence and increase characterize the different cohorts of women from different family enterprise environments. From a difference between those whose fathers were self-employed or family workers and those whose fathers worked for others of 32% and 65% in the 1960–64 cohort, the 1980–84 cohort difference is only 87% and 92%. Women whose fathers work for themselves or in family enterprises are thus only slightly less likely to work outside their families in contemporary Taiwan. Moreover, the likelihood of working outside the home has become independent of educational attainment in the later years. Each of the marriage cohorts before 1980–84 shows an expected positive relationship between education and the likelihood of working outside

TABLE 5.5 Percentage of Respondents Who Worked at Jobs Organized outside the Family by Area of Early Socialization, Organization of Father's Work, and Education by Marriage Cohort, 1986 Survey

	MARRIAGE COHORT						
	1955– 59	1960– 64	1965– 69	1970– 74	1975– 79	1980– 84	Total
Where grew up							
Country	20	31	39	61	83	88	61
Town	50	47	48	70	82	94	71
City	42	64	69	74	83	87	78
For whom father worked							
Self/family/relative	25	32	41	61	81	87	63
Worked for others	35	65	59	76	86	92	78
Education							
No formal schooling	20	25	23	32	58	a	27
Primary level	32	40	45	64	80	89	62
Jr. high level	a	74	63	66	85	90	82
Sr. high level	a	a	82	86	87	90	88
College/university	a	a	a	88	95	87	90

Note: For this table the cell entries indicate the percentage of people in each particular strata-cohort who had the characteristic of interest. See table 5.1 for number of respondents. Question wording for premarital work experience appears in table 5.1.

[a]For these cells the number of cases is below thirty and no estimates are reported.

the family before marriage; for the 1980–84 cohort there is little difference by educational attainment beyond primary school.

The implications of these transformations across all regional, family environment, and educational strata are that daughters throughout Taiwanese society today are exposed at similar levels to the nonfamily influences of their work environments.

Living arrangements while working. In order to explore the impact of work on whether or not daughters remain in the family environment, table 5.6 looks at cohort trends for the two major categories of residence for working women: with family and relatives or in a dormitory. The cohort patterns reveal interesting differences among the various strata of interest. First, women raised in cities and towns are more likely to live at home while working than those raised in the country and this is true of every cohort in spite of a decline across time for each category. Furthermore, there has been a more rapid decline in home living among rural and town women than among their urban sisters. This is likely the result of the differential availability of work close to home in urban and nonurban settings. Thus, while 62% of rural women, 74% of town

TABLE 5.6 Premarital Living Arrangements of Taiwanese Women while Working (Nonhome Workers Only) by Marriage Cohort, 1986 Survey

	MARRIAGE COHORT						
	1955– 59	1960– 64	1965– 69	1970– 74	1975– 79	1980– 84	Total
A. *Lived at home or with relative*							
Type of area grew up in							
Country	67	62	60	39	44	42	46
Town	a	74	76	65	63	57	65
City	a	88	76	76	75	76	76
For whom father worked							
Self/family/relative	71	69	65	47	52	49	53
Worked for others	a	75	73	63	63	65	66
Educational attainment							
No formal schooling	a	60	a	a	a	a	56
Primary level	74	73	65	47	50	48	54
Jr. high level	a	a	65	52	49	45	51
Sr. high level	a	a	84	68	68	62	66
College/university	a	a	a	79	70	71	72
B. *Lived at dormitory*							
Type of area grew up in							
Country	17	26	29	48	49	51	45
Town	a	11	16	28	30	40	28
City	a	8	20	16	21	21	19
For whom father worked							
Self/family/relative	15	20	26	41	40	44	38
Worked for others	a	12	19	28	33	30	28
Educational attainment							
No formal schooling	a	19	a	a	a	a	28
Primary level	18	20	25	43	44	47	39
Jr. high level	a	a	35	40	44	48	43
Sr. high level	a	a	13	21	26	32	28
College/university	a	a	a	9	20	24	17

Note: For this table the cell entries indicate the percentage of people in each particular strata-cohort who had the characteristic of interest. See table 5.1 for number of respondents. Question wording for living arrangements appears in table 5.1.

[a] For these cells the number of cases is below thirty and no estimates are reported.

women, and 88% of urban women married in 1960–64 lived with family members when working, the percentages declined strikingly to 42%, 57%, and 76% of those married in 1980–84.

For women from different family enterprise environments, the differences between strata increase with age. Of the women whose fathers were self or family employed in the 1960–64 marriage cohort, 69% lived with family members while working and 20% lived in dormitories compared to 75% and 12% of those women whose fathers worked for others. By the 1980–84 marriage cohort, 49% of the women from self- or family-employed parental backgrounds live with kin compared to 65% of the women whose fathers worked for others. Meanwhile, the positive relation between education and the likelihood of living at home or with relatives is maintained across all cohorts, although there is a decline in family living during work for all education levels. Corresponding to these patterns is the increase in dormitory living for all groups. The relationship of these trends with those for family living suggests a general pattern of living apart from the family but in the relatively supervised environment of women's work dormitories.

These striking patterns suggest first that work does not operate by itself in exposing women to nonfamily influences. For an increasingly large percentage, in fact a majority percentage for rural women, starting to work involves a simultaneous change in living arrangements from family to nonfamily surroundings. The high percentages of women who work and live apart from their families are exposed to a degree of autonomy virtually unknown in the past. Moreover, it is precisely those women from rural backgrounds who might be expected to be more protected and constrained from exposure to new ideas and circumstances who are most likely to live apart from their families. We have mentioned the differential quality of supervision in dormitories and families and the possibilities of exposure to new ideas from peers with different family backgrounds. Indeed, for women from rural areas, dormitory living may be similar in effect to the impact of universal military service on males at a similar point in their life courses.

Income flows. We might expect the increasing exposure to education and nonfamilial work environments to alter the relationship of these daughters with their families. This would be reflected in a variety of ways, including a possible change in the use of their earnings. In table 5.7 we explore changes in income flows by the various strata. This table presents figures only for those women who worked for pay, since the relationships found for all women were largely expected. That is, looking at the percentage of all women who gave most of their earnings to their parents, we found a steady increase across cohorts for virtually every category of rural-urban background, family enterprise background, and education. In addition, expected relationships across strata were maintained throughout most birth cohorts. Thus, urban-raised women were less likely to turn most of their income over to their parents than their town and country sisters. This was also the case for women whose fathers worked for nonfamily members and for more highly educated

TABLE 5.7   Taiwanese Women Giving Most Premarital Earnings to Parents
(Workers for Pay Only) by Marriage Cohort, 1986 Survey

	MARRIAGE COHORT						
	1955– 59	1960– 64	1965– 69	1970– 74	1975– 79	1980– 84	Total
Where grew up							
Country	89	84	88	79	79	76	79
Town	a	85	78	82	73	75	77
City	a	78	78	70	72	65	70
For whom father worked							
Self/family/relative	78	81	83	78	77	74	77
Worked for others	a	88	83	76	74	69	75
Education							
No formal schooling	a	96	100	a	a	a	90
Primary level	82	88	88	85	89	88	87
Jr. high level	a	74	67	72	78	80	78
Sr. high level	a	a	74	58	60	63	61
College/university	a	a	a	57	41	49	48

Note: For this table the cell entries indicate the percentage of people in each particular strata-cohort who had the characteristic of interest. See table 5.1 for number of respondents. Question wording for use of earnings appears in table 5.1.

ᵃFor these cells the number of cases is below thirty and no estimates are reported.

women. Since these are relationships we have already seen in table 5.1, the question we examine here is whether there have been changes in the propensity to turn over income among those women making money.

The data presented in Table 5.7 provide strong evidence not only that working daughters are increasingly less likely to turn over most of their income to their parents but also that the strongest effects are from educational attainment. Comparing strata in the total column of the table reveals some differentiation along the rural-urban continuum, where 79% of the women raised in rural areas turned their earnings over to their families compared to 70% of those raised in urban areas. Employment status of fathers, on the other hand, appears to be without much impact on the propensity of daughters to give most of their earnings to the family fund.

The single most powerful variable affecting the propensity to hand over earnings to the natal family is educational attainment. Looking at differences among strata in the total column, we see a smooth and deep decline with educational attainment in the percentages giving most of their wages to the family fund. Thus, where 90% of working daughters with no formal education and 87% of those with only primary education turn over their wages, the percentages drop to 61% and 48% for daughters with senior high and college levels of schooling. A look within each marriage cohort reveals that this direction of effect is quite stable through time—in all but the 1965–69 cohort, the percentages of working daughters giving most of their earnings to their parents declines with education. Finally, we note that cohort trends indicate a clear decline in the likelihood of turning earnings over to parents for all early residential strata, for working daughters whose fathers worked outside the family, and for those attaining at least senior high school levels of education. Other strata show more stable or mixed patterns across the marriage cohorts represented here.

Thus, although the picture we have of work and income flows is still one in which the majority of daughters behave filially—that is, they turn their earnings over to the family—a large and growing minority of women working before marriage have not done so. Although the cohort trends are not as striking as in other familial activities, the relationship among education and rural-urban strata is as we would expect from the theoretical discussion in the last chapter. What cannot be explored with these data, unfortunately, is whether those turning their money over to their parents do so with the implicit understanding that it will enhance their own dowries at marriage as Chen (1985) suggests or whether they do so with no expectation of such return. Similarly, we are uncertain about whether women who have not turned over most of their earnings have done so with or without parental approval. If the household economy does not require children to contribute, as has begun to be the case with rising incomes in Taiwan, then one would expect that parents would begin to acknowledge their children's "right" to keep their earnings, as parents do in North America (Bachman 1983).

Marital work. Table 5.8 shows that the tendency for daughters-in-law to work has been increasing in Taiwan for every strata until the most recent marriage cohort, of which over half of the married women raised in urban and town environments worked in the early years of marriage. The increase in the propensity to work has, however, been most dramatic for women raised in rural and urban areas where, of those women married in 1955–59, only 15% and 13% worked at nondomestic tasks between marriage and first birth compared to 55% and 60% of those married in the 1980–84 period.

We might expect the propensity to work at this period to vary by husband's employment, especially if we take that employment as an indicator of the nature of the larger marital family economy. Looking at trends in women's work in the early years of marriage by whether the

TABLE 5.8   Women's Work Experience in Marital Home between Marriage and First Birth by Marriage Cohort, 1986 Survey

| | MARRIAGE COHORT | | | | | | |
	1955–59	1960–64	1965–69	1970–74	1975–79	1980–84	Total
I. Any work at all							
Where grew up							
Country	15	20	23	30	41	55	34
Town	25	24	25	34	48	60	40
City	13	38	40	37	46	60	45
For whom husband worked							
Self	13	20	22	22	36	47	28
Family/relative	a	22	34	23	34	45	33
Worked for others	16	25	26	36	48	63	42
Education							
No formal schooling	16	14	20	24	31	a	18
Primary level	15	23	21	27	37	49	30
Jr. high level	a	45	35	33	40	57	45
Sr. high level	a	a	52	44	51	59	53
College/university	a	a	a	76	79	74	78
II. Work outside home							
Where grew up							
Country	8	9	14	21	28	42	23
Town	8	15	15	26	55	47	30
City	8	27	27	29	39	51	37
For whom husband worked							
Self	3	8	9	12	20	31	15
Family/relative	a	10	12	16	18	22	17
Worked for others	8	18	21	29	39	51	35
Education							
No formal schooling	8	8	13	17	19	a	11
Primary level	7	10	12	18	27	37	19
Jr. high level	a	34	24	24	27	42	33
Sr. high level	a	a	42	36	43	48	44
College/university	a	a	a	74	68	71	72

Note: For this table the cell entries indicate the percentage of people in each particular strata-cohort who had the characteristic of interest. See table 5.2 for number of respondents. Question wording for work experience appears in table 5.2.

ªFor these cells the number of cases is below thirty and no estimates are reported.

husband is self-employed, works for relatives, or works for others indicates that the propensity for work dramatically increases in all these groups although there are differences in level. Husbands who work outside the family are most likely to have wives who themselves work. The relationship of this postmarital work with education is made clear by the table as well. Although the propensity to work is increasing for all levels of education across time, those women with greater education are in every cohort more likely to work than others.

The last three panels of table 5.8 show trends in the percentage of all women who worked outside their marital homes between marriage and first birth. Again, the general pattern for all groups, as above, is toward an increase across marriage cohorts. The levels reached, however, are lower than for women engaged in any work at all although the differences between the two become smaller among later cohorts for more highly educated women, urban-raised women, and women whose husbands worked for other than family members. For these groups especially, then, we can say that the propensity to engage in nondomestic work tasks at all has become associated with work outside the home.

Summary

In this chapter we have documented the vigorous and protracted trend toward the increasingly nonfamily organization of activities which have historically been organized by and often conducted within family groups. Most of the trends we document have to do with public schooling and a set of activities revolving around living arrangements; our explorations have focused on the familial contexts pivoting around marriage and shown to be the most significant for women's lives in Taiwan. And we have also looked within the marital family context at the activities of women before and after the onset of their own family-building careers. The results indicate a mixture of compelling change and continuities in the organization of these activities.

Taken in order of magnitude, the single most powerful change—and the one with the greatest significance for later life course transitions—is the educational revolution for both men and women. By the 1960s Taiwan had transformed itself from a society in which a substantial minority of its women received no formal education, and one where the great majority of those who did attended only up to some point in the primary grades, into a society of near-universal attendance in which a majority of women went to junior high school levels and above. For men, the transformation had begun even earlier and involves even higher levels of attainment for the majority.

Only slightly behind education in the magnitude of change, the trend toward increasing nonfamilial organization of work activities is similarly dramatic for Taiwan. Premarital work experience outside the home has been transformed from an activity engaged in by about a third of the women in the earliest marriage cohort to an activity engaged in by over 90% of the women of recent cohorts. Moreover, the experience of nonfamilial work has spread to a majority of women of every background, from rural to urban, and every educational level. Similarly, women's employers today are overwhelmingly more likely to be unrelated to them than in the past at only slightly lower levels than work experience outside the home.

The rise of nonfamilial living arrangements before marriage is a third powerful trend. From a society in which over 90% of the women married in 1955–59 lived their entire premarital lives within kin contexts, Taiwan has become a society in which only about half do so. Strikingly, nearly all of the rise in nonfamilial living before marriage takes place in work dormitories, where 40% of all women in the most recent marriage cohort have lived. When one looks at the experience of only those women who have worked outside the home, we see that the experience of nonfamilial living before marriage has come to characterize almost half of them.

Slightly less striking have been the changes in nonfamily work after marriage, but even here the changes are powerful. The experience of work outside the home has increased fivefold across the cohorts we examine for the period between marriage and first birth. For the period between the birth of a first and second child there has been a fourfold increase in this activity.

TABLE 5.1 SUPPLEMENT: The Organization of Premarital Activities by Birth Cohort, 1986 Survey (Replication of Table 5.1 Using Birth Cohort)

	BIRTH COHORT						
	1935– 39	1940– 44	1945– 49	1950– 54	1955– 59	1960– 64	Total
Number of wives[a]	373	604	691	1,001	1,004	575	4,290
Number of husbands	517	644	721	949	795	170	4,290
I. Contexts of socialization							
Type of area in which wife grew up							
Country	62	59	61	57	53	60	58
Town	18	23	19	20	20	18	20
City	20	18	20	23	26	22	22
Total	100	100	100	100	100	100	100
Wife's father's occupation							
Farm	61	57	57	50	46	49	52
Nonfarm	39	43	44	50	54	51	48
Total	100	100	100	100	100	100	100
For whom wife's father worked							
Self/family/relative	77	73	73	70	67	69	71
Other	23	27	27	30	33	31	29
Total	100	100	100	100	100	100	100
II. Educational attainment							
Wife's education							
Illiterate/no formal	42	30	14	7	4	2	13
Primary level	45	51	59	58	37	30	47
Jr. high level	7	9	12	10	20	35	16
Sr. high level	4	6	10	18	32	29	19
College/university	2	4	6	7	8	5	6
Total	100	100	100	100	100	100	100
Husband's education							
Illiterate/no formal	14	11	6	2	2	1	5
Primary level	54	50	48	40	31	21	39
Jr. high level	11	12	16	18	17	31	18
Sr. high level	13	16	18	22	29	37	24
College/university	9	11	13	17	22	11	15
Total	100	100	100	100	100	100	100
III. Employment before marriage[b]							
Wife's work pattern before marriage							
No work	17	13	12	5	4	2	8
Worked at home, no wages	41	37	29	17	6	4	19
Worked at home for wages	6	4	4	5	2	3	4
Worked outside the home	36	46	55	73	89	91	69
Total	100	100	100	100	100	100	100
Women's employer at first job							
No work for pay	58	50	41	22	10	7	27
Self/family/relative	4	5	6	5	3	5	4
Other	39	45	53	72	87	88	68
Total	100	100	100	100	100	100	100
Women's employer at first job— workers for pay only							
Self/family/relative	9	10	10	7	4	5	6
Other	91	90	90	93	96	95	94
Total	100	100	100	100	100	100	100

TABLE 5.1 continued

	BIRTH COHORT						
	1935–39	1940–44	1945–49	1950–54	1955–59	1960–64	Total
Husband's employer at first job							
Self/family/relative	44	38	30	26	21	19	29
Other	56	62	70	74	79	81	71
Total	100	100	100	100	100	100	100
IV. Living arrangements[c]							
Women's living arrangements while working							
No nonhome work	64	54	45	27	12	10	31
Home/relative	28	31	36	41	48	44	40
Dormitory	6	9	14	27	34	41	24
Other	2	6	5	5	6	5	5
Total	100	100	100	100	100	100	100
Women's living arrangements while working—nonhome workers only							
Home/relative	78	69	66	56	54	48	58
Dormitory	17	19	25	36	38	46	35
Other	5	12	9	7	7	6	8
Total	100	100	100	100	100	100	100
V. Income flows before marriage[d]							
Women's use of earnings							
No earnings	57	50	41	22	10	7	27
Mostly to parents	33	40	46	59	68	71	56
Not mostly to parents	10	10	14	19	22	22	17
Total	100	100	100	100	100	100	100
Women's use of earnings—workers for pay only							
Mostly to parents	78	80	77	75	75	76	76
Not mostly to parents	22	20	23	25	25	24	24
Total	100	100	100	100	100	100	100

[a]The number of respondents is based on total respondents by birth cohort. The total includes cases within cohorts not reported in the table because of their small samples. Individual cells have slightly different bases because of missing data.

[b]For these panels we have used information from a series of questions. The English translations of question wording are:

"Did you work for money outside the home before you were [first] married? For how long?"

"Did you work for money at home before you were [first] married? For how long?"

"Did you help in a family business or farm but not for money before you were [first] married? For how long?"

[c]For these panels we have used information from a series of questions. The English translations of question wording are:

"Did you live at home while you were working?"

"Did you live in a dormitory while you were working?"

"Did you live with relatives while you were working?"

"Did you live in places other than your home, dormitory, or with relatives while you were working?"

A hierarchical form of coding was used for this panel; if the answer to all questions was yes, the respondent was placed in the "other" category.

[d]The English translation of this question's wording is, "Besides room and board, what did you mostly do with the money you earned when you were working and living away from home before marriage?"

Six

From Arranged Marriage toward Love Match
A. Thornton, J. S. Chang, and H. S. Lin

Introduction

The historical Chinese marriage system was organized and directed by
the parental generation (chap. 2). In the past there were several different
ways in which marriages could be arranged. In so-called major marriages, the culturally preferred pattern, the wife joined the husband's
family at the time of marriage; in the minor marriage pattern, culturally
less desirable but still not infrequent, the future wife was adopted into
the parents-in-law's family as a young child, where she was raised to
adulthood; and in uxorilocal marriage, the husband joined the wife's
family at the time of marriage. Although the type of marriage had very
important implications for both parent-child and husband-wife relationships, all three marriage systems had at least one important thing in
common—the marital decisions and arrangements were made largely by
the parental generation (Wolf and Huang 1980).

The so-called minor marriage system probably was the most extreme
in excluding young people from the marital decision, since the marriage
choice and the move of the bride-to-be into the new home took place
when the prospective bride and groom were still infants or young children. Although major and uxorilocal marriages were contracted and
instituted after the couple had entered their teenage years, the prospective
husband and wife still had little say in the marital decision. Romance
and courtship by starry-eyed young adults had no place in the marriage
process. Instead, mate selection involved complex negotiations carried
out in full rationality by the parental generation. Relatives and friends
often assisted the parental negotiations, and professional matchmakers
were sometimes hired to assist in these important decisions. Since husbands and wives in major and uxorilocal marriages usually were raised
in different villages, they first became acquainted during the marriage
negotiations or at the time of the ceremonies sealing the marriage (Schak
1975).

In its preferred form the negotiation and contracting of marriages involved six events or rites (Chang 1991; Freedman 1970a). The process began with inquiries of interest—frequently through a go-between. If interest was reciprocated, the necessary genealogical and horoscopic data were sought. Then the horoscopes of the prospective bride and groom were matched. If all went smoothly to this point, the agreement was clinched by transferring gifts. The next step occurred with the setting of the wedding date. Finally, the wedding occurred and the bride moved to her new home.

In this system, marriage was a process of agreements and rituals rather than an event. In fact, the marriage agreement was established at the first transfer of gifts between the two families. After this event a marriage existed which could only be broken with great difficulty. In fact, if either the prospective bride or prospective groom died after this agreement, the rest of the marriage ceremonies were sometimes completed with the surviving spouse acting as a widow or widower. The final steps of the process, therefore, only completed the marriage that was contracted at the initial exchange of gifts (Chang 1991; Freedman 1970).

There are numerous reasons to expect a transformation of the marriage system in Taiwan (chap. 4). The expansion of educational attainment and urban living, the shift to nonfamilial employment and industrial work, and new experiences with nonfamily living arrangements before marriage have enormous implications for the roles of young people and their interactions with peers and parents. The young people have been reoriented from a world organized almost entirely by family elders to one which offers the chance to participate in nonfamily institutions. These provide opportunities for independence from parents and chances to interact with those of the opposite sex. These changes began before World War II but have been particularly rapid during the last four decades. There has also been a widespread diffusion of the Western ideal of marriage, which emphasizes both the involvement of young people in mate selection and the importance of love, romance, dating, and courtship in that process. Given these changes in Taiwanese society, a transformation from parentally controlled and arranged marriages toward a love match system seems likely.

Data and Methods

The data for the analysis of the transformation of the Taiwanese marriage system primarily come from the series of island-wide surveys of married women. These surveys are supplemented by information from three island-wide surveys of unmarried women, in 1971, 1978, and

1984. Information from a school study conducted in 1983–84 also allows a more intensive examination of the behavior and values of unmarried young people. Finally, the household registration system provides data concerning childbearing outside marriage.

In the surveys of married women, the respondents were asked to report on the process of mate selection in their (first) marriage. Our analysis of change using these data classifies women according to their birth or marriage cohort and then compares the nature of marital arrangements for the different cohorts. Since this approach considers experience at approximately the same time in the life course for each of the birth and marriage cohorts, it is possible to interpret cohort differences as reflecting changes across historical time.

Both marriage and birth cohorts have been used as markers of historical time as a partial solution to an important methodological problem that confronts both approaches—the differential truncation of marriage ages as one moves across both birth and marriage cohorts. All the data used to study trends in marital arrangements were collected from women of childbearing years who had married by the time of the survey in question, thereby eliminating from analysis the marital experience of all those who would marry after the survey. This has implications for both the birth and the marriage cohort analyses because the percentage of each cohort that was married and eligible for inclusion in the study varies by birth and marriage cohort. The earliest birth cohorts include a nearly full array of ages at marriage while the later birth cohorts are increasingly limited to women married at younger ages. The marriage cohort truncation problem works in the opposite direction in that the most recent marriage cohorts include a nearly full array of ages at marriage while earlier marriage cohorts are increasingly limited to women married at younger ages. Thus, whereas the birth cohort approach truncates *later* cohorts toward younger marriages, marriage cohort analyses truncate *earlier* cohorts toward younger marriages. Comparing analyses using the two approaches, therefore, allows one to place some bounds on the magnitudes of the trends observed. Further discussion of these issues, including relevant examples, is provided in appendix B.

Results

Data concerning the process of mate selection and marital arrangements are cross-tabulated by birth cohort in table 6.1, while table 6.2 cross-tabulates the data by marriage cohort. Our observations begin with the birth cohort of 1933–34, which reached adulthood in the late 1940s

TABLE 6.1 The Process of Mate Selection, by Birth Cohort, 1986 Survey

	PERCENTAGE DISTRIBUTIONS BY BIRTH COHORT						
	1933–34[a]	1935–39	1940–44	1945–49	1950–54	1955–59	1960–64
Number of respondents	402	373	604	691	1,001	1,004	575
Who decided marriage[b]							
Parents	68	57	47	42	30	19	11
Both parents and couple	18	29	37	39	49	51	57
Couple	14	14	15	19	21	30	32
Total	100	100	100	100	100	100	100
How first became acquainted with husband[c]							
Through parents or relatives	—	35	34	35	28	22	16
Through prof. matchmaker	—	26	24	20	14	9	5
Same neighborhood	—	8	8	6	6	6	6
Through friends	—	23	23	28	32	30	32
Through work	—	4	9	8	13	20	23
At school	—	2	2	1	3	5	4
By self	—	3	3	4	6	8	14
Dating husband before marriage[d]							
No dates	—	64	52	40	22	12	4
Dated with parental approval	—	29	37	47	60	62	61
Dated without parental approval	—	7	11	13	18	26	35
Total	—	100	100	100	100	100	100
Dating someone besides husband before marriage[e]							
No	—	94	88	83	76	67	64
Yes	—	6	12	17	24	33	36
Total	—	100	100	100	100	100	100
Number of engagement ceremonies (Ding huan)[f]							
None	—	8	8	5	5	5	6
One	—	76	73	74	77	80	80
Two	—	16	19	20	18	16	13
Total	—	100	100	100	100	100	100

[a]Data for 1933–34 birth cohort were obtained in the 1973 survey.

[b]The English translation of the question wording is, "Would you say that your [first] marriage was mainly decided by you and your husband, or mainly decided and arranged by your parents and your husband's parents? Or were both the couple and the parents involved in the arrangement?"

[c]The English translation of the question wording is, "How did you first become acquainted with your first husband? Did he live in the same neighborhood as you, or did you meet him through work, at school, through friends, through parents or relatives, or what?" Some respondents volunteered other ways of meeting their husbands, of which "by self" was the only major category. Numbers do not add to 100 because respondents could give more than one answer. Also a few "other" responses are not shown in the table. Some of these may have included people who met their husbands on their own.

[d]The English translation of the question wording is, "Did you date your husband before you were married?" (If yes): "Did you get your parents' permission when you first began to date him?"

[e]The English translation of the question wording is, "Besides your husband, did you date anyone else before you were married?"

[f]The English translation of the question wording is, "Did you and your husband have one or more ceremonies before your wedding that publicized the marriage decision" (Ding huan)? (If yes): "Did you have a small ceremony involving only the close relatives of you and your husband (Hsiao ding), a large ceremony involving a larger group of people (Dah ding), or what?" For the data presented we counted the number of different ceremonies.

TABLE 6.2   The Process of Mate Selection, by Marriage Cohort, 1986 Survey

	PERCENTAGE DISTRIBUTIONS BY MARRIAGE COHORT					
	1955–59	1960–64	1965–69	1970–74	1975–79	1980–84
Number of respondents	236	538	647	773	964	978
Who decided marriage						
Parents	62	52	44	34	23	13
Both parents and couple	23	35	39	46	49	56
Couple	16	13	17	20	28	31
Total	100	100	100	100	100	100
How first became acquainted with husband[a]						
Through parents or relatives	30	38	35	30	25	18
Through professional matchmaker	32	24	22	16	10	8
Same neighborhood	9	9	7	8	6	4
Through friends	17	22	26	30	32	32
Through work	6	5	8	11	19	21
At school	0	2	1	3	3	6
By self	6	3	4	5	7	11
Dating husband before marriage						
No dates	68	59	44	28	13	6
Dated with parental approval	26	32	43	55	62	65
Dated without parental approval	6	9	13	16	25	29
Total	100	100	100	100	100	100
Dating someone besides husband before marriage						
No	94	91	88	81	70	60
Yes	6	9	12	19	30	40
Total	100	100	100	100	100	100
Number of engagement ceremonies						
None	11	8	5	6	5	5
One	74	74	77	71	80	81
Two	15	18	18	22	16	14
Total	100	100	100	100	100	100

Note: For wording of the questions see table 6.1.

[a]Numbers do not add to 100 because respondents could give more than one answer; also, a few "other" responses are not shown in the table.

and early 1950s, and extend through the birth cohort of 1960–64, which reached adulthood in the late 1970s and early 1980s. Our marriage cohorts extend from 1955 through 1984.

A comparison of tables 6.1 and 6.2 shows that the general nature and magnitude of trends are very similar in the birth and marriage cohort approaches. Since the biasing effect of age at marriage truncation works in the opposite direction in the two analyses, there are some differences in the nature of the trends estimated by the two approaches; nevertheless, the differences are small and have no impact on the overall conclusions. The discussion that follows notes any differences which seem particularly significant.

Arrangement of Marriages

Parental involvement in the arrangement of marriages declined steadily and rapidly across all the birth and marriage cohorts surveyed.[1] Fully two-thirds of the marriages of the women born in the early 1930s were totally arranged by the parents, and in another one-sixth of the marriages the parents had significant involvement. The fraction of marriages totally arranged by parents declined steadily over all the cohorts so just over one-tenth of the marriages of the women born during the early 1960s were arranged by parents.

Although parents no longer entirely determine the marital choices of their children, many of them are still involved in that decision. Marriages decided by both the parents and the couple increased from 18% for the oldest women in the survey to 57% for the youngest. When the 57% of marriages with partial involvement of parents is added to the 11% with total parental control, we can see that parents still have some involvement in two-thirds of the marriages of the youngest women. Nevertheless, one-third of the youngest women report they and their husbands made the marital decision themselves.

The dramatic shift from parental- to couple-arranged marriages has been accompanied by marked trends in preferences concerning mate selection. In a 1971 survey of unmarried women aged 18 to 29, nearly one-third said the best procedure for finding a spouse was for the parents to choose alone but with the couple's consent, nearly two-thirds said the young couple should choose but receive the parents' consent, and only 4% said the young couple should choose without parental consent (not in tables).[2] Between 1971 and 1978 the fraction saying the parents

1. Data concerning who decided whom a single person should marry were obtained in 1973, 1980, and 1986, allowing an evaluation of aggregate shifts in reports for the same period made at different points in time. This can be done by limiting the universe of women in two adjacent surveys to those eligible for selection in both years and then comparing the distributions of responses in the two years. This analysis suggests that there may have been an increased reporting of couple involvement between 1973 and 1980 but a decreased reporting of such involvement from 1980 to 1986. The data reported in table 6.1 are taken exclusively from the 1973 and 1986 surveys, and any effect of differential reporting across time in these two surveys is very small.

2. The English translation of the question wording is, "Nowadays, what do you think is the best procedure for finding a spouse: parents making the choice alone but with the young people's consent, young people making their choice alone but with parents' consent, or young people making the choice alone without parents' consent?"

should make the choice declined from about one-third to about one-tenth. The decrease from one-third to one-tenth in those saying parents should make the choice was matched by an increase of similar magnitude in the percentage preferring the choice to be made by the couple but with parental consent. The continuing desire for parental involvement is reflected in the fact that the percentage preferring the young people to choose without parental assistance remained constant at less than 5% across the seven years.

Since age at marriage increased across this time period, age distribution differences in the two surveys might account for the observed trend. However, a cross-tabulation of the answers by age in each of the surveys revealed only a small association between age and mate choice preferences, and the trends observed across the overall age range also occurred at each age level. Consequently, the changing preferences about marital arrangements are not merely an artifact of shifting ages at marriage.

Introduction of Spouses

The historical arranged marriage system is consistent with the way parents and their official agents introduced the prospective husband and wife. Over one-third of the women born in the late 1930s were introduced to their husbands by their parents or other relatives, and one-fourth were introduced by professional matchmakers (table 6.1). The percentage of women introduced to their husbands by professional matchmakers declined steadily across all of the birth cohorts, reaching a low of 5% for the youngest women. There have also been declines in introductions by adult relatives, although that decline began only in the birth cohorts of the early 1950s.

Helping friends with marriage arrangements is an honorable tradition in Chinese society. There is a Chinese saying that, "if you succeeded in matchmaking for your friends three times, thereby accumulating unpublicized good, you will have a better life in the afterworld and bring happiness for your offspring." Chinese people have historically enjoyed matchmaking and are proud of becoming successful marital go-betweens for their friends.

Friends have played a role in the mate selection process across the entire postwar period. Nearly 30% of all women participating in our 1986 survey reported being introduced by friends. Even among the oldest women in our surveys, more than one-fifth were introduced to their husbands by friends, and this number increased to nearly one-third for the youngest women.

The composition of friends and the nature of their involvement as marital go-betweens probably has been shifting in Taiwan, although that cannot be demonstrated from the survey data. In the past a substantial fraction of the friends involved in the process were probably friends of the parents. Although friends of parents probably continue to be active in the introduction process, there has probably been a shift toward introductions by peers of the couple.

The workplace, which increasingly has employed large numbers of young people, has become a very important place for meeting future spouses. Only one in twenty-five of the oldest women in the 1986 survey reported meeting their future husbands at work while over one in five of the youngest women met their husbands at work. For the marriage cohorts of the early 1980s the workplace is more important than adult relatives or matchmakers as a source of introductions to future husbands. Only friends are now more important than the workplace as a source of matchmaking.

Since school enrollment has increased dramatically in Taiwan, one might have expected schools, like paid employment, to operate as marriage markets today. The data in tables 6.1 and 6.2 suggest some movement in this direction, but currently schools are much less important than workplaces as marriage markets.

Workplaces have probably outpaced schools as marriage markets because of the timing of employment and schooling in the life course. Even among the most recent birth cohort of married women, the majority have not gone beyond junior high school, and these women were not in school during the period of their life courses when marital choices were being made. Also, both junior and senior high schools are mostly sex segregated; male and female students usually attend separate schools. While colleges and universities are mostly integrated, college attendance is still low enough in Taiwan so that it provides mating opportunities for only a limited number of couples.

Paid employment, unlike attendance at high school and college, has become a very common experience in the Taiwanese life course, with the vast majority now working away from home before marriage. Large numbers even live in factory-related dormitories before marriage. Since this work experience usually follows school attendance, it occurs at a more propitious moment for meeting a future spouse.

One limit to the potential of the workplace as a marriage market is its high degree of sex segregation. Although we have no systematic data about sex segregation, we know that young women and young men often do not work together in the same work teams. Nevertheless, as Yang (1978, 1982a, 1982b, 1987) has described in fictional stories based on his factory experience, females and males often work in the same organization, even if not within the same small group. This provides excellent opportunities for interactions during work breaks, during lunch hours, in the evenings, and on weekends.[3]

The fraction of women saying that they met their husband at school or work probably understates the importance of schools and workplaces as marriage markets. Many of the young women who said they were introduced to their husbands by a friend undoubtedly became acquainted with the friend at school or work.

Women now meet their husbands more frequently by themselves. Starting from a low of about 3% for the oldest women, more than 10% of the youngest women now report that they became acquainted with their husbands without any introduction.[4]

Dating

The involvement of young people in the mate selection process has been accompanied by the emergence of dating. Two-thirds of the women born in the late 1930s reported that they had never had a date with their future husband, and only 7% dated without parental permission. Dating expanded dramatically across subsequent birth cohorts of women, reaching 60% for women born only ten years later. In recent years dating has become nearly universal; 94% of the women of the most recent marriage cohort had dated their prospective husbands.

The emergence of universal dating has not necessarily removed parents from supervision of their children's courtship activities. Even among the youngest married women participating in our 1986 survey, three out of five reported that they had parental approval to date their future husband. Nevertheless, dating without parental approval has increased markedly. While only 7% of the women born in the late 1930s reported dating their husband without parental approval, this percentage doubled during the next ten years and then doubled again to 26% for the birth cohort of 1955–59.

Perhaps the most significant indicator of the existence of a dating culture is the number of young women dating men whom they did not marry. This phenomenon was limited to 6% of the women born in the late 1930s but included over one-third of the married women born during the early 1960s. Dating has clearly become an important part of the

3. Informal interviews with factory executives and dormitory supervisors revealed at least one company with an explicit policy encouraging marriage among its employees.
4. This category was not included as one of the potential ways of meeting a husband in the original questionnaire but was a very frequent volunteered response.

life course for significant fractions of young Taiwanese women. Nevertheless, the continuity with the past is still evident in that 60% of the women marrying in the early 1980s had dated only their husbands (also see Schak 1975).

There is a substantial association between age at marriage and dating someone other than the husband; older marrying women were significantly more likely than others to have dated someone else. Since the youngest women in the 1986 data collection included only that small minority who married relatively young, it is very likely that the fraction of this birth cohort that will eventually date someone besides their future husbands will be substantially higher than the current 36%. For example, among the most recent marriage cohort, 40% have dated someone other than their husband.

Engagement Ceremonies

Ceremonies publicizing the marriage decision are common features of the marriage process in Taiwan. In addition to such ceremonies at the wedding itself, there may be multiple ceremonies at other times between the initial marital agreement and the wedding. These may occur in conjunction with the agreement of marriage or when the date of the wedding is set. There may be small ceremonies involving only the close relatives of the bride and groom or larger and more elaborate events involving a wider range of associates. Respondents in the 1986 survey were asked about the number and timing of such ceremonies before marriage—events that we refer to here as "engagement ceremonies."

The final panel of table 6.1 shows that, despite the transformation of the marriage system from parentally arranged matches toward unions contracted by the young people themselves, there has been little shift in the number of engagement ceremonies. There may have been a small decrease in the number of couples having no engagement ceremonies, but the percentage of marriages preceded by at least one ceremony to publicize the marriage before the wedding has always been very high.

In recent decades formal engagement has come to mark an important transition in the autonomy of the couple (Schak 1975). With engagement, young couples have more freedom to date and more opportunities for privacy, a life course change with importance for levels of intimacy.

Earlier Change

Although the data in table 6.1 are limited to women born in the 1930s and later, they suggest considerable change in the marriage system before the oldest women in our surveys reached adulthood. This speculation is

supported by several observations: one-third of the oldest women reported that they had some say in the selection of their husbands; nearly
10% of the women born in the late 1930s reported meeting their husbands through work, through school, or by themselves; and one-third
of these same women reported having dated their husbands before marriage. While these numbers are very low compared to later figures, they
are significantly higher than one would expect from the ethnographic
and historical accounts of Chinese marriage patterns (see chap. 2). Furthermore, all of these numbers were increasing within the first birth
cohorts of women observed in our surveys. This interpretation of earlier
changes is consistent with the observations of other researchers reporting
significant trends in Chinese marriage patterns prior to World War II
(Wolf and Huang 1980).

Differentials by Education and Childhood Residence

Further insights into the transformation of the Taiwanese marriage system can be obtained from table 6.3, where selected indicators of the mate
selection process obtained during the 1986 survey are cross-tabulated by
birth cohort, education, and the place where the respondent grew up.
Important linkages between education, urban living experience, and the
transformation of the Taiwanese marriage system are suggested by these
data. For the overall sample, the historical parentally organized and
directed marriage system is much more prevalent among uneducated
women and those who grew up in the countryside. Such women were
considerably more likely than others to have had their marriages arranged by parents, to meet their husbands through parents, relatives, or
professional matchmakers, and not to date. To illustrate the magnitude
of these differentials, 60% of all uneducated women had their marriages
arranged by their parents, while only 8% of the college-educated women
had arranged marriages. These findings are consistent with the theoretical framework outlined in chapter 4 suggesting that school attendance
and urban living are associated with the involvement of children in the
mate selection process.

Most of the educational and rural-urban differentials in the mate
selection system were present among the oldest women participating in
the 1986 survey. For example, in the 1940–44 birth cohort two-thirds
of the uneducated women had their marriages arranged by their parents,
as compared to only one-sixth of the marriages of the senior high graduates in the same birth cohort. Even larger differentials exist for dating:
whereas three-fourths of the uneducated women born between 1940 and
1944 had never dated, only one-tenth of the senior high graduates of

TABLE 6.3   The Process of Mate Selection, by Birth Cohort, Education, and Place Where Grew Up, 1986 Survey

	BIRTH COHORT						
	1935– 39	1940– 44	1945– 49	1950– 54	1955– 59	1960– 64	Total[a]
A. Percentages of Marriages Arranged by Parents							
Education							
None	65	63	62	49	47	*	60
Primary	57	49	46	37	26	17	39
Junior high	*	27	34	21	22	10	21
Senior high	*	15	22	13	8	7	11
College/university	*	*	11	9	7	*	8
Where grew up							
Country	65	57	49	34	24	14	38
Town	48	42	40	31	15	8	28
City	44	24	25	18	11	6	18
B. Percentage of Marriages Arranged by the Couple							
Education							
None	12	10	8	10	6	*	10
Primary	13	15	16	17	26	29	19
Junior high	*	15	21	29	32	28	28
Senior high	*	38	28	30	35	39	34
College/university	*	*	45	30	39	*	36
Where grew up							
Country	12	11	16	19	27	32	21
Town	13	13	18	19	30	29	22
City	17	30	26	28	38	34	31
C. Percentage Meeting Husband through Parents or Relatives							
Education							
None	34	37	29	45	54	*	36
Primary	39	35	36	33	25	21	32
Junior high	*	31	38	22	24	14	23
Senior high	*	28	40	21	15	15	19
College/university	*	*	18	7	18	*	16
Where grew up							
Country	40	37	35	32	26	19	30
Town	26	33	38	29	18	14	26
City	28	27	31	20	19	11	22
D. Percentage Meeting Husband through a Professional Matchmaker							
Education							
None	40	38	48	33	11	*	37
Primary	19	22	21	17	15	7	18
Junior high	*	13	10	6	9	6	8
Senior high	*	3	0	6	5	2	4
College/university	*	*	0	3	2	*	2
Where grew up							
Country	26	28	24	16	10	6	17
Town	31	27	20	17	14	4	18
City	23	11	8	6	4	2	7

TABLE 6.3 continued

	BIRTH COHORT					
	1935–39	1940–44	1945–49	1950–54	1955–59	1960–64	Total[a]

E. Percentage Meeting Husband through Friends							
Education							
None	14	12	18	18	14	*	15
Primary	26	25	26	30	26	33	28
Junior high	*	35	33	39	35	35	34
Senior high	*	28	34	39	34	31	34
College/university	*	*	50	34	25	*	32
Where grew up							
Country	17	20	25	30	27	29	26
Town	35	23	21	27	30	40	28
City	29	30	45	43	36	35	37

F. Percentage Meeting Husband through Work							
Education							
None	1	3	2	8	11	*	4
Primary	6	9	8	10	18	19	12
Junior high	*	10	7	18	19	24	18
Senior high	*	28	15	18	26	26	23
College/university	*	*	11	19	15	*	15
Where grew up							
Country	3	6	6	11	21	23	13
Town	4	8	11	13	21	27	15
City	7	16	10	16	19	19	16

G. Percentage Meeting Husband at School							
Education							
None	1	0	0	0	3	*	1
Primary	2	0	0	0	1	1	0
Junior high	*	0	2	2	2	1	2
Senior high	*	10	3	2	8	10	6
College/university	*	*	11	27	25	*	21
Where grew up							
Country	3	1	1	2	4	2	2
Town	0	1	2	2	3	4	2
City	0	5	1	4	11	10	6

H. Percentage Meeting Husband by Self							
Education							
None	4	3	5	0	0	*	3
Primary	2	3	3	4	8	16	5
Junior high	*	0	4	7	6	11	7
Senior high	*	3	9	9	9	13	10
College/university	*	*	8	10	13	*	12
Where grew up							
Country	3	3	4	6	8	16	7
Town	1	2	4	6	9	11	6
City	3	4	4	6	9	11	7

TABLE 6.3 continued

	1935–39	1940–44	1945–49	1950–54	1955–59	1960–64	Total[a]
			Birth Cohort				

	1935–39	1940–44	1945–49	1950–54	1955–59	1960–64	Total[a]
I. Percentage with No Dates with Husband before Marriage							
Education							
None	81	76	81	55	44	*	73
Primary	62	52	43	27	20	9	34
Junior high	*	19	19	13	8	3	10
Senior high	*	11	9	4	4	1	5
College/university	*	*	3	1	0	*	2
Where grew up							
Country	71	61	48	26	16	5	34
Town	63	48	37	24	11	5	27
City	47	28	18	8	4	1	13
J. Percentage Dating Husband without Parental Approval before Marriage							
Education							
None	5	8	2	4	18	*	7
Primary	6	11	10	15	25	29	16
Junior high	*	10	21	21	21	41	26
Senior high	*	14	25	24	29	34	28
College/university	*	*	29	34	38	*	33
Where grew up							
Country	5	9	11	17	23	37	18
Town	8	10	15	14	26	36	19
City	9	16	16	25	33	28	24
K. Percentage Dating Someone besides Husband							
Education							
None	2	2	4	12	3	*	4
Primary	8	9	12	16	20	25	15
Junior high	*	21	22	33	32	34	31
Senior high	*	49	42	37	47	51	45
College/university	*	*	47	53	51	*	48
Where grew up							
Country	5	9	11	19	28	34	20
Town	6	17	19	23	29	36	23
City	9	17	32	36	46	39	34
L. Number of Respondents							
Education							
None	155	182	99	67	35	9	547
Primary	168	306	405	576	368	172	2,009
Junior high	27	52	81	105	197	201	678
Senior high	15	39	68	183	319	166	803
College/university	7	23	38	70	85	27	250
Where grew up							
Country	229	352	420	567	534	346	2,474
Town	68	139	131	205	205	105	859
City	75	110	137	228	264	124	948

Note: The cell entries indicate the percentage of people in each particular education/birth cohort or residence/birth cohort group who had the mate selection experience listed in that panel of the table.

* For these cells the number of cases is less than 30, and no estimates are reported.

[a] In addition to the cases listed in the body of the table for the birth cohorts of 1935–64, the total column includes a few people who were born in 1965–66.

the same cohort had never dated (panel I of table 6.3). Similarly, while nearly 40% of the marriages of the uneducated women in this same birth cohort of women were introduced by a professional matchmaker, only 3% of the introductions of the senior high graduates of this birth cohort were made by matchmakers (panel D). The rural-urban differentials among the same birth cohort are similarly large.

A more detailed examination of the data in table 6.3 demonstrates that many features of the overall marriage system observed among the marriage cohorts of the 1980s (table 6.2) were already apparent both in the marriages of the earliest cohorts of women growing up in urban areas and in the marriages of women who had attended at least junior high school. Although the number of highly educated urban women in the birth cohorts of the late 1930s and early 1940s was relatively small, most of these women were involved in the selection of their own husbands and were dating their future husbands. Substantial numbers were introduced by their friends, and very few were introduced by professional matchmakers.

Table 6.3 also shows that the shift from arranged marriages to love matches across the birth cohorts from 1935 through 1964 was both rapid and pervasive. Virtually all of the education and residential groups participated in this transformation of the marriage system. However, among the dimensions of the mate selection system documented across the birth cohorts participating in the 1986 survey, the observed changes are greatest among the less-educated and more rural segments of the population. In fact, among the most recent birth cohorts, arranged marriages, introductions by professional matchmakers, and not dating were quite rare even among the least educated and most rural women (panels A, D, and I of table 6.3).[5]

One plausible interpretation of these data is that the transformation of the marriage system in Taiwan began first among the urban and better-educated segments of the population, and was already well along by the time the birth cohorts of the late 1930s reached adulthood. Subsequently, however, the transformation spread to the more rural and less-educated segments of society, and today virtually all groups have been influenced.

Another possibility is that the rural-urban and educational differentials among the oldest women in our survey are longstanding. This alter-

5. The old, parentally directed mate selection system may still be predominant among those women who have never been to school. However, there are so few of these uneducated women among the most recent cohort that they have little impact on the total system.

native explanation suggests that well-educated urban people have always had considerable involvement in the mate selection process but that their previous small numbers minimized their impact on the overall marriage system.

Several more specific dimensions of the marriage transformation in Taiwan are apparent from table 6.3. Paid employment may have become important as a marriage market in urban areas sooner than in the countryside, but it then spread to women from the countryside. In the earlier years women reared in cities were more likely than rural women to meet their husbands at work, but in recent years this phenomenon has been reversed (panel F of table 6.3). This reversal is probably related to the increased migration of rural women to the city to gain employment, where they then met their future husbands.

School has never been an important marriage market for women who have not gone beyond junior high school, both because the lower schools are highly sex segregated and because such young girls are too immature to consider marriage. As children mature into high school and college, schools become more relevant as marriage markets. Six percent of all those with senior high education and 21% of the college educated met their husbands at school (panel G of table 6.3). Both high schools and colleges in Taiwan are integrated, thus enhancing the opportunities for interaction with the opposite sex. However, most school-based marriage markets are limited to urban areas because high school and college attendance is higher for urban women, and only women with considerable education are meeting their husbands in school.

Finally, in the earliest cohorts, women in all segments of the population rarely found a husband on their own. However, self introductions now have increased quite uniformly across all educational groups, except for women with no schooling.

Premarital Sexual Relations and Pregnancy

One of the expected concomitants of the transformation of a marriage system from arranged unions to love matches is increased premarital sexual relations and bridal pregnancies. As young people are brought directly into the mate selection process through dating and courtship, their behavior is less subject to parental control. In addition, the increase of schooling, nonfamily employment, and nonfamily living arrangements gives young people more opportunity to interact with peers without familial supervision.

The increased independence of young people, their greater involvement in activities outside the home before marriage, and the shift of marital arrangements from the control of parents to that of their children are clearly reflected in a strong trend toward increased premarital sexual relations (tables 6.4 and 6.5).[6] The percentage of women who reported having sex before marriage with their future spouse increased from 9% for the birth cohort of 1935–39 to over one-third for the birth cohort of 1955–59. And among the women born in the early 1960s and married by the 1986 survey date, over one-half reported premarital sex with their husbands.

Respondents were asked whether their first sexual relations with their husbands occurred before or after their first engagement ceremony. Those data indicate that the incidence of sexual relations with the future spouse has increased both before and after that first engagement ceremony. The number reporting premarital sex after a ceremony rose from 3% among the birth cohort of 1935–39 to 21% of the cohort of women born in the early 1960s, while the comparable increases in premarital sex before a ceremony across the same years was from 4 to 27%. The increase in sexual relations before a ceremony is particularly important, indicating that premarital sexual relations have increased even in situations where the couple's relationship has not yet progressed to a formal engagement ceremony.

Although there have been substantial increases in premarital sexual relations both before and after engagement ceremonies, the increase apparently occurred earliest in situations where the couple's relationship had been publicized with an engagement ceremony. The incidence of premarital sex before an engagement ceremony increased by only one percentage point across the 1935 to 1949 birth cohorts, while the number initiating sexual relations after a ceremony increased from 3 to 8% during the same period. Apparently, changes in premarital sexual experience occurred first in situations legitimated by formal agreements of marriage. However, the increase in premarital sexual relations among the later birth cohorts has been most dramatic in the period before rather

6. Since we have data on premarital sex and pregnancy from both our 1980 and 1986 surveys, it is possible to check the consistency of reports across years. In order to accomplish this check, subsets of the two samples were defined to include women who were both born and married at the right times to be eligible for both surveys. Since the actual behavior being reported by these women could not have changed between 1980 and 1986, any observed differences would have to be due to either recall bias or sampling error. This exercise revealed that the percentages reporting premarital sex and premarital pregnancy were approximately 3 to 4 points higher in the 1980 survey than in the 1986 survey. This suggests that there may be a tendency for women to underreport their earlier experiences somewhat as they become older. If this is true, the estimates of trends could be biased somewhat toward overestimating the increase in premarital sex and pregnancy.

TABLE 6.4   Premarital Sex and Pregnancy, by Birth Cohort, 1967, 1973, and 1986 Surveys

	PERCENTAGE DISTRIBUTIONS BY BIRTH COHORT[a]								
	1921–24	1925–29	1933–34	1935–39	1940–44	1945–49	1950–54	1955–59	1960–64
Number of respondents	234	961	402	373	604	691	1,001	1,004	575
Premarital sex with husband[b]									
No	—	—	—	91	87	86	77	63	47
Yes	—	—	—	9	13	14	23	37	53
Total	—	—	—	100	100	100	100	100	100
Premarital sex with husband[b]									
No	—	—	—	91	87	86	77	63	47
Yes, after engagement ceremony	—	—	—	3	7	8	11	17	21
Yes, before engagement ceremony	—	—	—	4	5	5	10	17	27
Yes, no engagement ceremony (or timing unknown)	—	—	—	2	1	1	2	2	5
Total	—	—	—	100	100	100	100	100	100
Premarital sex with someone besides husband before marriage[c]									
No	—	—	—	98	99	99	98	97	97
Yes	—	—	—	2	1	1	2	3	3
Total	—	—	—	100	100	100	100	100	100
Premarital pregnancy (direct measure)[d]									
No	—	—	—	92	89	90	84	70	54
Yes	—	—	—	8	11	10	16	30	46
Total	—	—	—	100	100	100	100	100	100
Timing of first birth[e]									
Before marriage	0	1	1	1	1	0	1	1	2
1–7 months after marriage	0	5	6	7	8	8	14	23	35
8 months after marriage or no birth	99	94	93	92	91	91	85	76	64
Total	100	100	100	100	100	100	100	100	100

[a] The data for the 1921–29 birth cohorts come from the 1967 and 1973 surveys, and all data for all subsequent cohorts come from the 1986 survey.

[b] The English translation of the question wording is, "Before you were married, did you have sexual intercourse with your future husband?" (If yes and respondent had been engaged): "Did you have intercourse with your future husband before you were engaged?"

[c] The English translation of the question wording is, "Before you were married, did you have sexual intercourse with anyone other than your husband?"

[d] The English translation of the question wording is, "How long did you take to become pregnant after you were married?" Respondents either reported the number of months or volunteered that they were pregnant at marriage.

[e] Includes only women who were married ten or more months at the time of interview.

than after ceremonies publicizing the marriage agreement. While more of the premarital sexual relationships among the women born in the 1940s were initiated after an engagement ceremony, the majority among the most recent cohort were initiated before a ceremony (table 6.4). This general reversal of the incidence of the initiation of premarital sex from

TABLE 6.5 Premarital Sex and Pregnancy by Marriage Cohort, 1986 Survey[a]

	PERCENTAGE DISTRIBUTIONS BY MARRIAGE COHORT					
	1955–59	1960–64	1965–69	1970–74	1975–79	1980–84
Number of respondents	236	538	647	773	964	978
Premarital sex with husband						
No	89	89	84	78	65	60
Yes	11	11	16	22	35	40
Total	100	100	100	100	100	100
Premarital sex with husband						
No	89	89	84	78	65	60
Yes, after engagement ceremony	5	4	8	12	17	16
Yes, before engagement ceremony	4	6	6	9	16	20
Yes, no engagement ceremony (or timing unknown)	2	2	2	1	2	3
Total	100	100	100	100	100	100
Premarital sex with someone besides husband before marriage						
No	98	99	99	98	97	97
Yes	2	1	1	2	3	3
Total	100	100	100	100	100	100
Premarital pregnancy (direct measure)						
No	92	91	88	84	73	67
Yes	8	9	12	16	27	33
Total	100	100	100	100	100	100
Timing of first birth[b]						
Before marriage	1	1	1	0	1	1
1–7 months after marriage	9	7	10	14	23	24
8 months after marriage or no birth	91	92	89	86	76	75
Total	100	100	100	100	100	100

[a] For wording of the questions, see table 6.4.

[b] Includes only women who were married ten or more months at the time of interview.

after to before an engagement ceremony is also evident in the marriage cohort data (table 6.5). Thus, the initiation of premarital sexual relations appears to be moving earlier in the process of mate selection and marriage.

Although the dating culture has expanded dramatically in Taiwan in recent decades, 40% of the recently married women having dated someone besides their future husbands (table 6.2), there is no evidence in these data that premarital sexual relations have extended to these dating relationships. The percentage of women reporting premarital sex with someone other than the future husband has never exceeded 3% for any cohort, and only a very few had this experience before age 18.[7] This suggests that premarital sexual initiation is still occurring primarily within the context of courtship leading to marriage and that there is moderately little sexual intercourse between young people who are not contemplating marriage at least somewhat seriously.

Important increases have also occurred in the percentage of women who are pregnant at marriage. In the 1986 survey women were asked to report how soon after marriage they first became pregnant, with the option of volunteering that they were pregnant at marriage. Eight percent of the women born in the late 1930s reported being pregnant at marriage. This percentage increased steadily over time, reaching 30% for the birth cohort of 1955–59 and 46% for married women from the 1960–64 birth cohort.[8]

An indirect measure of premarital pregnancy, the timing of the first birth relative to marriage, enables us to extend our analysis of premarital pregnancy back to the birth cohort of 1920–24. Those data indicate that less than 5% of the women born in the 1920s were pregnant at marriage. There was a small, steady increase in premarital pregnancies across the birth cohorts from 1920 through 1949, but bridal pregnancies increased rapidly among all later cohorts.[9]

7. Questions about premarital sexual experience, especially with someone other than the future husband, are still sensitive in Taiwan. In the interviews we tried to mitigate against this sensitivity by asking the questions about premarital sex with someone other than the husband in a self-administered questionnaire. Nevertheless, it is still possible that the reported figures underestimate the prevalence of this experience.

8. Since the questions about premarital sex and pregnancy were asked in different parts of the survey, there is considerable opportunity for inconsistency in responses. We checked the extent of such inconsistency and found it to be very limited. Only 1% of those whose first pregnancy came before marriage failed to report premarital sexual experience.

9. Studies using household registration data report substantially higher levels of premarital pregnancy among women born before World War II than is implied in the estimates reported in tables 6.4 and 6.5. For example, Pasternak (1983) and Wolf and Huang (1980) studied women born in three Taiwanese villages between 1891 and 1920 and reported that from 12 to 20% were pregnant at marriage. There are a number of possible explanations for this difference in estimates of levels of premarital pregnancy, including problems with the reliability of both the survey and the household registration data. On the survey side, premarital pregnancy remains a sensitive topic in Taiwan, and women may simply be underreporting its incidence. On the household registration data side, we know of no island-wide estimates from this source of the fraction of women experiencing a premarital pregnancy. We know that there are geographical variations in nonmarital pregnancy, and the local areas that have been studied may not adequately represent the island-wide experience. Also, even though the registration data are generally of high quality, there may be errors in reports of marriage and birth timing. Unfortunately, we have not been able to find data that would allow us to resolve this discrepancy.

TABLE 6.6   Nonmarital Birthrates in Taiwan, 1960–85

	Rate (per 1,000 unmarried women)[a]
1960	10.7
1964	8.8
1968	6.0
1972	4.4
1976	3.7
1980	3.8
1984	3.5
1985	3.2

Source: Lin 1987.

[a] The rate is calculated by dividing the number of births to unmarried women by the total number of unmarried women between the ages of 15 and 49. Nonmarital births in these calculations include all births without an official legitimate status of marriage. They could include children from concubine relationships and from prostitution.

With the rapid increases in dating, premarital sex, and premarital pregnancy, one might expect an increase in out-of-wedlock childbearing as well. However, the survey data do not support this expectation. The percentage of women reporting a child before marriage has been less than 3% across all birth cohorts of women, with no apparent increases with time (tables 6.4 and 6.5).[10]

A time series of nonmarital birthrates estimated from household registration data also show no increase in out-of-wedlock childbearing in Taiwan since 1960, the earliest date since World War II for which such estimates are possible (table 6.6). Instead, those data suggest that nonmarital birthrates have *declined* substantially since 1960. Between 1960 and 1972 the nonmarital birthrate declined from 10.7 per thousand unmarried women to 4.4, and declined further to 3.2 between 1972 and 1985. An explanation for this decline is discussed later in this chapter.

Although the increases in premarital sex and pregnancy clearly exist across both birth and marriage cohorts, the trends are smaller for the marriage cohort approach. The primary difference is that the birth cohort estimates suggest much higher levels of premarital sex and pregnancy among the most recent birth cohort than among the most recent marriage cohort; 53% of the women born in the early 1960s (and married by 1986) reported premarital sex and 46% reported being pregnant at marriage while the comparable figures for the marriage cohorts of the early 1980s were 40 and 33%, respectively.

10. For an excellent analysis of nonmarital childbearing during the Japanese period, see Barrett (1980). Barrett reported fairly significant levels of nonmarital childbearing during that period.

TABLE 6.7 Premarital Sex and Pregnancy by Birth Cohort and Age at Marriage, 1986 Survey

Age at Marriage	BIRTH COHORT						
	1935–39	1940–44	1945–49	1950–54	1955–59	1960–64	Total
A. Percentage Reporting Premarital Sex with Husband							
17 or younger	11	26	8	22	48	61	31
18–19	10	12	16	28	46	65	33
20–21	6	10	14	22	44	52	28
22–24	10	12	16	26	34	40	25
25 or older[a]	11	12	16	16	21	—	16
B. Percentage Reporting a Premarital Pregnancy (direct measure)							
17 or younger	11	19	2	15	43	55	25
18–19	9	7	13	23	37	61	28
20–21	5	11	9	14	36	40	21
22–24	8	11	11	18	24	36	19
25 or older[a]	9	10	12	12	18	—	13
C. Number of Respondents							
17 or younger	36	71	87	110	92	80	476
18–19	78	111	140	156	137	141	763
20–21	108	164	168	240	246	190	1,116
22–24	102	161	173	295	336	160	1,227
25 or older[a]	47	94	122	200	193	—	659

Note: The cell entries indicate the percentage of people in each particular age at marriage group that had the mate selection experience listed in that panel of the table.

[a]The oldest women in the 1960–64 birth cohort were only age 26 at the 1986 survey. Consequently, there is no information about women marrying at later ages among this birth cohort. The few women age 26 are included in the total.

Since the data from the birth cohort of the 1960s are heavily weighted toward women who married young, these results suggest an important association between premarital sex, pregnancy, and age at marriage. Birth cohort trends, reported within age-at-marriage groups (table 6.7), clearly show that among the birth cohorts from 1935 through 1949 premarital sex and pregnancy were not more prevalent among those marrying at younger ages. Of course, the expected negative association of premarital sex and pregnancy to age at marriage could be obscured somewhat, since women from the same birth cohort who marry at older ages also marry at later time periods. With the secular rise in premarital sex and pregnancy, the levels for the women marrying at older ages could be adjusted upward, since they married at later periods. Women marrying at older ages also have more years of exposure to premarital sex and pregnancy.

Although the same confounding of age at marriage and period effects exists for the birth cohorts of the late 1950s and early 1960s, the negative association between age at marriage and premarital sex and pregnancy is clearly evident for those birth cohorts. While more than 45% of the birth cohort of 1955–59 marrying before age 20 reported premarital sex with their husbands, only 21% of those marrying at age 25 and older so reported. Differentials of similar magnitude also exist for the youngest group of women (table 6.7).

Another view of the interrelationships between birth cohort, age at marriage, and premarital sex and pregnancy looks at how time trends across birth cohorts vary by age at marriage. While recent increases in premarital sex and pregnancy have occurred at all marriage ages, these increases have been much larger for those marrying at young ages.

The changing association between age at marriage and premarital sex and pregnancy may reflect changes in the causal forces interrelating marriage and premarital pregnancy. Because of the strong role of parents in marital arrangements in the past, premarital sexual relations and pregnancy probably occurred after the marital decision with little effect on the timing of marriage. More recently, with the emergence of dating and the involvement of young adults in the mate selection process, premarital sex and pregnancy are more likely to precede the decision to marry. Some of the women who initiate sexual relations and subsequently become pregnant may marry earlier than they would have otherwise. Of course, a pregnancy-hastened marriage can occur at any age. This phenomenon, however, produces a correlation between young age at marriage and bridal pregnancy because relatively few women now marry early unless they become pregnant, while at older ages large numbers marry without this motivation.

The emergence of a strong correlation between age at marriage and premarital pregnancy with the birth cohorts of the 1950s is consistent with the rapid increase in premarital sex before an engagement ceremony which occurred at the same time. This suggests that premarital sex was beginning to occur earlier in the courtship process and affected marital timing for those women who became pregnant.

The negative association between age at marriage and premarital sex and pregnancy has clear implications for our estimates of the experiences of the most recent birth cohorts of women. The truncation of the experience of the most recent birth cohorts to those who marry at young ages probably produces substantial overestimates of the percentage who will experience premarital sex and pregnancy. Since the women from these birth cohorts who marry at later ages will probably have a lower incidence of premarital sex and pregnancy, the inclusion of their experience will substantially lower the overall estimates for those birth cohorts below those suggested by the truncated data reported in table 6.4. However, this speculation assumes that any period increases in premarital sex and pregnancy occurring after 1986 will not be so large as to negate the emergent age at marriage effect.[11]

Education and Rural-Urban Childhood Residence

Marriage arrangements, dating, and the ways of becoming acquainted with a future spouse were shown earlier to be associated in predictable ways with education and rural-urban residence. However, the relationships of premarital sex and pregnancy with education and place of childhood residence appear to be more complex (table 6.8). Education has an inverse U-shaped relationship with both premarital sex and pregnancy. The incidence of premarital sex and pregnancy in each birth cohort is lowest among those with no education or with university training and highest among those with junior high education. The increase in premarital sex and pregnancy across birth cohorts is also basically replicated within each of the five education groups, suggesting a fairly uniform trend across all education groups.

The overall association between place of childhood residence and premarital sex and pregnancy is very modest. Women growing up in the countryside have almost the same overall distributions on these premarital experiences as those who grew up in cities. But this overall lack of association masks an interesting birth cohort/place of residence interaction. Among the older women there was a greater tendency for those growing up in cities to have experienced premarital sex and to be pregnant at marriage. For the more recent birth cohorts, however, this association was reversed; women who grew up in the countryside actually had somewhat more premarital sex and pregnancy than city women. These observations indicate that there were greater increases in premarital sex and pregnancy among women growing up in the countryside than in the cities. One possible explanation is that the recent migration of women from rural-to-urban areas has given them more autonomy from their parents and more opportunities to experience premarital sexual relations and pregnancy.

11. This expectation is also supported by comparing the estimates from the 1980 and 1986 surveys for the 1955–59 birth cohort. The fraction of women reporting premarital sex and premarital pregnancy in 1986 was substantially lower than the percentage in 1980, reflecting the addition to the sample of women from the birth cohort who married at older ages.

TABLE 6.8 Premarital Sex and Pregnancy by Birth Cohort, Education, and Place Where Grew Up, 1986 Survey

	BIRTH COHORT						
	1935– 39	1940– 44	1945– 49	1950– 54	1955– 59	1960– 64	Total
	A. Percentage Reporting Premarital Sex with Husband						
Education							
None	10	9	3	13	20	*	10
Primary	10	14	16	24	41	55	26
Junior high	*	18	15	25	40	57	37
Senior high	*	16	19	25	33	51	33
College/university	*	*	18	14	32	*	21
Where grew up							
Country	7	11	12	23	38	55	26
Town	16	14	15	25	32	56	27
City	9	19	19	21	38	45	28
	B. Percentage Reporting a Premarital Pregnancy						
Education							
None	8	7	3	5	22	*	8
Primary	8	13	11	18	34	51	21
Junior high	*	14	10	19	32	49	30
Senior high	*	13	13	16	25	42	25
College/university	*	*	8	4	24	*	12
Where grew up							
Country	6	9	8	16	31	48	21
Town	14	11	14	16	27	47	21
City	10	17	11	16	28	40	21

Note: The cell entries indicate the percentage of people in each particular education/birth cohort or residence/birth cohort group that had the mate selection experience listed in that panel of the table. See table 6.3 for the number of respondents.

*For these cells the number of cases is less than 30, and no estimates are reported.

The Intimate Behavior and Attitudes of Teenagers

A broader view of the experiences of young people before marriage is shown in data from two island-wide surveys that contain an extensive array of attitudinal and behavioral information collected from single women and men. One survey sampled never-married women and collected information in face-to-face interviews in 1984. The other sampled male and female students in 1983–84 and collected information through anonymous questionnaires administered to groups of students in their classrooms (Cernada et al. 1986). Although both surveys obtained information from older respondents, our analysis focuses on men and women between the ages of 15 and 19. Unfortunately, comparable data were not collected in earlier studies, making it impossible to document trends.

TABLE 6.9 Intimate Attitudes and Behaviors of Unmarried Taiwanese, Ages 15–19, 1984

	Single Women	SCHOOL SURVEY	
		Women	Men
A. Percentage Reporting Following Experience[a]			
Having had a close boyfriend/girlfriend	23	24	42
Kissing or embracing	9	9	17
Caressing	2	4	11
Sexual relations	2	1	5
B. Percentage Saying Kissing or Embracing Is Appropriate for an Unmarried Woman			
If the relationship is a casual one	3	11	27
If she likes the man	21	30	62
If she loves the man	45	63	84
If she is engaged to the man	69	96	91
C. Percentage Saying Caressing Is Appropriate for an Unmarried Woman			
If the relationship is a casual one	2	1	9
If she likes the man	4	6	26
If she loves the man	10	18	50
If she is engaged to the man	26	37	73
D. Percentage Saying Sexual Relations Are Appropriate for an Unmarried Woman			
If the relationship is a casual one	1	0	3
If she likes the man	1	1	9
If she loves the man	2	3	19
If she is engaged to the man	6	6	36

Note: The cell entries indicate the percentage of people with each intimate experience or who would permit each intimate experience.

[a] Two questions were used. The first was, "Do you have or have you ever had a close boyfriend/girlfriend?" The second question was, "Have you had the following experiences with someone of the opposite sex: embracing and kissing; caressing; sexual intercourse?"

Looking first at the behavior of the sample of never-married women, 23% reported having had (or presently having) a close boyfriend (table 6.9). However, only 9% reported ever embracing or kissing a boyfriend, and just 2% reported having had sexual relations. These numbers contrast sharply with a 1982 study in the United States, where fully 45% of the unmarried women of the same ages reported having had sexual relations (Hofferth, Kahn, and Baldwin 1987).

Juxtaposing the relatively low levels of sexual experience reported by the unmarried teenagers with the relatively high levels of premarital sex reported by married women in their twenties raises questions about the quality of the data from the single women. The data from the unmarried women were collected in face-to-face interviews; the sensitivity of the subject may have caused an underreporting of premarital sex. However, the distributions of behavioral responses in the student study were very similar to those in the more general study even though the student information was collected in a more anonymous format, making it unlikely that the low level of reported sexual experience is due to underreporting caused by the face-to-face format of the general survey of unmarried young women. Of course, underreporting of sexual experience is still possible in both surveys.

The 1984 island-wide survey also asked unmarried teenage women their opinions about the appropriateness of certain intimate behaviors in different kinds of relationships with men. Those data, as reported in table 6.9, demonstrate that the acceptance of intimate behavior depends upon both the level of intimacy involved and the nature of the relationship. Only a small minority of these teenage women believed that any form of intimate behavior should be permitted in casual relationships. The acceptance of kissing or embracing rises rapidly as the level of the relationship becomes more serious: 21% said it was permitted if the woman was fond of the man, 45% if the woman loved the man, and 69% if the couple were engaged. A similar pattern of permission exists for caressing: 4% would permit such behavior if the woman were fond of the man, 10% if she loved him, and 26% if they were engaged. But these women indicated that sexual relations should be almost entirely limited to engaged situations; only 2% of the women said that sexual relations are permitted if the woman loves the man, while 6% said that they are permitted if the couple is engaged. Note that the percentage (6%) saying that sex is permitted for an engaged couple is substantially lower than the percentage of Taiwanese women currently experiencing sexual relations before marriage. These women may have underreported their true acceptance of sexual relations for engaged couples, or their attitudes may become less restrictive as they grow older and become more involved in the mate selection process.

Another explanation of the discrepancy between what young women see as permissible intimate behavior and what they are likely to experience is the significant difference in attitudes between males and females participating in the school survey. With one exception, the young men had substantially more permissive attitudes toward intimate behaviors at all levels of male-female relationships than did the young women. For example, only 6% of the young women students participating in the school study considered sexual relations permissible for an engaged woman, while 36% of the young male students said they were permissible. Also, although very few female students said sex was acceptable if the couple were not engaged, 19% of the men said it was okay if the couple loved each other, 9% said it was okay if they liked each other, and 3% said it was permissible even if the relationship was a casual one. Since the percentages of male students approving sexual relations among engaged couples is similar to the percentage of young women currently reporting premarital sex with their husbands, the actual behavior of young couples is more like the ideas of acceptable behavior held by young men than those held by young women.

The school survey also documents a substantial male-female difference in reported intimate relationships. Whereas 9% of the female students reported embracing or kissing and 1% reported sexual intercourse, the comparable percentages for male students were 17 and 5%. These differences could be due to a number of explanations, including differential reporting bias, different patterns of school attendance, different age patterns of entrance into intimate relationships, and different patterns of sexual behavior between men and women.

The 1984 island-wide survey of unmarried teenage women also ascertained views about how to resolve an unplanned pregnancy. Those women were asked, "What do you think is the best solution if an unmarried person becomes pregnant?" Four out of five said that it would be best to try to get married to the person making her pregnant, suggesting the high priority of marriage as the best solution to such pregnancy (not shown in tables). Twelve percent of the women said abortion was the best solution. Particularly relevant to the relatively low nonmarital birthrate in Taiwan is the finding that only 3% of the women favored bearing and rearing the child, while another 4% favored bearing the child but giving it to others to rear.

Alternative Explanations

We observed earlier in this chapter that premarital sex and pregnancy have been increasing in Taiwan during recent years while out-of-wedlock birthrates have been declining. We also noted that the level of sexual intimacy among unmarried teenage women is relatively low, certainly much lower than levels of premarital sex reported by married women.

One approach to this problem of apparently discrepant results accepts the validity of the data at face value. This approach suggests that premarital sexual relations occur almost exclusively in relationships where marriage is already in process or considered to be a real possibility and that the increase in premarital sexual experience in Taiwan has primarily been limited to such relationships. In the relatively infrequent cases where a couple becomes sexually involved before they are serious about the possibility of marriage, it is likely that a premarital pregnancy would precipitate serious consideration of marriage, an outcome supported by the reports young Taiwanese women give of what they would do if faced with a premarital pregnancy.

This interpretation suggests that bridal pregnancies would increase without a concomitant increase in premarital births. Linking these insights with the dramatic increases in age at marriage to be documented in chapter 8, we can see that the *rate* of nonmarital childbearing could actually decline. If the fraction of women having a premarital birth remained steady and age at marriage increased, the nonmarital fertility rate would decline because the denominator of the measure would increase while the numerator remained constant.

An alternative approach discounts the quality of some of the data and emphasizes the importance of abortion to unmarried women in Taiwan. If premarital sex among teenagers, premarital sex with someone other than the man the woman married, and out-of-wedlock childbearing in Taiwan continue to be sensitive topics that are underreported in survey studies, then the levels of premarital sex outside the marriage process or outside relationships leading to marriage probably are substantially greater than reported. In addition, the use of contraception and abortion by unmarried Taiwanese women may have been sufficiently great to prevent increases in out-of-wedlock childbearing—perhaps even great enough to cause nonmarital childbearing to decline. While no systematic data are available about the contraceptive and abortion behavior of unmarried people, there is evidence that contraception and abortion have become very prevalent among married people (see chap. 11). In addition, anecdotal data from medical people in Taiwan suggest that there may be considerable abortion among unmarried Taiwanese women as well.

These two approaches, posed here as alternative explanations, are not mutually exclusive and could be operating in tandem to produce the observed data. Unfortunately, we have insufficient information to test the relative importance of the different factors.

Summary

This chapter documents a dramatic revolution in intimate relations in Taiwan. The historical system of arranged marriages and the introduction of husbands and wives by the older generation have largely ended; young people are now directly involved in mate selection, and dating has become a common feature of the process. This transformation of the system from being parentally directed to having substantial involvement of the young people themselves has been accompanied by a large increase in sexual intimacy before marriage and a proliferation of pregnant brides.

While the marriage system in Taiwan has moved substantially from arranged marriage, it has not become a simple love match system, certainly not by the standards of contemporary Western societies. The older generation retains considerable involvement in the choice of a spouse; most Taiwanese brides dated only with parental consent; and most dated only their husband. Premarital sexual relations are apparently still quite rare among Taiwanese teenagers, and very few Chinese brides say that they have had sexual relations with anyone besides their husband-to-be. And out-of-wedlock childbearing rates are still low and may actually be decreasing. Apparently, many of the historical Chinese patterns of mate selection and marriage have persisted into the present and old systems still have considerable influence on the behavior of young people.

Seven

Determinants of Historical Changes in Marital Arrangements, Dating, and Premarital Sexual Intimacy and Pregnancy

A. Thornton, J. S. Chang, and L. S. Yang

The transformation of the marriage system in Taiwan from arranged marriage toward love match during the last several decades is consistent with the theoretical framework outlined in chapter 4. The family mode of organization in Taiwan has been substantially modified since World War II. Taiwanese society has been transformed from a family mode of production with its economic base in rural agriculture to an urban industrial society employing many people outside their family unit. Accompanying the expansion of wage employment has been an increase in dormitory residence. Similarly, the school system, initiated in the prewar period, expanded rapidly after World War II so that most Taiwanese youths now devote many of their maturing years to formal education. Many Taiwanese have also been integrated into a sophisticated network of mass media, which provide access to many ideas originating outside their families and local communities—both from Taiwan's urban centers and from abroad. The transformation of the life experiences of many Taiwanese women and men from a locus within familial relationships and obligations to numerous nonfamilial activities and relationships has been accompanied by substantial changes in marital patterns.

Although the concurrent transformations of the family mode of organization and mate selection customs are consistent with the theoretical framework outlined in chapter 4, the aggregate-level data provide little information about which social and economic forces are most closely associated with the transformation of mate selection in Taiwan. To investigate which social and economic forces and processes are related to marriage and marital change in Taiwan, we constructed and estimated multivariate individual-level models of the mate selection process, using the series of island-wide surveys. The independent variables examined in these analyses included education, father's occupation, premarital employment, and premarital living arrangements.[1] These multivariate individual-level models were constructed and estimated for several aspects of the mate selection process, including who decided the marriage, how the woman first became acquainted with her husband, dating experience, premarital sexual experience, and premarital pregnancy. The estimated effects of the predictor variables in these models show the influence of each of these variables on the various dimensions of mate selection.

By including measures of historical time in these multivariate individual-level models of the mate selection process, we can determine the extent to which the individual-level explanatory variables account for the historical changes observed. We do this by comparing the unadjusted or observed effect of historical time period with the effect of historical time after controlling for the individual-level explanatory variables. The differences between the unadjusted and adjusted effects of historical time represent the amount of historical change accounted for by the explanatory variables included in the equations.

The data for this analysis come primarily from the series of island-wide surveys of married women. Whenever the same dependent variables were measured in more than one such survey, we pooled the data across surveys to increase both the number of cases and the amount of historical time covered in the analyses. For all analyses using the surveys of married women, we utilized marriage cohort as our indicator of historical time. We used marriage rather than birth cohort because of the smaller amount of truncation bias associated with using marriage cohort. We limited the effects of truncation bias by excluding all women from marriage cohorts where no surveyed woman could have been married at ages 25 and above.[2] We used marital cohort for our indicator of historical time rather than the period of the survey because all of the marriage process variables analyzed refer to behavior at the time of marriage rather than at the time of the survey.

1. We also considered including age at marriage as an explanatory variable in this research and did so in preliminary analyses. However, we decided not to include these results in the tables because of the ambiguity of the causal interconnections between age at marriage and the dependent variables examined. While age at marriage could be a determinant of these other variables, it could also be an outcome of them. In addition, the preliminary analyses demonstrated that the inclusion of age at marriage did not materially change any of the conclusions made from the analyses that exclude it.

2. See appendix B for a full discussion of the truncation bias issue, including the relative magnitudes and directions of the biases associated with marriage and birth cohorts. The marriage cohorts included in the analysis for the respective surveys are as follows: 1946–65 marriage cohorts for the 1965 survey; 1948–67 cohorts for the 1967 survey; 1959–73 cohorts for the 1973 survey; 1966–80 cohorts for the 1980 survey; and 1962–84 cohorts for the 1986 survey.

We also analyzed attitudes toward mate selection using pooled data from two island-wide surveys of single young women. However, since the marriage attitude variables in the young women's surveys refer to the time of the interview, we used survey date rather than birth cohort as the indicator of historical time.

For dichotomous dependent variables, we used logit regression to estimate the parameters of the equations. For ordinal-level variables, we treated the variables as interval-level measures and estimated the equations using Multiple Classification Analysis, a form of dummy variable regression. We summarized the results of the analyses by indicating the predicted value of the dependent variable within categories of the explanatory variables.

Our initial analysis focused on the marital preferences of unmarried women aged 18–29 in 1971 or 1978. These women were asked to indicate "the best procedure for finding a spouse," with three suggested alternative response categories: parents choose with couple's consent; young people choose with parental consent; and young people choose without parental consent. We coded the three categories from zero to two, with zero indicating low couple involvement and two indicating total choice by the younger generation.

Table 7.1 summarizes the results of the multivariate analyses of these marital decision preferences. Since a relatively small number of variables were collected in the 1971 survey, this analysis is limited to three explanatory variables: survey year; education; and age. Age was controlled because age at marriage was changing in Taiwan during these years. The second column of the table lists the observed or unadjusted means on the dependent variable for each category of the independent variables; each subsequent column indicates the adjusted or predicted means estimated from multivariate equations containing the variables listed in each column.

These data confirm the strong shift toward preferences for the involvement of young people in the mate selection process. Between 1971 and 1978 the mean of the dependent variable increased from .72 to .93, a shift of .21 in the direction of young people wanting more choice in a marital partner. Education also displayed a strong effect on mate selection preferences. The education-preference association was both monotonic and strong; the college educated had twice the score of those with no formal education in both the single-variable and multivariate equations. Age had only a modest and statistically insignificant effect on mate selection preferences.

The increase in female education can explain a substantial portion of

TABLE 7.1   Multivariate Analysis of Mate Selection Preferences of
Unmarried Women

	N (1)	Unadjusted Means[a] (2)	ADJUSTED MEANS[b]		
			(3)	(4)	(5)
Year of interview					
1971	1,537	0.72	0.72	0.74	0.74
1978	698	0.93	0.93	0.89	0.89
Eta²/beta²		0.038	0.036	0.019	0.019
Significance[c]		***	***	***	***
Age					
18–19	881	0.77	0.79		0.80
20–21	714	0.77	0.77		0.77
22–24	493	0.84	0.82		0.80
25–29	147	0.78	0.77		0.74
Eta²/beta²		0.003	0.001		0.001
Significance[c]					
Education					
None	64	0.44		0.47	0.47
Primary	848	0.64		0.66	0.66
Junior high	284	0.83		0.82	0.82
Senior high	676	0.89		0.87	0.87
College/university	362	0.97		0.97	0.97
Eta²/beta²		0.081		0.064	0.065
Significance[c]		***		***	***

Note: The dependent variable is coded as follows: 0, parents choose with couple's consent; 1, young people choose with parents' consent; and 2, young people choose without parents' consent. The data came from 1971 and 1978 island-wide surveys of single women.

[a] These are the observed means on the dependent variable within categories of the predictor variables.

[b] The adjusted means are predicted values on the dependent variable within categories of the predictor variables. The predicted values were estimated from a multiple classification analysis (dummy variable regression) encompassing all of the variables included in each column as predictor variables.

[c] These rows designate statistical significance under the assumption of simple random sampling: * = 0.05; ** = 0.01; *** = 0.001.

the change in mate selection preferences across time. Controlling education reduces the difference between the 1971 and 1978 means from .21 (.93 minus .72) to .15 (.89 minus .74). Thus, education alone explains nearly 30% of the total change between 1971 and 1978. Adding age to the equation provides no further explanation of the historical trends.[3] However, if other important predictors of mate selection preferences such as work patterns and place of residence were available for analysis, they might also account for some of the unexplained trend across time.

3. We also did an analysis that collapsed the mate selection variable into a two-category dichotomy. That analysis was done using logistic regression. The results from that analysis were very similar to those reported in table 7.1.

Table 7.2 summarizes an analysis of the actual marital decision process experienced by married women interviewed in 1973, 1980, or 1986. In this analysis, parentally arranged marriages were coded as one, couple-arranged marriages as three, and marriages involving both parents and couple as two.

These data show a substantial shift of marital arrangements across time; for the marriage cohort of 1959, the mean score on the marital arrangement variable was 1.55, while the comparable score for the 1980–84 cohort was 2.17. The difference of .62 between the two marriage cohorts represents the aggregate shift across these several decades—the change we want to explain with our multivariate models.

Shifting to the other independent variables, we see results consistent with our theoretical expectations. Young women who grew up in agricultural families were more likely than others to have their marriages parentally arranged; the mean difference on the variable is .28. The woman's education was also strongly and monotonically related to marital arrangements. On a numerical scale extending only from 1 to 3, women with college educational experience scored 2.39, compared to an average score of 1.52 for women with no formal education.

The women's premarital work experience is also related to their marital arrangements. As expected, women who worked outside the home were significantly more involved in the arrangement of their marriages than were those with no work experience outside the home before marriage, a difference of about .4. However, the premarital residences of working women had little influence on who arranged the marriage. Employed women who lived in a factory dormitory or other nonfamily arrangement had a score of 2.08 on the marital arrangement variable, which was only .05 higher than the score for employed women who lived with parents or other relatives. Also, women who worked at home for wages had marital arrangements very similar to those with no wage experience.

Focusing on the full multivariate model in the last column of table 7.2, we see that wife's education, premarital work experience, and father's occupation demonstrate the expected relationship with marital arrangements, even after controlling for the other variables. The largest observed effect is for education—with the difference between the lowest and highest educational groups being .6 units on the marital arrangement variable, a very substantial shift for a dependent variable that ranges only from 1 to 3.

How much of the .62 change in marital arrangements between the marriage cohorts of the late 1950s and the early 1980s can be explained

TABLE 7.2 Multivariate Analysis of Who Decided the Marriage

	N (1)	Unadjusted Means[a] (2)	Adjusted Means[b]				
			(3)	(4)	(5)	(6)	(7)
Marriage cohort							
1959	266	1.55	1.56	1.68	1.65	1.64	1.73
1960–64	1,760	1.67	1.68	1.77	1.74	1.74	1.81
1965–69	3,003	1.78	1.79	1.83	1.83	1.82	1.86
1970–74	2,751	1.92	1.92	1.92	1.91	1.91	1.91
1975–79	2,170	2.13	2.12	2.04	2.06	2.06	2.00
1980–84	976	2.17	2.15	2.01	2.08	2.08	1.96
Eta^2/beta^2		0.059	0.051	0.018	0.027	0.028	0.009
Significance[c]		***	***	***	***	***	***
Wife's father's occupation							
Farmer	5,554	1.77	1.78				1.84
Nonfarmer	4,937	2.05	2.02				1.96
Eta^2/beta^2		0.033	0.024				0.007
Significance[c]		***	***				***
Wife's education							
None	1,566	1.52		1.59			1.66
Primary	5,934	1.82		1.83			1.85
Junior high	1,412	2.07		2.03			1.99
Senior high	1,469	2.26		2.20			2.14
College/univ.	542	2.39		2.33			2.26
Eta^2/beta^2		0.101		0.070			0.045
Significance[c]		***		***			***
Wife's work before marriage							
No wage work	3,464	1.64			1.71		
Wage work/home	584	1.65			1.69		
Wage work outside home	6,716	2.06			2.02		
Eta^2/beta^2		0.072			0.042		
Significance[c]		***			***		
Wife's premarital work & living arrangements							
No nonhome work	4,112	1.65				1.71	1.77
Parents/relatives	4,088	2.03				2.01	1.94
Dormitory/others	2,621	2.08				2.03	2.04
Eta^2/beta^2		0.068				0.039	0.021
Significance[c]		***				***	***
Unadjusted R^2			0.083	0.115	0.094	0.092	0.140

Note: The dependent variable is coded as follows: 1, parents; 2, both parents and couple; and 3, couple. The data came from 1973, 1980, and 1986 island-wide surveys of married women.

[a] These are the observed means on the dependent variable within categories of the predictor variables.

[b] The adjusted means are predicted values on the dependent variable within each category of the predictor variables. The predicted values were estimated from a multiple classification analysis (dummy variable regression) encompassing all of the variables included in each column as predictor variables.

[c] These rows designate statistical significance under the assumption of simple random sampling: * = 0.05; ** = 0.01; *** = 0.001.

by the explanatory variables examined here? By comparing the observed marriage cohort means in column 2 of table 7.2 with the adjusted means in columns 3–7, we can see that the wife's education, work experience, and father's occupation can each individually explain some of the trends in mate selection. That is, the observed difference in mate selection across marriage cohorts is larger than the adjusted difference estimated with any of these variables controlled.

Education is the single most important variable for explaining the historical trends in marriage arrangements in Taiwan. Controlling education reduces the difference between the youngest and oldest marriage cohorts from .62 to .33, suggesting that educational changes alone can explain nearly 50% of the time trend in marital arrangements. Each of the two premarital work experience variables individually accounts for approximately 30% of the historical trends, while the father's occupation accounts for a very small fraction of the change. The inclusion of all the variables in the equation reduces the differences across marriage cohorts from .62 to .23. Thus, all of the variables together account for almost two-thirds of the entire observed trend. The remaining one-third of the historical trend is due to other factors that have not been explicitly measured and considered here or to measurement errors in the variables available for analysis.

A similar set of findings emerges when we examine how women meet their husbands,[4] using the woman's marriage cohort, father's occupation, and her own schooling and employment experience as predictor variables. While this causal ordering of variables is appropriate for most couples, it may not be for those who could have met their future spouse long before finishing school and beginning employment. Consequently, the effects shown for schooling and employment may be somewhat biased.

Table 7.3 shows educational attainment as the strongest predictor of how these Taiwanese women met their husbands. Eighty-three percent of the college-educated women met their husbands without the assistance of relatives or matchmakers; the comparable figure was only 28% for women with no formal education (col. 2). While the multivariate controls reduce the differential somewhat, the women with the most education remain twice as likely as the least educated to meet their husbands by themselves.

Both agricultural roots and the lack of premarital wage employment

4. The dependent variable is coded as a dichotomy: meeting husband through parents, other relatives, or matchmakers coded as zero; all others coded as one.

TABLE 7.3 Multivariate Analysis of How Wife First Became Acquainted with Husband

	N (1)	Unadjusted Proportions[a] (2)	Adjusted Proportions[b] (3)	(4)	(5)	(6)
Marriage cohort						
1962–64	325	0.42	0.43	0.53	0.48	0.56
1965–69	607	0.44	0.45	0.51	0.49	0.54
1970–74	751	0.55	0.56	0.58	0.56	0.59
1975–79	934	0.67	0.67	0.65	0.65	0.64
1980–84	953	0.75	0.74	0.69	0.72	0.67
Significance[c]		***	***	***	***	***
Wife's father's occupation						
Farmer	1,732	0.53	0.54			0.58
Nonfarmer	1,703	0.68	0.68			0.65
Significance[c]		***	***			**
Wife's education						
None	328	0.28		0.34		0.38
Primary	1,706	0.53		0.55		0.56
Junior high	608	0.71		0.69		0.68
Senior high	710	0.78		0.75		0.73
College/univ.	218	0.83		0.81		0.79
Significance[c]		***		***		***
Wife's premarital work and living arrangements						
No paid work	826	0.40			0.46	0.52
Paid work at home	127	0.62			0.65	0.64
Nonhome work, live home, give parents money	1,105	0.64			0.63	0.62
Same, keep money	342	0.72			0.70	0.61
Nonhome work, live dorm, give parents money	864	0.67			0.65	0.68
Same, keep money	247	0.75			0.72	0.70
Significance[c]		***			***	***

Note: The dependent variable is coded as follows: 0, parents, relatives, and matchmakers; 1, all others. All women whose parents were not alive and in Taiwan at the time of marriage were excluded from analysis. The data came from the 1986 island-wide survey of married women.

[a] These are the observed proportions meeting husband independently within categories of the predictor variables.

[b] The adjusted proportions are predicted values on the dependent variable within each category of the predictor variables. The predicted values were estimated from logistic regression equations encompassing all of the variables included in each column as predictor variables.

[c] These rows designate statistical significance under the assumption of simple random sampling: * = 0.05; ** = 0.01; *** = 0.001.

inhibit self introductions. But among women with premarital work experience, keeping substantial parts of their earnings had no additional effect on marital introductions once the other variables were controlled (col. 6, table 7.3).

There is, however, an additional modest effect of dormitory living. In the full multivariate model, women who both worked and lived away from home were somewhat more likely than those who worked but lived at home to meet their husbands without the introductions of the senior generation (col. 6, table 7.3). This suggests that dormitory living provides young women the autonomy to interact with men that they would not have residing in the parental home. Nevertheless, the effect of dormitory living is not particularly large, which is consistent with Kung's observation that factory dormitories in Taiwan are paternalistic. Young women in Taiwan's work-related dormitories are closely supervised, which limits their opportunity for independent decision making. This apparently prevents dormitory experience from having a strong influence on the locus of control in the mate selection process.

The variables in this analysis substantially explain the increases between the early 1960s and the early 1980s in the percentage of women who met their husbands with no assistance from relatives or matchmakers. Controlling education alone reduces the difference between the marriage cohorts of the early 1960s and the early 1980s from 33 percentage points (.75 minus .42) to 16 percentage points (.69 minus .53), a reduction of 52%. All the variables together reduce the difference between the youngest and oldest cohorts to 11 percentage points, accounting for two-thirds of the observed trends in meeting a future spouse.

In tables 7.4 and 7.5 we shift to dating behavior; table 7.4 focuses on dates with the future husband, while table 7.5 summarizes dates with someone else. Dating with the husband is coded on a three-point scale—no dating is scored zero, and dating without parental permission is coded two. For dating with others, we scored the variable as a dichotomous zero-one variable, with one representing such dating experience.

Dating behavior is related to a woman's education, premarital employment, and father's occupation. Women with agricultural roots, as compared to those from city backgrounds, experienced less freedom in dating their husbands and were less likely to have dated someone else. These differences, however, were sharply reduced in the multivariate models, particularly when education and work experience were in the equations, suggesting that the effects of parental origins operate at least partially through these two factors.

TABLE 7.4 Multivariate Analysis of Dating Husband before Marriage

	N (1)	Unadjusted Means[a] (2)	Adjusted Means[b] (3)	(4)	(5)	(6)
Marriage cohort						
1962–64	330	0.53	0.54	0.68	0.65	0.75
1965–69	619	0.68	0.69	0.78	0.78	0.84
1970–74	759	0.88	0.89	0.91	0.90	0.92
1975–79	943	1.12	1.11	1.08	1.07	1.04
1980–84	956	1.23	1.22	1.12	1.16	1.08
$Eta^2/beta^2$		0.132	0.120	0.054	0.065	0.028
Significance[c]		***	***	***	***	***
Wife's father's occupation						
Farmer	1,759	0.87	0.90			0.94
Nonfarmer	1,711	1.08	1.05			1.00
$Eta^2/beta^2$		0.027	0.012			0.002
Significance[c]		***	***			**
Wife's education						
None	336	0.38		0.53		0.62
Primary	1,723	0.86		0.90		0.90
Junior high	614	1.17		1.12		1.09
Senior high	714	1.23		1.14		1.11
College/univ.	219	1.32		1.25		1.22
$Eta^2/beta^2$		0.151		0.079		0.055
Significance[c]		***		***		***
Wife's premarital work and living arrangements						
No paid work	834	0.56			0.69	0.76
Paid work at home	130	0.89			0.92	0.92
Nonhome work, live home, give parents money	1,118	1.04			1.01	0.99
Same, keep money	348	1.15			1.09	0.98
Nonhome work, live dorm, give parents money	869	1.14			1.09	1.11
Same, keep money	249	1.22			1.15	1.09
$Eta^2/beta^2$		0.127			0.060	0.037
Significance[c]		***			***	***
Unadjusted R^2			0.144	0.194	0.180	0.225

Note: The dependent variable is coded as follows: 0, no date; 1, dated with parental approval; 2, dated without parental approval. All women whose parents were not alive and in Taiwan at the time of marriage were excluded from analysis. The data came from the 1986 island-wide survey of married women.

[a] These are the observed means on the dependent variable within categories of the predictor variable.

[b] The adjusted means are predicted values on the dependent variable within each category of the predictor variables. The predicted values were estimated from a multiple classification analysis (dummy variable regression) encompassing all of the variables included in each column as predictor variables.

[c] These rows designate statistical significance under the assumption of simple random sampling: * = 0.05; ** = 0.01; *** = 0.001.

TABLE 7.5 Multivariate Analysis of Dating Someone besides Husband before Marriage

	N (1)	Unadjusted Proportions[a] (2)	ADJUSTED PROPORTIONS[b] (3)	(4)	(5)	(6)
Marriage cohort						
1962–64	335	0.09	0.09	0.12	0.11	0.14
1965–69	619	0.11	0.11	0.14	0.13	0.15
1970–74	760	0.19	0.19	0.20	0.19	0.19
1975–79	950	0.30	0.29	0.26	0.27	0.24
1980–84	961	0.40	0.38	0.30	0.35	0.27
Significance[c]		***	***	***	***	***
Wife's father's occupation						
Farmer	1,766	0.19	0.18			0.18
Nonfarmer	1,721	0.33	0.29			0.24
Significance[c]		***	***			***
Wife's education						
None	339	0.05		0.06		0.08
Primary	1,729	0.16		0.16		0.16
Junior high	617	0.30		0.27		0.25
Senior high	720	0.45		0.39		0.36
College/univ.	220	0.50		0.45		0.40
Significance[c]		***		***		***
Wife's premarital work and living arrangements						
No paid work	840	0.09			0.12	0.14
Paid work at home	132	0.14			0.14	0.11
Nonhome work, live home, give parents money	1,121	0.26			0.24	0.21
Same, keep money	349	0.39			0.34	0.22
Nonhome work, live dorm, give parents money	870	0.30			0.26	0.27
Same, keep money	252	0.42			0.37	0.31
Significance[c]		***			***	***

Note: The dependent variable is coded as follows: 0, no; 1, yes. All women whose parents were not alive and in Taiwan at the time of marriage were excluded from analysis. The data came from the 1986 island-wide survey of married women.

[a] These are the observed proportions of the dependent variable within categories of the predictor variables.

[b] The adjusted proportions are predicted values on the dependent variable within each category of the predictor variables. The predicted values were estimated from logistic regression equations encompassing all of the variables included in each column as predictor variables.

[c] These rows designate statistical significance under the assumption of simple random sampling: * = 0.05; ** = 0.01; *** = 0.001.

Educational experience had a strong influence on dating behavior. The college-educated women scored more than three times higher than women without formal education on dates with the husband. Also, ten times as many of the highly educated women had dated someone besides their future husband. While these differentials were reduced somewhat in the multivariate equations, they still remained important, suggesting that education has a powerful independent influence on dating.

Finally, paid employment was also related to dating behavior. Those with wage jobs outside the home before marriage scored approximately twice as high on dating the future husband as those with no paid employment, while the differential between these two groups was even greater for dating with others. As with marital introductions, dating shows some response to premarital living arrangements while employed. Those who lived in work-related dormitories had somewhat more dating experience than those who were employed but lived at home, providing further evidence of the additional autonomy associated with dormitory living.

The effect of the work variable is reduced, but not eliminated, in the multivariate equations. This suggests that the observed correlation of this variable with dating can be partially explained as the result of both dating and employment experience being caused by the other variables in the model.

The historical trends in parental background, education, and premarital work and living arrangements can also account for a substantial fraction of the cohort trends in dating behavior. Whereas the unadjusted difference between the earliest and latest marital cohorts on the husband dating scale was .7 units, it reduces to .33 with the full controls, suggesting that historical changes in these three explanatory variables can account for slightly more than 50% of the historical change occurring in dating of the husband. Similarly, the unadjusted cohort shift of 31 percentage points in dating someone besides the husband was reduced to 13 percentage points. Thus, nearly 60% of this substantial shift stems from the three variables included in this analysis, with the single most important explanation of changing dating behavior being the dramatic increase in education.

Shifting now to premarital sexual intimacy and pregnancy (tables 7.6–7.7), we find an important new pattern of relationships. Educational attainment, which had been strongly and monotonically related to mate selection, introductions, and dating, displayed a strong inverse-U relationship with premarital sexual experience and pregnancy. Thus, the lowest reported levels of premarital sexual experience and pregnancy were from college-educated women and those without formal education,

TABLE 7.6 Multivariate Analysis of Premarital Sex with Husband

	N (1)	Unadjusted Proportions[a] (2)	ADJUSTED PROPORTIONS[b]				
			(3)	(4)	(5)	(6)	(7)
Marriage cohort							
1960–64	346	0.10	0.10	0.10	0.10	0.10	0.11
1965–69	1,371	0.18	0.18	0.18	0.19	0.19	0.19
1970–74	1,830	0.27	0.27	0.26	0.27	0.26	0.26
1975–79	2,172	0.36	0.36	0.35	0.34	0.34	0.34
1980–84	973	0.40	0.40	0.40	0.38	0.38	0.38
Significance[c]		***	***	***	***	***	***
Wife's father's occupation							
Farmer	3,290	0.28	0.28				0.26
Nonfarmer	3,186	0.30	0.28				0.29
Significance[c]							
Wife's education							
None	623	0.15		0.20			0.21
Primary	3,435	0.29		0.30			0.30
Junior high	1,000	0.37		0.32			0.32
Senior high	1,190	0.32		0.26			0.26
College/univ.	442	0.17		0.14			0.14
Significance[c]		***		***			***
Wife's work before marriage							
No wage work	1,614	0.20			0.23		
Wage work at home	276	0.20			0.21		
Wage work outside home	4,746	0.32			0.30		
Significance[c]		***			***		
Wife's premarital work & living arrangements							
No nonhome work	1,910	0.20				0.23	0.23
Parents/relatives	2,811	0.29				0.26	0.27
Dormitory/others	1,920	0.38				0.35	0.34
Significance[c]		***				***	***

Note: The dependent variable is coded as follows: 0, no; 1, yes. The data came from the 1980 and 1986 island-wide surveys of married women.

[a] These are the observed proportions of the dependent variable within categories of the predictor variables.

[b] The adjusted proportions are predicted values on the dependent variable within each category of the predictor variables. The predicted values were estimated from logistic regression equations encompassing all of the variables included in each column as predictor variables.

[c] These rows designate statistical significance under the assumption of simple random sampling: * = 0.05; ** = 0.01; *** = 0.001.

while junior high school women displayed the highest levels. Furthermore, the differences between those with junior high educations and those at the ends of the educational distribution were substantial (col. 2 of the two tables). The same basic inverse-U relationships also persisted in the multivariate models. However, since many of the women without formal education came from the earlier marriage cohorts, controlling for

TABLE 7.7 Multivariate Analysis of Premarital Pregnancy

	N (1)	Unadjusted Proportions[a] (2)	ADJUSTED PROPORTIONS[b]				
			(3)	(4)	(5)	(6)	(7)
Marriage cohort							
1960–64	336	0.09	0.09	0.09	0.09	0.09	0.10
1965–69	1,357	0.14	0.14	0.14	0.15	0.15	0.15
1970–74	1,814	0.19	0.19	0.18	0.20	0.19	0.19
1975–79	2,151	0.27	0.27	0.27	0.26	0.26	0.26
1980–84	931	0.33	0.33	0.33	0.31	0.31	0.32
Significance[c]		***	***	***	***	***	***
Wife's father's occupation							
Farmer	3,237	0.22	0.22				0.20
Nonfarmer	3,139	0.23	0.21				0.22
Significance[c]							
Wife's education							
None	594	0.12		0.16			0.16
Primary	3,400	0.23		0.24			0.24
Junior high	987	0.29		0.25			0.24
Senior high	1,174	0.24		0.19			0.19
College/univ.	432	0.10		0.08			0.08
Significance[c]		***		***			***
Wife's work before marriage							
No wage work	1,584	0.15			0.18		
Wage work/home	268	0.16			0.17		
Wage work outside home	4,684	0.25			0.23		
Significance[c]		***			***		
Wife's premarital work and living arrangements							
No nonhome work	1,870	0.15				0.18	0.18
Parents/relatives	2,773	0.22				0.20	0.20
Dormitory/others	1,898	0.30				0.27	0.26
Significance[c]		***				***	***

Note: The dependent variable is coded as follows: 0, no; 1, yes. The data came from the 1980 and 1986 island-wide surveys of married women.

[a] These are the observed proportions of the dependent variable within categories of the predictor variables.

[b] The adjusted proportions are predicted values on the dependent variable within each category of the predictor variables. The predicted values were estimated from logistic regression equations encompassing all of the variables included in each column as predictor variables.

[c] These rows designate statistical significance under the assumption of simple random sampling: * = 0.05; ** = 0.01; *** = 0.001.

cohort in the multivariate equations adjusted estimates for the uneducated women strongly upward. Because of the curvilinear relationship of education to premarital sex and pregnancy, changes in educational attainment across marriage cohorts cannot account for the substantial changes observed in premarital sex and pregnancy in Taiwan. We will return to the issue of education and premarital sex and pregnancy later.

The occupation of the wife's father had virtually no effect on the three measures of sexual and pregnancy experience. Consequently, this factor also could not explain any historical trends in these dependent variables.

We also estimated equations of premarital sex and pregnancy that substituted the wife's rural and urban experience for the wife's father's occupation. The rural-urban experience variable displayed virtually no relationship with premarital sex or pregnancy, nor did it influence the other parameters estimated in the analysis (data not shown).

The only substantive variable in tables 7.6–7.7 with even a modest monotonic effect on premarital sex and pregnancy was premarital work and living arrangements. Women with wage employment outside the home more often reported premarital sexual and pregnancy experience, and such reports were slightly higher among workers who lived in factory dormitories than among those who lived in their parental home.

The lack of strong monotonic relationships between the predictor variables and premarital sex and pregnancy makes it impossible for the measured predictor variables to explain historical trends in premarital sex and pregnancy. The full multivariate models account for only 10% or less of the shifts across marital cohorts, all of which are due primarily to premarital work and living arrangements. Apparently, one cause of the increase in premarital sex and pregnancy is the new independence associated with nonhome work and residence.

The process of mate selection can have strong implications for premarital intimacy and pregnancy. When marriages are entirely arranged by parents, and young people are introduced to their future spouse through parents or matchmakers with no prior dating, there is little opportunity for sexual intimacy before marriage. However, when young people independently meet and choose their future spouses and experience extensive unsupervised dating, premarital intimacy seems much more probable. The new trends in mate selection and dating could thus account for a significant part of the historical changes in premarital sex and pregnancy.

We addressed these questions by estimating equations predicting premarital sex and pregnancy which included three dating and mate selection variables: dating the future husband; who decided the marriage; and how the future husband was met. Although we recognize that the three mate selection and dating variables are intertwined with premarital sex and pregnancy in complex and potentially multidirectional ways, we have chosen this specification of the relationship because we believe that the bulk of the causal influence flows from the dating and mate selection variables to premarital sex and pregnancy. This specification is especially appropriate for dating and introductions to the future husband, because both are expected to precede premarital sex. However, the causal interrelationships between who chose the husband and premarital sex may be more complex since the marital decision may occur after premarital sex and even pregnancy have been experienced, a sequencing of experiences that may have become more common in recent decades (see previous chapter). While these considerations suggest that there may be some reciprocal causal influence of premarital sex and pregnancy on the marital decision, we believe that most of the causation is from who chose the spouse to premarital sex and pregnancy—a causal ordering that legitimizes the empirical equations estimated. Nevertheless, the potential reciprocal causation requires additional caution in interpreting these equations.

Tables 7.8 and 7.9 summarize the equations adding who decided the marriage, how the future husband was met, and dating to our earlier equations predicting premarital sex and pregnancy. Unlike the prior analysis of premarital sex and pregnancy (tables 7.6 and 7.7), which included information from both the 1980 and 1986 surveys, the present analysis is limited to women interviewed in 1986 because some of the detailed information about the mate selection variables was not ascertained in the 1980 study.

The 1986 data strongly support ideas which link the mate selection process with premarital sexual intimacy and pregnancy. All three of the mate selection variables—who decided the marriage, who made the introduction, and dating—have the expected relationship to the sex and pregnancy variables. Furthermore, the unadjusted relationships (col. 2 of tables 7.8 and 7.9) are very strong and there is very little weakening of the effects when marriage cohort and the wife's education, work experience, and father's occupation are added to the equations (cols. 5–7). For example, premarital sexual intimacy was reported for only 12% of the parentally arranged marriages, while among women who chose their own spouse 42% reported premarital sexual intimacy (adjusted percentages in col. 5 of table 7.8). Similarly, 15% of those who were introduced to their future husbands by parents or matchmakers reported premarital sexual intimacy, compared to 33% of those who met their husband independently (col. 6, table 7.8). The effect of dating was even stronger; only 7% of those with no dating experience reported premarital sexual intimacy, compared to 47% of those who dated without parental permission (col. 7, table 7.8).

Each dimension of the mate selection process apparently has an independent effect on premarital sex. The last columns of tables 7.8 and 7.9

TABLE 7.8 Multivariate Analysis of Premarital Sex with Husband, including Mate Selection and Dating as Predictor Variables

	N (1)	Unadjusted Proportions[a] (2)	Adjusted Proportions[b] (3)	(4)	(5)	(6)	(7)	(8)
Marriage cohort								
1962–64	335	0.09	0.10	0.11	0.11	0.11	0.12	0.11
1965–69	616	0.16	0.16	0.17	0.17	0.17	0.17	0.16
1970–74	757	0.22	0.22	0.22	0.21	0.21	0.20	0.20
1975–79	951	0.35	0.34	0.32	0.30	0.30	0.28	0.27
1980–84	956	0.40	0.39	0.37	0.34	0.34	0.32	0.30
Significance[c]		***	***	***	***	***	***	***
Wife's father's occupation								
Farmer	1,764	0.26		0.24	0.24	0.24	0.22	0.22
Nonfarmer	1,716	0.30		0.27	0.25	0.26	0.24	0.23
Significance[c]		**						
Wife's education								
None	337	0.09	0.14	0.15	0.17	0.17	0.19	0.19
Primary	1,729	0.27	0.28	0.28	0.28	0.28	0.27	0.27
Junior high	611	0.38	0.32	0.31	0.28	0.28	0.26	0.24
Senior high	718	0.33	0.25	0.25	0.21	0.22	0.20	0.18
College/univ.	220	0.20	0.16	0.15	0.12	0.12	0.10	0.09
Significance[c]		***	***	***	***	***	***	***
Wife's premarital work and living arrangements								
No paid work	834	0.15		0.20	0.21	0.21	0.22	0.22
Paid work at home	132	0.20		0.20	0.18	0.18	0.18	0.17
Nonhome work, live home, give parents money	1,120	0.28		0.24	0.22	0.23	0.21	0.20
Same, keep money	346	0.28		0.25	0.24	0.24	0.22	0.22
Nonhome work, live dorm, give parents money	871	0.39		0.33	0.30	0.31	0.28	0.26
Same, keep money	251	0.37		0.32	0.29	0.29	0.26	0.25
Significance[c]		***		***	***	***	**	*
Who decided marriage								
Parents	1,041	0.12			0.12			0.17
Parents/couple	1,705	0.29			0.26			0.22
Couple	854	0.46			0.42			0.32
Significance[c]		***			***			***
How met future husband								
Relatives/matchmakers	1,412	0.15				0.15		0.18
Others	2,141	0.37				0.33		0.26
Significance[c]		***				***		***
Dating husband before marriage								
No date	848	0.06					0.07	0.09
Date—parental approval	2,008	0.29					0.26	0.25
Date—no parental approval	734	0.51					0.47	0.40
Significance[c]		***					***	***

Note: The dependent variable is coded as follows: 0, no; 1, yes. The data came from the 1986 island-wide survey of married women. All women whose parents were not alive and in Taiwan at the time of marriage were excluded from analysis.

[a] These are the observed proportions of the dependent variable within categories of the predictor variables.

[b] The adjusted proportions are predicted values on the dependent variable within each category of the predictor variable. The predicted values were estimated from logistic regression equations encompassing all of the variables included in each column as predictor variables.

[c] These rows designate statistical significance under the assumption of simple random sampling: * = 0.05; ** = 0.01; *** = 0.001.

TABLE 7.9 Multivariate Analysis of Premarital Pregnancy, including Mate Selection and Dating as Predictor Variables

	N (1)	Unadjusted Proportions[a] (2)	ADJUSTED PROPORTIONS[b]					
			(3)	(4)	(5)	(6)	(7)	(8)
Marriage cohort								
1962–64	326	0.09	0.09	0.10	0.10	0.10	0.10	0.10
1965–69	612	0.12	0.12	0.13	0.12	0.13	0.13	0.12
1970–74	751	0.16	0.15	0.15	0.14	0.14	0.14	0.13
1975–79	935	0.27	0.26	0.24	0.23	0.23	0.21	0.20
1980–84	917	0.33	0.32	0.30	0.28	0.28	0.26	0.25
Significance[c]		***	***	***	***	***	***	***
Wife's father's occupation								
Farmer	1,724	0.21		0.19	0.18	0.18	0.17	0.17
Nonfarmer	1,682	0.23		0.21	0.19	0.19	0.18	0.17
Significance[c]		*						
Wife's education								
None	320	0.07	0.10	0.11	0.12	0.13	0.14	0.14
Primary	1,706	0.22	0.23	0.23	0.23	0.23	0.22	0.22
Junior high	599	0.31	0.25	0.24	0.22	0.22	0.20	0.19
Senior high	705	0.24	0.18	0.17	0.15	0.15	0.14	0.13
College/univ.	211	0.11	0.08	0.08	0.06	0.06	0.05	0.05
Significance[c]		***	***	***	***	***	***	***
Wife's premarital work and living arrangements								
No paid work	815	0.11		0.14	0.15	0.14	0.16	0.15
Paid work at home	126	0.15		0.15	0.14	0.14	0.14	0.13
Nonhome work, live home, give parents money	1,099	0.22		0.19	0.18	0.18	0.17	0.16
Same, keep money	340	0.21		0.20	0.19	0.19	0.18	0.17
Nonhome work, live dorm, give parents money	856	0.32		0.26	0.23	0.24	0.21	0.20
Same, keep money	246	0.29		0.24	0.22	0.22	0.20	0.20
Significance[c]		***		***	**	***	*	
Who decided marriage								
Parents	1,023	0.10			0.10			0.13
Parents/couple	1,673	0.23			0.20			0.17
Couple	830	0.35			0.31			0.23
Significance[c]		***			***			***
How met future husband								
Relatives/matchmakers	1,375	0.12				0.11		0.13
Others	2,105	0.29				0.25		0.20
Significance[c]		***				***		***
Dating husband before marriage								
No date	830	0.05					0.06	0.08
Date—parental approval	1,965	0.23					0.20	0.19
Date—no parental approval	721	0.39					0.35	0.29
Significance[c]		***					***	***

Note: The dependent variable is coded as follows: 0, no; 1, yes. The data came from the 1986 island-wide survey of married women. All women whose parents were not alive and in Taiwan at the time of marriage were excluded from analysis.

[a] These are the observed proportions of the dependent variable within categories of the predictor variables.

[b] The adjusted proportions are predicted values on the dependent variable within each category of the predictor variable. The predicted values were estimated from logistic regression equations encompassing all of the variables included in each column as predictor variables.

[c] These rows designate statistical significance under the assumption of simple random sampling: * $= 0.05$; ** $= 0.01$; *** $= 0.001$.

show that all three mate selection variables maintain measurable effects even when they are entered simultaneously into the prediction of premarital sex and pregnancy. However, the pattern of dating appears to be a stronger determinant than mate introductions and choice. Even with full controls for all of the other variables, those who dated without parental permission are approximately four times as likely as those with no dating experience to report premarital sexual intimacy and pregnancy.

These data also suggest that changes in mate selection and dating between the early 1960s and the early 1980s can help to explain historical trends in premarital sexual intimacy and pregnancy. Looking at the marriage cohort variable, we see that between the early 1960s and the early 1980s the number reporting premarital sexual intimacy increased by 31 percentage points—from 9 to 40% (col. 2 of table 7.8). With controls for the wife's education, premarital work experience, and father's occupation, this difference is reduced to 26 percentage points (col. 4). When the mate selection and dating variables are added, the difference between the youngest and oldest cohorts is reduced to 19 percentage points (col. 8), with the dating variable alone accounting for most of this extra reduction (col. 7). All together, the full model predicting premarital sexual experience accounts for 12 of the 31 percentage point shift in premarital sexual experience between the early 1960s and the early 1980s—a reduction of nearly 40%.

For premarital pregnancy, there was a 24 percentage point increase (from 9 to 33%) between the early 1960s and early 1980s (table 7.9). This difference was reduced to 20 percentage points with the introduction of controls for the wife's education, her premarital work experience, and her father's occupation. By introducing mate selection and dating, this difference was reduced further to 15 percentage points. Thus, the full model explains 38% of the historical shift in premarital pregnancy during this time period—a fraction similar to that for the change in premarital sexual experience.

Although we can account for about one-third of the historical shift in premarital sexual and pregnancy experience, two-thirds of that historical transformation still remains unaccounted for by our rather extensive model. There must have been dramatic changes occurring in Taiwan that had important implications for premarital sexual behavior but were largely independent of the kinds of social and economic experiences of young women analyzed in this chapter. Another possibility is that measurement errors in the variables limit our ability to account for a larger fraction of the changes occurring in premarital sexual intimacy and pregnancy.

The data in tables 7.8 and 7.9 also suggest that who decided the marriage, dating, and how one meets her husband help account for some of the effect of premarital employment on premarital sex and pregnancy. When the dating and marriage arrangement variables are added to the models, the effects of the work and residence variables are substantially reduced. This suggests that one reason why women with nonhome work and residential experience before marriage have higher rates of premarital sex and pregnancy is their greater independence in the marriage market and more extensive dating experience.

Tables 7.8 and 7.9 also provide further information concerning the influence of education on premarital sexual intimacy and pregnancy. As noted above, the relationship between education and premarital sexual intimacy and pregnancy is clearly and strongly inverse-U-shaped when there are no controls for other variables. But this strong inverse-U relationship is sharply modified when controls are introduced.

Among the least educated women, especially those with no formal schooling, we see that the introduction of controls sharply adjusts upward their apparently low levels of premarital sexual experience and pregnancy. For example, controlling for marriage cohort increases the predicted percentage of women reporting premarital sex from 9 to 14% (col. 3 of table 7.8). Adding premarital work experience and father's occupation increases the percentage to 15%, while the number rises to 19% when the three mate selection and dating variables are added along with the other predictor variables (col. 8 of table 7.8). Similar adjustments to the percentage reporting premarital pregnancy among the women without formal schooling shifts the percentage from 7 to 14% (col. 8 of table 7.9).

On the high end of the educational continuum, the introduction of controls sharply decreases the already low observed premarital sex and pregnancy of the well-educated, especially those with a college education. With the full multivariate controls, the percentage of college-educated women reporting premarital sex decreases from 20 to 9% (table 7.8) and the percentage reporting a premarital pregnancy decreases from 11 to 5% (table 7.9). Thus, these controls transform the observed inverse-U relationship into an effect that is largely negative, although it still retains some of the inverse-U shape.

These results suggest several reasons why women with little or no education have low levels of premarital sex and pregnancy. First, this relationship is partially spurious; women with no formal education have low levels of premarital sex and pregnancy at least partially because they grew up during a period when these behaviors were relatively uncommon. Thus, if the more recent marriage cohorts included significant numbers of women without formal schooling, the experience of these cohorts with premarital sex and pregnancy would be greater than observed for the actual sample of women with no formal education.

Second, low educational levels can restrict the involvement of women in activities outside the family—both paid employment and residence in nonfamily living arrangements. Since exclusive involvement in family work and home living restrict premarital sex and pregnancy, women with little or no formal education have relatively low levels of premarital sex and pregnancy. Finally, as we saw earlier in this chapter, women with no formal educational experience tend to be excluded from choosing their own spouses and have little opportunity to date their future husbands, behaviors that are likely to foster premarital sex and pregnancy. Once all of these factors are taken into account, the predicted levels of premarital sex and pregnancy among the less-educated women are actually moderately high.

These three mechanisms can also explain why the low observed levels of premarital sex and pregnancy of most highly educated women are depressed even further once the multivariate controls are applied. These women tend to be among the more recent marriage cohorts and grew up when levels of premarital sexual intimacy were historically high. They also have more extensive opportunities for paid employment and high involvement in the mate selection and dating process—behaviors which frequently lead to high levels of premarital sex and pregnancy. Despite these characteristics, highly educated women have low levels of reported premarital sex and pregnancy, and their predicted levels become even lower when the other variables are adjusted. There are thus elements in high levels of education in Taiwan that limit premarital sexual intimacy and pregnancy.

Several features of Chinese culture and the ways in which young Taiwanese mature to adulthood may be helpful for understanding the restrictive influence of high educational attainments on premarital sex and pregnancy. Our earlier analyses (chap. 6) suggest that the great majority of reported experiences with sexual intercourse and pregnancy before marriage occur within the context of courtship and entrance into marriage. The completion of school is also an important prerequisite for thinking about marriage in the Chinese context today. Very few couples meet in school, and most marriages occur after the completion of schooling. Consequently, school attendance is a powerful inhibitor of entrance into the process of marriage (J. S. Chang 1990). Similarly, young women who are still in school also have lower rates of experiencing premarital sexual intercourse than do women of the same age who have discontinued school attendance (J. S. Chang 1990). As a result, high educational attainment tends to delay the initiation of serious courtship and premarital sexual intimacy until later in the lives of young women.

Of course, this delay of entrance into the marriage market is probably not the only explanation for the low levels of premarital sex and pregnancy among highly educated women, since all of the women included in these analyses had entered the marriage market and had, at least in principle, had the opportunity for premarital sexual intimacy. One possibility is that highly educated Taiwanese have shorter periods of courtship, allowing them less time for the development of sexual intimacy within the relationship. However, we know from other analyses (J. S. Chang 1990) that there are no educational differences in the length of the engagement period itself.

Another speculation concerning the reported low premarital sex and pregnancy of the well-educated focuses on birth control and the potential misreporting of sexual experience. It is likely that educated sexually active unmarried women would be more effective users of contraception than their less educated peers. The data provide some support for this idea as the differential between the women with the most and least education is somewhat larger for premarital pregnancy than for premarital sex (compare cols. 8 of tables 7.8 and 7.9). Well-educated women with an unplanned premarital pregnancy are also probably more likely than the less-educated to terminate the pregnancy through abortion. If premarital sexual experience resulting in a birth is more fully reported in surveys than premarital sexual experience that does not result in a birth, as we expect, the higher levels of contraceptive use and abortion among sexually active college-educated women could result in larger underestimates of sexual relations among the well-educated. As a result, the educational differential in premarital sex and pregnancy could be caused, at least in part, by differences in the use of contraception and abortion.

In an effort to gain further insights into the determinants of premarital sex, we disaggregated the opportunity for premarital sex into two time periods: before and after an engagement ceremony publicizing the marriage. This analysis first examined whether or not the woman experienced sexual intercourse before her engagement ceremony. The second part of the analysis examined premarital sexual experience occurring after an engagement ceremony among those who did not experience sexual intercourse before the ceremony.

This analysis revealed considerable continuity of influences before and after an engagement ceremony. The estimated parameters for the variables during the preceremony period are very similar to those for the period between an engagement ceremony and marriage (data not shown). Having an engagement ceremony does not modify substantially the nature of the causal forces operating.

Conclusions

The analyses reported in this chapter provide extensive support for the theoretical model underlying this research. The modes of organization experienced by young people during their growing-up years strongly influence how their marital arrangements are made, their dating activity, and their experience with premarital sexual intimacy and pregnancy. Experiences with activities organized outside the familial network are associated with young women wanting and having more say in the choice of their husbands, less involvement of the senior generation in making introductions of future spouses, and more experience with dating. In addition, the more involvement young people have in the mate selection and courtship process, the greater the prevalence of premarital sexual intimacy and pregnancy.

A consistent theme of this chapter is the overwhelming influence of education in the mate selection process. Overall, highly educated women want and have much more say in who they will marry, have more involvement in dating, and are less likely to meet their future husbands through the introductions of parents or matchmakers. Furthermore, these relationships are generally large and monotonic over the entire range of educational attainments from the least to the most highly educated. The effects of education also remain strong even when other important variables are controlled. The effects of education on premarital sex and pregnancy, however, are much more complex, the relationship being an inverse-U shape rather than monotonic. Premarital sex and pregnancy are highest among junior high graduates and lowest among college graduates and those without formal schooling.

While education is the most important determinant of the mate selection processes examined in this chapter, the occupation of the woman's father and her experience with nonfamily employment and living arrangements also have their own independent effects. Agricultural families have significantly more involvement than others in the marital arrangements of their daughters. Their daughters also date less than young women who do not grow up in farming households. The daughter's own involvement in employment outside the family unit also affects her marital arrangements—increasing her say in the choice of her husband, the extent of her dating activity, and the likelihood that she will experience premarital sex and pregnancy.

Perhaps the most important conclusion of this chapter is that the trends in farm background, education, and premarital nonfamilial employment and living arrangements take us a long way toward explaining the remarkable changes that have occurred in the mate selection process during the past several decades. As a group, this set of variables is able to explain about two-thirds of the historical change in the ways husbands are selected and in how husbands and wives are introduced to each other. Nearly three-fifths of the historical change in dating behavior can also be explained by these same variables. The unexplained part of these trends is probably due primarily to other factors that were not measured in the data sets available to us in this analysis.

Since education is such a powerful determinant of the mate selection process and since education has increased so dramatically across time, this one variable can account for much of the change observed in mate selection. By itself, education can account for nearly 50% of the time trends in marital arrangements, over 50% of the change in introductions, and nearly 40% of the dating trend. It can also account for nearly one-third of the observed trend in the mate selection preferences of unmarried women. These results indicate that the transformation of the modes of socialization and education in Taiwan is a major part of the story explaining the remarkable changes in marriage since World War II.

Interestingly enough, however, the increases in education, paid employment, and nonfarm residence can account for very little (10% or less) of the increase in premarital sex and pregnancy during recent years. This is because these variables have either a small or nonmonotonic influence on premarital sex and pregnancy. But changes in mate selection and dating can explain approximately one-third of the historical trends in premarital sex and pregnancy. Over the past several decades Taiwanese young people have become increasingly involved in dating and the mate selection process, and that has resulted in increased sexual intimacy before marriage. However, the increased involvement of young Taiwanese in the mate selection process is only part of the story about increased premarital sex and pregnancy. Unfortunately, explanation for the remaining part cannot be achieved within the bounds of the data available for the current analysis.

Eight

Trends in the Timing and Prevalence
of Marriage

H. S. Lin, M. L. Lee, and A. Thornton

Introduction

Marriage was a central event in the life courses of most Chinese men and women. This was particularly true for women, since in the Chinese social system unmarried females were viewed as temporary residents in their natal homes. It was only through marriage and acceptance into their husband's family that women were permanently integrated into the ancestral chain, ensuring acceptance and care both in this life and in the world to come (Ahern 1971; Freedman 1979; Hsu 1971; Wolf 1972; Wolf and Huang 1980). Marriage was also important for both men and women because it provided the opportunity to extend the family line into the future through childbearing. Failure to marry and have children was viewed in Chinese culture as the most serious breach of filial piety since it threatened the continuation of the family chain (Hsu 1971; Lang 1968). Consequently, early and universal marriage was encouraged, this imperative being particularly important for women (Pasternak 1989; van der Valk 1939).

The parent-run marriage system in Taiwan's past was very effective in bringing men and women together in matrimony. Marriage was very nearly universal for Taiwanese women at the beginning of this century, and most married while still teenagers. The vast majority of Taiwanese men also married but later in the life course.

The timing and prevalence of marriage in Taiwan have been greatly modified during the twentieth century. The new system of social, economic, and familial relations has delayed the advent of marriage for both men and women. Marriage timing for women has shifted from the late teens into the middle twenties, while marriage age for men has shifted from the early to the late twenties. While the great majority of men and women continue to marry, recent data suggest that there may be an emerging trend for some people to go through life without marrying.

Our discussion of changing nuptiality in Taiwan will begin by considering the prevalence of first marriage. Using marital status distributions derived from censuses and household registrations, we estimate the percentage of the population that has ever been married at specific ages. This provides an overall view of changes in first marriage across the century. We also examine age-specific rates of entrance into marriage, an approach that provides more detailed information about the precise timing of marriage changes and the ways in which those changes have differentially affected people at different points in the life course. Finally, we speculate about the future incidence of persons never marrying. We do so by extrapolating current first marriage rates into the future and examining their implications for the number of people who will never marry.

Prevalence of Marriage

A summary view of marriage change in twentieth-century Taiwan is provided by table 8.1, where the percentages of men and women who were ever married at different ages are listed for various years. The data from 1905 through 1980 are taken from Taiwan censuses, while the data for 1985 and 1990 come from the household registers. Switching from using the 1905 to 1980 censuses to the household registers for 1985 and 1990 introduces a slight data incomparability, since the percentages reported as ever married are slightly lower in the household registers than in the censuses. This inconsistency leads to overestimates of the decline in marriage occurring in the 1980s.[1]

As table 8.1 indicates, marriage in 1905 was universal and occurred at young ages among Taiwanese women. Large fractions of women married during their teenage years, and most had married before they reached 30. In fact, in 1905 47% of the women aged 15–19 had married; among those 20–24 the fraction was 92%. At ages 30 and above, the number of women who had been married was 99% or greater.[2]

Marriage began significantly later for men. In 1905, only one-tenth of the men aged 15–19 had ever been married; this number increased to nearly one-half for the men aged 20–24, a figure nearly matching the

1. Evaluation of the differences between the census and household register information is made possible by the availability of data from both sources in 1966, 1975, and 1980. In all three years the percentage ever married among women at ages over 30 was from 1 to 3 percentage points higher in the census. At the younger ages, however, the discrepancy was smaller, and for ages 15–19 was in the opposite direction.

2. The ages shown in table 8.1 were calculated as the number of complete years lived. These ages, thus, are generally one year less than the historical Chinese method of calculating age, which assigned a person the age of 1 at birth.

TABLE 8.1 Percentage Ever Married by Gender, Age, and Year

A. Women

Age	1905	1915	1920	1925	1930	1935	1956	1966	1970	1975	1980	1985	1990
15–19	47.3	34.6	31.6	29.4	32.6	28.1	11.4	8.6	7.1	5.5	5.3	3.1	2.5
20–24	91.6	87.6	85.6	84.4	86.3	83.0	70.6	59.5	49.6	43.3	41.5	33.5	25.6
25–29	98.2	96.8	96.2	96.2	96.1	95.9	95.2	92.9	91.2	85.9	82.7	76.5	68.0
30–34	99.2	98.6	98.0	98.3	98.0	97.7	97.8	98.1	97.7	97.4	94.3	90.6	87.7
35–39	98.8	99.2	98.6	99.0	98.8	98.4	98.5	98.9	98.8	98.7	97.9	94.3	92.5
40–44	99.3	99.4	99.0	99.2	99.2	98.9	98.7	99.1	98.8	99.1	98.8	96.7	94.5
45–49	99.6	99.6	99.3	99.0	99.4	99.3	99.0	99.1	98.8	99.2	99.1	97.4	96.2
50+	99.8	99.8	99.7	99.6	99.6	99.2	99.4	99.3	98.8	98.9	99.0	97.1	96.9

B. Men

Age	1905	1915	1920	1925	1930	1935	1956[a]	1966	1970	1975	1980	1985	1990
15–19	10.2	5.6	6.0	5.3	7.3	5.7		1.0	0.8	0.7	0.9	0.6	0.7
20–24	45.7	39.9	41.9	44.7	51.6	49.8		16.1	12.2	12.7	12.6	10.0	8.6
25–29	77.4	72.7	75.3	78.2	82.9	83.1		66.0	65.0	61.7	60.5	52.7	43.7
30–34	89.4	88.0	87.6	89.7	91.3	91.9		86.6	89.1	90.7	87.5	83.8	77.3
35–39	97.9	93.2	92.3	93.4	94.2	94.4		78.5	91.3	95.4	93.6	92.1	89.4
40–44	98.2	95.1	94.8	95.5	95.6	95.7		77.3	83.3	94.8	94.9	94.3	93.2
45–49	98.4	96.0	95.9	96.2	96.7	96.3		82.7	83.6	89.1	93.5	95.1	94.7
50+	96.8	97.0	97.0	97.4	97.6	97.0		91.3	91.8	90.7	85.9	88.5	90.8

Note: Data for 1905 through 1980 are from the censuses. Data for 1985 and 1990 are from the household registers.

[a]Data for 1956 are not included for men because of the exclusion of military men from the 1956 census reports.

TABLE 8.2 Ratio of Men to Women (times 100) by Year and Age

Age	YEAR											
	1905	1915	1920	1925	1930	1935	1966	1970	1975	1980	1985	1990
15–19	126	116	112	109	106	104	106	106	104	105	105	105
20–24	123	122	116	112	108	106	101	104	102	103	105	105
25–29	122	124	120	114	111	108	104	102	99	105	104	105
30–34	119	120	121	118	114	110	112	100	99	107	104	105
35–39	116	114	115	118	116	112	143	114	100	106	105	104
40–44	112	108	108	110	114	114	149	145	114	104	105	105
45–49	100	100	99	101	105	109	142	145	146	116	102	103
50+	73	73	73	75	77	81	108	114	120	129	123	115

Note: Data for 1905 through 1980 are from the censuses. Data for 1985 and 1990 are from the household registers.

percentage of women married at ages 15–19. This suggests an average gap of about five years in marriage ages between men and women in 1905. Marriage was much more prevalent among older men, reaching nine-tenths by ages 30–34. While the fraction of men who ever married was below that for women, marriage was still nearly universal for men at the turn of the century—including at least 95% of those who were 35 or older in 1905.

The prevalence of marriage by age and gender in Taiwan in 1905 was probably influenced by the unusual distribution of the population by gender at different ages. Table 8.2 shows a strong preponderance of men under age 45 in 1905, the number of men exceeding the number of women by 12 to 26%.[3] The surplus of men compared to women would have produced a marriage squeeze, making it easier for women than men to find a spouse and accounting, at least in part, for the young and universal marriage among Taiwanese women (Barclay 1954). Other researchers have shown that regional variations in the sex ratio in Taiwan were related to regional differences in the prevalence of marriage (Barrett 1985; Casterline 1980).

Marriage was nearly universal among men in Taiwan despite the imbalanced sex ratio. This probably was made possible, in part, by the wide age difference between men and women, an age gap which, in turn, may have been enlarged by the high ratio of men to women. High rates of widowhood and divorce also made many previously married women available for remarriage (see chap. 10). As a consequence of the high

3. Several factors could have contributed to this gender imbalance: high rates of male migration to Taiwan from the mainland; the larger number of males than females at birth; and young females having higher mortality than young males (Barclay 1954; Barrett 1985).

sex ratio and high rates of marital dissolution, 18% of the men marrying for the first time in 1906 married a divorced or widowed woman—a figure twice the percentage of new brides marrying a previously married man (Barclay 1954, 226).

The high prevalence of marriage among Taiwanese men and women at the beginning of the twentieth century contrasts sharply with Western European experience, where marriage propensities were considerably lower. Marriage took place earlier in Taiwan than in Western Europe in the same period. For example, over 90% of the Taiwanese women aged 20–24 in 1905 had been married, while the percentage married at the same ages in fifteen Western European countries studied by Hajnal ranged from 14 to 42%. Similarly among men, the 45% ever married at ages 20–24 in Taiwan was substantially higher than the 4–17% married among men of the same ages in Western Europe (Hajnal 1965, 102).

The universality of marriage in Taiwan also contrasts with Western Europe. Less than 1% of the women aged 45–49 in Taiwan in 1905 had never married, while 10 to 29% of women of the same ages in the Western European countries had not married. The fraction of young men in Western Europe who went through life without marrying was similar to that for Western European women (Hajnal 1965, 102).

The propensity to marry in Taiwan in 1905 also exceeded that in Eastern Europe—a region frequently noted for having substantially higher rates of marriage than Western Europe. The percentage of women married at ages 20–24 in six Eastern European countries studied by Hajnal (1965) ranged from 56 to 84%, less than the 90% of Taiwanese women aged 20–24 married in 1905. While marriage among older Eastern European women was nearly universal, the fraction never married was still slightly lower in Taiwan,

Although the universality and youthfulness of marriage in Taiwan at the turn of the century contrasted sharply with patterns in Western Europe, marriage in Taiwan was well within the range observed in Asia. Data from mainland China before World War II suggest that marriage may have been even more prevalent on the mainland than in Taiwan at the same time (Barclay et al. 1976; Barrett 1985). At the older ages marriage was nearly universal for both men and women on the mainland before World War II. Marriage on the mainland also appears to have occurred at younger ages; whereas 33% of women aged 15–19 and 86% of those aged 20–24 in Taiwan in 1930 had been married, from 38 to 52% of mainland women aged 15–19 and 92 to 94% of those 20–24 had been married at about the same time period.

Nearly universal marriage has also been reported in many other Asian populations, including Japan, Korea, India, and Turkey (Hajnal 1965; Smith 1980; Taeuber 1958). Although marriage prevalence was lower in some Asian countries than in Taiwan—for example, in Japan, the Philippines, and Sri Lanka—other Asian populations, including Korea and India, had even lower ages at marriage than Taiwan (Hajnal 1965; Smith 1980; Taeuber 1958). In Korea in 1930, 98% of the women aged 20–24 had been married, compared to 86% in Taiwan the same year. The prevalence of early marriage among men was also greater in Korea than Taiwan (Hajnal 1965). An even sharper contrast is with Bangladesh, where in 1975 70% of women aged 15–19 had been married, a figure considerably higher than that for Taiwan early in this century (Durch 1980).

There were significant trends in marriage in Taiwan between 1905 and World War II—trends which were different for men and women. While there was an overall trend toward a lower prevalence of marriage for women, marriage increased for men.

The data for women show persistent declines in the prevalence of marriage between the ages of 15 and 24 (table 8.1). From 1905 through 1935, the fraction of older teenagers who had ever been married declined from 47 to 28%, while the percentage married by their early 20s declined from 92 to 83%. This decline was most marked in the decade between 1905 and 1915. There were, however, no strong declines in the percentage married at ages 25 and older, as more than 95% of the women aged 25 and older had been married during all years before World War II. The near-universality of marriage at the older ages also continued; more than 99% of the women who were 45 and older had been married in all years through 1935. Of course, since the birth cohort of women over 45 in 1935 experienced their young adult years early in the century, when most married before age 25, it would have been difficult for subsequent changes in the social environment to have markedly reduced their marriage universality. Nevertheless, the data suggest that the important change for women during the years before World War II was an increase in age at marriage, with little or no decline in the universality of marriage. Furthermore, the increase in marriage ages only marginally affected the postponement of marriage into the late 20s.

The trends between 1905 and 1915 were similar for men and women, as the prevalence of marriage declined for both sexes. The decline for men was somewhat more pervasive across age groups than for women. However, after 1915 there was a sharp divergence in the prevalence of marriage between men and women, as the percentage of men aged 20 to 34 who had ever been married increased during the subsequent two decades. There was no increase at the older ages, which suggests that this change was primarily a decline in age at marriage without an accompanying increase in the universalism of male marriage. But the steady level of teenage marriage among men suggests that the decline in male ages at marriage did not extend below age 20.

The trends in marriage during the years before World War II were probably related to concurrent trends in the sex ratio of the population (Barclay 1954). As table 8.2 documents, the ratio of men to women between ages 15 and 34 generally declined over the years between 1905 and 1935. In fact, by 1935 the number of men relative to women between the ages of 15 and 24 had nearly declined to what one would expect on the basis of the sex ratio at birth, thereby ameliorating the marriage squeeze which had favored women in 1905. Consequently, the difficulty of locating a husband in this period probably increased while the problem of finding a wife probably declined, and this could have increased the marriage ages for women and decreased them for men.

The declining sex ratio and declines in mortality also reduced the need and possibility for single men to marry divorced or widowed women. Thus, the percentage of never-married men marrying divorced or widowed women declined from 18% in 1906 to 6% in 1935 while the percentage of new brides marrying widowed or divorced men declined from 9 to 6% (Barclay 1954, 226).

The increases in female age at marriage before World War II may also have been linked to changing distributions of marriage types. Early in this century large fractions of marital unions in Taiwan were matrilocal (uxorilocal) and "minor" rather than "major" marriages, but over the course of the prewar years the prevalence of major marriage increased (Barclay 1954; Wolf and Huang 1980).[4] Since women in minor and matrilocal marriages were, on average, younger when they married than those in major marriages, this change could have led to older female ages at marriage (Barclay 1954; Pasternak 1983, 1989; Wolf and Huang 1980). The shift toward major marriage would not have had the same effect for men since grooms in matrilocal marriages were generally older rather than younger than those in major marriages (Pasternak 1983; Wolf and Huang 1980).[5]

4. Parish and Whyte (1978) report that the practice of adopting future daughters-in-law (minor marriage) has disappeared in Kwangtung in mainland China as well.

5. A clear prediction of the effect of the shift toward major marriage for men's marriage ages is not possible because men in major marriages were older than those in minor marriages and younger than those in matrilocal marriage (see Wolf and Huang 1980 and Pasternak 1989).

Of course, the increase in major marriage may have been influenced by the changing gender composition of the population. As the relative number of men declined and their bargaining position in the marriage market improved, they may have become less willing to enter minor or matrilocal marriage (Barclay 1954). If true, the changing gender composition in Taiwan before World War II could have simultaneously led to more major marriage, younger male marriage, and delayed female marriage.

This analysis of the central role of the changing sex ratio in determining marriage trends suggests that there may have been no fundamental change in the marriage system of Taiwan before World War II. Instead, the trends in marital timing in those years may represent an adaptation of the system to the changing availability of men and women in the marriage market.[6] The history of marriage in Taiwan during the early decades of this century, as in other countries, including Australia (McDonald 1975), may largely be the story of difficulties of the marriage market in adjusting to an imbalance in the number of men relative to women—an imbalance that itself changed over these decades. While we cannot discount the possibility that other factors influenced marriage during these years, these conclusions suggest that the major transformation of marriage timing occurred after World War II rather than before.

The numerical balance between men and women in Taiwan was disturbed again following World War II—this time by the defeat of the Nationalist government on the mainland and the removal of the government and military to Taiwan. While there were many married couples in this migration, there were also a substantial number of unmarried young men in the military. This resulted in more men than women in the prime marrying years, a surplus greater than that in 1905. For those aged 35–49 in 1966, a group which would have been aged 18–32 in 1949, men exceeded women by more than 40% (table 8.2). These cohorts, with their inordinately high sex ratios at each successive age bracket, are also apparent in subsequent years (M. C. Chang 1990).

The influx of large numbers of single men into the population following World War II had an immediate and lasting influence on the marriage distribution of men. Among the cohorts of men directly involved in the postwar migration from the mainland—those 35–49 in 1966—the fraction remaining single was unusually high in every year. For example,

---

6. See Guttentag and Secord (1983) for an extended discussion of potential influences of the sex ratio on human behavior.

in 1966 only four-fifths of this group had married, a number significantly lower than that for any preceding or following cohort of men, and their low marriage prevalence persisted through subsequent years. These data suggest that large numbers of these military migrants never married—a conclusion supported by information gathered from elderly men at the end of the 1980s (Hermalin, Ofstedal, and Li 1991).

Since the influx of these men from the mainland produced a large surplus of men relative to women, one would expect it to lower marriage prospects for other men as well. The data are consistent with this, since the prevalence of marriage among men of all ages declined between 1935 and 1966.

The data for women, however, suggest caution in attributing the post-war marital decline among men to the marriage squeeze caused by the large in-migration of single men. One would expect the large surplus of men to create an unusually positive marriage market for women, causing female marriage to increase during these years. But the observed trend for women was in the opposite direction; the prevalence of marriage declined sharply over time. This suggests that there were other causal forces that counteracted the positive influence of the relatively small number of women on the prevalence of female marriage.

Several factors could have limited the influence of the large in-migration of single military men on female marriage prevalence. First, the Mainlanders had little access to local Taiwanese society; many came with no family members, which limited their access to marriageable Taiwanese women. Second, mandatory military service probably limited their ability to marry and thus decreased the competition for wives. Finally, a program of military service for Taiwanese men was initiated soon after the arrival of the Nationalist government. This removed many Taiwanese men from the marriage market, which helped negate the addition of Mainlander men.

The data in table 8.1 demonstrate that the economic and social changes occurring in Taiwan after World War II were accompanied by large declines in the prevalence of marriage, which continued for both men and women across the entire postwar period. The percentage of women married at ages 20–24 declined from 83% in 1935 to just 26% in 1990. Among men aged 25–29, the percentage married declined from 83% in 1935 to 44% in 1990.

While the data are not precise enough to pinpoint the exact timing of the historical decline in marriage, they indicate that the trend had begun by the 1956 census. In 1956 only 11% of the teenage women had been married—down from 28% of the same age group who had been married in 1935. The number of women married by ages 20–24 also declined, from 83 to 71% during the 1935–56 period. The decrease in marriage at these ages persisted through 1990.

Table 8.1 shows that the changes in the percentages ever married through 1980 were overwhelmingly the result of increases in age at marriage and not of an increase in the number who never married (also see Feeney 1991). The increase in marriage age is indicated in the declining percentage of both sexes married at every age below 30. Over time, the percentage of teenagers married declined first, followed by those 20–24, and then by those 25–29—reflecting the increase in the central marrying ages. However, at the same time that the prevalence of marriage was declining at ages below 30, the percentages of men and women aged 40–44 in 1980 who had ever married were very similar to the levels observed before World War II. Thus, despite the substantial increase in age at marriage, the trend before 1980 apparently represented only an increased postponement of marriage and not an increasing number of people never marrying.

Trends during the 1980s suggest that marriage may be less universal in the future. Between 1980 and 1990 there were steady, although small, decreases in the percentage married between the ages of 35 and 49. Between 1980 and 1990, the percentage of women aged 35–39 who had ever married decreased from 96.1 to 92.5%, while the decline among those 45–49 was from 97.4 to 96.2%.[7] These data suggest that nearly 4% of all Taiwanese women are now remaining single at least through their 40s, which marks a slight departure from the period before World War II.[8]

While it is too early to tell whether these recent changes represent only another upward shift in age at marriage or an increase in the number who never marry, one emerging possibility is that significant numbers of today's young adults may not marry. This would represent a shift in the centrality of marriage in the lives of Taiwanese men and women. Even if marriage remains almost universal, the continued upward shift in age at marriage means that substantial fractions of Taiwanese men and women will remain single during a large part of their early life

7. The data for these 1980–90 comparisons all come from the household register data in order to negate differences that were due to the incomparability between census and household register data. Thus, the data for 1980 in the text do not match those shown in table 8.1.

8. Note, however, that in 1980 the estimate of the percentage still single at ages 45–49 from the census was 0.9%, or 1.7 percentage points lower than the 2.6% estimate from the household register. If this 1.7 percentage point difference between data sources persisted through 1990, the percentage still single in the 1990 census would be only 2.1.

courses. We will return to the issue of changes in the universality of marriage in subsequent paragraphs.

Rates of Entrance into Marriage

Information about marriage change in Taiwan during the twentieth century can be obtained from the 1980 census, in which age at first marriage was ascertained for every woman and cross-tabulated by her current age. That cross-tabulation, which provides both current age and age at marriage by single years, permits calculation of annual age-specific probabilities of marriage for many years before 1980. These data allow more detailed insights concerning the exact timing of historical trends and the age groups most closely associated with those changes.

There are several factors that could produce bias in these data, including inaccurate recall of age at first marriage, differential mortality by age at first marriage, and differential calculations of marriage ages across birth cohorts. We evaluated the combined influence of these sources of bias using the 1980 census information to calculate alternative estimates of the percentage of women aged 15–19 and 20–24 who were married in the previous census years between 1920 and 1975. This was done by identifying the women in the 1980 census who would have been 15–24 at the census years and then ascertaining from their ages at marriage whether they had already been married then.

A comparison of these alternative estimates of previous marital status from the 1980 census with the estimates of marital status reported in table 8.1 reveals some systematic bias in the data (comparisons not shown). The alternative estimates derived from the 1980 census information underestimate the percentage of women ever married between 1920 and 1935; this discrepancy is greatest in 1920 and declines across the years to 1935. The alternative estimates from the 1980 census for 1956 are almost identical to those from the actual 1956 census, but beginning with the 1966 census the alternative estimates overestimate the actual percentage ever married, and these overestimates increase over the later years. Since the alternative 1980 calculations underestimate the prevalence of marriage in the more distant past and overestimate it for more recent years, they also underestimate the magnitude of the decline in marriage over time.[9]

9. In making these comparisons, we assumed that the reported ages at marriage were calculated by respondents using the Chinese counting system that assigns newborn babies an age of 1. In order to adjust this system to the Western procedure used in table 8.1, we subtracted one year from the reported ages. However, we suspect that many of the younger women reported their ages at marriage using the Western system. If so, this could help to

Despite these biases, the alternative estimates of the percentages of women married at ages 15–19 and 20–24 are generally consistent with those from table 8.1 in that they show dramatic declines in the prevalence of marriage in the twentieth century (data not shown). The declines in female marriage across the twentieth century are also apparent in the age-specific rates of first marriage estimated from the retrospective 1980 census data and shown in figure 8.1 for selected birth cohorts of Taiwanese women.[10] All the age-specific rates through age 21 decline with each successive birth cohort. The data in figure 8.1 are also consistent with table 8.1 in documenting that the declines in marriage were more marked for recent years than for earlier in the century. All these comparisons suggest that the age-specific marriage rates estimated from the retrospective 1980 data generally track the historical declines in marriage estimated from data collected at the time of occurrence.

However, figure 8.1 also reveals a second problem with these data—a tendency for women to report a disproportionate number of marriages at ages 20 and 25. Though there is a general tendency for observed marriage rates to increase monotonically from age 15 through the early 20s for all marriage cohorts, the rates around age 20 depart from this pattern, the observed marriage rates at age 20 being substantially higher than those at either age 19 or 21. In fact, for some cohorts the rates at age 20 are several times higher than the rates at the two adjoining ages. Although less marked, there is also a similar tendency for the same phenomenon to occur at age 25, with higher marriage rates at age 25 than at ages 24 and 26 for some of the cohorts.

This age heaping of marriage rates declines with time, the drop being most striking at age 20, where the spike in marriage rates drops substantially with each successive birth cohort and almost disappears by the

---

explain why the alternative estimates from the 1980 census overstated marriage for the young women. For those young women who reported their ages at marriage in Western years, our procedure of subtracting 1 from the reported age produced too low an age at marriage and too high a prevalence of marriage. Subtracting 1 from reported ages at marriage was probably more appropriate for the older women, since they were probably more likely to have used the Chinese counting system. It is not clear why the alternative estimates from the 1980 census underestimated marriage for the older women.

10. The marriage rates in figure 8.1 and all other figures derived from the 1980 census were calculated using reported ages at marriage with no adjustments made. Although we refer to the information in figure 8.1 as marriage rates, it is more technically correct to call them first marriage probabilities as labeled in the figure. These marriage probabilities were calculated by dividing the number of marriages occurring in a year by the number of women who had not previously married. We refer to these probabilities in the text as rates in order to facilitate exposition. This procedure is followed for figures 8.2–8.6 as well.

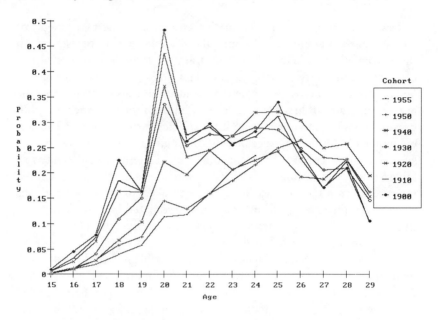

Figure 8.1   Age-specific first marriage probabilities for women by birth cohort.

youngest cohort. Similarly, the spike at age 25 is reduced among more recent birth cohorts. This age heaping, and its differential association with birth cohort, must be taken into account in considering the trends in first marriage rates derived from these data.[11]

Figures 8.2 through 8.6 show age-specific marriage probabilities for single years across most of the twentieth century. Consistent with the data in table 8.1, these data show a fairly steady decline in female mar-

11. Other researchers have reported a similar irregular pattern of age at marriage from both Taiwan and mainland China earlier in this century (Barclay et al. 1976; Coale 1971, 1977). These researchers, however, have emphasized the relative paucity of reported marriages at age 19 rather than the large number of marriages at age 20. One explanation of this pattern is that the numeral "9" has the same pronunciation in some Chinese dialects as the word used for "dog," which would make people reluctant to report that age at marriage (Barclay et al. 1976; Coale 1977). But Barrett (1985) argues that this pattern was neither general in Taiwan before World War II nor existent in recent data from the mainland. For our data from the 1980 Taiwan census greatest caution must be exercised in interpreting trends in marriage rates at ages 19, 20, and 21, since those are the most affected by the age heaping of reported marriage ages. More specifically, since age heaping declines over birth cohorts, the trend lines for age 20 will be biased toward representing a steeper decline in marriage than actually occurred, while the trend lines for ages 19 and 21 will be biased toward showing less decline.

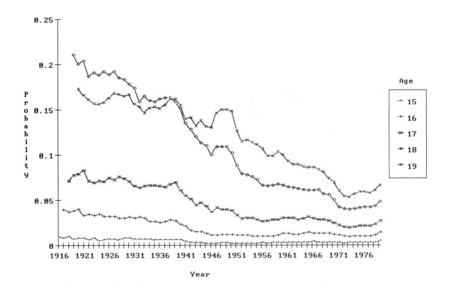

Figure 8.2 Age-specific first marriage probabilities for women by year, ages 15–19.

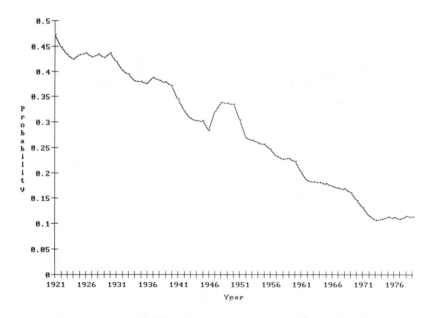

Figure 8.3 Probability of first marriage for women at age 20 by year.

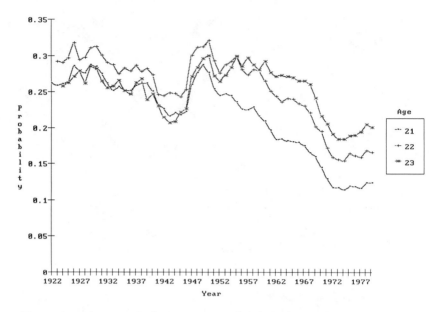

Figure 8.4 Age-specific first marriage probabilities for women by year, ages 21–23.

Figure 8.5 Age-specific first marriage probabilities for women by year, ages 24–25.

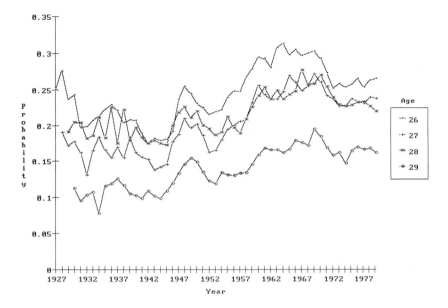

Figure 8.6   Age-specific first marriage probabilities for women by year, ages 26–29.

riage rates across the entire period before World War II. This reduction appears to be fairly general at all ages through about age 25, but not at older ages.

The data in figures 8.2 through 8.6 also provide an important new insight not available from table 8.1: World War II had a significant disruptive effect on the transition to marriage in Taiwan. Although female marriage had been declining for many years before World War II, the war brought further declines in marriage rates so that many of the age-specific time series hit new historical lows at the end of the war. The effect of World War II was felt all across the life span, as the rates for virtually all ages from 15 through 29 were strongly affected during this period.

There was a noticeable marriage boomlet immediately after World War II. Marriage rates increased at virtually every age, returning many of the age-specific marriage propensities back to their prewar levels. However, the postwar marriage boomlet up through age 20 was short-lived, and by the early 1950s marriage rates at these younger ages had returned to the levels recorded at the end of World War II. The postwar boomlet appears to have been more powerful at the older ages; even though marriage propensities at these ages also declined in the early 1950s, they remained generally higher than at the end of World War II. The postwar boomlet apparently was a partial compensation for the low marriage rates during World War II, since those who postponed marriage during the war apparently married more rapidly when the war ended.

The wartime decline in marriage and the subsequent marriage boomlet undoubtedly influenced childbearing during these years. As documented in chapter 3, fertility rates during and after World War II declined and then increased in a swing remarkably parallel to the trends in marriage. The marital decline during the war probably reduced the exposure of women to childbearing, while the subsequent marriage boom produced increased numbers of children.

Despite the marriage boomlet following World War II, teenage marriage rates during the early 1950s fell below the levels observed during the war (fig. 8.2). The extent and rapidity of this decline in the early 1950s suggest that the decline in living standards after the war may have depressed the rate of marriage formation among young people.

However, the recovery of the economy in the 1950s and 1960s did not reverse the low marriage rates among teenagers. Instead, there was a continuing decline in teenage marriage rates across the 1950s, a decline that continued into the 1960s and 1970s and also occurred among women aged 20 and 21. Consequently, the 1979 marriage rates through age 21 were very low when judged by historical standards (figs. 8.2–8.4).

While marriage rates at the younger ages declined steadily during the middle 1950s, marriage rates increased from ages 22 through 29 (figs. 8.4–8.6). The increase in marriage rates at ages 22 and 23 lasted for only a few years and was then followed by a long-term decline (fig. 8.4). The increase in rates at ages 24–25 persisted only into the early 1960s, while the increase at ages 26–29 persisted until the late 1960s and then declined (figs. 8.5 and 8.6).

The temporary increases in marriage rates among women 22–29 during the 1950s and 1960s probably represent a response to earlier declines in marriage rates at younger ages. The group eligible to marry after postponing marriage at the younger years then included many of the most marriageable people in the population, namely those who would have married at younger ages in earlier times. Marriage rates at these ages actually increased as this group rapidly entered marriage after their earlier postponements.

The postponement of marriage became so extensive by the end of the 1960s that the rates of marital formation declined at all ages up through

TABLE 8.3 Age-Specific First-Marriage Rate (times 1,000) by Gender, Age, and Year

A. Women

Age	1980	1981	1982	1983	1984	1985	1986	1987	1988	1989
15–19	21	21	18	15	13	12	11	10	10	11
20–24	160	153	137	127	113	108	96	86	90	87
25–29	303	299	266	272	257	254	229	229	233	226
30–34	135	132	124	124	114	109	110	112	121	124
35–39	43	49	57	55	49	47	47	46	44	42
40–44	23	25	33	33	24	19	25	22	20	20
45–49	16	17	22	21	16	11	14	12	9	9

B. Men

Age	1980	1981	1982	1983	1984	1985	1986	1987	1988	1989
15–19	4	4	3	3	3	2	2	2	2	2
20–24	47	46	42	38	33	30	27	24	24	25
25–29	263	248	214	207	186	179	158	150	152	146
30–34	280	261	232	219	202	199	183	176	181	175
35–39	85	86	87	94	93	90	87	82	81	81
40–44	37	37	39	41	36	31	32	33	33	38
45–49	22	19	20	21	20	19	17	18	19	17

Note: Data from household registration information.

29.[12] However, the declines at the older ages appear to have leveled off during the later 1970s.

Our analysis of age-specific marriage rates extends into the 1980s, using data from the household registration system. Those data, reported in table 8.3, include information for men as well as women. They indicate that marriage rates continued to decline from 1980 through 1989 for women younger than 30. In fact, between 1980 and 1989 the marriage rate at ages 20–24 fell by 46% for women. And at ages 25–29 the decline during the same time period was about one-fourth.

Table 8.3 also shows that the trends for men during the 1980s were very similar to those for women. Male marriage rates declined at all ages up through 34. Furthermore, these declines were very substantial, reaching nearly one-half for men in their 20s.

12. Casterline (1980) used a sample of household registration records to estimate age-specific marriage rates for ages 18 through 25 for the 1956 through 1974 period. Casterline's conclusions are generally consistent with those reached above, the most notable exception being his conclusion that marriage rates at ages 18 and 19 plateaued or rose in the middle 1960s. However, data in table 8.1 for this same time period indicate that the percentage of women 15–19 not yet married increased during this period, which would be consistent with the conclusions we reached in the text about teenage marriage trends in the 1960s.

Another indication of the increasing age at marriage is the distribution of first marriages by the ages of the bride and groom in 1989 (Ministry of the Interior 1990). In that year the median age of first marriage was 25.4 for women and more than a quarter of first marriages occurred after age 27 (data not shown). Similarly for men, the median age at first marriage in 1989 was 28.1 and one-quarter of their first marriages occurred after age 30. As recently as 1980, the median age at first marriage was 23.5 for women and 27.1 for men (Ministry of the Interior 1981).

Attitudes and values concerning marriage timing have been changing along with marriage behavior. These changes are documented in two series of cross-sectional surveys in Taiwan—one of unmarried women aged 18–29 and the other of married women aged 20–39. In the surveys of unmarried women, conducted in 1971, 1978, and 1984, respondents were asked, "What do you feel is the best age for a young woman to marry?" The mean preferred age at marriage, which was 24.2 in 1971, increased to 24.8 in 1978 and to 25.2 in 1984, an increase of one year across the thirteen-year period between the first and last surveys.

In each of the surveys of married women, conducted in 1973, 1980, and 1986, respondents were asked, "What do you think is the best age for a girl to get married these days?" In 1973 the mean age at marriage given by these married women was 23.1, and this number increased to 24.0 in 1980 and to 24.6 in 1986. These data indicate that actual and ideal ages at marriage were changing in parallel directions during this period.

We noted in the beginning of this chapter that Taiwanese marriages during the early years of this century were generally within a larger Asian pattern of young and universal marriage. Despite Taiwan's substantial increases in age at marriage, the island's marriage prevalence is still similar to that in several other Asian populations, including Korea, Japan, Singapore, and Hong Kong, which also experienced increases in age at marriage (United Nations 1989). As a result, Taiwan and these other East Asian societies now have a significantly lower prevalence of marriage than many other Asian populations, including India, the Philippines, Nepal, Pakistan, and Bangladesh (United Nations 1989). This has occurred despite some declines in marriage in many of these other Asian populations as well (Smith 1980). Marriage among young adults also continues to be less prevalent in Taiwan than in mainland China, where age at marriage has also increased (Barrett 1985; United Nations 1989; Whyte and Parish 1984).

The impressive increases in age at marriage in Taiwan have also changed marital comparisons with Europe and North America. Although marriage prevalence among young adults was persistently higher in Taiwan than in many Eastern European countries during the early 1900s, the prevalence of marriage under age 25 in many Eastern European countries in the mid-1980s was much higher than that in Taiwan. For example, while two-thirds of Taiwanese women aged 20–24 in 1985 had never been married, the comparable numbers during the 1980s for Czechoslovakia, Hungary, Poland, and Yugoslavia ranged from 36 to 46% (calculated from United Nations 1989).[13] Marriage among men below age 30 was also significantly lower in Taiwan than in these Eastern European populations.

The substantial increases in age at marriage in Taiwan brought the prevalence of marriage at young ages into the range observed for Western Europe and North America—societies long known for their delayed marriage. For men under age 30 and women under 25 the fraction still single in Taiwan in the middle to late 1980s was similar to those in France and Italy, and at these ages marriage prevalence was even lower in Taiwan than in the United Kingdom, Canada, Belgium, East Germany, and the United States. However, several Western and Northern European countries, including Denmark, Finland, West Germany, the Netherlands, Norway, Sweden, and Switzerland, had smaller fractions married at these ages than Taiwan (United Nations 1989).

While marriage prevalence during the earliest years of young adulthood in Taiwan is now squarely within the Northern and Western European pattern, the prevalence of marriage at the older ages remains higher in Taiwan. As noted earlier, marriage has remained nearly universal at older ages in Taiwan—a phenomenon that separates Taiwan from Western populations. For example, in 1985, 94% of women in Taiwan aged 35–39 had been married, a number equaled by only two of the Western populations listed above, namely Belgium and East Germany. The prevalence of marriage at the older ages in Taiwan more resembles that in Eastern Europe.

Potential Increases in the Number Never Marrying

To assess the potential decline in the universality of marriage we used life table procedures and the 1989 age-specific marriage rates (table 8.3) to estimate the percentage of people who would remain single at age

13. In the middle to late 1970s the comparable percentages in Bulgaria, Romania, and the Soviet Union ranged from 28 to 36% (calculated from United Nations 1989).

50 if those marriage rates continued indefinitely into the future. These calculations show that if a hypothetical cohort were to experience a lifetime of marrying at the 1989 rates, 7% of the women and 9% of the men would remain single at age 50.[14]

These estimates of singleness at age 50 are nearly double the percentage single at ages 45–49 in 1990, suggesting a considerable potential for continued increases in the percentage never marrying. Of course, marriage rates may increase in the future so that the percentage single at age 50 may remain significantly lower than the 7–9% implied by the synthetic cohort estimates using the 1989 marriage rates. However, it is probably more likely that marriage rates will continue to decline in the future. If this happens, the 7–9% projected to remain single would be a significant underestimate of the percentage who will never marry. If there were a permanent across-the-board decline of 20% in age-specific marriage rates from their 1989 values, the number of women and men remaining single at age 50 would increase to 12 and 14%, respectively, a plausible projection given the history of declining marriage rates.[15] These estimates, therefore, suggest the distinct possibility that significant numbers of Taiwanese men and women will never marry.

Taiwan is not the only East Asian population facing a potential decline in the universalism of marriage. Marriage was nearly universal in Japan at the beginning of this century but has since declined somewhat (Feeney and Saito 1985). Recent estimates project that as many as 8% of Japanese women may never marry (Feeney 1990; Feeney and Saito 1985). There is also serious speculation that there will be increases in the number never marrying in Singapore (Cheung 1988, 1990).

A substantial increase of singleness in Taiwan would probably have many significant ramifications for social relationships. Of great importance would be the exclusion of many women from participation in the family chain linking the ancestors, the living, and future generations. Childlessness would also increase for both men and women, which would isolate them from the advantages of parenthood both in this life and in the hereafter. It is also likely that these negative consequences of

---

14. These estimates assume no mortality. Also note that these estimates of the percentage remaining single at age 50 using 1989 data are substantially higher than Feeney's (1991) estimates of the percentage who never marry based on 1988 estimates derived using a different methodology. We have not yet determined the source of the difference between our estimates and those of Feeney.

15. This assumed 20% further decline is completely arbitrary and was chosen entirely for the purpose of illustrating the effect of potential further declines in age-specific marriage rates.

singleness would prevent the number never marrying from increasing rapidly.

Summary

The material presented in this chapter has documented impressive changes in the timing and prevalence of marriage in Taiwan during the twentieth century. At the beginning of this century marriage was both universal and young—with the prevalence among women enhanced and the prevalence among men depressed by the significant surplus of males. During the years before World War II the sex ratio became more balanced and the prevalence of marriage increased for men and decreased for women. Thus, the main story of trends in the prevalence and timing of marriage in Taiwan before World War II appears to be the adjustment of the marriage market to the changing balance of the numbers of men and women. The decline in matrilocal and minor marriage and the increase in major marriage may also have had an influence on marital timing trends before World War II.

World War II had a significant but temporary effect on marriage in Taiwan. Marriage rates fell during the war years but increased for a short period after the war. These swings in marriage apparently resulted in a similar trend in childbearing.

The influx of many young single military men from the mainland in the late 1940s and early 1950s again upset the numerical balance between the sexes, depressing the marriage market for men so that many of these Mainlanders never married. While this influx should have facilitated women's marriages, there is no evidence of general increases in female marriage after the influx of the Mainlanders to Taiwan.

Despite the favorable marriage market for women during most of the years following World War II, marriage rates have significantly declined for both women and men. The declines in marriage between 1950 and 1990 have been so substantial that many young men and women now spend a significant part of young adulthood as single persons. There may even be an emerging trend toward remaining single well into the middle ages—or even toward never marrying—and there is no evidence that these trends toward lower marriage prevalence have begun to stabilize.

These trends indicate a formidable restructuring of marriage formation in Taiwan during the past four decades. While the declines in marriage in the 1950s may have been due to the economic disruptions of World War II, the sustained declines of subsequent decades probably were the result of the economic and social forces transforming the island.

These were years of rapid industrialization and urbanization, income growth, educational expansion, and increasing contacts with other societies, particularly those of the West. As we argued in chapter 4, there are many reasons to believe that these economic and social changes have led to later marriage.

The strength of the social and economic forces depressing marriage in Taiwan during recent decades is very impressive because the surplus of men relative to women across all these years alone should have increased the prevalence of female marriage. Those social and economic forces apparently were strong enough both to negate a demographically driven increase in female marriage and to produce a substantial decline in marriage. An evaluation of the precise forces causing these recent changes in marriage is the subject of the next chapter.

Nine

Determinants of Historical Changes in Marital Timing

A. Thornton, H. S. Lin, J. S. Chang, and L. S. Yang

Recent changes in the timing and prevalence of marriage in Taiwan occurred during the same time period as the social and economic transformation of the island. Taiwan has changed from a rural agricultural society with low levels of economic production and consumption to an urban industrialized society with a rapidly expanding standard of living. Educational levels have expanded dramatically, and Taiwan has been integrated into the world economy, wherein it has had substantial contact with Western societies and their different patterns of family life.

Our thesis is that the temporal linkage between the extensive changes in the timing and prevalence of marriage and the social and economic change in Taiwan was not coincidental. In chapter 4 we noted many theoretical reasons to believe that pressures toward delayed marriage in Chinese populations would be associated with increases in educational attainment, the shift from rural and agricultural economic organization to an urban industrial economy, and the change from family employment to involvement in the paid labor force. We also suggested that contact with Western societies and their different family patterns, including later ages at marriage and more people never marrying, might also provide an impetus toward a decline in marriage in Taiwan. All these forces have probably combined to produce the recent changes in the timing and prevalence of marriage in Taiwan.

Prior research confirms this interpretation of Taiwanese marriage trends. Barclay (1954) has shown that the prevalence of marriage was higher in rural areas than in cities during the Japanese colonial period, and Casterline (1980) has shown the extension of this pattern into the second half of the century. Casterline also suggested that the marital changes occurring in the 1961–76 period began first in areas geographically proximate to cities.

Education has played a major role in explaining marriage trends in

Taiwan. Using decomposition techniques, Freedman and Casterline (1979) estimated that at least two-thirds of the decline in the prevalence of marriage among young adult women between 1966 and 1976 could be attributed to changes in education. Casterline (1980), using aggregate-level areal data to study the determinants of marriage in Taiwan between 1961 and 1976, identified female education as an extremely powerful predictor of nuptiality—strongly related to both marriage and marital change.

Casterline also reported relationships between nonagricultural employment and marriage. However, the relationship of marriage with nonagricultural employment was stronger for men than for women. Female employment had a very weak association with marriage, which may have been due in part to a deficient measurement of women's employment. Casterline also found that levels of child mortality and the ratio of men to women influenced marriage levels.

In this chapter we provide new information on the determinants of marital timing in Taiwan. We evaluate the empirical importance of several theoretical predictors of marriage by estimating models of marriage preferences and behavior and examining the extent to which these determinants of marriage can account for the dramatic transformation of Taiwanese marriage in recent decades. To investigate these questions, we use information about the marriage behavior and preferences of multiple birth and marriage cohorts of Taiwanese women interviewed in our series of surveys over the past three decades.

Though our data lack measures of some theoretically appropriate variables, we have indicators of several pertinent factors, including educational attainment, city residence experience, and position in the economic structure, with particular emphasis upon labor force participation. By estimating the effects of each of these factors on individual marital preferences and behavior, we can better understand which ones most influence marriage formation. To do this we estimated several multivariate models predicting the rate of marriage, age at marriage, and desired marital timing.

We also examined the extent to which historical trends in educational attainment, rural-urban residence, labor force experience, and residential patterns could account for the observed changes in actual and desired marital timing. As outlined in chapter 1, we did this by comparing historical trends in marriage preference and behavior in equations that control for the relevant social and economic predictors of marriage with historical trends estimated without controls. The differences between these two sets of estimated historical effects reflect the amount of historical change that can be explained by the included social and economic determinants of marriage.

To analyze the determinants of marital timing we relied heavily on our two series of island-wide surveys—both the surveys of married women and those of young unmarried women. We maximized the sample sizes and historical coverage in both data series by pooling the multiple individual-level data sets. We also utilized information from a panel study of young women who were interviewed in both 1971 and 1978.

These analyses assume that educational attendance occurs prior to marriage—that education influences marriage timing rather than marriage influencing educational achievements. In Western societies, where there is great potential for marriage and childbearing to truncate school attendance, this assumption has been seriously questioned. Such reciprocal influences of marriage on education may also be possible in Taiwan, but probably at a minor level since Taiwan's cultural customs place great emphasis upon education and the importance of finishing school before marriage. As chapter 6 documents, relatively few Taiwanese couples meet at school. Taiwanese women also tend to finish school before they marry and rarely truncate marriage or reenter school for more education after marriage. Lin (1987) reports that very few of the women in the 1980 survey of married women had a marital age below that at which they were likely to graduate from their highest educational level, while most married at an age substantially higher than when they had left school. Lin (1988) also reported that only a few of the young married women participating in the 1971 island-wide survey were still attending school. These findings validate our confidence about the causal priority of educational attainment—a confidence that is reinforced by data from a panel study which will be presented later in this chapter.

We begin our discussion of the determinants of marital timing by looking at subjective indicators. As noted in the previous chapter, both the married women's and young women's surveys asked respondents for their views about the best ages for a woman to marry. In analyzing these variables, we used the survey period as our indicator of historical time because the subjective views of ideal marital timing refer to current ideas about marriage rather than to the women's ideas at the time of their marriage.

The women participating in the surveys of married women conducted in 1973, 1980, and 1986 were asked, "What do you think is the best age for a girl to get married these days?" Table 9.1, which summarizes our analysis of those data, provides strong support for several of our hypotheses about the determinants of individual views of the best timing

TABLE 9.1 Multivariate Analysis of Women's Desired Age at Marriage, 1973–86 Surveys

	N (1)	Unadjusted Means[a] (2)	Adjusted Means[b]				
			(3)	(4)	(5)	(6)	(7)
Year of survey							
1973	5,487	23.1	23.1	23.3	23.3	23.3	23.3
1980	3,800	24.0	24.0	24.0	24.0	24.0	24.0
1986	3,187	24.7	24.7	24.4	24.4	24.5	24.5
Eta²/beta²	—	0.136	0.127	0.065	0.072	0.074	0.075
Significance[c]		***	***	***	***	***	***
Wife's father's occupation							
Farmer	6,512	23.5	23.5	23.7	23.7	23.7	23.7
Nonfarmer	5,451	24.2	24.1	23.9	23.9	23.9	23.9
Eta²/beta²	—	0.039	0.029	0.004	0.005	0.002	0.002
Significance[c]		***	***	***	***	***	***
Wife's education							
None	2,157	22.8	—	23.1	23.3	23.2	23.4
Primary	6,767	23.5	—	23.6	23.7	23.6	23.7
Junior high	1,477	24.4	—	24.2	24.1	24.2	24.1
Senior high	1,523	25.1	—	24.8	24.4	24.7	24.4
College/univ.	547	25.7	—	25.4	24.8	25.2	24.8
Eta²/beta²	—	0.188	—	0.111	0.045	0.089	0.045
Significance[c]		***		***	***	***	***
Husband's education							
None	842	22.7	—	—	23.3	—	23.4
Primary	5,695	23.3	—	—	23.6	—	23.6
Junior high	1,915	23.8	—	—	23.8	—	23.8
Senior high	2,486	24.4	—	—	24.1	—	24.1
College/univ.	1,523	25.1	—	—	24.3	—	24.2
Eta²/beta²	—	0.139	—	—	0.024	—	0.017
Significance[c]		***			***		***
Rural/urban living experience							
Always farm	4,012	23.2	—	—	—	23.5	23.6
Farm now/been in city	1,510	23.9	—	—	—	23.7	23.7
City now/been on farm	3,687	24.0	—	—	—	23.9	23.9
Always in city	3,134	24.2	—	—	—	24.0	24.0
Eta²/beta²	—	0.052	—	—	—	0.013	0.011
Significance[c]		***				***	***
Unadjusted R^2	—	—	0.165	0.243	0.250	0.262	0.271

Note: The dependent variable is the woman's desired age at marriage. The data came from 1973, 1980, and 1986 island-wide surveys of married women.

[a] These are the observed means on the dependent variable within categories of the predictor variables.

[b] The adjusted means are predicted values on the dependent variable within each category of the predictor variables. The predicted values were estimated from a multiple classification analysis (dummy variable regression), including all of the variables in each column as predictor variables.

[c] These rows designate statistical significance under the assumption of simple random sampling: * = 0.05; ** = 0.01; *** = 0.001.

for marriage. As expected, women with farm backgrounds reported lower preferred ages of marriage than those from nonfarm origins, with an observed difference of about seven-tenths of a year. This difference declines to one-fifth year when controls for interview year and education are introduced, with much of the reduction attributable to the inclusion of wife's education. Thus, a substantial part of the effect of farm background on ideal age at marriage operates through the wife's education, since farm-reared women are usually less educated, which, in turn, leads them to favor lower ages at marriage.

Women with mixed rural and urban experience preferred higher ages at marriage than those who had always lived on farms. Women with mixed rural-urban experience had an average desired age at marriage of 23.9 or 24.0, about three-fourths of a year higher than the average of 23.2 years for women with continuous farm experience. Women with continuous city experience had an even higher average preferred age at marriage of 24.2. These differentials are reduced, but not eliminated, with the very extensive controls used in the multivariate equations (table 9.1).

The effect of education on marital timing preferences is particularly powerful, since without controls the differential between women with the least and most formal educational experience is almost 3 years. With father's occupation and the year of survey controlled, the difference is still 2.3 years, and with all the variables in table 9.1 controlled, the difference in desired age at marriage between the most and least educated remains at 1.4 years (cols. 4 and 7 of table 9.1).

Husband's education also is strongly related to the wife's beliefs about ideal marital timing. Without controls for other variables the wives of men with the highest education reported a mean desired age at marriage of 25.1, compared to a mean of 22.7 for women married to men with no formal education. This differential is only slightly below that observed for the wife's own education. While the effect of the husband's education is dramatically reduced by the multivariate controls, including the wife's own education, husband's education still has an effect after controlling for the other variables (col. 7 of table 9.1).

Several other variables, including work experience before marriage and premarital living arrangements, were also considered. With controls for survey year, father's occupation, and education, they displayed only small net effects on the marriage timing variable and only marginally added to the explanation of the trends in preferred marriage ages.

How well does this individual-level model of preferred marriage ages account for changes in marital timing attitudes between 1973 and 1986?

Column 2 of table 9.1 shows that ideal age at marriage increased from 23.1 in 1973 to 24.0 in 1980 and finally to 24.7 in 1986, an increase of 1.6 years over the entire period of thirteen years. Taking into account education and farm background reduces the difference between 1973 and 1986 from 1.6 to 1.1 years (col. 4). Note that this reduction is entirely due to education: there is still a difference of 1.6 years between the earliest and latest survey when only the wife's father's occupation is controlled (col. 3). The addition of the other variables into the equations does not further reduce the historical time effect (cols. 5–7). Thus, the range of variables included here can account for about one-third of the total observed change in desired age at marriage between 1973 and 1986 (reducing it from 1.6 to 1.1 years). Of course, while these individual-level variables can account for a substantial fraction of the change in desired age at marriage, they also fail to explain much of that trend.

Further insights into the determinants of desired age at marriage come from data collected from both single and married women in Taiwan in 1971, 1978, and 1984. In those surveys, women were asked, "What do you feel is the best age for a young woman to marry?" Table 9.2 provides an analysis of the data from all three surveys, with separate panels provided for married and unmarried women. Table 9.3 provides a more detailed investigation of the 1978 and 1984 data, limited to women still single at the time of the surveys.[1]

Looking first at table 9.2, which summarizes all three surveys, we see a strong confirmation of the importance of education as a determinant of preferred marital timing. For the total sample of women in 1971 and 1984, we observe a 3-year difference in preferred age at marriage between those with the lowest and those with the highest education, and that relationship is reduced only about four-tenths of a year when the survey year is controlled (col. 3).

As one would expect, the association between education and preferred age at marriage is smaller when married and single women are considered separately. Nevertheless, for both single and married samples, the average difference in preferred age at marriage between those with the least and those with the most formal education is between 2.2 and 2.8 years. These differentials are reduced to 1.9 and 2.3 years, respectively,

1. All of the surveys drew comparable samples of single women, which makes it possible to study the preferences of single women at all three time points. The samples of married women in 1971 and 1984 were also comparable with each other. However, the 1978 married sample was not comparable to the other two years, which prevents making comparisons of this sample with the others. See appendix A for more details concerning the designs of the respective data collections.

TABLE 9.2 Multivariate Analysis of Desired Age at Marriage from the 1971, 1978, and 1984 Young Women's Surveys

	ALL WOMEN[a]			MARRIED WOMEN[a]			UNMARRIED WOMEN[b]		
	N (1)	Unadjusted Means (2)	Adjusted Means (3)	N (4)	Unadjusted Means (5)	Adjusted Means (6)	N (7)	Unadjusted Means (8)	Adjusted Means (9)
Year of survey									
1971	3,532	23.5	23.8	1,984	22.9	23.1	1,548	24.2	24.4
1978	—	—	—	—	—	—	698	24.8	24.8
1984	2,508	24.8	24.5	1,300	24.4	24.1	1,208	25.2	25.0
$Eta^2/beta^2$		0.140	0.042		0.184	0.081		0.088	0.032
Significance		***	***		***	***		***	***
Respondent's education									
None	450	22.5	22.8	394	22.4	22.7	63	23.4	23.7
Primary	2,539	23.4	23.5	1,732	23.2	23.3	957	24.0	24.1
Junior high	871	24.2	24.0	519	24.0	23.8	471	24.4	24.3
Senior high	1,532	24.9	24.7	505	24.7	24.3	1,321	25.0	24.9
College/univ.	647	25.5	25.4	134	25.2	25.0	641	25.6	25.6
$Eta^2/beta^2$		0.260	0.185		0.196	0.102		0.181	0.135
Significance		***	***		***	***		***	***
Unadjusted R^2			0.296			0.263			0.209

Note: The dependent variable is the woman's desired age at marriage.

[a]The sample includes women aged 18–29 in 1971 and 1984 Young Women's Surveys.

[b]The sample includes unmarried women aged 18–29 in 1971, 1978, and 1984 Young Women's Surveys.

TABLE 9.3 Multivariate Analysis of Desired Age at Marriage from the 1978 and 1984 Young Women's Surveys (single women only)

	N (1)	Unadjusted Means (2)	ADJUSTED MEANS		
			(3)	(4)	(5)
Year of survey					
1978	698	24.8	24.9	24.9	24.9
1984	1,208	25.2	25.2	25.2	25.2
Eta²/beta²		0.017	0.016	0.007	0.009
Significance		***	***	***	***
Father's occupation					
Farmer	549	24.8	24.9		25.0
Self/family employed	573	25.2	25.3		25.2
Employed by others	749	25.2	25.1		25.1
Eta²/beta²		0.022	0.012		0.003
Significance		***	***		***
Father's education					
Illiterate	149	24.7	24.8		25.0
Literate	195	24.9	25.0		25.2
Primary	923	25.0	25.0		25.0
Junior high	252	25.2	25.2		25.0
Senior high	234	25.4	25.3		25.1
College/univ.	135	25.7	25.7		25.4
Eta²/beta²		0.037	0.028		0.005
Significance		***	***		***
Respondent's education					
Primary and under	254	24.5		24.6	24.6
Junior high	305	24.4		24.4	24.5
Senior high	940	25.1		25.1	25.1
College/univ.	407	25.8		25.8	25.7
Eta²/beta²		0.124		0.117	0.099
Significance		***		**	***
Unadjusted R²			0.063	0.131	0.139

Note: The dependent variable is the woman's desired age at marriage. The sample includes unmarried women aged 18–29 in 1971 and 1984 Young Women's Surveys.

when the survey year is controlled. This indicates that a small part of the correlation between education and preferred age at marriage is due to both variables changing at least somewhat independently across time. Table 9.3 also demonstrates that education remains a strong determinant of marital timing preferences among single women even with the introduction of controls for their father's occupation and education, suggesting an important causal connection between a woman's education and marriage preferences (col. 5).

Table 9.3 also documents a relationship between ideal age at marriage and the occupation and education of a woman's father. Daughters of farmers or of men with little formal educational experience have a lower average preferred age at marriage. The magnitudes of these associations are smaller in the multivariate analyses, suggesting that at least some of the effects of paternal education and occupation operate through the woman's own schooling achievements. However, even with the full controls, both variables maintain a modest but observable influence on desired age at marriage (col. 5 of table 9.3).

Tables 9.2 and 9.3 also demonstrate that the educational and occupational variables considered here provide some success in explaining historical trends in preferred age at marriage. Over the entire period from 1971 through 1984 for the total sample of women, we see that ideal age at marriage increased by 1.3 years—from 23.5 to 24.8 (table 9.2, col. 2). When education is controlled, this difference is reduced to .7 years, suggesting that education alone can account for 46% of the trend across these thirteen years (col. 3). The separate analyses of the married and unmarried women reveal that one-third to two-fifths of the 13-year trend in preferred marital ages can be accounted for by increased education.

Our next analysis deals with the actual ages at which women marry, using data from the 1965–86 series of married women surveys with information about the marital timing of women married between 1950 and 1984. We used marriage cohort instead of birth cohort as our indicator of historical time to minimize the truncation bias associated with a sample limited to married women.[2] Table 9.4 summarizes the effects of the wife's educational attainment on the ages at which women married between 1950 and 1984, and table 9.5 adds the wife's father's occupation to the equation using a smaller range of marriage cohorts.[3]

Table 9.4, which includes the full range of marriage cohorts, shows that educational attainment has a strong and nearly monotonic effect on age at marriage. Women with no formal education had an average age at marriage of 20.7, compared to an average age at marriage for the college educated of 24.9—a difference of more than 4 years. Some of this difference among educational groups results from the more educated women having been born and matured in later years, when age at marriage was higher. However, when marriage cohort is controlled, the dif-

2. See appendix B for a full discussion of the truncation bias issue, including the relative magnitudes and directions of the biases associated with marriage and birth cohorts. The marriage cohorts included in the analysis for the respective surveys are as follows: 1950–65 marriage cohorts for the 1965 survey; 1950–67 cohorts for the 1967 survey; 1959–73 cohorts for the 1973 survey; 1966–80 cohorts for the 1980 survey; and 1962–84 cohorts for the 1986 survey.

3. The occupation of the wife's father was not ascertained in the 1965 and 1967 surveys, making it impossible to include this information for the earliest marriage cohorts.

TABLE 9.4   Multivariate Analysis of Female Age at Marriage, 1965–86 Surveys

	N (1)	Unadjusted Means[a] (2)	Adjusted Means[b] (3)
Marriage cohort			
1950–54	1,843	20.1	20.4
1955–59	2,268	20.6	20.9
1960–64	3,746	21.2	21.4
1965–69	3,535	21.1	21.2
1970–74	2,766	21.7	21.6
1975–79	2,173	22.5	22.0
1980–84	978	23.0	22.3
$Eta^2/beta^2$	—	0.064	0.027
Significance[c]		***	***
Wife's education			
None	4,150	20.7	21.0
Primary	9,011	21.0	21.0
Junior high	1,844	21.8	21.5
Senior high	1,715	23.1	22.7
College/univ.	586	24.9	24.5
$Eta^2/beta^2$	—	0.100	0.068
Significance[c]		***	***
Unadjusted R^2			0.122

Note: The dependent variable is the woman's age at her first marriage. The data came from 1965, 1967, 1973, 1980, and 1986 island-wide surveys of married women.

[a]These are the observed means on the dependent variable within each category of the predictor variables.

[b]The adjusted means are predicted values on the dependent variable within each category of the predictor variables. The predicted values were estimated from a multiple classification analysis (dummy variable regression), including all of the variables in each column as predictor variables.

[c]These rows designate statistical significance under the assumption of simple random sampling: * = 0.05; ** = 0.01; *** = 0.001.

ference between women with the most and women with the least formal educational attainment remained at 3.5 years (col. 3).

Reducing the number of marriage cohorts and adding the wife's father's occupation does not substantially change the estimated effects of the wife's education on age at marriage (table 9.5). Though women from farm backgrounds married significantly younger than others, much of the farm background effect apparently operated through educational attainment; the introduction of education into the equation substantially reduced the farm background effect (compare cols. 3 and 4).

Tables 9.4 and 9.5 also show that the historical trends in farm background and educational attainment can partially account for the trends in age at marriage. The observed difference in age at marriage between

TABLE 9.5   Multivariate Analysis of Female Age at Marriage,
1973–86 Surveys

	N (1)	Unadjusted Means[a] (2)	ADJUSTED MEANS[b] (3)	(4)
Marriage cohort				
1959	267	20.5	20.5	20.8
1960–64	1,769	21.0	21.0	21.2
1965–69	3,011	20.9	21.9	21.1
1970–74	2,766	21.7	22.7	21.7
1975–79	2,173	22.5	22.4	22.2
1980–84	978	23.0	22.9	22.5
Eta^2/beta^2	—	0.061	0.055	0.027
Significance[c]		***	***	***
Wife's father's occupation				
Farmer	5,568	21.2	21.2	21.4
Nonfarmer	4,957	22.1	22.0	21.7
Eta^2/beta^2	—	0.022	0.016	0.003
Significance[c]		***	***	***
Wife's education				
None	1,576	20.9	—	21.3
Primary	5,955	21.1	—	21.2
Junior high	1,414	21.7	—	21.5
Senior high	1,472	23.1	—	22.7
College/univ.	574	24.9	—	24.5
Eta^2/beta^2	—	0.110	—	0.072
Significance[c]		***		***
Unadjusted R^2			0.077	0.136

Note: The dependent variable is the woman's age at her first marriage. The data came from 1973, 1980, and 1986 island-wide surveys of married women.

[a] These are the observed means on the dependent variable within each category of the predictor variables.

[b] The adjusted means are predicted values on the dependent variable within each category of the predictor variables. The predicted values were estimated from a multiple classification analysis (dummy variable regression), including all of the variables in each column as predictor variables.

[c] These rows designate statistical significance under the assumption of simple random sampling: * = 0.05; ** = 0.01; *** = 0.001.

the earliest and latest marriage cohorts in the surveys (early 1950s through early 1980s) is reduced by 34%—from 2.9 to 1.9 years with a single control for wife's education (table 9.4). A similar reduction results when the change from the late 1950s through the early 1980s is analyzed controlling for the wife's education and father's occupation (table 9.5).

One difficulty with the analyses of age at marriage reported in tables 9.4 and 9.5 is that the sample of respondents was restricted to ever-married women so that women unmarried at the survey dates were ex-

TABLE 9.6   Multivariate Analysis of Women's Marriage Rates, 1971
and 1984

	N (1)	Unadjusted Effects[a] (2)	Adjusted Effects[b] (3)
Birth cohort			
1941–45	946	1.00	1.00
1946–50	1,480	0.94	1.16**
1951–55	1,498	0.69***	1.03
1956–60	1,031	0.67***	1.20**
1961–66	1,099	0.43***	0.98
Education			
None	455	1.00	1.00
Primary	2,547	0.64***	0.62***
Junior high	873	0.43***	0.41***
Senior high	1,532	0.21***	0.20***
College/univ.	646	0.10***	0.09***

Note: The dependent variable is the rate of marriage for women aged 18–29 in 1971 and 1984
Young Women's Surveys. Statistical significance: * = 0.05; ** = 0.01; *** = 0.001.

[a] The unadjusted effects are estimated without controls for any other variables.

[b] The adjusted effects are estimated in multivariate equations including all of the variables listed as
predictor variables. The equations are estimated by using the Cox proportional hazard model.

cluded from the analysis. This truncation of the sample by the occurrence
of marriage could bias the conclusions.

To provide a view of the determinants of marital timing which is not
influenced by truncation bias, we also analyzed data from the 1971 and
1984 young women's surveys which contained samples of both married
and unmarried women between the ages of 18 and 29. We pooled the
data from the two surveys and estimated multivariate models of the rate
of marriage using the Cox proportional hazards model. By estimating
marriage rate models containing education and birth cohort, we could
examine the effect of education on the marriage rate and investigate the
extent to which education could account for any trends in that rate.
Birth cohort was used in these analyses instead of marriage cohort, since
many of the women had not yet married. The results of these analyses
are summarized in tables 9.6 and 9.7.[4]

The Cox proportional hazards model is a tool for investigating the

4. An essential component of the estimation of hazard models is identification of the
waiting time to marriage. For those women who had married by the time of the interview,
we identified this waiting time as the number of months between the time the woman
reached age 12 and the date of her first marriage. All women who had not yet married by
the time of the interview were treated as censored in the analysis, with their waiting time
defined as the number of months between their 12th birthday and the time of the interview.

TABLE 9.7   Multivariate Analysis of Marriage Rates, 1984

	N (1)	Unadjusted Effects[a] (2)	ADJUSTED EFFECTS[b] (3)	(4)	(5)
Birth cohort					
1951–55	382	1.00	1.00	1.00	1.00
1956–60	1,031	0.99	1.11	0.98	1.11
1961–66	1,099	0.69***	0.95	0.71***	0.95
Father's occupation					
Farmer	899	1.00		1.00	1.00
Self/family employed	667	0.68***		0.69***	0.92
Employed by others	874	0.59***		0.59***	0.95
Education					
None and primary	609	1.00	1.00		1.00
Junior high	512	0.75***	0.75***		0.75***
Senior high	1,027	0.34***	0.34***		0.34***
College/univ.	364	0.15***	0.15***		0.15***

Note: The dependent variable is the rate of marriage for women aged 18–29 in 1984 Young Women's Survey. Statistical significance: * = 0.05; ** = 0.01; *** = 0.001.

[a] The unadjusted effects are estimated without controls for any other variables.

[b] The adjusted effects are estimated in multivariate equations, including all of the variables listed as predictor variables. The equations are estimated by using the Cox proportional hazard model.

determinants of a continuous time model of individual transitions from one state to another (Cox 1972; Namboodiri and Suchindran 1987; Teachman 1982). The hazard or rate of marriage can be written as $h(a) = ho(a) \times \exp(B_k Z_k)$, where $h(a)$ is the rate of marriage, $ho(a)$ is an underlying baseline rate, Z_k represents the explanatory variables included in the equation, and the B_k values are the effect parameters associated with the explanatory variables. In the model the underlying hazard rate, $ho(a)$, is not estimated but is adjusted multiplicatively by the effects of the predictor variables. To facilitate interpretation of results, we report $\exp(B_k)$ in the tables. For interval-level predictor variables, this quantity can be interpreted as the amount by which the underlying hazard is multiplied for each unit change in the explanatory variable. For categorical predictor variables, which are treated in these analyses as dummy variables, the quantity $\exp(B_k)$ represents the amount by which the underlying hazard for the omitted category is multiplied to obtain the hazard rate for the specified category. The percentage change in the underlying hazard associated with each unit of change in the explanatory variable or with each category of the dummy variable is equal to $100(\exp[B] - 1)$.

Both tables 9.6 and 9.7 document a large influence of education on the rate of marriage, with the rate of marriage declining dramatically with each level of education. Junior high school graduates have marriage rates that are only 43% as high as the rates for women without formal school, while the rates for college women are less than a fourth of those of junior high educated women (col. 2 of table 9.6). These observed effects are largely unaffected by controls for birth cohort or the father's occupation (cols. 3–5 of table 9.7). These substantial and persistent effects attest to the powerful influence of educational attainment on the tempo of marriage.

The woman's father's occupation also has a substantial influence on her propensity to marry (table 9.7). Women from farm origins have significantly higher rates of marriage than those from nonagricultural families. In addition, women whose fathers were self- or family-employed had higher rates than women whose fathers were employed by others. Controlling birth cohort does not affect this differential. However, the introduction of the wife's education into the equation reduces the estimated effect of farm origins to a small and statistically insignificant magnitude. This suggests that women from farm backgrounds have high marriage rates primarily because of their low educational attainments.

Perhaps the most remarkable result of tables 9.6 and 9.7 is the extent to which educational attainment can account for historical trends in the rate of marriage. Table 9.6 shows a steady monotonic trend toward lower marriage rates across the birth cohorts from the early 1940s through the early 1960s, with the marriage rate for the youngest women only 43% as high as the rate for the oldest (col. 2). The multivariate model controlling education completely eliminates the negative correlation between birth cohort and marriage rates (col. 3 of table 9.6). In fact, with education controlled, some of the later birth cohorts have higher rates of marriage than the oldest women. Apparently Taiwan's increasing levels of educational attainment, along with the substantial negative effect of education on the rate of marriage, can account for all the change in marriage rates during the past few decades, suggesting that marriage rates have declined primarily because educational levels have expanded so dramatically.

Further insights into the determinants of marital timing in Taiwan are provided by the panel design of the 1971 Young Women's Survey. In 1978, the study staff used the household registers to identify the women from the 1971 survey who had subsequently married. All of these ever-married women were reinterviewed in 1978, which allowed their date of marriage to be ascertained. This follow-up design thus allowed identification of women who had ever married as well as the

TABLE 9.8 Multivariate Analysis of Marriage Rates, 1971–78

	Unadjusted Effects[a]	Adjusted Effects[b]		
	(1)	(2)	(3)	(4)
Age	1.26***	1.25***	1.24***	1.29***
Urban birthplace	0.50***	0.71***	0.51***	0.72***
Educational level[c]	0.67***	0.71***		0.69***
Years of nonfamilial employment	1.07*		1.02	0.94*

Note: The dependent variable is the rate of marriage between 1971 and 1978 for single women aged 18–20 in 1971. The number of respondents is 882. Statistical significance: * = 0.05; ** = 0.01; *** = 0.001.

[a] The unadjusted effects are estimated without controls for any other variables.

[b] The adjusted effects are estimated in multivariate equations, including all of the variables listed in each column as predictor variables. The equations were estimated using the Cox proportional hazards model.

[c] Educational level was coded as follows: 0, no formal education; 1, primary; 2, junior high; 3, senior high; and 4, college or university.

date of their first marriage. The panel design permitted use of the 1971 interview data as independent variables in the prediction of the 1971–78 marital experience of those women still single in 1971. This design feature allowed us to investigate a broader range of marriage determinants than was possible with just the cross-sectional information.[5]

We limited this analysis to single women aged 18–20 in 1971 to specify a birth cohort in which few members had married prior to the 1971 survey. For this group of single women we defined the dependent variable as the marriage rate subsequent to the 1971 interview. For those who subsequently married, the waiting time to marriage was defined as the number of months between the 1971 interview and the date of first marriage. Those still single at the time of the 1978 follow-up survey were treated as censored as of March 1978.[6] The predictor variables included in this analysis were the woman's age, place of birth, education, and several dimensions of work experience, with all of the variables measured in 1971. Several of these explanatory variables, including age, education, and the amount of nonfamilial employment, were treated as interval-level variables in this analysis, while birthplace and employment status in 1971 were treated as categorical dummy variables. Tables 9.8 and 9.9 summarize the results.

5. For more information concerning both the study design and results of this analysis, see Lin (1988).

6. By limiting the sample to birth cohorts of women who had experienced little marriage before 1971, we minimized the biases associated with left censoring. That is, since there were few women aged 18–20 who had been married by 1971, there was very little chance for the unmarried group to be highly selective of those who did not marry early.

TABLE 9.9 Multivariate Analysis of Marriage Rates, 1971–84

	Unadjusted Effects[a] (1)	Adjusted Effects[b] (2)
Age	1.17**	1.24***
Urban birthplace	0.58**	0.72**
Educational level[c]	0.75***	0.82***
Employment status		
Family farm	2.08***	1.76***
Family business	1.24	1.30
Employed by relatives	1.24	1.18
Employed by others	1.00	1.00

Note: The dependent variable is the rate of marriage between 1971 and 1978 for single women aged 18–20 in 1971 who reported working in past months. The number of respondents is 640. Statistical significance: * = 0.05; ** = 0.01; *** = 0.001.

[a] The unadjusted effects are estimated without controls for any other variables.

[b] The adjusted effects are estimated in multivariate equations, including all of the variables listed in each column as predictor variables. The equations were estimated using the Cox proportional hazards model.

[c] Educational level was coded as follows: 0, no formal education; 1, primary; 2, junior high; 3, senior high; and 4, college or university.

The strong association between educational attainments and marriage is reconfirmed in this panel analysis. Women with high levels of education have much lower marriage rates than others, and this association is only slightly attenuated by the introduction of controls for age and rural-urban birthplace. With these controls, each increase in level of education is associated with a 29% reduction in the marriage rate (col. 2 of table 9.8).[7]

The substantial negative association between educational attainment in 1971 and subsequent rates of marriage provides strong support for treating education as the explanatory variable in analyses of marriage. In this panel design, where schooling is clearly prior to marriage, the strong association between the two variables can only be interpreted as the effects of education on marriage. There is no possibility that the observed association between education and marriage was due to the reciprocal causation of marriage influencing educational achievement.

The magnitude of the effect of education on marriage using the panel design is also very important. In the bivariate analysis reported in table 9.8 each level of education in 1971 is associated with a 33% lower level

7. The successive levels of education used in this analysis are the following: no formal schooling; primary; junior high; senior high; and college or university. Extensive analysis by Lin (1988) demonstrates that the relationship between these levels of education and the rate of marriage is linear, which justifies treating them as an interval variable in this analysis. See footnote c of table 9.8 for the explicit coding.

of marriage between 1971 and 1978 (col. 1). This estimated association of marriage with educational level is only somewhat less than that estimated earlier using levels of education ascertained during a survey to predict earlier rates of marriage. For example, using the pooled 1971 and 1984 data we found that each level of education at the time of the survey was associated with a 42% lower marriage rate prior to the survey.[8] Lin (1988, 75) estimated a 38% reduction in that rate using 1971 education reports to predict lifetime marriage rates through 1978 for women aged 18–29 in 1971. The similarity of the panel design estimate to those from retrospective designs provides further support for the conclusions reported in tables 9.6 and 9.7.

The rural-urban nature of the woman's birthplace also has an important influence on marriage rates. Marriage rates among women born in urban places are only one-half those of women with rural origins (col. 1, table 9.8). However, with controls for age and education, the differential associated with birthplace is reduced to 29% (col. 2). This leads to the conclusion that one of the reasons for the lower marriage rates of the urban born is their greater educational achievements.

Nonfamilial employment before 1971 demonstrates an interesting and complex relationship with subsequent marriage rates. Looking first at the unadjusted or zero-order effect, we see that each year of nonfamilial employment is associated with a 7% *higher* rate of marriage, an association which is reduced to statistical insignificance with controls for age and birthplace (cols. 1 and 3 of table 9.8). The reduced magnitude of the effect with these controls occurs because younger women and those from urban backgrounds accumulated fewer years of paid employment prior to their late teenage years, and urban background and later historical periods are both negatively associated with marriage rates during the early 20s (Lin 1988).

Furthermore, in the multivariate equation that includes age, birthplace, and education the effect of nonfamilial employment on the marriage rate reverses direction and becomes negative. With all of these variables controlled, each additional year of nonfamily employment is associated with a decrease of 6% in the marriage rate, providing strong support for the idea that nonfamilial employment delays marriage (col. 4, table 9.8).

The effect of nonfamilial employment becomes negative with the introduction of education into the equation because at ages 18–20 educa-

8. We also estimated the education effect separately for the 1971 and 1984 data sets. The estimates from the two surveys were almost identical, being .42 and .44, respectively.

tion is negatively associated with paid employment. Single women with primary schooling in 1971 had accumulated an average of 2.7 years of nonfamilial employment in 1971, compared to the average of 1.1 years experienced by high school graduates (Lin 1988). The reason for this negative correlation between education and paid employment is that teenagers in Taiwan rarely combine paid employment with school enrollment because employment outside the family is generally viewed as incompatible with school attendance. Controlling for this negative association and the negative influence of education on marriage results in the expected negative effect of nonfamilial employment on marriage.

Further insights into the influence of female employment are provided by table 9.9, which summarizes the effects of 1971 current work status on the subsequent rate of marriage. The work status variable was created from a series of three questions asked of respondents in 1971. The first was, "Have you been working during the past months, either for pay or in a family business or farm?" Those who had been working were asked, "What type of work is it—a family farm, a family business, or employment by others?" All who were employed by others were asked if their employers were relatives. All women who reported working were coded into the four categories shown in table 9.9; those who had not worked in recent months were excluded from this analysis.

Table 9.9 demonstrates that women who were working in family farm activities in 1971 had by far the highest rates of marriage during the subsequent seven years—more than double the rate for those working for nonrelatives outside of agriculture (col. 1). This differential was reduced somewhat with the multivariate controls, but even in an equation containing age, birthplace, and education the rate of marriage for women working on family farms remains 76% higher than the rate for women working for nonrelatives (col. 2). Women who worked in family businesses or for relatives had marriage rates intermediate between those working on family farms and those employed by unrelated persons. While premarital work experience apparently had no influence on the ideal ages of marriage of women who were already married, as reported earlier, such experience seems to have a powerful influence on the marriage behavior of young women. Furthermore, even though the effect of an agriculturally employed father operates primarily through the woman's education, there appears to be a strong independent effect of the woman's own agricultural employment during her transition to adulthood years.

Although there are no indicators of historical time in tables 9.8 or 9.9, the data summarized in those tables have important implications for understanding historical trends in marriage rates in Taiwan. In recent decades Taiwan has changed both from a rural agricultural society whose economic activities were organized primarily within family units to an urban industrialized society with extensive paid employment and from a society with minimal schooling to a population with high education levels. Tables 9.8 and 9.9 demonstrate that a rural birthplace, involvement in family economic enterprises, and low levels of formal education are associated with high marriage rates, while urban origins, high levels of education, and wage employment are associated with low marriage rates.

We have noted the large effects of the individual predictor variables in table 9.9. Even in the multivariate models there is a 28% reduction in marriage propensity associated with urban as compared to rural birthplaces, an 18% decline in marriage associated with each level of education, and a 43% decline moving from family farm work to employment by a nonrelative.[9] Taken together, the effects of these three variables on marriage rates are exceptionally large. For example, the multivariate equation in table 9.9 implies that women from urban origins who have a high school education and work for unrelated employers would have marriage rates only 28% of those for women from rural origins who have primary school educations and work in family enterprises.[10]

Conclusions

The data presented in this chapter provide strong support for the idea that urbanization, industrialization, and the expansion of education have been major factors in the decline in marriage in Taiwan during recent decades. Our analyses consistently show that at the individual level each of these variables influences the attitudes and behavior of Taiwanese women, with some effects being very strong. We have also shown that these variables can account for substantial fractions of the historical

9. The 28 and 18 percentage declines for birthplace and education are calculated using the formula presented earlier in the text. In order to calculate the 43% figure for employment status, it is necessary first to transform the coefficient for that variable so that family farm work is the base and the marriage rate for those employed by others is expressed relative to that base. The coefficient for the employed versus those working on family farms is 1.00 divided by 1.76, which equals .57. Converting this to a percentage reduction gives the figure of 43%.

10. The estimate of .28 was calculated by multiplying together the coefficient for urban birthplace (.72), the coefficient reflecting the difference between primary and high school education (.82 × .82), and the coefficient for employment by others relative to family farm work (1.00/1.76).

changes in individual preferences in marital timing in Taiwan. Perhaps the most startling finding is that these variables can account for virtually all of the change in actual marriage rates across a significant range of cohorts of Taiwanese women.

Education is the most important determinant of marriage in Taiwan. It is a very strong predictor of individual marriage attitudes and behavior—with these educational effects extending to a wide range of marriage indicators, including marital timing desires, age at marriage, and marriage rates. The educational effects have been strong in all the analyses and were reduced only slightly by a range of controls for other variables.

Education also stands out as the most important explanation of recent marriage trends in Taiwan. In all our analyses the changing levels of educational attainment provide the predominant explanation of historical change in marriage. In fact, for one key analysis, which focused on marriage rates from samples of women studied in 1971 and 1984, changing education accounted for the entire historical change in the rate of entrance into marriage. This conclusion is consistent with the earlier work of Freedman and Casterline (1979), which used decomposition techniques to study the effects of changing education between 1966 and 1976, and with Casterline's (1980) analyses of marriage change using aggregate-level data. This suggests the need for further investigation into the specific dimensions of education that influence marriage.

While education is the crucial determinant of the recent marriage decline in Taiwan, it is not the only important variable. Occupational origins and geographical location are also related to marriage; women in rural areas and from farm backgrounds have higher marriage rates and lower marriage ages than women with no agricultural and rural backgrounds. However, much of this effect operates through education: women from urban and nonagricultural backgrounds attend school longer, leading to later ages at marriage.

We also found evidence suggesting that a woman's participation in the nonfamilial work force influences marriage. The 1971–78 panel study showed that both the amount and the kind of work experience prior to the 1971 survey influenced subsequent marriage behavior, with long years of employment away from familial enterprises leading to lower rates of marriage. Our data also suggest that any effect of premarital employment on marriage is unlikely to operate through desired age at marriage, since marital timing preferences themselves are only weakly related to premarital employment.

Ten

Trends in Marital Dissolution

M. L. Lee, A. Thornton, and H. S. Lin

While the historical Chinese social system produced universal and young marriage, biological and social forces combined to ensure the fragility of individual marital unions. As documented in chapter 3, mortality was very high in Taiwan in the early 1900s, and the result was a high rate of marital dissolution caused by the death of the husband or wife.

Mortality was not the only cause of marital dissolution in Taiwan, since divorce had been accepted in Chinese culture for centuries. The Chinese classics both listed multiple circumstances that would permit divorce and provided conditions where it was not allowed (Dull 1978; Tai 1978). The household registration system established by the Japanese in the first decade of this century revealed that divorce was relatively common in Taiwan (Barclay 1954). Together, the high rates of divorce and the high rates of mortality resulted in substantial overall rates of marital dissolution.

In this chapter we trace the trajectory of marital dissolution across the twentieth century, documenting trends in both divorce and widowhood. We demonstrate a dramatic transformation in marital dissolution—both in its overall level and in the processes producing it. As a result of the significant improvements in health conditions, marital dissolutions caused by mortality declined substantially. There was also a long-term decline in voluntary marital disruption which extended from the beginning of this century through the end of the 1960s. However, there was an important reversal of this trend in the early 1970s, and divorce increased rapidly during the 1970s and 1980s.

Measuring Marital Dissolution

The censuses and household registration system provide the information necessary to estimate divorce rates across most of the twentieth century. A summary of annual crude divorce rates and marital divorce rates is

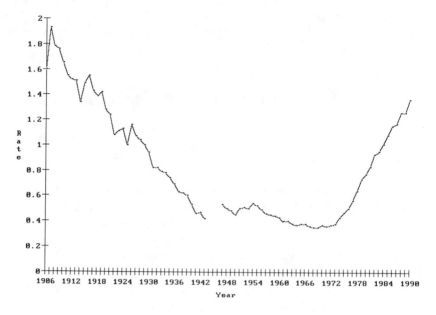

Figure 10.1 Crude divorce rate by year (times 1,000).

provided in figures 10.1 and 10.2, while table 10.1 lists age-specific divorce rates. These divorce rates were estimated from annual counts of divorce and the appropriate populations at risk.[1]

Table 10.1 also provides estimates of the fraction of marriages that would end in divorce within specified anniversaries of marriage if the age-specific divorce rates observed in a given year continued indefinitely. These estimates were calculated using life table procedures to project the divorce experience of a hypothetical or synthetic cohort of women who married at exactly age 20 and experienced the age-specific divorce rates of that year for the next thirty years. Since these estimates were designed to summarize the overall level of divorce in the population, they were calculated assuming no mortality. These estimates are also artificial in assuming a cohort of brides at exactly age 20. Calculations using other ages would, of course, produce different estimates of lifetime experience with divorce. The selection of an arbitrary starting age for these calculations was necessitated by the unavailability of marital duration-specific divorce rates.

1. The crude divorce rate is defined as the number of divorces divided by the total population, while the marital divorce rate divides the annual number of divorces by the number of married men. The age-specific divorce rates are indexed by the age of the wife.

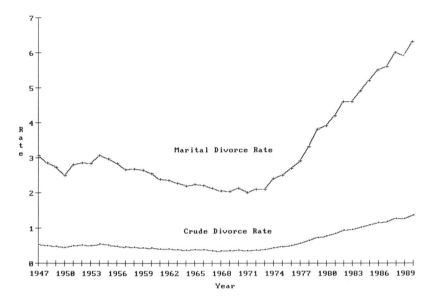

Figure 10.2   Crude divorce rate and marital divorce rate (times 1,000) by year.

While it was possible to estimate divorce rates directly from counts of divorces and the numbers of married people, the absence of counts of the annual number of marriages terminated by the death of the husband or wife necessitated the estimation of these rates from the death rates of men and women in the population. For the purposes of these estimates we assumed that wives were five years younger than their husbands and calculated age-specific mortality-caused dissolution rates by adding together the age-specific death rates for women and the age-specific death rates for men five years older and subtracting the product of the two rates.[2] The mortality rates used in these estimates were estimated from the life tables for the respective years. We also estimated the percentage of marriages that would terminate by the death of the husband or wife (or both) within specified anniversaries of marriage. These estimates were calculated from the mortality tables for the respective years using the assumption that a synthetic cohort of brides of exactly age 20 and grooms of exactly age 25 experienced indefinitely the mortal-

2. The five-year age gap between husbands and wives was chosen largely to simplify calculations. As documented in chapter 8, the gap in ages between husbands and wives was about five years in 1905 but has been reduced in subsequent years. These calculations also assume independence of mortality between husbands and wives.

TABLE 10.1 Age-Specific Rates of Marital Dissolution from Divorce and Mortality by Age and Year (per 10,000)

Age (females)	1906	1915	1920	1925	1930	1935	1975	1980	1985	1989
A. Marital Dissolution from Divorce										
15–19	189	226	217	173	146	132	75	57	80	94
20–24	102	145	129	105	97	85	56	72	94	116
25–29	55	91	84	61	53	47	40	70	92	108
30–34	37	61	56	37	30	23	29	58	78	92
35–39	39	48	38	29	25	16	18	32	59	69
40–44	28	38	29	15	18	13	14	20	29	41
45–49	19	30	22	16	16	9	9	13	19	19
Percentage ending in divorce within specified number of years[a]										
10	8	11	10	8	7	6	5	7	9	11
20	11	16	14	11	10	8	7	11	15	18
30	13	19	16	12	11	9	8	12	17	20
B. Marital Dissolution from Death[b]										
15–19	268	225	286	139	110	120	24	23	20	22
20–24	364	322	390	195	145	153	27	25	23	25
25–29	443	387	476	245	168	175	31	29	26	29
30–34	533	485	546	318	204	210	44	41	36	36
35–39	626	564	595	378	260	280	62	57	52	53
40–44	723	640	643	446	336	336	86	84	76	77
45–49	853	777	726	526	398	427	126	123	112	112
Percentage ending in death within specified number of years[c]										
10	33	30	35	20	15	15	3	3	2	3
20	63	59	64	44	32	34	8	7	7	7
30	84	80	82	66	53	55	17	16	15	15

[a] On the assumption that a marital cohort of 20-year-old brides experience the age-specific divorce rates of that age for a lifetime, with no mortality.

[b] Calculated by adding the age-specific death rates of women to age-specific death rates of men five years older and subtracting the product of the two.

[c] On the assumption that a marital cohort of 20-year-old brides and 25-year-old grooms experience the age-specific mortality rates of that year for a lifetime, with no divorce.

ity regimes of the life table. These projections assume no divorce. All of these mortality estimates are shown in table 10.1.[3]

Divorce and Mortality in the Early 1900s

Table 10.1 shows that mortality quickly disrupted many marriages contracted early in this century. Even at the youngest ages, the estimated

3. The mortality calculations in table 10.1 assume that the death rates of the total male and female populations also apply to men and women who are married. At ages when large fractions of the population are married, little error can result from using the death

annual marital dissolution rate from mortality in 1906 was 27 per thousand and rose to 85 per thousand for the oldest couples. This mortality regime would terminate one-third of the marriages of a synthetic cohort of 20-year-old brides and 25-year-old grooms within a decade. This number would reach nearly two-thirds within two decades and five-sixths within three decades. While mortality declined somewhat between 1906 and 1915, the fraction of a similar synthetic cohort experiencing the death of either the husband or wife (or both) within twenty years remained at 59% in 1915.

Precise comparisons of divorce and mortality-caused marital dissolution are difficult because of the assumptions required to estimate the mortality rates. Nevertheless, the data are sufficient to indicate that the rate of mortality-caused marital dissolution increases with age while the divorce rate declines across the life course. At ages 15–19, the divorce rate in 1915 was approximately equal to the dissolution rate caused by mortality, but at older ages mortality was substantially higher than divorce. For example, at ages 35–39 the mortality rate was nearly twelve times as large as the divorce rate. As a result, the overall incidence of the dissolution of marriages from divorce was much smaller in 1915 than the incidence of marital disruption from mortality. Whereas the mortality rates of 1915 would result in 30% of the marriages terminating within ten years and 80% within thirty years, the divorce rates of the same year imply that 11% would terminate within a decade and 19% within three decades.[4]

---

death rate of the total population as an estimate for the married population. However, in more recent years, when significant fractions of the population are unmarried at younger ages, there is more potential for bias in this procedure. Age-specific mortality rates are available by marital status for the most recent years in Taiwan. In 1989 the mortality rates for the married were lower than for the unmarried at every age over 20 (Ministry of the Interior 1990). This suggests that at least for recent years our calculations somewhat overstate marital dissolution from mortality. Thus, while reality departs at least somewhat from these assumptions, we believe they are sufficient to permit broad comparisons in mortality across time. Furthermore, while precise comparisons between estimates of divorce and mortality-caused marital dissolution are not possible, general comparisons of levels and trends are appropriate.

4. Note that the estimates of marriages ending by death within certain time periods after marriage assume no divorce, while the estimates of the fraction ending in divorce assume no death. Both sets of estimates would be lower if the other were treated as a competing risk rather than being assumed to be zero. The estimates also assume that a hypothetical cohort would experience the age-specific mortality or divorce of a single year across an entire lifetime.

Although divorce was much less important than mortality as a mechanism terminating marriages early in the century, a divorce regime high enough to terminate nearly one-fifth of all marriages within thirty years is clearly of importance. Furthermore, this estimate ignores the high rate of divorce among the many Taiwanese who were married as teenagers. The divorce rate among teenagers in 1915 was high enough to imply that 11% of the marriages to brides of age 15 would terminate within five years.[5] When added to the divorces that would occur between ages 20 and 50, these data imply that fully 27% of all marriages to 15-year-old brides would end in divorce by the time they reached age 50, assuming, of course, that neither they nor their husbands died first. There were also probably other voluntary marital disruptions which were not recorded in the household registration system.[6]

Taiwan's high divorce rate in the early 1900s contrasts sharply with the low levels of divorce reported for other Chinese populations. M. Freedman (1966, 60) reports that while there is no reliable statistical evidence about divorce from other Chinese populations, the available evidence for Fukien and Kwangtung on the mainland suggests that divorce was practically nonexistent or extremely rare. Pasternak (1983, 75) suggests that accounts from other parts of China are consistent with this view of infrequent divorce reported by Freedman.

M. Freedman (1966, 60–65) speculates that the high divorce rate in Taiwan may have been due to the relatively weak lineage organizations on the island. Such weak lineage organization may have combined with the scarcity of women in the population (see chap. 8) to enhance the independence of women (see Guttentag and Secord 1983). This may have limited the negative influence of divorce on women and enhanced their chances for remarriage. We also noted earlier (chap. 8) that matrilocal (uxorilocal) marriage and the adoption of future daughters-in-law (minor marriage) were both common in the early 1900s. Since both of these marriage forms were very susceptible to divorce, their prevalence may have contributed to the high divorce rates of the early 1900s (Freedman 1966; Pasternak 1983; Wolf 1975; Wolf and Huang 1980).

5. This estimate is consistent with the more detailed calculations of Barclay (1954, 221) concerning the number of marriages that would end in divorce. Using a cohort approach relating divorces to the actual marriages from which they came, Barclay estimated that between 8 and 14% of all marriages contracted between 1906 and 1925 ended in divorce within five years (also see Wolf and Huang 1980).

6. Our discussion of age-specific divorce rates and their implications focuses on 1915 rather than 1906 because 1906 was the first year of the household registration system and the crude divorce rates of that year were substantially lower than those in immediately succeeding years (see fig. 10.1).

Pasternak (1983, 80), however, suggests that the reported difference between Taiwan and the southeastern part of mainland China may be more apparent than real (also see Barrett 1985). He opines that the observed difference may be due to Taiwan's excellent household registration system that detects and records marital dissolutions that would not be observed without the registration system. This line of argument suggests that the prevalence of divorce in other Chinese populations may be greater than generally believed.

The divorce rate in Taiwan at the beginning of the century was also high by international standards of that time. During the first decade of the century the crude divorce rate in Taiwan was above 1.6 per thousand total population, as compared to a crude divorce rate of 1.2 during the same years in Japan (Taeuber 1958, 223). The divorce rate in the United States, a country long considered to have high levels of divorce, reached a crude divorce rate of 1.6 only in 1920, despite having experienced rapidly increasing divorce in the previous two decades (U.S. Department of Health, Education, and Welfare 1954). Of course, Taiwan is also not unique in having high divorce rates. Other societies such as Java, Malaysia, Japan in earlier years, and certain African societies have been reported to have high divorce rates (Brandon 1990; Barnes 1951; Goody 1962; Geertz 1961; Kumagai 1983).

The combination of high mortality and high divorce meant that marital dissolution was a common experience in the past—both for children and for adults. Many children undoubtedly experienced either the death or divorce of their parents. Large numbers of young people also experienced their own marital dissolutions soon after reaching adulthood and entering marriage—through their own death, the death of a spouse, or divorce.

With the near universality of first marriage and high rates of marital dissolution one would expect to find large numbers of previously married people in the population. This expectation is confirmed in table 10.2, which lists age-specific percentages of men and women who are currently widowed.[7] While the prevalence of widowhood is, as expected, fairly low in young adulthood, it increases substantially with age as death rates increase and people have longer exposures to mortality. The 1905 census indicates that 10% of the men aged 40–44 were widowed, and this number increased to 29% for those over age 50. With adult mortality lower among women than men, widowhood was more prevalent for

7. We use the term "widowed" to refer to both men and women whose spouse has died.

TABLE 10.2 Percentage Currently Widowed, by Gender, Age, and Year

A. Women

Age	1905	1915	1920	1925	1930	1935	1956	1966	1970	1975	1980	1985	1990
15–19	0.7	0.4	0.4	0.2	0.2	0.2	0.0	0.0	0.0	0.0	0.0	0.0	0.0
20–24	2.1	1.7	1.9	1.2	1.0	1.0	0.3	0.2	0.1	0.1	0.1	0.1	0.1
25–29	4.8	3.7	4.0	2.7	2.2	2.2	1.0	0.6	0.5	0.4	0.5	0.4	0.3
30–34	9.4	6.9	7.5	5.3	4.7	4.4	2.8	1.3	1.0	0.9	1.1	1.0	0.9
35–39	17.6	13.3	13.3	10.2	9.3	8.2	6.3	2.8	2.0	1.8	2.1	2.0	2.0
40–44	30.2	23.9	22.7	18.6	16.5	15.0	11.6	6.1	4.7	3.6	3.7	3.6	3.7
45–49	43.4	38.4	35.5	29.9	27.2	24.1	19.5	11.9	9.3	6.7	6.4	5.9	6.3
50+	72.2	71.5	69.5	65.1	61.6	57.9	53.4	43.3	41.0	34.7	31.4	27.2	25.6

B. Men

Age	1905	1915	1920	1925	1930	1935	1956[a]	1966	1970	1975	1980	1985	1990
15–19	0.2	0.1	0.1	0.0	0.1	0.0		0.0	0.0	0.0	0.0	0.0	0.0
20–24	1.0	0.7	0.8	0.5	0.5	0.4		0.1	0.0	0.0	0.0	0.0	0.0
25–29	2.5	2.1	2.4	1.4	1.2	1.1		0.2	0.2	0.1	0.1	0.1	0.1
30–34	4.3	4.1	4.2	2.9	2.3	1.9		0.6	0.4	0.3	0.2	0.2	0.3
35–39	6.8	6.2	6.6	4.9	4.0	3.4		1.0	0.8	0.6	0.5	0.4	0.5
40–44	10.1	8.8	9.2	7.7	6.5	5.7		1.8	1.2	1.2	1.1	0.9	1.0
45–49	14.0	12.2	12.5	10.7	10.1	8.8		3.2	2.1	1.7	2.1	1.7	1.8
50+	28.6	26.8	25.3	23.1	22.2	21.3		13.1	13.1	9.3	8.9	8.1	8.8

Note: Data for 1905 through 1980 are from the censuses. Data for 1985 through 1990 are from the household registers.

[a] Data for 1956 are not included for men because of the exclusion of military men in 1956 from the census reports.

women. At ages 40–44 in 1905, 30% of women were widowed, and the number reached nearly three out of four at ages over 50.

While the censuses in the early 1900s recorded large numbers of widows in the population, relatively few divorced people were enumerated. As table 10.3 shows, the number of men and women reported as divorced for any age group never exceeded 3% across all of the years before World War II. The low prevalence of divorcees in the population suggests that divorced men and women remarried quite rapidly, an expectation confirmed by analyses showing that remarriage was both common and rapid among the divorced during the colonial period (Barclay 1954; Barrett 1985). Since remarriage rates for the divorced were very high, relatively little time was spent divorced.

Remarriage rates were also high among young widowed men and women early in the century—a factor that reduced the amount of widowhood time (Barclay 1954; Barrett 1985). Remarriage, however, declined with age, the decrease being particularly rapid for women. As mortality increased and remarriage declined with age, the amount of time older women spent as widows was substantial. Since older men had both higher mortality and higher remarriage rates than older women, there were substantially fewer widowed men than women in the population.

The combination of high rates of widowhood, divorce, and remarriage meant that a substantial fraction of marriages contracted early in this century involved people who were previously married. Either the husband or the wife had been previously married in 42% of all marriages contracted in 1906 (Barclay 1954, 225). As a result, many people early in this century experienced what we now refer to as reconstituted or blended families.

Divorce and Mortality Trends before World War II

Both divorce and mortality declined steadily and markedly across the first four decades of this century. As Figure 10.1 documents, the crude divorce rate declined from nearly two per thousand early in the century to about one-half per thousand on the eve of World War II. The decline in divorce also occurred for every age group, with the percentage reductions ranging from 41 to 70% for the respective age groups between 1915 and 1935. Overall, the decline in divorce was large enough to reduce the fraction of marriages of a synthetic cohort of 20-year-old brides that would end in divorce within thirty years from 19% in 1915 to 9% in 1935, assuming, of course, no mortality.

TABLE 10.3 Percentage Currently Divorced, by Gender, Age, and Year

A. Women

Age	1905	1915	1920	1925	1930	1935	1956	1966	1970	1975	1980	1985	1990
15–19	0.7	0.3	0.4	0.3	0.3	0.2	0.1	0.1	0.0	0.0	0.1	0.0	0.0
20–24	1.2	0.8	1.1	0.9	0.9	0.7	0.7	0.7	0.3	0.4	0.5	0.6	0.6
25–29	0.9	0.8	1.1	1.0	1.1	0.9	1.0	1.3	0.7	0.7	1.4	1.8	2.0
30–34	0.8	0.8	1.0	1.0	1.0	1.0	1.2	1.6	0.9	0.8	2.1	2.6	3.5
35–39	0.7	0.7	0.9	1.0	1.0	0.9	1.3	1.9	1.1	1.0	2.0	2.8	4.2
40–44	0.4	0.7	0.9	1.0	0.9	1.0	1.5	2.3	1.3	1.2	2.0	2.2	3.9
45–49	0.3	0.6	0.9	0.9	0.8	1.0	1.4	2.4	1.6	1.2	1.9	2.0	3.1
50+	0.2	0.2	0.5	0.6	0.6	0.7	1.0	1.9	1.6	1.4	1.6	1.5	1.8

B. Men

Age	1905	1915	1920	1925	1930	1935	1956[a]	1966	1970	1975	1980	1985	1990
15–19	0.3	0.1	0.1	0.1	0.1	0.0		0.0	0.0	0.0	0.0	0.0	0.0
20–24	1.2	0.8	0.8	0.7	0.7	0.6		0.1	0.1	0.1	0.1	0.2	0.2
25–29	1.9	1.7	1.7	1.6	1.4	1.3		0.5	0.8	0.4	0.7	1.0	1.3
30–34	2.1	2.3	2.3	2.0	1.8	1.6		1.1	1.8	0.7	1.5	2.1	2.9
35–39	1.8	2.1	2.3	2.2	1.9	1.7		1.6	2.9	0.9	1.8	2.7	3.9
40–44	1.4	1.8	2.3	2.1	2.1	1.8		2.6	3.9	1.1	1.9	2.6	4.3
45–49	1.1	1.6	1.9	2.0	2.0	2.0		3.9	5.9	1.3	2.2	2.3	3.8
50+	1.2	1.2	1.4	1.5	1.5	1.6		5.0	6.7	2.7	3.1	2.3	2.7

Note: Data for 1905 through 1980 are from the censuses. Data for 1985 through 1990 are from the household registers.

[a]Data for 1956 are not included for men because of the exclusion of military men in 1956 from the census reports.

The reduction in divorce during the first half of the twentieth century may have been related to the decline in matrilocal and minor marriage during those years (Barclay 1954; Wolf and Huang 1980). As discussed earlier, both matrilocal and minor marriage were characterized by great fragility, and the reduction in the prevalence of these marriages may have contributed to the reduction in divorce.

In percentage terms the decrease in mortality before World War II was very similar to the reduction in divorce; age-specific rates of marital dissolution in 1935 were from 47 to 57% lower than those in 1915. However, since mortality was significantly higher than divorce in 1915, the subsequent mortality decline was also more important than the concurrent decrease in divorce. In a synthetic cohort of marriages experiencing the mortality of 1935 the number terminating from mortality would have reached only 15% in one decade and 34% in two decades, percentages that are considerably lower than the 30 and 59% for a similar synthetic cohort experiencing the mortality rates of 1915.

Marital Dissolution Trends after World War II

The mortality decline under way in the early 1900s has extended across the entire twentieth century. As table 10.1 documents, the age-specific mortality-caused marital dissolution rates of 1989 were between 80 and 88% lower than those recorded in 1935. These reductions in mortality have been so significant that the percentage of marriages in a synthetic cohort that would be terminated by the 1989 death rates reaches only 3% in ten years, 7% in twenty years, and 15% in thirty years. These figures indicate that the fraction of marriages ending in death within three decades in the late 1980s would only be about one-half as large as the fraction terminated by mortality within one decade at the beginning of the century.[8] Thus, compared to the early 1900s, it would be only a slight exaggeration to state that mortality has now been nearly eliminated as a cause of marital dissolution during the first decade or two of marriage.

The decline in mortality has also tremendously reduced the amount of time spent as a widow during the years of early and middle adulthood

---

8. However, since age at marriage has increased dramatically during the same years, the ages at which people live the first three decades of marriage is also higher. Because mortality increases with age, these calculations overestimate the actual declines in mortality-caused marital dissolution across the century. Also, our mortality measures are based on the total rather than the currently married population, which imparts an upward bias to the estimates of mortality levels, at least in recent years.

(table 10.2). These declines have occurred at every age and for both men and women. The declines in widowhood have also been very steady, with almost every new year of observation across the century bringing a reduction in the prevalence of widowhood.

By 1990, the prevalence of widowhood among men had fallen so low that at ages under 45 the percentage of the population widowed never exceeded 1% (table 10.2). Even at ages over 50, only 9% of all men were currently widowed. While the number of widowed women in 1990 was also very low by historical standards, the prevalence of widows remained much higher for women than for men. For example, at ages over 50, one-fourth of the women were widowed as compared to the 9% among men. The higher prevalence of widowhood among women as compared to men largely reflects their lower mortality rates. Since women frequently outlive their husbands, more women than men experience the deaths of their spouses. Higher male mortality also means that widowed men will die faster than widowed women, thereby leaving fewer widowed men in the population. Higher male mortality also leads to a preponderance of women at the older ages, which gives men more opportunities than women to remarry. The importance of the latter factor in Taiwan, however, has been negated to a great extent by the large influx of single men to the island in the late 1940s and early 1950s. In fact, at the oldest ages in Taiwan today there is a surplus of men over women (see table 8.2).

While the historical changes in divorce and mortality before World War II were very similar, trends in the two forms of marital dissolution began to diverge in subsequent years. At the same time that mortality was plummeting downward in the years following World War II, the decline in divorce continued but at a much slower pace. By the middle of the 1960s the long-term decline in divorce had been completely halted. Consequently, while mortality continued to be more important as a terminator of marriages at ages over 30 in 1975, at younger ages there were more marital terminations from divorce than death.

The 1970s witnessed a new trend in divorce—a rapid and substantial increase that was to extend through the 1980s (figs. 10.1 and 10.2). Just during the two decades from 1970 through 1990, the marital divorce rate tripled. The recent upturn in divorce also occurred across the entire age range, with the increases in individual age-specific rates between the ages of 20 and 44 ranging from between 2.7 and 3.8 times for the 1975–89 period (table 10.1). This maintained the overall negative relationship between age and the divorce rate. There is also no evidence that the increase in divorce in Taiwan is weakening.

The substantial increase in divorce in the 1970s and 1980s was sufficient to bring the respective divorce rates back to their levels at the beginning of the twentieth century. In fact, with the exception of the age group 15–19, which contained relatively few married couples in 1989, the age-specific divorce rates of 1989 were remarkably similar to those of 1915. The similarity between 1915 and 1989 also extends to the summary indicators of divorce. The divorce rates of both years imply that 11% of brides marrying on their 20th birthdays would divorce within ten years while 19–20% would divorce before their 30th wedding anniversary.

These estimates of the percentages of marriages ending in divorce, however, require a warning label: they are not predictions but projections of the implications of a set of rates and assumptions. The estimate of 20% of marriages ending in divorce within thirty years is based on a synthetic cohort experiencing a lifetime of divorce at the 1989 levels, and, of course, no group of couples has done that. If the divorce rates decline again in the future, this number will be a substantial overestimate of the level of divorce actually experienced in the population. But if divorce rates continue their recent upsurge, this projection of one in five marriages ending in divorce in thirty years will be a substantial underestimate. And if the tripling of divorce that occurred in the 1970s and 1980s repeats itself in the next two decades, the fraction of marriages terminating in divorce would soar to very high levels.

All of these projections assume marriage at age 20 for women, which is significantly lower than the current average (chap. 8). Since divorce declines with age, projections of marital dissolutions for those marrying at older ages would be significantly lower than for those marrying at age 20. Under the age-specific divorce rates of 1989, the fraction of brides marrying at age 25 who would experience divorce in thirty years would be approximately 16% rather than the 20% estimated for those marrying at age 20. These estimates also assume no mortality, but in a real rather than hypothetical world some of the marriages projected to end in divorce by our procedures would be terminated by mortality rather than divorce. However, the assumption of no mortality has only a limited effect, since mortality is now so low that few marriages are disrupted by death before experiencing many years at the risk of divorce. At the same time, these projections also cover only thirty years of marriage, and divorces at later marital durations would add to the fraction of marriages ending in divorce. But with divorce relatively rare at older ages, the addition of these divorces would not increase the total estimate substantially.

While the divorce rates of the late 1980s are very similar to those of the early part of this century, the overall rates of marital dissolution—combining both divorce and mortality—are still much lower than those recorded earlier. Thus, even the recent tripling of divorce has not returned the overall rates of marital termination back to their earlier high levels. In fact, given currently low rates of mortality, it would take another round of substantial increases in divorce for that to occur.

The recent increase in divorce and the continuing decline of mortality, however, have combined to make divorce a much more significant source of marital dissolution than mortality during early and middle adulthood. This can be seen from the 1989 data in table 10.1 showing that at every age below 40 the rate of divorce is higher than the rate of dissolution due to death. During the 20s this differential is dramatic, the divorce rate being several times higher than the mortality-caused rate of marital dissolution. In fact, the 1989 divorce rates imply that 11% of 20-year-old brides would divorce within a decade, while the death rates of the same year would terminate only 3% of such marriages in the same ten years. Even after thirty years, the 1989 mortality rates would terminate only 15% of the marriages as compared to the 20% that would end through divorce. Furthermore, since divorce is concentrated at the younger ages and mortality at the older ages, treating the two forms of dissolution as competing rather than separate risks would heighten the differences between the two forms of dissolution.

This shifting distribution of marital dissolutions from mortality to divorce is also reflected in important changes in the composition of the previously married in the population. Whereas the percentage of the population currently widowed declined dramatically across the entire length of the century, the percentage of the population currently divorced at each age remained fairly steady through 1975. In subsequent years, the rising divorce rate was accompanied by an increase in the prevalence of divorced people in the population—an increase that occurred at nearly every age and for both men and women. By 1990, at least 3% of all men and women between the ages of 30 and 50 were divorcees.

As a result of increasing divorce and declining mortality after 1975, the number of divorcees in 1990 exceeded widows and widowers at all ages under 45, with a striking differential at some ages. For example, at ages 30–34 the number of divorced men was nearly ten times as large as the number of widowed men. Among women of the same ages, divorcees outnumbered widows by nearly four to one.

As a result of the long-term trends in marital formation and dissolution, the prevalence of people in Taiwan who are currently single but who had been married is now substantially lower than it was early in this century. This decline is particularly marked at the older ages, at which high mortality rates resulted in a high prevalence of widowed people in the early 1900s. These changes, together with the dramatic increases in the ages at which Taiwanese get married discussed in chapter 8, have produced a major shift in the place of marriage in the Taiwanese life course. Whereas the great majority of young adulthood in the past was lived as a spouse, large fractions of middle and old age were spent unmarried. In today's world the situation has been largely reversed: large proportions of young adulthood are now spent single and more of the mature years are lived with a spouse. Now it is only as people reach very elderly years that the proportion unmarried again becomes substantial.

Marital dissolution trends in this century have also reduced the importance of remarriage. We noted earlier that fully 42% of the marriages in 1906 included either a bride or a groom who was previously married (Barclay 1954). By 1979, the number of marriages including a previously married spouse had been reduced to 7%, although the subsequent increase in divorce expanded this number to 11% by 1989 (Ministry of the Interior 1980b, 1990). As a result of these long-term changes, there are now many fewer reconstituted or blended families than in the early 1900s.

The divorce trends in Taiwan during the twentieth century have been very different than those in many Western countries. Whereas divorce in Taiwan declined rapidly before World War II, changed little between World War II and 1970, and then increased rapidly, the trend in many Western countries was generally upward, with the exception of perturbations associated with economic depressions and wars (Cherlin 1981; Chester 1977; Thornton and Rodgers 1987). Thus, while divorce rates in Taiwan at the end of the century were very similar to those at the beginning, most Western divorce rates were much higher at the end than at the beginning of the century. These divergent trends between Taiwan and most Western societies also resulted in Taiwan having a substantially lower divorce rate in the late 1980s than most societies in the West. The crude divorce rates of most Western and Northern European populations in the middle-to-late 1980s ranged from 1.4 to 2.8 times that of Taiwan during the same period.[9] Crude divorce rates in the Soviet Union and

9. The Western and Northern European countries included in this comparison were Denmark, Finland, France, East and West Germany, Iceland, Luxembourg, the Netherlands, Norway, Sweden, Switzerland, and the United Kingdom. Australia, Canada, and

United States were even higher than those in other European and North American populations, making comparisons with them and Taiwan even more extreme (United Nations 1991).

While divorce trends in Taiwan during the twentieth century were very different from those in many Western societies, they were remarkably similar to those in Japan during the same period (Kumagai 1983; Taeuber 1958). As noted earlier, divorce rates were generally very similar in the two societies at the beginning of the century. Both societies also experienced substantial declines in divorce before World War II as well as generally level trends in the years following the war. Like Taiwan, Japan has also experienced a substantial upturn in divorce in recent years, but with the timing of that upturn occurring somewhat earlier than in Taiwan. Finally, the crude divorce rates in the two countries in 1988 were nearly identical: 1.2 in Japan and 1.3 in Taiwan (United Nations 1991).

While Taiwan's rate of divorce is very similar to Japan's, divorce in Taiwan appears to be higher than in several other populations of East Asia. Korea, Hong Kong, and Singapore all recorded crude divorce rates just below 1.0 in the late 1980s, while the comparable Taiwanese rate was 1.3 (United Nations 1991).

Divorce Differentials

In earlier chapters we were able to utilize the extensive information from Taiwan about the determinants of marriage to explain substantial portions of the trends in spouse choice and marital timing (chaps. 7 and 9). While we aspired to conduct similar analyses of the determinants of divorce trends, the paucity of appropriate data linking divorce to its theoretical determinants makes it very difficult to conduct a thorough and detailed empirical documentation of the theoretical factors that caused divorce to increase in the 1970s and 1980s.

Nevertheless, there is information available that links together both divorce levels and trends with education and metropolitan residence. Lee (1984) documented divorce rates by education groups for the years from

---

New Zealand were also within the same range. Portugal and Italy were two Western European countries with lower crude divorce rates than Taiwan. Several Eastern European countries also had crude divorce rates that were similar to or lower than that recorded in Taiwan (United Nations 1991). Note that crude divorce rates permit only general comparisons of divorce propensities across societies since they also reflect differences in age and marital status distributions.

1977 through 1981 and found that divorce was positively related to educational level, that relationship being stronger and more monotonic for the husband's than for the wife's education. However, divorce increased sharply during this four-year period within each of the educational groups. In addition, the increases in educational attainment during those same years could not account for very much of the increase in divorce.

In table 10.4 we document a strong relationship between divorce and residential location. In that table we separate Taiwan's population into metropolitan and nonmetropolitan sectors, the metropolitan area being defined as Taiwan's five large cities and highly urbanized Taipei County. Table 10.4 lists age-specific and total marital divorce rates for selected years between 1970 and 1989.[10]

For every year between 1970 and 1989, the primary years for the upswing in divorce, the rate of voluntary marital dissolution was strongly related to residential location. Couples living in the most urbanized areas of Taiwan had divorce rates that were from 58 to 85% higher than the rates for people living outside the major urban areas. There is also no clear trend in the magnitude of this difference.

Note that the differences between the geographical areas are not the result of age differences between the areas, since there are important residential differences in divorce for every age group. However, table 10.4 also indicates that when the residential differences are measured in percentage terms, they are greater for older couples. Apparently, living outside the major urban areas has a less stabilizing effect on newly established marriages than on those that have survived for at least a few years. Table 10.4 also shows that there were substantial divorce increases within both the metropolitan and the nonmetropolitan areas, the increases being similar in both areas.

We examined the influence of increasing urbanization on the increase in divorce using direct standardization techniques. This analysis revealed that the shift from nonmetropolitan to metropolitan residence over this two-decade period can explain only a small proportion of the overall increase in divorce.[11] Of course, this analysis does not take into account the fact that all areas of Taiwan were being drawn into a more metropoli-

---

10. Age-specific rates were not available for 1970.

11. We estimate through direct standardization techniques that if there had been no changes in the distribution of the population between metropolitan and nonmetropolitan areas between 1970 and 1989, the increase in divorce would have still been about 93% as large as it was with the actual increases in metropolitan residence.

TABLE 10.4 Age-Specific Divorce Rates by Year and Residence (per 10,000)

	METROPOLITAN[a]					NONMETROPOLITAN[a]					RATIO OF METROPOLITAN TO NONMETROPOLITAN (TIMES 100)				
	1970	1975	1980	1985	1989	1970	1975	1980	1985	1989	1970	1975	1980	1985	1989
Total[b]	30.0	34.6	54.1	68.7	74.0	17.2	19.5	29.3	40.0	46.7	174	177	185	172	158
15–19	—	75.7	70.4	95.2	121.6	—	75.1	51.3	67.9	83.2	—	101	137	140	146
20–24	—	75.6	93.1	119.1	138.4	—	46.4	61.2	77.5	100.4	—	163	152	154	138
25–29	—	55.1	88.9	111.0	128.9	—	32.3	56.6	76.1	89.1	—	171	157	146	145
30–34	—	36.5	78.4	97.2	107.4	—	21.8	45.2	62.1	78.6	—	167	173	157	137
35–39	—	26.8	44.6	80.0	87.0	—	13.1	20.8	44.8	53.0	—	205	214	179	164
40–44	—	22.2	29.9	39.0	56.0	—	9.5	13.6	20.1	31.1	—	234	220	194	180
45–49	—	14.3	20.5	28.6	27.7	—	6.8	8.7	12.3	12.8	—	210	236	233	216

[a]"Metropolitan" is defined here as Taipei County and the cities of Taipei, Tainan, Taichung, Keelung, and Kaohsiung. All other areas are considered nonmetropolitan. Data are calculated from *Demographic Factbooks* for the respective years.

[b]The total rate is for married women of all ages and not just those between the ages of 15 and 49.

tan and cosmopolitan world between 1970 and 1989, changes that could also help to explain the increases in divorce during this period.

Thus, while the available data suggest that increasing education and urbanization may partially explain recent increases in divorce, they also indicate that there is much more to the explanation than that. The completion of that explanation, however, awaits the accumulation of additional data.

Eleven

The Fertility Transition in Taiwan

R. Freedman, M. C. Chang, T. H. Sun, and M. Weinstein

An Overview

Taiwan's transition from traditionally high fertility to low replacement levels occurred between 1956 and 1983. In this twenty-seven-year period the gross reproduction rate, a measure of fertility,[1] fell from 3.16 to the replacement level of 1.04. Then, between 1983 and 1986, fertility fell precipitously to 0.81, below replacement level (table 11.1). Since 1986 there has been no clear trend. The gross reproduction rate has varied between 0.81 and 0.89.

The aspect of the demographic transition involving mortality decline in Taiwan, as in other less developed countries (LDCs), began considerably before fertility began to decline in 1956. In Taiwan this decline started during the period of Japanese colonial rule, as we saw in chapter 3. After the disruption of the war years and the immediate postwar period, life expectancy rose rapidly, reaching 69.2 for males and 74.2 for females by 1983, when fertility was just at the level required to replace the population with such low mortality.

The relatively high fertility of the postwar years, up to 1956, was a continuation of the high fertility of the colonial period, which was rooted in the strong familial institutions central to Taiwanese society of that period. According to Barclay (1954), "The organization of livelihood,

The text of this chapter incorporates extensive passages excerpted, with the permission of the Population Council, from Chang, Ming-Cheng, Ronald Freedman, and Te-Hsiung Sun, 1987, "Trends in Fertility, Family Size Preferences, and Family Planning Practice: Taiwan, 1961–85." *Studies in Family Planning,* 18 (6) (November/December): 320–37.

1. The gross reproduction rate is a measure of the number of daughters each woman would have if she lived through the childbearing years subject to the fertility rate for each age prevailing at the specified date. A gross reproduction rate of 1.0 means that, under these conditions, women will, on average, just replace themselves with one daughter. It is a hypothetical rate indicating what would happen if current rates continue. It is not necessarily a measure of what actually will happen.

TABLE 11.1 Gross and Net Reproduction Rates (GRR and NRR), Taiwan, 1956–90

Year	GRR	NRR
1956	3.16	2.84
1960	2.79	2.52
1961	2.70	2.49
1965	2.34	2.20
1970	1.94	1.84
1975	1.37	1.32
1980	1.22	1.18
1983	1.04	1.01
1984	0.99	0.96
1985	0.91	0.89
1986	0.81	0.78
1987	0.82	0.79
1988	0.89	0.86
1989	0.81	0.78
1990	0.86	0.83

Sources for this and subsequent tables: *Taiwan and Taiwan-Fukien Demographic Fact Books* (1960–90); *Demographic Reference: Taiwan, Republic of China* (1965).

the inheritance of occupation, the immobility of the rural population and the character of migration to cities all reflected the influence of familial relationships in the decisions of individuals." The Japanese colonial policy was to maintain the strength of traditional familial institutions as a source of social stability and as the chosen instrument for controlling individual behavior.

Barclay estimated that gross reproduction rates were in the range of 2.93 to 3.39 during the colonial period, with the higher rates prevailing during the decade of the 1930s. The gross reproduction rate of 3.16, when Taiwan's sustained fertility decline began in 1956 (table 11.1), was in the middle of the range of rates which prevailed in family-centered Taiwan of the colonial period.

Since by 1956 mortality had already fallen considerably while fertility remained high, the net reproduction rate[2] of 2.84 that year was at an all-time high. It was considerably higher than in the Japanese period,

2. The net reproduction rate represents the rate at which women will replace themselves with daughters, if they are subject throughout the childbearing years to the age-specific fertility and mortality rates prevailing at the specified period. A net reproduction rate of 1.0 indicates that, if the current rates continue long enough, each woman will exactly replace herself with one daughter. The net reproduction rate is the gross reproduction rate adjusted for mortality. The greater the mortality rates, the greater the difference between the gross and net reproduction rates.

when much higher mortality kept the net reproduction rate well below the gross reproduction rate. Since fertility fell much faster than mortality after 1956, the net reproduction rate fell to a replacement level of 1.01 by 1983 and then further to 0.78 by 1986. By that time mortality was so low that there could only be a small difference between the gross and net reproduction rates.

The actual rate of natural increase, which is affected by the age-sex distribution as well as by age-specific fertility and mortality rates, was as high as twenty-five per thousand in the decade of the 1930s. But the high fertility of 1956, together with already much lower mortality, produced a high natural increase rate of thirty-seven per thousand.

By 1983, when the net reproduction rate was 1.01, the natural increase rate was still sixteen per thousand because the age distribution was still favorable to high birthrates and low death rates. By 1986–90 fertility had fallen so much further that the rate of natural increase was a low eleven per thousand. The 1990 age-specific fertility and mortality rates, if continued indefinitely, implied a negative intrinsic rate of growth of 17% per generation.

While the population of Taiwan continues to grow because of young age distributions produced by formerly high fertility, Taiwan's present low fertility rates imply, if continued, zero population growth some decades hence, followed by an actual population decline. Either of these assumptions would produce an aging population. Taiwan, having passed through both the fertility and the mortality aspects of the demographic transition, now faces many of the same problems as Japan and other developed countries.

This summary overview of Taiwan's demographic transition is the background for considering the fertility and family planning transition in Taiwan. Unless Taiwan's very low mortality rates rise unexpectedly, its future population growth and age distribution will depend mainly on fertility trends, the dynamic factor in a regime of very low mortality. Demographic trends in fertility and nuptiality will be considered first. Then we will consider the trends in preferences for number, sex, and timing of children and in fertility control measures to satisfy these preferences.

Fertility and Marriage Trends in Taiwan, 1956–90

Between 1956 and 1990 the total fertility rate[3] for Taiwan—another measure of fertility—fell by 72%. The crude birthrate[4] fell less (63%) because of an increase in the proportion of the population consisting of women in their prime childbearing years. In 1956, 11% of the total population consisted of women 20–34 years of age. In 1990 the proportion was 14%, representing an increase of 26%. This change was not gradual. Most of the change occurred in the 1970s, the percentage of women 20–34 years of age being relatively stable during the 1960s. Between 1970 and 1975 there was an increase of 16% and from 1975 to 1980 an increase of another 14%, whereafter the change was much slower. The timing of the increase in the 1970s is related to the brief baby boom after World War II and a faster mortality decline in the 1950s.[5]

In every period from 1956–61 through 1980–85, declining marriage[6] and marital fertility were each factors in the decline in the birthrate (table 11.2).[7] For the whole period (1956–90), considering only the effects of marriage and marital fertility, 55% of the decline in the birthrate was attributable to declining marital fertility and 45% to declining marriage.[8] However, the relative contributions of the two factors varied considerably during the thirty-year period. Initially (1956–61), decreasing marriage had an effect (44%) almost equal to that of declining marital fertility and considerably greater than in the next period (1961–65) when only 19% was attributable to marriage, the decline of which slowed

3. The total fertility rate is the number of children each woman will bear if she lives through the childbearing years subject to the age-specific fertility rates for the specific year in question. Since the sex ratio at birth is approximately 105 boys per hundred girls, the total fertility rate is approximately 2.05 times the gross reproduction rate. Often, as in table 11.4, the rate is expressed per thousand women. Like the gross and net reproduction rates, it is a hypothetical measure of the consequences of the continuation of current rates.

4. The crude birthrate is the number of births per thousand of the total population.

5. Life expectancy at birth for males in the Taiwan area rose from 52.90 in 1950 to 61.80 in 1960. The increase was much slower in the next decade, at the end of which life expectancy rose to 66.08.

6. The term "nuptiality" is more appropriate technically than the term "marriage," which we use in this chapter because it is more familiar to the general reader.

7. It is possible to reduce changes in the birthrate into four components: the proportion of the women married at each childbearing age, their age distribution, their marital fertility at each age, and the interaction between these three factors. The results of such a decomposition are shown in table 11.2.

8. In these calculations, the change in the crude birthrate due to percentage married or marital fertility is divided by the sum of the two. For example, for 1956–90, 14.5 and 17.8 are each divided by 32.3 to obtain the percentages cited in the text.

TABLE 11.2 Decomposition of Changes in Crude Birthrates and Percentage Changes in Crude and Standardized Birthrates, Taiwan, 1956–90

Rate	RATE CHANGES							
	1956–90	1956–61	1961–65	1965–70	1970–75	1975–80	1980–85	1985–90
Crude birthrate								
Beginning of period	44.8	44.8	37.7	32.1	27.2	22.4	23.3	18.0
End of period	16.6	37.7	32.1	27.2	22.4	23.3	18.0	16.6
Change in crude birthrate due to								
Age structure	10.5	-2.3	-1.1	-0.2	3.9	2.7	0.6	-0.7
Percentage married	-14.5	-2.3	-0.8	-1.5	-2.5	-1.5	-2.4	-2.9
Marital fertility	-17.8	-2.9	-3.4	-3.2	-5.6	-0.1	-3.4	1.9
Interaction	-6.4	0.4	-0.2	0.0	-0.4	-0.2	-0.2	0.3
All factors[a]	-28.2	-7.1	-5.6	-5.0	-4.6	0.9	-5.3	-1.4
Per annum change in crude birthrate due to								
Age structure	0.3	-0.5	-0.3	0.0	0.8	0.5	0.1	-0.1
Percentage married	-0.4	-0.5	-0.2	-0.3	-0.5	-0.3	-0.5	-0.6
Marital fertility	-0.5	-0.6	-0.9	-0.6	-1.1	0.0	-0.7	0.4
Interaction	-0.2	0.1	-0.1	0.0	-0.1	0.0	0.0	0.1
All factors[a]	-0.8	-1.4	-1.4	-1.0	-0.9	0.2	-1.1	-0.3
Crude birthrate, end of period, standardized[b] on age and marriage, beginning of period	27.0	41.9	34.3	28.9	21.6	22.3	19.9	19.9
Average annual change								
Crude birthrate	-0.8	-1.4	-1.4	-1.0	-1.0	0.2	-1.1	-0.3
Standardized birthrate	-0.5	-0.6	-0.9	-0.6	-1.1	0.0	-0.7	0.4
Percentage decrease per year								
Crude birthrate	1.8	3.2	3.7	3.1	3.5	-0.1	4.6	1.6
Standardized birthrate	1.1	1.3	2.0	2.0	4.1	0.0	2.9	-2.1

[a] Discrepancies are due to rounding.

[b] Standardized rates are computed by assuming that age-marital distributions remain constant during the period and that only the age/marital-specific fertility rates change.

TABLE 11.3 Percentage of Women Currently Married and Percentage Change, by Wife's Age, Taiwan, 1956–90

Wife's Age	PERCENTAGE CURRENTLY MARRIED								Percentage Change, 1956–90
	1956	1961	1965	1970	1975	1980	1985	1990	
15–19	11.3	12.5	9.2	8.0	5.8	5.0	3.2	2.5	−78
20–24	69.6	60.9	58.3	50.3	43.2	39.9	33.7	25.5	−63
25–29	93.2	89.3	88.8	88.1	82.8	78.9	75.0	66.9	−28
30–34	93.8	91.6	92.8	93.0	93.2	90.0	87.2	83.7	−11
35–39	90.8	89.8	91.5	93.2	93.8	92.8	89.9	86.7	−5
40–44	85.7	85.6	88.0	90.6	92.6	92.3	91.2	87.4	+2
45–49	78.1	80.2	83.3	85.7	88.9	90.1	89.7	87.4	+12

down temporarily (table 11.2). In 1975–80 the marriage effect accounted for almost all the birth rate decline due to a temporary slowing down of the marital fertility decline. With a greatly accelerated fertility decline in the period 1980–85, marital fertility decline was again the major factor. In the most recent period, 1985–90, the continuing decline in the percentage married accounted for all of the birthrate decline, with marital fertility increasing in all of the prime childbearing years. It is clear that changes in marriage played an important role in the transition from high to low fertility.

As table 11.3 indicates, between 1956 and 1990 the proportions currently married decreased by 78% at age 15–19, 63% at age 20–24, 28% at age 25–29, and 11% at age 30–34. At age 35–39 the proportions currently married increased until 1975 because of declining mortality, but then decreased steadily through 1990. The composition of this group, however, changed during this period. In 1956, among women 35–39, 1.6% had never married, 1.3% were divorced, and 6.3% were widowed. By 1990 these percentages were 7.5, 4.3, and 2.0%, respectively. The decline in the proportion of widows is a result of the mortality decline and not to a higher remarriage rate. The rise in the proportion never marrying was too small to have much effect on the fertility decline as compared with the effect of the rising age at first marriage, which decreased greatly the proportions in the prime childbearing years (20–24 and 25–29) where marital fertility was very high. Aspects of these issues about marriage were discussed in chapter 8.

Taiwan's fertility decline began first among women at older ages and later among women at younger ages (tables 11.4 and 11.5). For the whole period 1956–90, 35% of the total fertility rate decline was attrib-

TABLE 11.4 Fertility Rates, Taiwan, 1956–90

Type of Rate	1956	1961	1965	1970	1975	1980	1985	1990
Crude birthrate	44.8	37.7	32.1	27.2	22.4	23.3	18.0	16.6
Total fertility rate (per 1,000 women)	6,528	5,608	4,825	4,000	2,765	2,515	1,885	1,805
General fertility rate[a]	197	177	152	120	92	91	68	62
Age-specific fertility rate for all women by age								
15–19	51	45	36	40	34	33	20	17
20–24	265	249	261	238	191	180	129	100
25–29	341	342	326	293	212	200	158	159
30–34	297	246	195	147	80	69	56	68
35–39	223	157	100	59	26	16	12	15
40–44	105	71	41	20	8	4	2	2
45–49	23	10	6	3	2	1	0	0
General fertility rate for married women	285	258	225	192	153	152	113	105
Age-specific fertility rate for married women by age								
15–19	451	362	390	502	595	670	604	682
20–24	381	409	447	473	441	453	383	394
25–29	366	384	368	332	255	253	210	237
30–34	317	269	210	158	85	77	64	82
35–39	226	175	109	64	28	17	14	17
40–44	122	83	47	22	8	4	2	2
45–49	29	13	8	4	2	1	0	0

Note: In this and subsequent tables, 1956 age-specific fertility rates are based not on mid-year population but on the census population. All rates are per 1,000 women of population.

[a]The general fertility rate is the number of births per 1,000 women of childbearing age.

TABLE 11.5 Percentage Changes in Fertility Rates, Taiwan, Selected Time Periods, 1956–90

Rate	1956–90	1956–61	1961–65	1965–70	1970–75	1975–80	1980–85	1985–90
Crude birthrate	-63	-16	-15	-15	-18	+4	-23	-8
Total fertility rate	-72	-14	-14	-17	-31	-9	-25	-4
General fertility rate	-69	-10	-14	-21	-23	-1	-25	-9
Age-specific fertility rate for all women by age								
15–19	-67	-12	-24	-11	-15	-3	-39	-15
20–24	-62	-6	+5	-9	-20	-6	-28	-22
25–29	-53	0	-5	-10	-28	-6	-21	+1
30–34	-77	-17	-21	-25	-46	-14	-19	+21
35–39	-93	-30	-36	-41	-56	-38	-25	+25
40–44	-98	-32	-42	-51	-60	-50	-50	0
45–49	-100	-57	-40	-50	-33	-50	-100	0
General fertility rate for married women	-63	-9	-13	-15	-20	-1	-26	-7
Age-specific fertility rate for married women by age								
15–19	+51	-20	+8	+29	+19	+13	-10	+13
20–24	+3	+7	+9	+6	-7	+3	-15	+3
25–29	-35	+5	-4	-10	-23	-1	-17	+13
30–34	-74	-15	-22	-25	-46	-9	-17	+28
35–39	-92	-23	-38	-41	-56	-39	-18	+21
40–44	-98	-32	-43	-53	-64	-50	-50	0
45–49	-100	-55	-38	-50	-50	-50	-100	0

utable to women over 35. However, the proportion attributable to such older women was 61% for 1956–61, 20% for 1970–75, and zero by 1985–90.

By 1990, fertility at age 45–49 had fallen to zero and at age 40–44 it was only 2 per thousand. At age 35–39 it had fallen to 15 per thousand from an initial 223 in 1956. The total fertility rate for ages 35 and older had fallen 95% in the thirty-four years under review. A further decline to zero fertility after age 35 could only reduce total fertility at all ages by 4%. That Taiwan's family planning program disproportionately re-cruited older women in its earlier period was a rational and effective strategy. However, from a demographic point of view, older women are no longer a significant target for the program. More than 85% of women over 30 were practicing contraception by 1985.

The concentration of births at younger ages means, of course, that the mean length of the generations has decreased significantly over the period under review, falling from 30.3 in 1956 to 26.5 in 1986. If there is a continuing negative rate of intrinsic growth, the shorter generation length means that an actual negative growth rate will be achieved more quickly than would otherwise be the case.

Over the whole period 1956–90, fertility at age 15–19 decreased by 67% (table 11.5). But this decline is entirely a result of the sharp decrease in the proportions married at that early age. Marital fertility actually increased sharply for the small group of married women who were 15–19 years old—only 2% of all women were 15–19 in 1990. This rise in marital fertility was caused by a higher age at marriage. As age at marriage rises, there are fewer second- and higher-order births among this age group. First birth intervals tend to be shorter than higher-order birth intervals. Hence, a rise in the proportion of first births in a certain age group usually leads to a rise in the marital fertility of that age group, other things being equal. Additionally, first birth intervals have been getting shorter.

The sharp decline in fertility for women 20–24 for the period 1956–90 as a whole was also entirely a result of the decline in the proportions married. For the period 1956–70, marital fertility actually increased 24% for this age group. This increase was probably also partly related to the rise in the age at marriage.[9] The marital fertility of women 20–24 began to decline in 1970–75 and has done so modestly since then, except

9. Part of this increase may also be related to less and shorter periods of breastfeeding (Millman 1986).

for small rises for 1975–80 and 1985–90. Age-specific marital fertility rates are shown in the bottom panel of table 11.4. At ages 25 and above, with a single exception, marital fertility declined throughout the period between 1956 and 1985. Between 1985 and 1990 marital fertility rose at all ages below 40.

During much of the period 1956–86, marital fertility as well as the proportions married declined simultaneously at ages over 24, suggesting that there exists a common determinant. One such determinant could be the existence of relatively attractive female employment opportunities that could raise the opportunity costs of childbearing. Relatively attractive employment may also serve as an alternative to early marriage.

Childbearing is now concentrated in a relatively short time period soon after marriage, because most couples have only two or three children and the first birth occurs soon after marriage. The concentration of small numbers of births in short time periods means that the potential for volatility is greater in response to short-run variations in timing of births and marriage and to the varying size of marriage cohorts resulting from past fertility changes.

The long-term fertility decline has been interrupted at least temporarily, with the gross reproduction rate varying up and down in the range of .81 to .89 between 1986 and 1990 (table 11.1). Griffith Feeney (1991) has pointed out that fertility may rise if births postponed because of a rising age at marriage are being made up. There is some support for this explanation in rising marital fertility rates for age groups from 25–29 through 35–39 between 1985 and 1990. However, the high gross reproduction rate for 1988 was probably a result of that year being a "Dragon Year," believed to be a favorable year for births.

Table 11.6 provides data comparing Taiwan's fertility for 1966 and 1986 with other Chinese populations in Hong Kong, Shanghai, and Singapore. Since Taiwan's population includes rural and small-town components not found in these other populations, data for Taipei, Taiwan's largest city, are also shown.

The pattern of concentration of fertility declines at older ages seen already for Taiwan as a whole, and here for Taipei, is similar to, but less extreme than, that in Shanghai, which was affected by the powerful family planning program in mainland China. This pattern differs from that for Singapore and Hong Kong, where fertility declines have been more concentrated in younger age groups. By 1986, when all of these populations had very low fertility rates, the proportions of their total

TABLE 11.6 Fertility Rates for Shanghai, Hong Kong, Singapore, Taiwan, and Taipei, 1966 and 1986

FERTILITY RATE

	1966					1986				
Age of Women	Shanghai	Hong Kong	Singapore	Taiwan	Taipei	Shanghai	Hong Kong	Singapore	Taiwan	Taipei
Age-specific fertility rate										
15–19	4	29	15	39	26	0	7	9	18	7
20–24	122	213	196	269	229	71	48	62	112	67
25–29	223	291	273	320	276	142	109	114	139	122
30–34	126	203	198	184	141	39	76	79	52	60
35–39	48	111	123	88	63	10	26	29	12	15
40–44	23	42	50	37	22	0	4	5	2	2
45–49	—	3	9	5	7	0	0	0	0	0
Total fertility rate per woman	2.72	4.46	4.32	4.71	3.82	1.34	1.33	1.49	1.68	1.36

Sources: Data for Hong Kong for 1966 are from Freedman and Adlakha (1968). Other data for Hong Kong and Singapore are from pertinent volumes of the United Nations *Demographic Yearbook*. Taiwan and Taipei data are from various volumes of the *Taiwan Demographic Fact Book*. The Shanghai data are from Coale and Li (1987).

fertility rates attributable to women at ages 30 and over were the following:

Shanghai	18%
Taiwan	20%
Taipei	28%
Hong Kong	39%
Singapore	38%

An important consequence of these patterns is that the mean length of generation is shorter for Shanghai than for any of the other populations, but it is also significantly shorter for Taipei and Taiwan than for Hong Kong and Singapore. As a result, at comparable levels of the net reproduction rate, the absolute value of the annual intrinsic rate of natural increase will be greatest in Shanghai, least in Hong Kong and Singapore, and intermediate for Taipei and Taiwan. This means, for example, that, with the fertility, mortality, and age distributions of a stable population, for net reproduction rates above 1, Shanghai's population would grow fastest, and for rates below 1 it would decline most rapidly.

It is notable that Shanghai's fertility rate was much lower than those of the other populations in 1966 as a result of a very sharp fertility decline following a major initiation of family planning programs in the cities of mainland China in 1963. Before this program and the Great Leap Forward immediately preceding it, Shanghai's fertility was similar to that of the other populations. By 1986 the rates of all of the cities had converged to very low levels.

Trends in Urban-Rural and Educational Differentials

For the whole period, 1961–86, the total fertility rate fell at about equal rates in the cities and in the rural townships, but somewhat more slowly in the urban townships. The fertility declines in the rural townships lagged in the early years, but in the period since 1975 have been greater than in the cities, with urban townships lagging behind both. The net result is that by 1986 the urban and rural township rates had almost converged, but the initial large differential between the cities and the townships persists:

Total Fertility Rates		
AREA	1961	1986
Taipei	4,467	1,350
Cities	4,902	1,495
Urban townships	5,637	1,815
Rural townships	6,128	1,860
Taiwan	5,608	1,675

TABLE 11.7   Total Fertility Rates by Education, 1966 and 1987, and Percentage Change, 1966–87, Taiwan Area, Republic of China

	Sr. High Grad. or Higher	Jr. High Grad.	Primary Grad.	Self-Taught Literate	Illiterate	Total
1966	2,604	3,023	4,600	5,377	5,446	4,676
1987	1,398	2,084	2,459	4,496	1,808	1,700
Percentage change, 1966–87	−46	−31	−47	−16	−67	−64

It is striking that by 1986 the total fertility rates of even the rural townships were substantially below replacement levels. Considering the whole period, 1961–86, the total fertility rates of the rural townships lagged behind those of the cities by a little less than five years, with a range of two to seven years. The fertility rates for Taiwan as a whole lagged behind those of the cities on the average only about two and one-quarter years. Diffusion from the urban to the rural areas has been very rapid, presumably as a result of Taiwan's small size, the excellent transportation and communication facilities which developed rapidly, and the considerable population mobility. Diffusion was found to be an important instrument of reproductive change in Taiwan, as demonstrated during an experiment in Taichung, one of Taiwan's important cities, early in the 1960s (Freedman and Takeshita 1969; Srikantan 1967).

Educational differentials in fertility were quite large in 1966 (table 11.7), when age-specific fertility rates by education of women were first published. Between 1966 and 1987 women who were either illiterate or literate without formal schooling had decreased from 42 to 4% of the women of childbearing age. Further, this relatively small group was concentrated at older, low-fertility ages by 1987. Nevertheless, the illiterate group was large enough so that their quite low fertility by 1987 must be taken seriously. We hypothesize that those still illiterate at that time were a highly selected, low-status group with fecundity (and perhaps other) impairments, high proportions unmarried, or both.

Since, by 1987, 96% of all women of childbearing age had at least a primary school education, we can concentrate on those. Between 1966 and 1987 the TFR (total fertility rate) fell at about the same high rate for both the primary-educated and senior-high-or-higher-educated women, so that the relative differential between these two extreme groups remained unchanged. The middle group—those with junior high education—had a somewhat slower rate of decline, so their TFR was closer to the primary school group by 1987. The fact that Taiwan's total fertility rate was substantially below replacement level by 1987 was a result of the very low fertility of the highest education group. The junior high group was just at the replacement level, and the primary school group was significantly above replacement. Nevertheless, by 1987 the TFR for the primary school group was lower than the 1966 rate for the best educated.

Although educational differences in contraceptive prevalence have virtually disappeared (see below), the continuing educational differentials in fertility are consistent with continuing differentials in fertility preferences and contraceptive effectiveness.

Trends in Family Size Preferences and Family Planning, 1965–85

The fertility trends just described resulted from fundamental changes in preferences regarding the timing of childbearing, in the number and sex of children, and in the use of fertility control measures to satisfy these changing preferences. Systematic data on these matters come from the series of sample surveys described in chapter 1 and appendix A and, therefore, begin in 1965 with the first of these surveys.

In view of the changes reported on marital fertility between 1956 and 1965, it is clear that a fairly rapid increase in the use of fertility control measures must have begun earlier. One approach to estimating the level and the effect of fertility control measures is the Coale and Trussell (1974) model, which essentially involves comparing the shape of the marital fertility schedule with that expected under a regime of natural fertility (i.e., fertility in a situation in which any influences affecting marital fertility are not parity-dependent and do not, therefore, involve deliberate fertility control to limit the number of births). In this model, m is an index of the departure of fertility patterns from natural fertility. The value of m is 0.0 if the shape of the fertility curve by age is identical with that of a model natural fertility schedule. An m value of 1.0 indicates that actual fertility differs from natural fertility to the same extent as the average deviation of 43 marital fertility schedules in the early 1960s, which represented a range of differences in the extent of fertility control.

In 1956 the value of m for Taiwan was 0.09, which is interpreted as a natural fertility level. By 1960 m was 0.375 and by 1965 it was 0.953. By 1978 it was 2.5. Differences in m by level of urbanization in 1961 and 1965 correspond roughly to the differentials already noted in fertility rates. It should be no surprise that m rose rapidly in Taiwan, since the concentration of declines at older ages characteristic initially of the fertility decline in Taiwan is built into the natural fertility model for estimating m.

Trends in Preferred Number of Children

Mean preferred family size of married women decreased monotonically from 4.0 in 1965 to 2.6 in 1985 (table 11.8).[10] Preferred family size decreased little between 1965 and 1970, while the adoption of birth control was very rapid. We speculate that preferred family size in 1965 was not much lower than in earlier periods, but that rapidly falling mortality motivated many women to adopt contraception to avoid childbearing beyond the desired number of children.

For two reasons it is also useful to examine preferred family size by cohort. First, if respondents adjust their reports of desired numbers of children on the basis of their past reproductive experience, then the preferences of the older respondents at each period may differ from the younger women at the same period even if at a comparable age they would have been similar. Second, it is of interest to determine whether the fertility transition represents smooth changes across cohorts or whether successive cohort trajectories differ.

In our cohort analysis we limit the samples at each period to currently (once) married respondents, married by age 25, and at least 25 years old at each survey date. The mean preferred number of children was considered at successive ages for five-year birth cohorts beginning with 1925–29 (unpublished table). The results confirm that at each age successive cohorts preferred fewer children. At ages 25–29, for example, respondents born between 1935 and 1939 reported a desired mean of 3.9 children, while twenty years later their counterparts desired 2.4 children. More dramatically, at ages 35 to 39, respondents born in 1925–29 preferred a mean of 5.4 children, while 20 years later the birth cohort of 1945–49 reported a preferred mean of 2.9 children—a change of 2.5, or 46%.

A comparison of the experience of each cohort at successive ages

10. In the tables of survey data that follow, the data are for married women 22–39 years of age instead of the more customary 20–39. The observations in these tables were calculated and added sequentially in periodic reports as the surveys were done. The standard use of 22–39 was to preserve comparability with an early survey. We have chosen not to recompute the data for other years on a 20–39 basis, because the shift from 22–39 to 20–39 made no difference for any trend statements and little difference in overall levels when we tested the differences for a range of variables for 1965 and 1985.

TABLE 11.8 Mean Preferred Number of Children for Married Women Aged 22–39, by Wife's Age, Number of Living Children, and Marriage Duration, Taiwan, Selected Years, 1965–85

Item	MEAN PREFERRED NUMBER OF CHILDREN[a]					NUMBER OF RESPONDENTS				
	1965	1970	1976	1980	1985[b]	1965	1970	1976	1980	1985[b]
Wife's age										
22–24	3.7	3.6	2.7	2.6	2.3	380	285	276	497	876
25–29	3.8	3.6	2.7	2.7	2.5	975	821	513	1,266	2,596
30–34	4.0	3.8	3.0	2.9	2.6	879	734	445	987	2,782
35–39	4.3	4.1	3.2	3.1	2.9	815	651	444	858	1,856
Total	4.0	3.8	2.9	2.8	2.6	3,049	2,491	1,678	3,608	8,110
Wives Aged 22–29										
Number of living children										
0	3.7	3.2	2.5	2.4	2.1	106	60	70	145	235
1	3.6	3.3	2.5	2.4	2.2	247	196	176	426	988
2	3.6	3.3	2.6	2.6	2.3	404	356	233	562	1,279
3	3.8	3.8	2.9	2.9	2.8	354	307	222	470	755
4	4.1	4.1	3.4	3.2	3.3	185	134	75	135	193
5 or more	4.7	4.3	c	3.8	2.8	59	53	13	25	22
6 or more	3.8	3.6	2.7	2.7	2.4	1,355	1,106	789	1,763	3,472
Wives Aged 30–39										
Number of living children										
0	2.7	c	c	2.3	1.8	21	13	3	23	53
1	3.2	3.2	2.6	2.3	2.0	42	25	25	96	332
2	3.2	3.1	2.4	2.4	2.2	110	113	99	332	1,284
3	3.7	3.4	2.9	2.9	2.8	238	284	274	668	1,790
4	4.1	4.0	3.3	3.4	3.3	447	423	266	474	890
5 or more	4.6	4.4	3.6	3.6	3.4	836	526	222	252	288
6 or more	4.2	3.9	3.1	3.0	2.7	1,694	1,384	889	1,845	4,637
Wives Aged 22–29										
Marriage duration (years)										
Less than 5	3.6	3.4	2.6	2.5	2.3	578	478	387	920	1,826
5–9	3.8	3.7	2.8	2.8	2.6	659	542	342	677	1,424
10–14	4.4	4.1	3.2	2.9	2.9	117	86	56	160	219
Wives Aged 30–39										
Marriage duration (years)										
Less than 5	3.2	2.9	3.2	2.3	2.2	23	22	78	86	319
5–9	3.7	3.6	2.9	2.7	2.5	218	204	158	367	1,288
10–14	4.1	3.9	3.1	3.0	2.7	638	538	356	724	1,693
15–19	4.3	4.1	3.2	3.2	3.6	661	499	298	556	1,135
20 and over	4.5	4.1	u	3.3	3.1	154	122	u	112	198

Note: u = unavailable.

[a] Indeterminate responses estimated for less than 2% of all cases.

[b] The 1985 data in tables 11.8 to 11.27 were based on a special survey which included aboriginal areas. The aboriginal areas are excluded in all of these tables, since they were excluded from the samples in all of the surveys for the other years.

[c] Mean not calculated for fewer than twenty cases.

suggests that later cohorts (those born in 1940 and later) differed from the earlier respondents in this respect: while the preferred number of children of earlier cohorts remained fairly stable or possibly increased slightly with increasing age, later cohorts reported smaller preferred numbers of children with increasing age. There is little evidence that the respondents adjusted their reported preferences upward to match their actual reproductive experience: actual fertility exceeded the reported number of desired children at all but the youngest ages.

The rapid increase in contraceptive practice began before much of the change in preferred number of children, because the actual number was beyond the preferred number. After 1970, by which time contraceptive use levels had already increased considerably, a rapid rate of decline in preferred family size also occurred. This rapid decline slowed down between 1975 and 1980, as did the actual fertility decline. In 1980 (Chang, Freedman, and Sun 1981) we expressed the belief that the slowing of the declines might indicate a leveling-off of fertility preferences, with strong traditional familial relationships retarding further declines. That conclusion was premature, since the more rapid decline resumed in 1980–85. The decline occurred for almost every category of age, parity, marital duration, and the rural-urban and educational variables (tables 11.8 and 11.9).

By 1985, two rather than three children had become the modal preferred family size for both younger and older women (table 11.10). Among women under 30, the preference for only two children increased from 6% in 1965 to 56% by 1985. In the five years from 1980 to 1985 the increase was from 41 to 56%. It continued to be true, however, that very few preferred one child—only 3% in 1985.[11] At the opposite extreme, preferences for large families have almost disappeared. In 1965, of women under age 30, 58% preferred four or more children; by 1985 it was only 6%, and no woman under 30 expressed a preference for more than four.

Another indication of smaller family size preference is the proportion of women at each parity saying that they wanted no more children (table 11.11).[12] Between 1965 and 1985 those saying that they wanted no more

11. While 14% of those with only one child said they want no more children, this was only 2.3% of the total sample, and a large majority of these were older women with relatively long open birth intervals.

12. Throughout this chapter, yes and no answers to the question, "Would you like to have more children?" are the basis for classifying women as wanting or not wanting additional children.

TABLE 11.9 Preferred Number of Children and Percentage Ever Practiced Contraception for Married Women Aged 22–39, by Education and Urbanization, Taiwan, Selected Years, 1965–85

Modernization Indicator	Preferred Number of Children					Percent Ever Practiced Contraception[a]					Number of Respondents				
	1965	1970	1976	1980	1985	1965	1970	1976	1980	1985	1965	1970	1976	1980	1985
Education															
None	4.1	4.0	3.4	3.2	3.1	19	51	78	83	89	1,449	839	393	536	511
Primary	3.9	3.8	2.9	2.9	2.8	32	54	73	81	91	1,311	1,325	962	2,033	3,847
Junior high	3.6	3.3	2.6	2.7	2.5	51	71	80	80	89	181	194	158	380	1,411
Senior high or more	3.2	3.0	2.3	2.4	2.2	60	79	78	85	90	108	133	171	695	2,477
Urbanization															
Rural township	4.2	3.9	3.2	3.0	2.8	21	48	73	79	90	1,227	1,004	574	1,123	2,371
Urban township	3.9	3.8	3.1	3.0	2.9	26	54	72	79	90	902	753	376	815	1,366
Small city[b]	3.8	3.6	2.7	2.7	2.5	32	62	78	86	91	303	199	221	664	1,959
Large city[c]	3.7	3.5	2.7	2.6	2.4	43	69	81	85	91	617	535	514	1,051	2,514
Total	4.0	3.8	2.9	2.8	2.6	28	56	76	82	90	3,049	2,491	1,685	3,653	8,246

[a]Includes sterilization.

[b]Small cities are defined administratively.

[c]Large cities are the five largest.

TABLE 11.10 Percentage Distribution of Preferred Number of Children for Married Women Aged 22–39 by Wife's Age, Taiwan, Selected Years, 1965–85

Wife's Age and Survey Year	Less than 2	2	3	4	5 or More	Indeterminate[a]	Total Percent	Number of Respondents
	PERCENTAGE DISTRIBUTION BY PREFERRED NUMBER OF CHILDREN							
22–29								
1965	—	6	33	46	12	1	100	1,355
1970	—	8	41	40	11	—	100	1,107
1976	1	37	49	12	1	0	100	790
1980	1	41	45	12	0	0	100	1,773
1985	3	56	33	6	0	2	100	3,545
30–39								
1965	—	4	18	48	28	1	100	1,694
1970	—	4	24	52	19	—	100	1,385
1976	1	25	40	31	3	1	100	895
1980	1	27	43	26	1	2	100	1,880
1985	2	41	38	15	1	3	100	4,792
22–39								
1965	—	5	25	48	21	1	100	3,049
1970	—	6	32	47	15	1	100	2,492
1976	1	31	44	22	2	—	100	1,685
1980	1	34	44	19	1	1	100	3,653
1985	3	47	36	12	1	3	100	8,337

Note: Figures may not sum to 100 because of rounding in this and subsequent tables. Dashes indicate less than 1% in this and subsequent tables.

[a]Answers of "up to the gods," "up to fate," or not ascertained.

children increased from 17 to 74% among second-parity women and from 50 to 90% at the third parity.

The proportions of women who said they wanted no more children increased steadily at each parity and marital duration from 1965 through 1976. Between 1976 and 1980 and then between 1980 and 1985, these proportions leveled off and even decreased at levels near saturation. By 1985, 64% of younger, second-parity women and 83% of older, second-parity women said that they wanted no more children. The corresponding figures for third-parity women were 86 and 91%. These recent trends probably have been affected by shifts in age at marriage, spacing behavior, and parity distributions, whose effects will require more detailed analysis than is possible for this trend review.

The decline in fertility preferences was found in all rural-urban and educational categories (table 11.9). However, in absolute terms the differentials were almost as large in 1985 as in 1965, and in relative terms

TABLE 11.11   Percentage of Married Women Aged 22–39 Who Want No Additional Children, by Wife's Age, Number of Living Children, and Marriage Duration, Taiwan, Selected Years, 1965–85

	Age 22–29					Age 30–39					Age 22–39				
Variable	1965	1970	1976	1980	1985	1965	1970	1976	1980	1985	1965	1970	1976	1980	1985
Number of living children															
0	1	—	—	2	—	33	34	a	a	2	6	6	—	3	—
1	1	0	15	14	11	21	35	20	33	25	4	4	16	17	14
2	13	19	58	57	64	34	56	77	86	83	17	28	63	68	74
3	45	50	84	86	86	58	80	98	96	91	50	64	92	92	90
4	74	66	89	93	94	84	88	95	97	95	81	82	94	96	95
5 or more	88	83	79	84	96	93	94	96	96	99	93	93	95	95	99
Marriage duration															
Less than 5 years	7	10	28	27	29	22	28	76	49	44	8	11	36	29	31
5–9 years	42	44	78	78	74	53	60	81	81	80	45	48	79	79	77
10–14 years	69	75	84	90	89	76	84	95	94	90	75	83	93	93	90
15–19 years[b]						91	95	97	98	92	91	95	97	97	92
20 and over[b]						92	95	u	95	95	92	95	u	95	94
Total	30	32	54	53	51	79	84	92	91	85	57	61	74	73	71

Note: Yes and no answers to the question, "Would you like to have more children?" are the basis for classifying women as wanting or not wanting additional children. One to two percent indeterminate were classified as wanting additional children. Dashes indicate less than 1%. u = unavailable.

[a] Fewer than twenty-two cases in base.

[b] Women were too young to be married this long, for age 22–29.

they were larger. The convergence of educational differentials in contraceptive practice discussed below did not extend to preferences.

The differences by education in preferences are not merely a function of educational differences in achieved parity or age. The negative relation of preference and education persisted, although it diminished by about half with control for age and parity. Further, when first preferences are controlled, the Coombs Number Preference (IN) Scale[13] is still negatively related to education. This indicates that the lower the educational level, the greater the probability that any specific preference statement has an underlying tilt toward higher fertility.

Differentials were greater for education than for the rural-urban dimension. Apart from the evidence in table 11.9, this is clear from the eta coefficients[14] measuring the association of preferences and education, which is considerably greater than for the rural-urban dimension (table 11.12). Further, while the eta for the rural-urban dimension decreased substantially between 1980 and 1985, that for education actually increased slightly, and there was a substantial increase in the eta for the education relationship between 1965 and 1985.

Since, throughout most of the twenty-year period under review, actual fertility was greater than preferred fertility at older ages, we might expect that preferences were adjusted upward over the life course to rationalize actual fertility preferences. This was definitely not the case for several age cohorts that we were able to follow over successive surveys.

The Preference for Sons

Along with the downward shift in the preferred number of children, there was a decrease in the preference for sons. Between 1965 and 1985 the percentage preferring two or more sons decreased from about 92% to about 45% (table 11.13). Most recently, between 1980 and 1985, the proportion wanting only one son increased significantly, especially among the younger women (49% of women aged 22–29 chose one son in 1985 compared with 35% in 1980). There was a decrease in the proportion wanting two sons, from 55% to 36% among women aged

13. The Coombs Scale asks respondents a series of questions on family size (IN) and sex (IS) preferences. The number preference scales are numbered from 1 to 7 to represent increasing bias for larger family size. See Coombs (1974) and Coombs, Coombs, and McClelland (1975) for more detailed explanations.

14. Eta is a measure of association from one-way analysis of variance. It is the square root of the percentage of variance in the dependent variable explained by the predictor variable.

TABLE 11.12 Eta Values for Correlations, within Age Groups, of Education and Urbanization with Preferred Number of Children, Number of Live Births, Practice of Contraception, and Wife's Age, Taiwan, Selected Years, 1965–85

Modernization Indicator and Wife's Age	ETA VALUES[a]														
	Mean Preferred Number of Children					Mean Number of Live Births					Percentage Who Ever Practiced Contraception				
	1965	1970	1976	1980	1985	1965	1970	1976	1980	1985	1965	1970	1976	1980	1985
Education and age															
22–29	.19	.27	.33	.31	.32	.13	.25	.28	.39	.44	.23	.26	.12	.08	.03
30–39	.22	.23	.34	.35	.37	.21	.24	.30	.39	.46	.27	.15	.07	.05	.00
Total, 22–39	.21	.26	.38	.35	.37	.17	.25	.38	.42	.48	.23	.15	.07	.04	.01
Urbanization and age															
22–29	.15	.22	.29	.20	.10	.03	.04	.12	.13	.09	.19	.20	.16	.12	.02
30–39	.16	.17	.25	.24	.13	.17	.18	.19	.20	.12	.19	.13	.03	.05	.02
Total, 22–39	.15	.20	.26	.22	.11	.08	.15	.13	.15	.08	.18	.16	.09	.08	.00

[a]Eta is a zero-order correlation coefficient where one of the variables is categorical.

TABLE 11.13 Percentage Distribution of Preferred Number of Sons for Married Women Aged 22–39, by Wife's Age, Taiwan, Selected Years, 1965–85

	PERCENTAGE DISTRIBUTION BY PREFERRED NUMBER OF SONS						
Wife's Age and Survey Year	Less than 2	2	3 or More	Either Sons or Daughters[a]	Indeterminate[b]	Total	Number of Respondents
22–29							
1965	6	72	18	3	1	100	1,355
1970	7	77	11	4	1	100	1,107
1976	29	57	2	12	1	100	790
1980	35	55	1	9	0	100	1,764
1985	49	36	1	11	3	100	3,545
30–39							
1965	4	61	32	2	1	100	1,694
1970	5	71	21	2	—	100	1,385
1976	19	65	5	10	1	100	895
1980	25	66	3	6	0	100	1,845
1985	35	49	2	10	5	100	4,792

Note: Figures may not sum to 100 because of rounding. A dash indicates less than 1%.
[a] No special preference; either sex is all right.
[b] Answers of "up to the gods," "up to fate," or not ascertained.

22–29. Nevertheless, the continuing preference for sons was evident in a number of ways. First, there is the simple evidence of the mean preferred numbers of sons and daughters in 1985:

Wife's Age (years)	Mean Preferred No.	
	Sons	Daughters
22–29	1.4	1.1
30–39	1.6	1.2

Distributions of family composition preferences are even more revealing than averages (table 11.14). In 1985, only 37% of the respondents expressed a preference for one son, but 67% were satisfied with one daughter. The modal preference in 1985 (37%) was for two children—one son and one daughter—a shift from the modal preference for two sons and one daughter in 1980. In 1965 only 4% had chosen one son and one daughter. The modal preference then was for two sons and two daughters. Chang (1989) reported that the proportion of wives who were willing to have more than the number of children they preferred in order to have a son decreased from 50% in 1973 to 22% in 1985, after adjustment for the effect of changing educational distributions.

Significant behavioral evidence of the continuing preference for sons in 1985 was that, among couples with similar numbers of children, desire

TABLE 11.14 Percentage Distribution of Family Composition Preferences, Taiwan, Selected Years, 1965–85

PREFERRED NUMBER		PERCENTAGE DISTRIBUTION				
Daughters	Sons	1965	1970	1976	1980	1985
1	1	4	5	23	28	37
1	2	23	30	40	41	30
2	2	40	41	20	17	11
1	3	6	5	1	1	0
2	3	13	8	1	0	0
3	3	4	0	0	0	0
Other combinations		6	8	3	3	8
Either sex all right		2	3	11	8	11
Indeterminate[a]		1	1	1	1	3
Total		100	100	100	100	100

Note: Figures may not sum to 100 because of rounding.

[a] Answers of "up to the gods," "up to fate," or not ascertained.

for more children and practice of contraception were related to the number of sons they had (see table 11.15), although differentials were smaller than in earlier years. In earlier years differentials by number of living sons were very large for those with two or more living children. By 1985, in all population strata, contraceptive prevalence rates for limiting and spacing births were so high and preferred numbers of children so low that differentials by sex of children inevitably were much smaller. While the preference for sons was still very evident, its force was constrained by the preference for few children.

There is probably further striking evidence of son preference in the rise of the sex ratio at birth from 106 to 110 in the past decade. In 1990, the sex ratio at birth was 119 for third births and 128 for fourth and fifth births, compared with the normal, expected 105. This probably results from a combination of prenatal sex determination and abortion. These new techniques may reduce the higher-fertility effect of son preference but at the cost of unbalanced sex ratios at adult ages. In Korea, this practice had produced by 1988 a sex ratio at birth of 115 with a ratio of 170 for third births (Lee and Cho 1991). With modern technology, very low fertility is theoretically compatible with almost everyone having a son, but the social costs of the resulting unbalanced sex ratio deserve serious consideration.

The Increase in Birth Control Practice

A substantial minority of couples were already practicing contraception when the survey series began in 1965. Ever-use and current use of contra-

TABLE 11.15 Percentage of Married Women Aged 22–39 Who Want No Additional Children and Percentage Who Are Currently Practicing Contraception, by Number of Living Children and Living Sons, Taiwan, Selected Years, 1965–85

Number of Living Children and Living Sons	Percentage Wanting No Additional Children					Percentage Currently Practicing Contraception[a]					Number of Respondents				
	1965	1970	1976	1980	1985	1965	1970	1976	1980	1985	1965	1970	1976	1980	1985
0 children	6	6	0	3	0	0	6	8	16	20	127	73	73	166	292
1 child															
0 sons	3	1	14	12	12	4	6	21	32	47	153	96	97	241	660
1 son	5	6	17	22	17	6	9	29	44	52	136	126	104	267	675
2 children															
0 sons	9	5	50	39	50	11	20	48	54	73	128	93	52	152	471
1 son	19	31	67	73	80	12	29	53	68	81	252	244	184	423	1,301
2 sons	22	37	63	77	78	13	34	70	80	85	134	133	97	273	850
3 children															
0 sons	14	12	46	60	82	9	10	49	58	80	70	56	35	71	208
1 son	29	51	87	88	85	17	40	65	74	88	185	179	145	338	884
2 or more sons	69	79	99	98	94	31	55	83	84	92	337	356	317	712	1,523
4 children															
0 sons	42	b	b	74	96	13	b	b	76	79	31	17	17	27	70
1 son	54	54	88	93	90	20	43	80	83	91	132	121	93	159	360
2 or more sons	91	93	97	99	98	40	63	75	90	93	469	418	234	429	705
5 or more children															
0 sons	61	58	b	45	100	21	36	b	36	76	33	22	7	11	30
1 son	78	77	92	95	98	27	43	75	78	90	107	75	60	84	90
2 or more sons	96	97	98	98	100	36	63	74	87	90	755	482	170	201	213
Total	57	61	74	73	71	24	44	63	70	78	3,049	2,491	1,685	3,554	8,332

[a]Includes sterilization.

[b]Fewer than twenty cases in base.

ceptives increased rapidly after that. This increase continued between 1980 and 1985 at all ages, parities, marital durations, and urban-rural and education strata (tables 11.9, 11.16, and 11.17).

In 1965 few women under 25 years of age were using contraception and even at age 35–39 only 36% were current users. While the increase in ever- and current use was rapid in all age groups, it was increasingly notable at the youngest ages as more and more women began use for spacing the small number of children they wanted. The age differentials in contraceptive prevalence rates narrowed very considerably over the twenty-year period. A majority of women at all ages were practicing contraception in 1985. In 1965, no childless wives reported ever practicing contraception (table 11.17). By 1985, 51% reported ever-use and 22% were currently using.

In 1965, the proportion ever using contraception was strongly related to education and degree of urbanization. These differentials narrowed steadily over the years. By 1985 the percentage ever practicing contraception was uniformly high for women with different degrees of urbanization and educational levels, ranging from 89 to 91% (table 11.9). For ages 30–39 current use varied only from 85 to 86%. As in previous periods, the increases in contraceptive use between 1980 and 1985 were slightly greater in the less educated and more rural strata of the population. This meant a continuing decrease in the correlation between these two variables and contraceptive use, as indicated by eta values in table 11.12. Between 1980 and 1985 the convergence (as indicated by eta) continued, both for younger and for older women, for these two measures. In other words, education and urban-rural differentials continued to decrease and almost disappeared by 1985.

Analyses of contraceptive use by birth cohort underscore these results (unpublished table). The percentage of respondents who reported that they had ever used contraception consistently follows the expected pattern: aggregate use increases with increasing age, and successive cohorts sampled at the same age show rapidly increasing use of contraception. At ages 25–29, of the cohort born between 1935 and 1939, just under 25% had used contraception, while of the cohort born twenty years later, 93% of women the same age had done so. At ages 35–39, 41% of the 1925–29 cohort had used contraception, while 96% of the 1945–49 cohort had. The sharpest increase occurred for the cohort born between 1940 and 1944.

Between ages 25–29 and 30–34, in the cohort born in 1935–39, the proportion who reported having used contraception nearly doubled from 25 to 49%, while in the next five years it increased again to 85% of the

TABLE 11.16 Percentage of Married Women Aged 20–39 Who Have Ever Practiced Contraception, Ever Had an Abortion, or Were Ever Sterilized, by Wife's Age, Taiwan, Selected Years, 1965–85

Wife's Age	Percentage Ever Practiced Contraception					Percentage Currently Practicing Contraception					Percentage Ever Had an Induced Abortion				
	1965	1970	1976	1980	1985	1965	1970	1976	1980	1985	1965	1970	1976	1980	1985
20–21	5	u	33	54	68	3	u	19	37	51	0	u	5	12	16
22–24	5	18	45	59	80	4	13	28	41	61	2	1	6	8	20
25–29	20	41	72	78	89	17	30	55	64	72	6	6	16	19	26
30–34	35	69	86	89	94	31	55	76	78	85	13	16	28	28	36
35–39	41	74	89	92	92	36	63	79	84	86	13	19	29	34	42

Wife's Age	Percentage Sterilized					Number of Respondents				
	1965	1970	1976	1980	1985	1965	1970	1976	1980	1985
20–21	1	u	1	1	1	139	u	97	173	207
22–24	0	1	2	3	4	380	289	276	502	884
25–29	3	3	7	12	13	975	821	514	1,271	2,632
30–34	6	9	15	26	30	879	734	449	993	2,835
35–39	9	15	19	27	37	815	651	446	887	1,816

Note: u = unavailable.

TABLE 11.17 Percentage of Married Women Aged 22–39 Who Have Ever Practiced Contraception or Had an Abortion, by Wife's Age, Number of Living Children, and Marriage Duration, Taiwan, Selected Years, 1965–85

Variable	Percentage Ever Practiced Contraception					Percentage Currently Practicing Contraception					Percentage Ever Had an Abortion				
	1965	1970	1976	1980	1985	1965	1970	1976	1980	1985	1965	1970	1976	1980	1985
Wives Aged 22–29															
Number of living children															
0	0	3	20	38	51	0	3	7	18	22	0	0	4	1	4
1	4	16	44	58	81	2	7	26	38	52	1	1	4	6	15
2	12	36	68	80	91	9	26	52	65	77	4	4	9	18	27
3	23	40	79	84	95	20	32	63	73	85	6	6	21	27	36
4	31	53	75	90	96	25	44	57	78	89	8	10	24	21	28
5 or more	34	66	a	73	96	30	41	71	62	83	8	13	a	23	17
All numbers	16	35	62	73	87	13	26	46	58	69	4	5	12	16	24
Wives Aged 30–39															
Number of living children															
0	0	19	a	17	26	0	a	a	4	7	5	4	a	0	2
1	19	30	20	62	67	19	16	16	37	43	5	8	0	13	17
2	27	52	81	88	94	21	39	71	76	84	6	8	20	24	37
3	32	72	92	94	97	30	61	86	84	92	13	21	32	37	44
4	44	76	92	96	98	39	62	80	90	92	15	17	28	34	40
5 or more	40	76	87	92	95	35	62	74	84	89	13	19	33	28	35
All numbers	38	72	87	90	93	33	58	77	81	85	13	17	29	31	39
Wives Aged 22–39															
Marriage duration (years)															
Less than 5	8	22	53	62	80	6	14	38	44	58	2	2	8	8	15
5–9	24	47	78	85	93	21	36	63	72	82	7	8	19	24	32
10–14	36	72	87	92	96	31	59	78	84	89	11	17	28	30	43
15–19	41	76	93	93	94	36	63	80	86	88	15	18	35	37	45
20 or more	35	77	—	90	93	32	65	—	81	82	11	22	—	38	45
Total	28	56	76	82	90	24	44	63	70	78	9	12	21	24	32

[a]Fewer than twenty cases.

TABLE 11.18   Percentage of Married Women Aged 22–39 Who Ever
Practiced Contraception by Wife's Attitude toward Additional
Children, Taiwan, Selected Years, 1965–85

	PERCENTAGE WHO EVER PRACTICED CONTRACEPTION				
Wife's Attitude	1965	1970	1976	1980	1985
Wanted no additional children	30	52	86	93	95
Wanted additional children	5	12	41	54	78

population who reported use. While we lack information on the cohort
of 1940–44 at ages 25–29, we can compare their behavior with the
previous cohort at ages 30–34. At those ages, of the 1940–44 birth
cohort, 79% had used contraception (49% of the previous cohort had
done so at the same age).

Use of contraception by later cohorts occurred early and at high levels:
over 90% of cohorts between 1945 and 1954 used contraception at ages
30–34, while over 90% of the 1955–59 cohort did so by ages 25–29.
This report of contraceptive use at early ages reflects the widespread use
of contraception for the purpose of spacing births: over half the women
of the cohorts of 1950–59 who had used contraception by ages 25–29
reported that they had begun the use of contraception for the purpose
of spacing births.

Reports of induced abortion among younger women and of sterilization among older women increased slowly but steadily from 1965–70
onward (table 11.16). The increases in the reported use of abortion,
concomitant with the rapid increase in contraceptive practice at all ages,
may indicate either an increasing incidence of accidental pregnancies due
to contraceptive failure or less tolerance of such failures. The substantial
increase in the adoption of sterilization may be due in part to the fact
that many women who had experience with abortion were sterilized
to avoid the necessity of aborting additional pregnancies. The use of
sterilization had a strong negative correlation to education.

Desire to Space and Stop Childbearing

In the early 1960s contraception was practiced almost entirely for stopping rather than spacing childbearing. In 1965 only 5% of women who
still wanted more children had ever practiced contraception (table
11.18). This proportion practicing contraception before they wanted to
stop childbearing increased slowly until 1970 and then increased very
rapidly, so that by 1980 the proportion was 54%, and by 1985 it in-

TABLE 11.19 Percentage of Married Women Aged 22–39 Ever Using Contraception, Who First Used Contraception to Space Births, by Wife's Age, Taiwan, Selected Years, 1970–85

Wife's Age	PERCENTAGE WHO FIRST PRACTICED TO SPACE BIRTHS			
	1970	1976	1980	1985
22–29	30	47	62	75
30–39	7	23	34	50
22–39	17	32	46	61

creased to 78%. These are remarkable shifts from stopping to spacing behavior in a very short time period. Among those wanting to stop, 30% had practiced contraception in 1965. This proportion increased rapidly to near-saturation levels of 93–95% by 1980–85.

Table 11.19 shows a different measure of spacing—self reports by those ever practicing contraception as to whether they began use for spacing. Among younger women this series, which began in 1970, shows 30% starting to practice contraception for spacing. This increased rapidly to 75% by 1985.

Contraceptive Methods Currently Being Used

While effective methods have dominated contraceptive practice since at least 1967 (table 11.20), there have been continuing substantial method shifts. The most notable changes have been a substantial decrease in the use of IUDs and a substantial increase in sterilization, which became the modal method by 1985. The increase in sterilization in Taiwan corresponds to increases in many countries around the world. The increases in Taiwan were facilitated by the easing of some legal barriers and easier

TABLE 11.20 Percentage of Current Users Reporting Selected Methods of Contraception, Taiwan, Selected Years, 1967–85

Method	PERCENTAGE REPORTING			
	1967	1976	1980	1985
IUD (including Ota ring)	57	44	32	25
Pill	8	11	9	7
Sterilization	17	18	25	33
Condom	5	6	12	18
Other	13	21	22	18
All current users	100	100	100	100

availability of services. Presumably, in Taiwan, as in the United States, as the number of children ever born has decreased and the period for which protection was required lengthened, sterilization became popular as a permanent stopping method, requiring no further action and no worries about the possible long-term effects of other methods. Norplant implants[15] are now receiving clinical and field tests in Taiwan and may become a substitute in Taiwan and elsewhere for sterilization.

The pill has never been an important method in Taiwan. The increase in the use of the condom from 5% in 1967 to 18% in 1985 makes it the third most commonly used method. The marked increase in the use of condoms is probably due largely to the efforts made in the island-wide army reservists' training program, in which condoms were offered. On the other hand, the small decrease in the use of the pill may be partly due to frequent reports in the Taiwan press of side effects, as reported in the world press.

The Decline in Breastfeeding

Breastfeeding, which reduces fecundability by extending the duration of postpartum anovulation, was initially important in keeping birth intervals longer and, therefore, fertility lower than the potentially higher fertility levels that might otherwise have been reached. During the period of the fertility transition, the prevalence and duration of breastfeeding have declined precipitously (Millman 1986). In 1967–68, among married women of reproductive age, 93% of infants were breastfed for an average duration of 13.6 months. By 1980, these numbers had fallen to 50% and 4.4 months and, by 1985, to 38% with a mean duration of 2.0 months. Thus, breastfeeding changed from a significant antinatalist factor to a negligible factor in just twenty years. This means that the decreased protection from pregnancy by breastfeeding must be compensated for by increased effectiveness of contraception if Taiwan couples are to achieve their small family goals without resort to abortion.

Discrepant Behavior

Women who want no additional children but are not practicing contraception may be said to be acting irrationally, in the sociological sense of not using available means to reach their desired goals. The proportion

---

15. Norplant is the registered trademark of the Population Council for contraceptive subdermal implants.

of all women who want no additional children and are not practicing contraception—that is, the discrepant group—is a function of two components: (1) the proportion of women who want no additional children and (2) the proportion of women not practicing contraception among those who want no additional children.

Among women who wanted no more children, there was a continuing decrease in the proportion not currently practicing contraception. Together with a small decrease in the proportion who wanted no more children, this resulted in a further decrease in the proportion whose behavior and attitudes were discrepant (table 11.21). This segment, 35% in 1965 among those 22–39 years of age, decreased to 12% by 1980 and 8% by 1985. The very low proportion for 1985 would be even lower if we excluded women who were pregnant, were in postpartum amenorrhea, were separated from their husbands temporarily, or believed they were subfecund.

Cumulative Fertility and the Open Birth Interval

The results of the increase in birth control practice are evident in a continuing decline of cumulative fertility. Both the mean number of children ever born and the mean number of living children continued to decrease between 1980 and 1985 for women over 25 (table 11.22). For women over 30, the decreases in the mean number of children ever born or living fell more than the decline in preferred number of children, so that the excess of births over preferred number of children continued to decrease between 1980 and 1985 (table 11.23). Since infant and child mortality rates continued to drop between 1980 and 1985, the difference between mean number of live births and mean number of surviving children also decreased during this period. The correlation (eta in table 11.12) between children ever born and urbanization and education continued to increase between 1980 and 1985, as it had from 1965 on for both younger and older women. The persistent and even growing differentials in preferred and cumulative fertility indicate that almost universal use of birth control does not necessarily mean that fertility will be homogeneous and low.

Until 1980, the increases in contraceptive practice for stopping childbearing had resulted in monotonic increases in the length of open birth intervals for women over age 25 (table 11.22). Between 1980 and 1985, however, there was a decrease in the mean open birth interval for two age groups, 25–29 and 30–34.

TABLE 11.21 Percentage of Women Who Want No Additional Children, Percentage among Those Who Are Not Practicing Contraception, and Percentage of Women Who Want No Additional Children and Are Not Practicing Contraception, for Married Women Aged 20–39, by Wife's Age, Taiwan, Selected Years, 1965–85

Wife's Age	Percentage Who Want No Additional Children					Percentage among Those Who Want No Additional Children Who Are Not Practicing Contraception					Percentage Who Want No Additional Children and Are Not Practicing Contraception				
	1965	1970	1976	1980	1985	1965	1970	1976	1980	1985	1965	1970	1976	1980	1985
20–21	5	u	23	26	18	80	u	68	43	27	4	u	15	11	5
22–24	10	13	30	29	36	84	46	55	38	19	8	6	16	11	7
25–29	37	38	67	62	57	65	45	34	20	14	24	17	23	13	8
30–34	71	77	87	86	81	59	33	20	13	9	42	26	17	11	7
35–39	88	92	96	96	90	61	33	19	14	12	54	30	19	13	10
22–29	30	32	54	53	51	67	45	38	23	15	20	14	20	12	7
30–39	79	84	92	91	85	60	33	20	13	10	48	28	18	12	8
22–39	57	61	74	73	71	61	36	26	17	11	35	22	19	12	8

Note: u = unavailable.

TABLE 11.22 Mean Number of Children Ever Born, Mean Number of Living Children, and Mean Open Birth Interval for Married Women Aged 22–39, by Wife's Age, Taiwan, Selected Years, 1965–85

Wife's Age	Mean Number of Children Ever Born					Mean Number of Living Children					Mean Open Birth Interval (months)[a]				
	1965	1970	1976	1980	1985	1965	1970	1976	1980	1985	1965	1970	1976	1980	1985
22–24	1.5	1.8	1.9	1.5	1.5	1.4	1.7	1.6	1.5	1.5	13.0	13.4	15.3	14.2	17.2
25–29	2.8	2.7	2.6	2.3	2.1	2.7	2.6	2.4	2.3	2.1	18.2	20.4	26.1	27.9	26.9
30–34	4.3	4.0	3.6	3.0	2.7	4.0	3.8	3.4	3.0	2.7	33.4	41.0	54.7	57.0	53.3
35–39	5.5	4.9	4.3	3.7	3.2	5.0	4.6	4.0	3.6	3.2	52.8	73.4	90.8	92.5	93.5
Total, 22–39	3.8	3.6	3.3	2.8	2.5	3.5	3.4	3.0	2.7	2.5	31.2	39.5	49.1	50.1	51.8

[a] Interval since last birth; for zero-parity women, it is the interval since marriage.

TABLE 11.23   Mean Number of Live Births and Living Children and Mean Preferred Number of Children for Married Women Aged 30–39, Taiwan, Selected Years, 1965–85

	MEAN NUMBER			
Wife's Age	1965	1976	1980	1985
30–34				
Live births	4.3	3.6	3.1	2.7
Living children	4.0	3.4	3.0	2.7
Preferred number of children	4.0	3.0	2.9	2.6
35–39				
Live births	5.5	4.3	3.7	3.2
Living children	5.0	4.0	3.6	3.2
Preferred number of children	4.3	3.2	3.1	2.9

Taiwan's Family Planning Program

The rapid rise of contraceptive use in Taiwan was achieved, to a substantial extent, by the acceptance of modern methods supplied by Taiwan's family planning program. It is estimated that the proportion of married women 20–44 years of age currently using a program-supplied contraceptive rose from 4% in 1965 to 59% in 1988 (table 11.24).

Although the program did not begin officially until May 1968, an unofficial series of family planning activities began much earlier. In 1959 a "Pre-Pregnancy Health Program" was begun on a small scale to provide family planning services and information as part of the Maternal and Child Health Program. In 1962–63 a large-scale experimental ac-

TABLE 11.24   Number of Current Program Method Users and Proportion of Current Program Method Users among Married Women 20–44, Taiwan, Selected Years, 1965–88

Year	IUD	Pill	Condom	Sterilization	TOTAL	
					Number	Percent
1965	71,696	—	—	—	71,696	4.4[a]
1970	281,135	31,214	14,995	—	327,344	18.0
1975	415,043	64,006	51,533	39,673	570,255	27.9
1980	535,637	70,507	155,645	278,866	1,040,655	44.0
1985	615,853	88,790	233,156	537,859	1,475,317	55.7
1988	615,000[b]	76,707	253,204	687,945	1,632,856	59.4

Source: Data and estimates in tables 11.24–11.27 are by Dr. T. H. Sun, based on the service statistics of the Taiwan Provincial Institute of Family Planning.

[a] Percentage of current program method users among married women aged 15–44.

[b] A rough estimate.

tion-research program in the city of Taichung evaluated different methods of providing information and services about family planning (Freedman and Takeshita 1969). A significant number of women accepted contraception (mainly the IUD), and the lessons learned from the experiment became the basis for the rapid development and expansion of the program. Perhaps the most important findings from the study were that there was a significant demand for such services and that providing them in an intensive and well-publicized program was not politically risky for the program leaders.

The program was rapidly expanded to 120 of the 361 local areas of Taiwan and then throughout the island. It operated through full-time female pre-pregnancy health workers who visited eligible women in their homes to offer information about services, which were then made available on a subsidized low-cost basis by qualified private physicians under contract with the program. Over time, the program was innovative in many ways, including mailings to recent mothers and an extensive program of messages through a variety of mass media, through group education in factories, through schools, through neighborhoods, and in the armed forces. The program is well known for its use of systematic research and evaluation as the basis for developing population policies and programs.

The program operated with a carefully designed system of annual targets for areas and for individual workers. In all five program periods between 1964 and 1988, targets usually were exceeded by achievements, although there was a modest shortfall in some periods. Overall, for 1964–88, the targets cumulated to 7,471,543, while the actual number of acceptors cumulated to 7,511,194. This close correspondence was not accidental. Targets were set to stretch the efforts of the workers, while being realistic. This is in contrast to programs in some other countries in which targets are so unrealistic as to result in poor worker morale and a general belief that the targets are not to be taken seriously.

Although other methods were offered in both the Taichung experiment and the subsequent expanded program, the IUD initially was the method of choice (table 11.24). According to Dr. Sun's estimates, about 6% of eligible married women (with no previous IUD) had a first IUD insertion in 1965 (table 11.25). From then on, annually through 1987, about 8–11% of such women had a first IUD insertion. The result was that about 59% of all women 20–44 between 1965 and 1987 had an IUD insertion (table 11.25). In addition, a considerable number of women had IUD reinsertions some time after a previously inserted IUD had been expelled or removed for some reason.

TABLE 11.25 Annual Rate of First IUD Insertions as a Percentage of All Married Women and of Eligible Married Women 20–44, and Proportion of Reinsertion, Taiwan, Selected Years, 1965–87

Year	Annual Rate of 1st Insertions per 100 Married Women	Annual Rate of 1st Insertions per 100 Married Women Eligible for 1st Insertion	Cumulative Rate of 1st Insertions per 100 Married Women in This or Any Previous Year	Proportion of IUD Acceptors Who Are Having a Reinsertion
1965	6.1	6.3	9.0	2.8
1970	5.6	8.0	32.1	30.9
1975	5.4	9.9	44.1	36.5
1980	4.2	9.6	52.9	36.7
1985	4.3	10.6	57.9	39.2
1987	3.4	8.9	59.1	44.0

The contraceptive pill, offered from 1967 onward, was accepted by a minority of women and never became the leading method. Sterilization, initially available through private physicians without program endorsement, became a program method in 1972. As increasing numbers of women have had the two or three children most wanted early in married life, more and more have turned to sterilization as a permanent way to terminate childbearing. By 1988 the number of women currently protected from additional pregnancies by sterilization exceeded the number protected by the IUD (table 11.24).

For the whole period from 1966 to 1988, it is estimated that there were about seven million program acceptors of one of the four principal methods. Among these, 41–45% had not previously used contraception when they adopted the specific method shown (table 11.26).

Dr. T. H. Sun, director of the program for many years, has estimated that the use of program-supplied methods averted about 5 million births that would otherwise have occurred (table 11.27). This is about 65% of all the births prevented by contraception obtained from either program or nonprogram sources, according to his estimates.

The success of Taiwan's family planning program and the transition from high to low fertility to which it contributed are closely related to the profound social and economic transformation of Taiwan, described in the preceding chapters. The early decline in mortality decreased the number of births needed for any desired number of children. At the same time, the number of children desired decreased, partly because of the increasing reliance on nonfamilial institutions to achieve important life values and partly because rising levels of aspiration for children and parents increased the cost of children. The satisfactions derived from

TABLE 11.26 Proportion of Program Method Acceptors Who Had No Previous Contraceptive Experience, Taiwan, Selected Years, 1966–87

| Year | PERCENTAGE OF PROGRAM ACCEPTORS WHO HAD NO PREVIOUS CONTRACEPTIVE EXPERIENCE | | | |
	IUD Acceptors	Pill Acceptors	Condom Acceptors	Sterilization Acceptors
1966	83.0	—	—	—
1970	61.5	32.0	26.5	—
1975	50.8	47.6	41.1	40.6[a]
1980	50.6	51.8	49.5	46.5
1985	46.2	48.0	45.0	43.6
1987	41.1	52.0	46.8	40.6
1966–87	44.9	42.7	40.6	42.3

[a] 1976 data.

TABLE 11.27 Number of Births Averted by Use of Program Methods, Taiwan, Selected Years, 1965–88

Year	IUD	Pill	Condom	Sterilization	Total	Cumulative Total
1965	3,688	—	—	—	3,688	3,688
1970	75,147	5,275	—	—	80,422	271,841
1975	114,124	15,184	8,819	5,060	143,187	868,288
1980	155,128	14,875	28,326	73,393	272,222	1,942,150
1985	176,062	19,429	45,908	160,642	402,041	3,669,272
1988	183,814	18,690	51,927	208,502	462,933	4,998,699
1965–88						
Number	2,830,523	287,708	460,683	1,419,785	4,998,699	
Percent	56.6	5.8	9.2	28.4	100.0	

Note: For the method of calculation of the number of births averted by each method, see table 5 in Sun (1987). The calculation for 1988 was supplied by Dr. Sun for this book.

parenthood in industrialized and urban societies do not require large numbers of children. Moreover, having a small number of children, providing one of them is a son, is not necessarily inconsistent with maintaining such traditional Chinese familial values as co-residence with parents early in marriage.

In addition to the impact of rapid structural changes on fertility preferences, contraceptive use, and fertility, the influence of mass-media messages of Western origin, pervasive in Taiwan, must have been considerable. Watkins (1986b: 448), in summarizing the Princeton study findings on the causes of fertility decline, concludes that "the European experience suggests that modernization is sufficient but not necessary." The rapid pace and high levels of social and economic change in Taiwan were also sufficient for a fertility decline in time. But in Taiwan there were two other factors not present in Europe which probably accelerated the fertility decline and change: (1) the means of mass-media diffusion of general secular values and of modern small-family values were very much greater than in Europe, and (2) a highly efficient family planning program added a highly targeted transmission of family planning information and services, making these general messages relevant to the Taiwan couples.

Social and economic transformations have been so rapid and so broad-based in Taiwan that it is likely that fertility eventually would have declined with or without a family planning program. However, it is unlikely that this would have occurred so rapidly or so equitably as it did with the program.

The large social differentials in contraceptive prevalence found in the 1962 Taichung study (Freedman and Takeshita 1969) and in the first island-wide survey in 1965 decreased rapidly, as we have seen. It is unlikely that contraceptive prevalence would have risen so rapidly among the disadvantaged strata—the poor, the less educated, and the rural—without the special efforts in this direction by the program. At the time of the Taichung study, among those who had more children than they wanted, one-third of the older women and one-half of the younger women had never used any method of fertility control. The situation was similar among those who had just the number they wanted but were likely to have more. Under these circumstances it is not surprising that it was precisely such groups who were likely to accept contraception in the Taichung intensive program, which offered them contraception under legitimate, safe, and inexpensive circumstances. As we have already seen, island-wide in 1965 there were considerable numbers of women who wanted no more children but were not using contraception, and this proportion declined to low levels between 1965 and 1985.

There is little doubt that the transformation of the Taiwanese family as part of the more general social and economic transformation of Taiwan—the theme of this book—was the most important basis for Taiwan's fertility decline. The independent role of the family planning program in the fundamental changes in reproductive behavior is too complex for adequate treatment in this chapter. Our goal in this necessarily brief section has been to establish that the program was, at a minimum, an important means by which changes in the family affected reproductive behavior. Beyond that it is likely that the fertility decline would have proceeded more slowly, less equitably, and with greater costs in human suffering without the program.

Taiwan's fertility is now as low as that of most Western countries. The question of how much further Taiwan's continuing socioeconomic change will lower fertility is in many respects similar to the unanswered question of whether Western fertility will continue to decline or whether it will level off not too far below replacement (Westoff 1978).

As we have seen, the long-term fertility decline was at least interrupted between 1985 and 1990, with a trendless oscillation of the gross reproduction rate between 0.81 and 0.89. Griffith Feeney (1991) has argued that such fertility will rise as births temporarily postponed as a result of later age at marriage are made up.

However, there are a number of forces which should continue to press fertility downward. For example, the educational distribution of women of childbearing age is changing rapidly. Sixty-one percent of the birth cohort of 1950–54 had only a primary education, but for some time now virtually all primary school graduates have been going on to junior and senior high school and the proportions going on to higher education have also been increasing rapidly. This means that, even if age-education-specific fertility rates remain unchanged, fertility will fall further because of the changing educational distribution. In the period from 1966 to 1980, 24% of the decline in the total fertility rate was a result of changes in the educational distribution rather than in age-education-specific marital fertility rates (Liu 1983). We have calculated that the projected changes in age-educational distributions expected between 1984 and 1994[16] would produce a 9% decline in the total fertility rate without any further decline in age/education-specific fertility rates.

We have already noted that the more poorly educated and the rural sectors of the population have, after a short time lag, reached the lower rates of the more urban and better educated strata. There is also a small potential for fertility decline if there is a further decrease in the small remaining number of women who are not practicing contraception although they want no more children.

Even without any further decline in age-specific fertility rates, the crude birthrate and, therefore, the rate of population growth are likely to decline after 1990, because women of childbearing age will begin to be more concentrated at older ages. This will counter the previous trend for the age distribution changes to retard the decline in the birthrate.

---

16. Projections were provided by Dr. Paul K. C. Liu of the Academia Sinica, Institute of Economics, Taipei.

Changes in fertility preferences should continue to put downward pressures on fertility for at least awhile. The recent decline in the numbers preferring three children and the increase in the numbers preferring two are likely to continue, especially since the number satisfied with one son continues to increase. Further, in 1985 Taipei couples had preferences 0.3 points below that for Taiwan as a whole, and in the past Taiwan has reached the Taipei level after a lag of a few years. That effective birth control is almost universal means that downward shifts in preferences are likely to be realized in actual fertility changes.

There continues to be some reason to expect a leveling-off of the fertility decline, however. There is still very little evidence of the preference for one child that has become so marked in Western societies. Even among young wives, only 3% indicated a preference for one child in 1985. This is no doubt affected by the continued, if diminishing, preference for sons.

The question of whether fertility preferences will fall further probably depends for the most part on the extent to which traditional family relationships are eroded. But even a further erosion, as suggested in the preceding chapters, need not carry fertility and fertility preferences to lower levels, since Taiwan's fertility is now at Western levels, which have leveled off near or below replacement levels now for some years.

Twelve

Co-Residence and Other Ties Linking Couples and Their Parents

M. Weinstein, T. H. Sun, M. C. Chang, and R. Freedman

Introduction

As discussed in chapter 2, historically, the co-residence of parents with their married sons and their families in a large, joint-stem household unit has been the Chinese ideal. The reality, in Taiwan and elsewhere, has deviated from the ideal for several reasons. First, for any given young couple, the relatives necessary for a joint-stem family may not have been available at particular stages of the family life cycle. Second, even when all the necessary relatives were available, the emphasis has been on the vertical filial tie rather than on the horizontal fraternal tie, so the predominant pattern has been co-residence of parents with one married son. Married brothers usually did not live together, but if they did, their co-residence occurred when the parent was or had been in the same unit. Finally, after a period of co-residence, young couples moved out for various reasons, for example, inadequate housing space, friction among family members, or simply a desire for independence. Some lived in nuclear units from the outset for such reasons. Even so, as recently as twenty years ago, a considerable majority of Taiwanese couples of childbearing age were living in extended households—almost always with the parents of the husband. Most of those living in nuclear units had previously lived in extended units.

Social and economic change has been very rapid in the last twenty years, and many aspects of Taiwanese life have been transformed (see chap. 3). Under these conditions, the general expectation is that the household will become Westernized and nuclear, because young couples are presumed to be increasingly economically and socially independent

The text of this chapter incorporates extensive passages excerpted with the permission of the Population Investigation Committee from Weinstein, Maxine, Te-Hsiung Sun, Ming-Cheng Chang, and Ronald Freedman, 1990, "Household Composition, Extended Kinship, and Reproduction in Taiwan: 1965–1985," *Population Studies* 44 (2) (July): 217–39.

of their parents and other relatives, and because the incorporation of Taiwan into the world system of communication and markets brings to its population life-style models that include the Western nuclear family.[1] Changes in household arrangements during this period of rapid development in Taiwan can be investigated with a time series on household composition. These data are unusual because they include information on (a) the availability of the relatives pertinent to household extension both at marriage and afterward; (b) the history of past extended co-residence for couples currently in nuclear units; and (c) whether parents not in the reference household are living with a married child elsewhere. These essential items are lacking in most studies of household composition, which depend on cross-sectional rosters of current household composition. Such data do not allow analysis of whether couples in nuclear units could live in extended units and whether filial co-residence obligations to parents are being fulfilled by other married sons if not by the reference couple.

We discuss the co-residential and commensal aspects of the family in Taiwan. But we also recognize that, while these aspects are important, family relationships are considerably more complex. Both before and after ritual and economic division of the Chinese family, there are a variety of other kinship linkages, even when familial subunits are living quite separately.[2] The linkage of separate households into larger familial networks is an important aspect of Taiwanese life which our data do not cover. Susan Greenhalgh (1982a, 1982b, 1984) has provided a good description and analysis of this suprahousehold familial network. The following quotation from her work indicates her view of the nature of the larger system in which households are a component:

> Taiwan's . . . urban life is structured by webs of social ties. . . . Family-centered, these personal networks bind urban residents to one another, to kin in the countryside, and to kin all over the globe. . . . The family, or *jia*, is a group of people related by blood, marriage or adoption, whose defining feature is the joint ownership of property by males . . . authority relations are hierarchically arranged with power and authority relatively centralized in the senior generation. . . .

1. The classic statement of this point of view is by W. J. Goode (1963). However, many scholars believe such a "convergence" theory does not take into account the persistent strength of different familial-cultural systems of many Third World countries.

2. This process is described for Taiwan by M. Cohen (1976). Susan Greenhalgh (1984) has described the process in which a married son lives with his parents for a time and then moves to another town, where he sets up a satellite household linked to the home unit by the remittance of funds, maintaining an interest in the estate which may not be divided for years. Y. C. Chuang (1973) has used the term "federal family" to describe such units.

Relations between generations are guided by a set of widely agreed upon . . . obligations, according to which parents have the duty to help provide for their children's education, jobs, spouses and, for sons, also shares of the family property. In return . . . children are duty bound to contribute to the family economy, and sons have the additional obligation of supporting their parents in their old age. Despite Taiwan's advanced level of modernization—or perhaps because of it—these norms are still widely followed. . . .

The family, a property-holding unit, must be sharply distinguished from the household, a co-residential unit [Greenhalgh 1984, 529, 533].

Although co-residence will be our primary focus, we will also provide some evidence on the residential proximity of parents and married sons not living with them, and on visiting and financial links between sons and parents who live separately.

Co-Residence: Data and Definitions

The data we analyze consist of households containing at least one couple of childbearing age (wife aged 20–39), so the study represents the kinship structure seen from the perspectives of such young married couples and their parents. We are covering the great majority of extended units from this perspective when we concentrate on links between the respondent, her husband's married brothers, and her husband's parents or grandparents. Only about 5% of the respondents were living in extended units with other relatives, mainly grandparents or the wife's parents.

The point of reference throughout is the respondent (a married woman aged 20–39) and her household, unless indicated otherwise.

We consider the following types of households:

1. *Nuclear.* Contains only one married couple, that of the respondent. May contain other unmarried relatives or nonrelatives (except parents of either the husband or wife).

2. *Extended.* Contains, in addition to the wife and husband, at least one other married couple related to the respondent or her husband or at least one parent or grandparent of the husband or wife.

   a. *Stem.* In addition to the husband and wife, contains one or more parents of the husband or wife or a grandparent of the husband or wife.
   b. *Joint.* Contains one or more other married couples related to the respondent or her husband of the same generation as the husband and wife, usually one or more married brothers of the husband.
   c. *Joint-stem.* Contains both vertical and horizontal linkages, that is, a married couple related to the respondent or her husband of the same genera-

TABLE 12.1 Percentage of Couples Who Lived with a Parent of the Husband at Least One Month after Marriage, Taiwanese Couples with Husband under Age 45 and at Least One of the Husband's Parents Available at Interview

Marital Duration	1967	1973	1980	1986
<5 years	88	78	72	67
N	755	1,101	986	731
5–9 years	89	86	77	69
N	873	1,109	854	743
10–14 years	92	89	82	71
N	764	889	587	573
15 + years	92	92	90	82
N	786	632	309	232
Total	90	85	78	70
N	3,178	3,731	2,736	2,279

tion as the husband and wife and one or more of their parents or grandparents.

Co-Residence from the Time of Marriage

We begin at the start of the life course for adult co-residence by examining the proportion of couples who began married life with the husband's parents.[3] These figures are displayed in table 12.1. In 1967, nearly all couples—92%—who had been married at least fifteen years began their marriage with the husband's parents. The percentage was lower for marriages of shorter duration but not substantially: in 1967, of couples married fewer than five years, 88% had lived with the husband's parents after marriage. By 1973, the differential between the most recently married couples and those married longest had increased: just 78% of couples married under five years in 1973 lived with the husband's parents after marriage. While this trend toward decreasing co-residence has continued, even in 1986, among those married under five years, 67%—the lowest figure—began marriage living with the husband's parents. While this figure represents a sharp decline from earlier periods, it still indicates that even quite recently two-thirds of the couples followed the traditional pattern.

At three of the survey dates, respondents were asked not only whether they began living with their husband's parents after marriage but also,

3. For comparability over time, we restrict the sample to couples with at least one parent available at the time of interview.

TABLE 12.2 Cumulative Household Dissolution Rates by Marital Duration, Taiwanese Couples Who Lived with a Parent of the Husband at Least One Month after Marriage, Husband under Age 45 at Interview, at Least One of the Husband's Parents Alive at Interview

Marital Duration	1973	1980	1986
Under 5 years			
Percentage of households dissolved by:			
1 year	14	17	20
3 years	30	34	36
N	860	711	489
5–9 years			
Percentage of households dissolved by:			
1 year	9	13	15
3 years	24	27	27
5 years	33	36	37
7 years	41	42	45
9 years	47	53	52
N	956	659	513
10–14 years			
Percentage of households dissolved by:			
1 year	4	13	13
3 years	14	26	23
5 years	22	33	32
7 years	29	38	42
9 years	36	41	47
N	790	479	406
15 + years			
Percentage of households dissolved by:			
1 year	3	8	14
3 years	9	15	26
5 years	15	21	33
7 years	19	26	41
9 years	24	31	47
N	632	309	232

Note: These estimates are based on the following questions. In each survey each respondent was asked, "At the time of your marriage did you and your husband's parents live or eat together for more than the first month after marriage?" If yes: (1973): "For how long did you live and eat together after you were married?" (1980): "For how long did you live together after you were married?" (1986): "How long was it after your marriage before you first began to live apart from your husband's parents?"

if they did so, how long they co-resided. These results are shown in table 12.2 by marital duration. The amount of time spent with the husband's parents follows a pattern similar to that found in table 12.1: the length of co-residence decreases with recency of marriage and at later dates of survey reference. For example, at the time of the 1973 survey, of those married fifteen years or more, only 3% had stopped living with the husband's parents by the end of one year, while the corresponding figure for those married fewer than five years was 14%. By 1986, 14% of couples married fifteen or more years had ended co-residence by the end of the first year, while 20% of those married fewer than five years had ended co-residence by one year. Still, this figure implies that even among the most recently married, co-residence continues for a not unsubstantial period following marriage: 80% of the most recently married couples (those married under five years in 1986) who lived with the husband's parents for at least one month after marriage were still residing with the parents after one year, while 64% continued for at least three.

In interpreting table 12.2 it is necessary to bear in mind that it refers to couples who lived with a parent of the husband for at least one month. Tables 12.1 and 12.2 together provide a picture of the considerable change that has occurred. For example, in 1973, of the 92% of couples married fifteen years or more who lived with the husband's parents for at least one month after marriage, only 3% had ceased co-residence by the end of one year. In other words, nearly 90% of all couples who had been married for fifteen or more years in 1973 had lived with their husband's parents for a least one year after marriage. By contrast, in 1986, only 80% of the couples married under five years who began marriage co-residing with the husband's parents (67% of all couples) were still co-residing at the end of one year. That is, the percentage of all couples who lived with the husband's parents for at least one year after marriage declined to about 54% from the 1973 value of 90% for the couples at the highest marital durations: a substantial decline, although even in 1986 the majority of newly married couples spent at least one year with the husband's parents.

Thus, while the practice of living with the husband's parents at marriage is decreasing, most young couples still do so. Among those who begin married life that way, the length of co-residence has decreased, but still a considerable portion continue with the husband's parents during the early years.

Only a very small percentage of couples who do not reside with the husband's parents at the time of marriage do so at a later date. Of Taiwanese couples with at least one of the husband's parents alive at the 1986 interview date, only a little over 3% (data not shown) lived with the parents at a later date although not at marriage.[4] It is difficult to assess indirectly the extent to which couples resume co-residence for the care of elderly parents: parental age is linked to the age of the respon-

---

4. This finding is based on respondents aged 20 to 49 at the date of the survey.

TABLE 12.3 Percentage Distribution by Household Type on Associative Basis, Taiwanese only, 1965–86

Household Type	1965	1967	1973	1980	1986
Nuclear	35	36	40	50	56
Stem	36	35	39	35	35
With husband's parents	32	30	35	32	32
With wife's parents	3	4	4	3	3
With other married relatives[1]	1	2	—	1	—
Joint-stem[2]	26	22	17	13	7
With husband's parents	25	21	17	13	7
With wife's parents	—	—	—	—	—
With other married relatives[1]	—	1	—	—	—
Joint	4	7	3	2	1
Total percentage	100	100	100	100	100
N	2,876	3,598	4,165	3,155	2,733

Note: — = less than 0.5%.

[1] Husband's or wife's grandparents for 1973 and 1980. For 1967 "other married relatives" may include grandparents, wife's married sibs, uncles and aunts, etc. For 1965 and 1986 wife's married sibs are excluded so that the category is essentially restricted to relatives of an earlier generation than husband's.

[2] For 1965 and 1967 classification as joint-stem or joint is based on presence of husband's married sibs; for 1973, 1980, and 1986 on presence of husband's married brothers. However, very few lived with married sisters at any time.

dent, there has been a decline in co-residence over time, and younger respondents are likely to be at an earlier stage in their marriages and, therefore, are more likely to be co-resident.

The Cross-Sectional View of Co-Residence

An initial view of the broad trends in co-residence patterns (table 12.3) indicates a steady trend toward nuclear households during the period 1965–86. The proportion in nuclear units, which increased from 36 to 50% between 1965 and 1980, increased further to 56% by 1986. A significant simplification of extended households has occurred over time with a steady decline of joint-stem and joint households (from 30% in 1965 to 8% in 1986). The percentage in stem households has remained around 35% throughout this period. Since most parents, as we shall see, continue to live with a married son, the breakup of joint-stem units is likely to add to the number of stem units as well as to the number of nuclear units. The proportion in stem units also tends to be increased by the increasing availability of parents for longer time periods as a result of declining mortality. The effects of increasing availability of parents and the fission of joint-stem units toward increasing the prevalence of stem units is counteracted to some extent by the increasing tendency of older parents to live separately from any married sons—a phenomenon we shall consider shortly.

Throughout our analysis we have considered the distribution of households by type. However, the proportion of all people who live in extended households will be greater than the proportion of households that are extended, since extended households are on average larger than nuclear households. For example, in 1986, while only 44% of the Taiwanese households were extended, 56% of the population was in extended units. The average number of persons that year per household was 4.7 for nuclear, 6.9 for stem, 8.2 for joint, and 11.7 for joint-stem.

While co-residence has been decreasing in Taiwan, it is still considerable in comparative perspective. Parish and Whyte (1978, 133) estimated that one-third of the households in rural mainland China were nuclear in preceding decades but that by 1973 over half were nuclear and only 2% were joint. This is close to our Taiwan estimates of 35% in 1965 and 56% in 1986. Further, they report, as we do, that the vertical dimension of extension was the dominant one. Lavely and Li (1985) reported that between 70 and 80% of households were nuclear in Fujian, Hebei, and Liaoning provinces in 1982, on the basis of the One-per-Thousand Survey of 1982.[5] Eighty-one percent were nuclear in the 1982 census (Yi 1986, 677). In a study of household co-residence in Malaysia in 1966–67, Palmore, Klein, and Marzuki (1970, 375–98) found that, among Chinese, 30% were currently co-resident with the husband's parents and 7% with the wife's, considerably less than in Taiwan at that same period and somewhat less than in Taiwan in 1986.

There is no evidence of any dilution of the strong patrilineal basis for co-residence in Taiwan. There has been essentially no change over the last twenty years in the small percentage co-resident with the wife's parents. One might have expected an increase on the basis of some ethnographic reports[6] and the hypothetical argument that economic and social change and contact with Western ideas might erode the operational significance of the patrilineal principle, because of the increasing economic independence of the couple from the husband's father. On the other hand, the work of Greenhalgh (1984, 529–52) indicates that extended family networks predominantly remain based on patrilineal

5. Those very low figures for extended households from the One-per-Thousand Survey and the 1982 census are somewhat misleading, because they do not take into account that the older parents and their married sons were likely to be living in very close proximity and with intimate daily contact in rural China.

6. E.g., B. Gallin and R. Gallin (1980).

principles, although she cites some possibilities that "an increase in women's job opportunities and economic importance has led families actively to cultivate female-linked ties in their search for urban housing, jobs, co-investors and the like."

Table 12.4 provides a more detailed view of changes between 1973 and 1986. In 1986, 42% lived in households extended on an associative basis. However, these gross figures do not take into account the effects of availability of the pertinent relatives, essential ethnic background differences, and position stages in the life course.

Taiwanese and Mainlander households[7] still differed substantially in 1986 on the prevalence of extended kinship co-residence, because Mainlanders are much less likely to have a parent of the husband available. Although the percentage of Mainlanders with a parent of the husband available has been increasing, in 1986 it was still only 56% for Mainlanders but 90% for Taiwanese. Although the proportion in extended units among those with a parent of the husband available in 1986 was very similar for Taiwanese and Mainlanders, the difference in availability and the continuing dominance of vertical patrilineal ties mean that Mainlander households were still much more likely to be nuclear. While the patrilineal principle was still dominant for both groups, Mainlanders were more likely to be living with the wife's parents, presumably because the husband's parents were less available. The overall percentage of Mainlanders living in extended units increased, despite the fact that the percentage of Mainlanders co-resident among those with at least one of the husband's parents alive decreased. This is because, with the increasing normalization of the Mainlander population structure, the percentage of Mainlanders with a husband's parent available is increasing rapidly.

For Taiwanese, the overall percentage living in extended units decreased. Of Taiwanese couples with at least one of the husband's parents alive at the time of the interview, 67% were in extended households in

---

7. The "Mainlanders" are those persons (and their children) who came to Taiwan when the Nationalist government of Chiang Kai-Shek and part of his army moved to Taiwan after World War II. They are carried in the Taiwan population register as natives of a mainland province. The Taiwanese are Chinese who came from the mainland several centuries earlier and are classified as either Fukienese or Hakka in ethnicity. In view of the patrilineal, patrilocal aspects of the kinship system, the ethnic classifications used here are those of the husbands. Many Mainlander men married Taiwanese women, since the sex ratio of the Mainlander migrants was very high. Our data on ethnicity are based on the respondent's report of her own and her husband's ethnic ancestry. We are unable to differentiate the small number of self-reported Fukienese and Hakka who came from the mainland. Such cases are classified here as Taiwanese.

TABLE 12.4 Household Structure on an Associative Basis, by Whether Parents Live with Married Brother, by Ethnicity, Taiwan, 1973, 1980, and 1986

Household Structure	Total			Taiwanese			Mainlander		
	1973	1980	1986	1973	1980	1986	1973	1980	1986
Nuclear	49.1	52.6	57.6	42.5	49.6	56.1	80.9	78.0	73.3
Husband's parent(s) live with husband's married brother(s)	14.7	18.0	21.2	17.5	20.4	22.4	1.8	4.9	8.2
Husband's parent(s) live alone	11.8	17.5	24.6	13.3	18.9	24.7	4.8	11.0	23.5
Could live with husband's married brother(s)	(6.3)	(11.4)	(17.5)	(7.3)	(12.6)	(18.0)	(1.8)	(6.3)	(13.6)
Could not live with husband's married brother(s)	(5.5)	(6.1)	(7.1)	(6.1)	(6.3)	(6.7)	(3.0)	(4.7)	(9.9)
Husband's parent(s) not available	22.6	17.1	11.7	11.7	10.3	9.0	74.8	62.1	41.6
Stem	34.1	33.6	34.3	37.5	35.0	35.0	17.9	20.6	24.2
Both husband's parents	14.2	16.6	17.8	16.2	17.9	18.4	4.1	8.6	11.9
Husband's father	3.8	2.9	4.4	4.3	3.3	4.5	1.6	0.5	3.3
Husband's mother	10.8	10.0	8.6	12.3	10.6	9.0	3.2	3.7	4.1
Wife's parents	5.0	3.6	3.3	4.3	2.6	2.9	8.7	7.7	4.9
Grandparents	0.3	0.4	0.2	0.4	0.5	0.2	0.3	0.0	0.0
Joint-stem	14.3	11.8	6.9	17.1	13.4	7.4	0.9	0.9	2.1
Both husband's parents	8.6	8.2	5.0	10.4	9.4	5.5	0.5	0.7	1.7
Husband's father	1.3	0.7	0.5	1.6	0.7	0.5	0.2	0.0	0.0
Husband's mother	4.2	2.8	1.2	5.0	3.2	1.2	0.2	0.2	0.4
Wife's parents	0.1	0.1	0.1	0.1	0.1	0.1	0.1	0.0	0.0
Grandparents	0.1	0.0	0.1	0.1	0.0	0.1	0.0	0.0	0.0
Joint	2.5	1.9	1.3	3.0	2.0	1.4	0.3	0.5	0.4
Total percentage	100.0	100.0	100.0	100.0	100.0	100.0	100.0	100.0	100.0
Number	5,543	3,818	3,101	4,568	3,155	2,733	931	428	243
Percentage with parents available	73.5	80.9	86.8	85.4	88.2	89.7	16.6	32.8	56.4
Percentage with parents and/or married brother(s) available	83.5	89.6	97.5	96.0	97.3	98.1	23.6	39.8	91.4
Percentage of respondents in extended units[1] among those with:									
Parents	69.2	58.6	48.9	67.3	57.1	48.9	84.3	67.0	47.3
Parents and/or married brother(s)	60.9	52.9	43.5	59.9	51.8	44.7		49.9	29.2

[1] Not necessarily same unit. Also, parents may live alone even when respondent lives in an extended unit.

1973 and 57% in 1980, but by 1986 this percentage had dropped to 49 (table 12.4). Overall then, when we control for availability of kin, we observe a decrease of extended households among couples of childbearing age and an increase in the likelihood that a parent lives alone even when a married son is available for co-residence.

The continuing dominance of the vertical over the horizontal extension is indicated by the fact that 89 to 90% of all Taiwanese extended units included the husband's parents. In addition to the decline of co-residence with a married brother of the husband already noted, in 1986 the great majority of married brothers lived together only if at least one of their parents was also present.

If we consider only couples with the husband's parents available, a similar picture of the dominance of the filial rather than fraternal tie emerges (data not shown). Among Taiwanese couples, the prevalence of stem households remained steady between 1980 and 1986 at about 38%. The greatest decline in the prevalence of a household type occurred among joint-stem households: the percentage declined from 17 in 1980 to 10 in 1986, with the largest decrease, a drop of 12%, observed among those married for more than ten years.

While nearly half of all Taiwanese households with available parental kin are still extended, a few indicators point to a continuing, if decelerating, tendency toward the nuclear model (data not shown). First, between 1980 and 1986 the percentage of households that were always nuclear increased from 16 to 21, while the percentage of respondents who always lived with the husband's parents declined from 44 to 37. Second, from the parental perspective, those living with a son declined from about 77 to 70% of the respondents' parents (see table 12.6 below).

To this point we have used information for 1986 that was clearly comparable with that available for previous years. In 1986 a special effort was made to add questions to discover cases of co-residence not revealed by the standard questions. The net result of taking this additional information into account increased the percentage of extended households by 1.1% among Mainlanders and 0.6% among Taiwanese. We have concluded that the standard questions used for the time series yield a picture of co-residence not likely to have been improved very much if the additional probing had been used in earlier surveys.

Correlates of Household Extension

Table 12.5 shows the relation between household extension and education, urbanization, and occupation in farming. For couples at longer

TABLE 12.5 Percentage of Couples in Various Living Arrangements, by Characteristics of Couple and Duration of Marriage: Taiwanese Couples with Husband's Parents Available, Respondents Aged 20–39

Characteristic	Percent Nuclear			Percent Stem			Percent Joint-Stem			Percent Joint			N		
	1973	1980	1986	1973	1980	1986	1973	1980	1986	1973	1980	1986	1973	1980	1986
Marital Duration 0–9 Years															
Wife's education															
None	28	30	33	49	48	48	23	20	15	1	3	4	363	101	27
Primary	35	40	50	45	41	37	18	17	12	2	1	1	1,428	1,014	486
Junior high	45	41	42	38	43	43	16	14	11	1	2	3	234	264	359
Senior high plus	44	49	47	43	39	40	11	11	11	1	1	2	209	447	638
Urbanization															
Rural twps.	27	27	34	50	51	47	21	21	17	1	1	1	796	562	460
Urban twps.	33	35	38	44	47	47	22	18	13	1	1	2	564	405	265
Small cities	45	53	56	41	33	32	11	12	9	2	1	3	271	313	373
Large cities	46	55	57	40	32	35	12	10	6	2	2	2	603	546	412
Farm status															
Farm occupation	20	25	20	54	52	59	25	22	18	1	1	2	1,019	757	152
Once on farm	57	58	52	31	29	36	10	10	11	2	3	2	736	710	856
Never on farm	37	45	45	46	42	42	16	12	11	1	1	2	479	359	502
Total Percentage	36	41	46	45	39	40	17	17	11	1	2	2	2,234	1,856	1,510[1]
Marital Duration 10–25 Years															
Wife's education															
None	29	39	53	43	39	46	26	20	1	1	1	0	624	251	93
Primary	40	50	59	40	36	36	18	13	4	2	1	1	849	563	615
Junior high	47	56	63	39	29	31	12	12	5	2	2	0	85	82	117
Senior high plus	57	64	71	25	28	25	18	7	3	0	1	1	28	75	115
Urbanization															
Rural twps.	27	31	50	48	44	45	24	23	5	1	2	0	663	313	304
Urban twps.	32	41	51	39	41	45	28	16	2	1	2	1	372	254	174
Small cities	56	70	73	34	24	23	9	5	3	1	1	0	175	170	206
Large cities	50	64	69	35	27	27	13	7	4	3	0	1	376	234	256
Farm status															
Farm occupation	24	31	36	47	46	59	28	22	4	2	1	1	910	469	197
Once on farm	61	71	69	28	23	27	9	6	3	2	0	1	416	336	560
Never on farm	42	53	60	43	34	34	14	10	5	1	3	1	260	166	183
Total Percentage	37	46	60	41	35	35	21	16	4	2	2	1	1,586	971	940[1]

Note: (1) For 1973 and 1980, farm occupation includes cases in which the husband's primary or secondary occupation is farming or where the couple currently lives on a farm. For 1985, it also includes cases in which farming is the primary occupation of the wife. (2) Values for 1980 differ slightly from previously published figures (R. Freedman, M.-C. Chang, and T.-H. Sun, "Household Composition, Extended Kinship and Reproduction in Taiwan, 1973–1980," *Population Studies* 36 (1982): 395–411).

[1]Total percentage each year for the four household types does not add to 100, as other living arrangements are not shown.

marital durations (ten to twenty-five years), at all three survey dates the greater the education of the wife, the lower the likelihood that the couple resided in an extended household. The percentage in nuclear households increased over time in all educational categories, while at each survey date the probability of residing in a nuclear household was positively related to the wife's education. On the other hand, the likelihood of living in a joint-stem household decreased over the period and was negatively related to the wife's education. The percentage living in stem households was negatively related to wife's education at each period, but showed a less clear-cut pattern over time, possibly reflecting a simplification in extension (i.e., a movement from joint-stem to stem) over the period. For the more recently married couples, those married under ten years at each survey date, the fundamental distinction was between those with no education and the remainder: when the wife was uneducated, the couple was less likely to reside in a nuclear household and more likely to be a member of a stem or joint-stem household.

Urbanization was also negatively related to household extension, although the primary distinction was between couples living in townships and those in cities. Among couples at both marital durations, the likelihood of residing in a nuclear household increased over the period in each type of place, while at each survey date the likelihood of residing in a nuclear household was greater for residents of cities than of townships. There was a corresponding decrease in the likelihood of residing in a joint-stem household over time, and couples in cities were less likely than those in townships to be in joint-stem households.

Occupation in farming was also linked to higher probabilities of co-residence. Couples who reported that they were currently farming were less likely to live in nuclear households and more likely to live in extended households than the remainder. For those formerly, but not now, on a farm, the likelihood of residing in a nuclear household was greatest at all three periods. This may have occurred because many were couples who had moved away from parental homes.

At the 1986 survey date, among couples at longer marital durations, only a small percentage were living in joint-stem households. We speculate that this finding may reflect both life course effects and an easing of the most traditional forms of co-residence.

Co-Residence from the Parental Perspective

So far we have examined trends in living arrangements from the respondent's viewpoint. These figures are subject to two competing influences:

TABLE 12.6 Living Arrangements of Husband's Parents on Associative Basis by Availability of Parent(s), Taiwanese Couples, Respondents Aged 20–39

	PERCENTAGE OF PARENTS WHO LIVE WITH A MARRIED SON		
	1973	1980	1986
At least 1 parent alive	82.1	76.5	70.2
N	3,782	2,829	2,452
Both parents alive	78.2	73.0	65.9
N	2,183	1,766	1,608
Father only alive	87.7	81.6	79.8
N	390	261	248
Mother only alive	87.3	82.7	77.8
N	1,209	802	596

first, the decline in household extension and, second, the decline in fertility, only partially offset by the lower mortality of siblings. With a decline in fertility and no change in the propensity for co-residence, each child would have a higher probability of living with a parent. From the parental perspective, though, lower fertility implies a smaller set of possible co-residential units, again only partially counterbalanced by the higher survival rate of children.

Table 12.6 explores co-residence from the parental perspective. Of the Taiwanese couples with at least one parent living at the date of interview, a large proportion had parents who resided with a married son—either with the respondent and her husband or with a married brother of the husband. Although this figure declined between 1973 and 1986 from 82 to 70%, even in 1986 the vast majority of Taiwanese parents who had at least one married son still resided with him. The likelihood of living with a married son was lower if both parents were alive than if only one parent was living, but it made little difference whether it was the mother or the father who was the sole surviving parent. In 1986, nearly four-fifths of widowed parents lived with a child, while two-thirds of parents with spouses did.

There is additional evidence that co-residence may possibly be linked to the needs of aging parents: between 1973 and 1986 the percentage of widowed parents living with a married son declined by 9 to 10% while the decline for parents with living spouses was 12%.

In 1986, data were collected on the age of the couple's parents. From these data, shown in table 12.7, we see additional evidence that co-residence may be related to the care of the parents. When we control for the respondent's age, the older the parents, the more likely they are

TABLE 12.7 Percentage of Parents Who Live with the Respondent and Her Husband or a Married Brother of the Husband by Age of (older) Parent and Respondent, Couples with at Least One Parent Alive at Interview, 1986 Survey

Age of Respondent	AGE OF (OLDER) PARENT			
	<50	50–59	60–69	70+
20–29	(63.6)	71.3	69.2	77.8
N	22	390	402	162
30–39		46.3	67.3	75.0
N		121	557	495
40–49			60.0	78.8
N			70	391

to be residing with a married son. Moreover, as mentioned earlier, if only one parent was alive, the likelihood of co-residence was higher than if both parents were alive (data not shown). While we lack direct evidence regarding parental disability or need, this relation is suggestive of the link of co-residence to parental care.

Expectations/Attitudes about Co-Residence

Attitudes toward co-residence have paralleled the declining proportions who have actually resided in extended households, at least until the time of the most recent survey, when there is some evidence of increased expectation of co-residence. Data from the surveys of young unmarried women allow us to examine the attitudes of unmarried women in addition to those participating in the surveys of married respondents. These data show a large decline in the percentage who report that they would be willing to live with their in-laws after marriage. In 1971, 64% of the respondents said that they would do so; by 1978 this percentage had declined to 52; and, by 1984, only 42% said they would be willing to live with their in-laws after marriage.

Corresponding to the decline in reported co-residence has been a decline in the percentage of respondents who report that newlywed couples should live with the husband's parents after marriage. There has also been a decline in the proportions who expect to reside with their own married sons. Generally, Taiwanese have more traditional attitudes than Mainlanders and attitudes are inversely related to education and urbanization; that is, respondents who were more highly educated and living in more urban areas were less likely to expect to live with their own sons or to report that couples should live with the husband's parents after marriage.

Table 12.8 shows the percentages of married women aged 20 to 39 who said that newlywed couples should live with the husband's parents. At each survey date, there is a substantial gap between the percentage who actually did live with their husband's parents after marriage and the percentage who thought that a newlywed couple should live with the husband's parents. In 1973, about 85% of Taiwanese couples lived with the husband's parents after marriage but only 59% of the respondents said that a newlywed couple should live with the husband's parents. At the time of the 1986 survey, although 70% of the Taiwanese respondents lived with one of the husband's parents after marriage, only 41.6% reported that the newlywed couple should live with the parent. This gap suggests that the decline in co-residence may continue. It also implies that the respondents are more traditional in their behavior than in the attitudes they report. While it would be interesting to compare the percentages who lived with their parents with their parents' expectations, data are not available for that task.

Table 12.8 shows that reported attitudes toward co-residence are inversely associated with age, wife's education, and urbanization.[8] Between 1980 and 1986 there was a slight increase in virtually all categories in the percentages reporting traditional attitudes. This increase in the percentage reporting traditional attitudes is greater for the responses to the question on whether the respondent expects to live with a married son.

The percentages of Taiwanese respondents who expect to live with a married son at some time after the son's marriage and in their old age are shown in table 12.9.[9] In 1967 just over 88% of the respondents reported that they expected to live with one of their sons after the son's marriage. By 1980 this percentage had declined to just under 42, rising in 1986 to 47. Most of the decline occurred between 1967 and 1973—a drop of nearly 30 points. Again, in most cases, the proportion voicing traditional attitudes was inversely associated with education and urbanization. Only a small percentage expected to live with the son only after marriage. For most, the expectation was linked to co-residence in old age (in addition to, or apart from, a period right after the son's marriage).

8. Results by husband's education are similar to those by the wife's.
9. In 1986, the wording and the skip pattern for the questions about attitudes toward co-residence were changed to ask counterfactual questions of women who did not currently have a son. There were only small differences between the answers of those who had at least one son and those of all respondents.

TABLE 12.8 Percentage of Married Women Aged 20–39 Who Said Newlywed Couple Should Live with Husband's Folks, by Ethnicity and other Characteristics, Taiwan: 1973, 1980, and 1986

Characteristic	TOTAL			TAIWANESE			MAINLANDER		
	1973	1980	1986	1973	1980	1986	1973	1980	1986
Wife's age									
20–24	54.7	40.5	35.6	56.4	42.2	36.6	44.9	23.9	42.3
25–29	55.6	36.0	36.5	57.7	36.8	38.7	46.4	28.2	15.6
30–34	56.9	38.2	41.4	60.2	39.8	42.8	43.0	32.7	33.3
35–39	59.8	41.0	44.8	61.0	43.3	46.3	46.3	30.4	35.4
Wife's education									
Illiterate	70.3	50.5	63.0	71.3	53.2	65.6	63.4	37.3	*
Literate, attended primary	64.3	42.2	52.8	67.3	43.0	56.4	51.6	36.8	38.1
Primary grad.	56.3	42.6	48.9	57.9	44.0	50.1	47.4	34.5	47.1
Jr. high	37.0	34.7	35.8	39.1	34.1	37.4	31.1	38.6	26.7
Sr. high	23.2	22.5	26.2	22.8	23.4	27.0	23.8	17.9	20.8
College or more	16.0	17.2	18.1	15.5	17.7	19.4	17.4	15.3	*
Type of area									
Large city	47.9	31.6	31.1	50.4	33.0	32.5	41.2	25.0	26.8
Small city	50.2	39.9	37.0	53.5	41.0	38.2	42.4	36.4	27.9
Urban township	59.9	43.4	40.6	62.4	44.4	42.1	43.8	25.8	19.2
Rural township	64.4	40.6	50.5	64.9	42.3	52.0	57.0	34.3	47.9
Total	56.6	38.5	40.0	59.0	40.0	41.6	45.2	29.9	30.4

*N < 20.

TABLE 12.9 Percentage of Taiwanese Respondents Aged 20–39 Who Expect to Live with a Married Son

	At Some Time after Marriage				In Old Age		
	1967	1973	1980	1986	1973	1980	1986
Wife's age							
20–24	84.6	56.7	42.2	43.0	53.3	40.4	41.2
25–29	86.8	55.4	36.6	44.0	53.5	34.5	42.4
30–34	90.3	58.7	42.1	45.1	56.5	38.5	42.7
35–39	89.7	62.5	48.2	54.0	59.8	47.1	52.5
Wife's education							
Illiterate	94.0	73.3	59.1	74.6	71.5	57.3	74.6
Literate, primary attended	92.9	64.3	45.1	66.4	61.0	43.0	65.8
Primary grad	88.0	56.5	44.2	55.5	54.0	42.3	52.5
Jr. high	61.8	38.0	37.3	43.8	35.2	33.6	41.5
Sr. high	46.7	23.9	26.7	31.4	20.3	24.7	29.2
College +	*	15.5	15.9	20.6	12.1	11.6	20.0
Urbanization							
Large city	—	53.2	27.8	36.5	50.8	25.1	35.0
Small city	—	47.3	37.2	45.4	46.2	32.5	43.7
Urban twp.	—	59.8	48.3	53.9	57.1	46.4	50.6
Rural twp.	—	65.1	51.3	53.2	62.2	48.8	51.7
Total	88.2	58.4	41.6	46.7	55.9	39.3	44.8

Note: — = data not available.

*N < 20.

The expectations of the Taiwanese respondents of childbearing ages regarding co-residence in their old age were substantially lower than their own parents' experience. As shown in table 12.6, in 1986, just over 70% of the respondents' husbands' parents lived with a married son. Of their parents aged 70 or above, more than three-quarters lived with a married son (table 12.7). Less than half the respondents (44.8% in 1986), though, expected to live with one of their own married sons.

Along with the decline in expectations of co-residence after marriage and in old age, expectations of financial support in old age have declined, although not as far. Taiwanese respondents continued to expect support in their old age from their married sons. In 1973, about 90% of Taiwanese respondents aged 20 to 39 expected their sons to contribute financially to their support in their old age. This percentage had declined to 84 by 1980, but even by 1986 just over three-quarters of the respondents expected financial support from their sons (data not shown). At the time of the 1986 survey, 85% of the couples not residing with parents themselves were giving money to the husband's parents—42% regularly

TABLE 12.10   Proximity of Parents of Husband and Wife to Respondent Couple, 1973, 1980, and 1986

Date	Same Household	Same Township or City	Farther Away	TOTAL Percent	N
		Proximity to Husband's Parents[a]			
1973	57.8	16.1	26.1	100	3,981
1980	52.6	16.9	30.5	100	3,079
1986	44.2	25.1	30.7	100	2,612
		Proximity to Wife's Parents[b]			
1980	4.5	33.0	62.5	100	3,573
1986	3.5	40.8	55.7	100	2,929

Note: For couples with wives aged 20–39.

[a] Omits cases with husband's parents unavailable.

[b] Omits cases with wife's parents unavailable.

and 43% occasionally (see table 12.15 and discussion below). Their expectations in this regard, therefore, are in closer conformity to their own behavior than their expectations about co-residence.

Proximity of Parents to Married Children

Evidence that kinship ties are extensive, even when young married couples are not co-resident with their parents, is provided by the residential proximity of couples to parents, the frequency of visiting, and the financial support flowing from the younger to the older generation. Although co-residence is decreasing, proximity to husband's parents and the frequency of visiting has not decreased, while the frequency of giving money has actually increased.

The proximity of young married couples to their parents is an important (albeit obvious) determinant of the frequency of face-to-face contacts and of various kinds of direct support for the parents. While co-residence with husband's parents decreased significantly between 1973 and 1986, the proportion living in the same place[10] as the husband's parents, co-resident or not, decreased only slightly. Sixty-nine percent were living in the same household with the husband's parents or in the same place in 1986 (table 12.10), but it has become more common to live in the same place as the husband's parents without co-residence.

Patrilocal principles affect the character of proximity. The proportion, co-resident or otherwise, living in the same place is greater for the hus-

10. This means living in the same city or township.

TABLE 12.11 Proximity of Parents of Husband and Wife to Respondent, for Respondents not Living with Parents, 1973, 1980, and 1986

Date	Same Township or City	Farther Away	TOTAL Percent	N
		Proximity to Husband's Parents		
1973	37.5	62.6	100	1,679
1980	35.7	64.3	100	1,461
1986	44.8	55.2	100	1,456
		Proximity to Wife's Parents		
1980	34.5	65.5	100	3,413
1986	42.3	57.7	100	2,811

Note: For couples with wives aged 20–39.

band's parents (69%) than for the wife's parents (44%) in 1986, because co-residence is almost entirely with the husband's parents. Among those not co-resident, the proportion living in the same place is about the same for the wife's parents and the husband's parents (table 12.11). However, among those living in the same place and not co-resident, the proportion living in the same neighborhood is much lower for the wife's parents (37%)[11] than for the husband's parents (58%; see table 12.12). Considering either co-residence or being in the same neighborhood as close proximity, the proportions in that class are 18% for the wife's parents and 59% for the husband's parents.

Characteristics associated in other analyses with weaker familial ties—higher education, premarital nonfamilial experience,[12] living in cities, being a migrant, and recent marriage—are all associated with less proximity to the husband's parents (table 12.12). Even when the couple apparently could choose to live close to the husband's parents, couples with these characteristics who live in the same place are less likely to live in the same neighborhood with the husband's parents.

Consider wife's education, which is negatively correlated with proximity. Compared with the least educated, the most highly educated are less likely to live in the same place as the husband's parents, less likely to live in the same neighborhood, and less likely to live in the same neighborhood even if they live in the same place. These findings hold

11. The data for the wife's parents are in an unpublished table.
12. The index of nonfamilial experience of the husband and wife before marriage is discussed in chapter 13.

whether the couple resides in a city or a township. The better educated appear to distance themselves from the husband's parents: even if they live in the same place, whether city or township, they are much less likely to live in the same neighborhood.

The patterns that we have described in detail for education also apply in general for several other important characteristics. Those whose premarital experiences are in a more nonfamilial context are farther away from the husband's parents by every measure used; more recent marriage has a similar effect. Similarly, income is negatively related to each measure of proximity.

Proximity to the wife's parents[13] has a much lower correlation with the determinants that we have seen to be strongly associated with proximity to the husband's parents. The operation of patrilocality is evident in the fact that important characteristics of the couple are related to proximity to the husband's parents rather than to the wife's parents.

Frequency of Exchange of Visits

The frequency of visits to or from the husband's parents is substantial. In 1986, if couples and their parents lived in the same city or township, 49% saw each other daily, 67% at least several times a week, 79% at least once a week. When they did not live in the same place, frequency of visits was much lower but still high: Among those living elsewhere, 21% saw each other at least several times a month and 49% at least once a month (table 12.13). The frequency of visits to the husband's parents or wife's parents changed little between 1973 and 1986.

Face-to-face contact with the husband's parents is considerable, considering those co-resident as seeing each other daily. On this basis, the percentage seeing each other frequently is as follows:

	LIVE IN SAME PLACE	ALL CASES
Daily	82	57
At least several times a week	88	62
At least once a week	92	66

For those living in the same place, in both 1980 and 1986, the frequency of visits to the wife's parents is very much lower than to the husband's parents. For those living elsewhere, the frequency of visits to the wife's

13. The data for the wife's parents are in unpublished tables.

TABLE 12.12 Percentage Distribution of Proximity to Husband's Parents by Characteristics of Couples and Parents, Excluding Couples Co-Resident with Husband's Parents or with Husband's Parents Not Available, 1986

	Same Nbhd.[a]	Same Twp.[a] or City	Farther Away	TOTAL %	TOTAL N	% in Same Nbhd. among Those in Same City or Twp.	% in Same Nbhd. among Those in Same City	% in Same Nbhd. among Those in Same Twp.	% in Cities
Wife's education									
Illiterate	47	14	38	100	104	77	67*	78	23
Pri. school	31	18	50	100	726	63	53	69	46
Jr. high	26	18	56	100	286	58	58	59	56
Sr. high	19	22	58	100	364	46	42	53	64
College & above	14	24	62	100	125	38	38	43*	79
Marriage cohort									
1962–64	40	19	41	100	108	67	50*	72	29
1965–69	33	19	47	100	216	63	52	69	39
1970–74	31	20	50	100	363	61	51	69	53
1975–79	26	19	55	100	480	57	50	64	55
1980–84	20	20	61	100	437	51	47	58	66
Premarital nonfamilial index									
4	63	9	28	100	46	88	0*	91	13
5	42	21	36	100	52	67	75*	67	21
6	36	14	50	100	123	72	80*	70	39
7	36	24	40	100	170	60	51	67	49
8	24	20	56	100	225	54	44	64	56
9	23	22	54	100	339	51	46	60	59
10	21	19	60	100	349	53	49	58	60
11	22	15	63	100	171	59	57	60*	61
12	22	25	53	100	32	47	25*	71*	59

Place of interview									
Rural township	36	14	50	100	409	72	—	73	—
Urban township	33	23	45	100	337	59	—	59	—
Small city	20	17	62	100	327	54	54	—	—
Large city	21	23	56	100	531	47	47	—	—
Migration history									
Nonmigrant	59	32	9	100	480	65	53	73	38
Migrant before marriage	16	15	69	100	351	50	51	47	74
Migrant after marriage[b]	7	9	83	100	513	44	46	42	49
N.A.	24	22	54	100	261	52	43	67	63
Family income (thousands)									
0–99 NT$	40	15	44	100	185	73	45*	84	38
100–199 NT$	32	18	49	100	342	64	59	67	46
200–299 NT$	25	18	57	100	504	58	52	64	54
300–399 NT$	22	21	56	100	292	51	47	58	59
400–499 NT$	26	22	52	100	161	54	54	52*	63
500+ NT$	16	29	55	100	115	36	30	53*	69
Total	27	19	53	100	1,605	58	50	66	53

Note: Data presented in the table include women aged 20–49 at the time of the interview. To adjust for truncation bias, only women of the 1962–84 marriage cohorts are included.

* Fewer than 30 cases.

[a] Nbhd. = neighborhood; twp. = township.

[b] Includes those who migrated both before and after marriage.

TABLE 12.13 Percentage Distribution of Frequency of Visits to or from Husband's Parents (HP) by Proximity of Residence, Women Aged 20–39, Excluding Couples Co-Resident with HP, 1973–86

Frequency	SAME TOWNSHIP OR CITY			ELSEWHERE IN TAIWAN			TOTAL		
	1973	1980	1986	1973	1980	1986	1973	1980	1986
Daily	52	44	49	3	2	2	21	17	23
Several times a week	19	21	18	6	5	4	11	11	10
Once a week	10	10	12	8	9	9	9	9	11
Several times a month	6	7	3	10	8	6	8	7	4
Once a month	6	10	9	20	21	27	14	17	19
Less often[a]	8	9	9	53	55	51	36	39	32
Total percentage	100	100	100	100	100	100	100	100	100
N	617	520	643	1,033	938	797	1,650	1,458	1,440

[a] Includes never visited.

parents also is lower than to the husband's parents but the differential is lower than when they are in the same place. A large part of the explanation of the greater frequency of visits to the husband's parents than to the wife's when they live in the same place is that the couple is much more likely to live in the same neighborhood as the husband's parents than the wife's parents. The causal direction is unclear: the greater tendency to live very close to the husband's parents may stem from a desire to facilitate closer and more frequent contact.

Face-to-face contacts between the couple and the wife's parents are much less frequent than with the husband's parents, because there is so much less co-residence with the wife's parents and because the couple is much more likely to live in the same neighborhood as the husband's parents. Considering co-residence as involving daily contact for the whole sample, the frequency of face-to-face contacts is as follows for the husband's and the wife's parents:

	HUSBAND'S PARENTS	WIFE'S PARENTS
Daily	58	13
At least several times a week	64	22
At least once a week	70	34

The difference is attributable partly to greater co-residence with the husband's parents but also to closer proximity to the husband's parents even when not co-resident.

Wife's education, marital cohort, husband's education, and the premarital nonfamilial index all are negatively related to daily visits to the husband's parents for those living in the same place (table 12.14). Daily visiting is much greater in townships than in cities, it is much lower among migrants than among nonmigrants, and those who migrated after marriage visit less frequently than those who migrated before marriage. These are differentials for those living in the same place for whom visits should not be difficult. These results are consistent with the view that many migrants are moving in pursuit of a different life-style, including less familial contact.

Frequency of Giving Money to Parents

A large proportion of young married couples have conformed to traditional values by giving money to the husband's parents, although these contributions often were neither essential to the parents nor a sacrifice to the givers. That patriarchal principles still dominate is evident in the much lower frequency of gifts of money to the wife's parents.

More specifically, 85% of all couples gave money to the husband's parents at least occasionally and 42% did so regularly in 1986 (table 12.15). There was actually a substantial increase in the regularity of giving to the husband's parents between 1973 and 1986. Regular giving increased from 32 to 42%, and couples who never gave decreased from 35 to 15% (table 12.15). This increase in giving money was probably a result, at least in part, of the large increase in per capita income in Taiwan during the 1970s and 1980s (see chap. 2).

The proportion giving regularly to the wife's parents is very much lower than the proportion giving to the husband's parents: 3% compared with 42%.

The strongest determinant by far of regular giving is income, and this positive effect of income is not diminished by multivariate controls (unpublished tables). The percentage giving regularly is 27–29 points greater for the highest than for the lowest income stratum, but giving money to the husband's parents is considerable in all strata. Even among the families with the lowest income, 75% gave at least occasionally, and 30% gave regularly in 1986.

Other variables that were related to proximity or visiting have either no effect or very small effects on monetary gifts.

TABLE 12.14 Percentage Distribution of Frequency of Visits to or from HP, by Various Characteristics, for Women Aged 20–49, Married 1962–84, HP Available and Living in the Same Place but Not Co-Resident with HP, 1986

	Daily	Several Times a Week	Once a Week	Several Times a Month	Once a Month	Less Often	TOTAL %	N
Wife's education								
Illiterate	62	14	3	5	6	9	100	64
Pri. school	53	16	11	3	8	9	100	364
Jr. high	50	17	13	3	9	8	100	124
Sr. high	40	18	16	5	11	10	100	153
College & above	35	20	12	2	18	12	100	49
Marriage cohort								
1962–64	58	8	6	12	8	8	100	64
1965–69	53	16	13	0	8	10	100	115
1970–74	49	17	11	4	7	11	100	184
1975–79	50	18	11	1	12	8	100	216
1980–84	43	18	16	5	10	8	100	174
Family income (thousands)								
0–99 NT$	60	13	5	4	11	8	100	103
100–199 NT$	52	23	9	3	6	8	100	172
200–299 NT$	50	15	12	4	9	11	100	219
300–399 NT$	41	16	20	2	15	5	100	127
400–499 NT$	47	14	13	6	9	11	100	79
500+ NT$	40	15	15	4	8	17	100	52
Premarital nonfamilial index								
4–5	75	6	8	4	3	4	100	67
6–7	52	20	9	2	6	10	100	163
8–9	48	15	11	3	14	8	100	256
10–12	40	19	17	4	10	10	100	219
Place of interview								
Noncity	62	13	9	3	5	8	100	395
City	35	20	16	4	14	11	100	358
Migration history								
Nonmigrant	61	16	8	4	6	6	100	438
Migrant before marriage	32	19	16	6	11	16	100	110
Migrant after marriage[a]	25	16	18	1	22	18	100	88
Whether in the nbhd.[b]								
Yes	72	14	6	2	3	3	100	441
No	18	20	20	6	18	18	100	313
Total percentage	50	17	12	4	9	9	100	754

[a] Includes those who migrated both before and after marriage.

[b] Nbhd. = neighborhood.

TABLE 12.15 Percentage of Frequency of Giving Money to HP and WP, for Those with Such Parents in Taiwan, Women Aged 20–39, 1973–86

	Regularly	Occasionally	Never	TOTAL %	N
		Gave to HP			
1973	32	33	35	100	3,921
1980	42	43	15	100	3,070
1986	42	43	15	100	2,680
		Gave to WP			
1973	—	—	—	—	—
1980	3	39	58	100	3,558
1986	3	49	48	100	2,917

ªNot available for WP in 1973.

Choices between Spending Money for Children and for Husband's Parents

Respondents were asked, "Aside from what you need for bare necessities, is it more important to spend money for children's needs or for husband's parents?" The choices were:

Children	30%
Husband's parents	3%
Equal	67%

Among those who chose the husband's parents or said "equal," about half said they would give less to the husband's parents if money was needed for their children's education.

While these choices are far from the Confucian ideal of absolute primacy of parents, still, a large majority give emphasis to obligations to both parents and children.

Summary and Discussion

Co-residence of a married couple with the husband's parents has continued to be an important aspect of family life despite Taiwan's industrialization and increased consumption levels and despite the increase in the prevalence of nuclear households over time.

Among Taiwanese couples, the percentage living in a nuclear household rose from 35% in 1965 to 56% in 1986.[14] Of couples with a parent

14. Among Mainlanders, the percentage has *declined* from 81 to 73, in part reflecting the increased availability of kin.

available for co-residence, about one-third were in nuclear units in 1973, 43% in 1980, and just over half in 1986. These increases in nuclear units are associated primarily with declines in the proportions living in households that are extended both laterally and across generations, but the percentage living with a parent in a stem household (of those with at least one of the husband's parents alive) declined by only 4 percentage points between 1973 and 1980, from 42 to 38, and remained at that level in 1986. In all, declines in co-residence notwithstanding, even in 1986 nearly half the respondents resided in extended units.

Current status data understate the prevalence of the extended family over the life course. From a life course perspective, more than two times the percentage evident from current levels reported living with the husband's parents at the time of marriage and for some time thereafter. From the perspective of the older generation, above two-thirds lived with a married son.[15]

It may be that only relatively low fertility is now required to fulfill traditional family values of filiality and the tradition of co-residence of parents with a married son at a number of life course stages. This results from several considerations. First, the predominance of the vertical tie for co-residence implies that only one son is necessary to provide the principal opportunity for an extended household. Second, it is likely that parents have a lesser need for children to work in familial enterprises and a greater need to invest in the costs of educating fewer children at the increasingly higher levels deemed necessary. Third, as a growing literature indicates, trends in mortality, fertility, and nuptiality have varying effects on co-residence potentials as they affect the age-sex-marital structure of the population (Atoh 1988; Bongaarts, Kurch, and Wachter 1987; Chen 1986; Hanada, Itoh, and Kono 1988; Hirosima 1988; Tu, Liang, and Li 1987; Yi 1986).

Briefly, declining mortality, which, in Taiwan, as elsewhere, preceded the fertility decline, has had the effect of increasing the survival of both potential co-resident generations—parents and married sons. In a patrilocal system which emphasizes stem co-residence the higher survival rate of the older generation makes for more stem families. However, the higher survival rate of sons makes for a countervailing increase of nuclearity, since only one son is needed for the stem family. With high fertility and low mortality it would be possible for all parents to be in stem families, while the proportion of married sons living in such families might be relatively low.

15. We observe in our samples, of course, only parents with at least one married son.

Later, as fertility declines, the decreased supply of married sons could have the effect of increasing the proportion of stem units if the propensity for living with one married son does not decrease.[16] Obviously, if fertility falls low enough, the potential for stem co-residence hits upper limits. Thus, on average, at least 50% of one-child families and 25% of two-child families will have no married sons to form a stem family. These limits are less stringent when co-residence with the wife's parents is possible. The effects will also depend on the parity distribution, even with low fertility.

In 1980–86, Taiwan had especially large cohorts of young married couples in the age group 20–39 (a result of formerly high fertility and low mortality). Apart from the moderate increase in the tendency of parents to live alone, these large cohorts, in combination with the stem emphasis, have made for increasing nuclearity. The rapidly falling fertility since the late 1950s is likely to have the reverse effect in coming decades.

Apart from the effect of demographic trends on the potential for co-residence, there is obviously a gradual erosion of the tendency toward co-residence. One piece of evidence is the small increase in the proportion of parents living alone, although they could live with married sons. We have seen that there has been a substantial decline in the percentage of respondents who report that newlywed couples should live with the husband's parents after marriage (from 59% in 1973 to 42 in 1986) and the percentage of respondents of childbearing age who themselves expect to live with a married son (from 88% in 1967 to 47% in 1986). Expectations not to co-reside are greater among younger, better educated wives, and among those who arranged their own marriages. Since these characteristics are becoming more prevalent, they suggest a continuing decline in co-residence in the next generation. The growing independence of the younger generation is further indicated by the decrease in the proportion of marriages reported as arranged by parents from 77% for the marriages of 1930–34 to 15% for the marriages of 1955–59 (Thornton et al. 1986, 185–97).

While the current generation of young married couples collectively expects co-residence to decrease, by no means do these couples' expectations suggest a disappearance of the extended family. For example, between 1980 and 1986 we observed a slight rise in the percentages reporting traditional attitudes and expectations. And even while the per-

---

16. During the period when mortality was falling rapidly prior to the decline in fertility, the potential for more complex household structures increased.

centages expecting co-residence decline, nearly half continue to expect to live with one of their married sons, while three-quarters expect the sons to contribute to their support in their old age.

The gradual erosion of the norms for co-residence may be accelerated by plans for universal health insurance and other social security measures actively being considered in affluent Taiwan. Together with the potential effects of below-replacement fertility, there seems to be a high probability of continuing declines in co-residence.

But kinship ties are extensive, even when young married couples are not co-resident with their parents. This is evident in the residential proximity to parents, in frequency of visiting, and in financial support flowing from the younger to the older generation. Although co-residence is decreasing, proximity to the husband's parents and the frequency of visiting have not declined, and the frequency of young couples giving money to the husband's parents has actually increased. Further, kinship ties transcending co-residence are extensive and are based on proximity of parents and their married sons. Patrilineal and patrilocal principles govern not only co-residence but these other ties as well. Young couples live closer to the husband's parents than to the wife's parents, visit the husband's parents more often, and are much more likely to give money to the husband's parents than to the wife's parents.

Characteristics associated with fewer familial ties—education, premarital nonfamilial experience, living in cities, and being a migrant— were associated in 1986 with less proximity to the husband's parents and with less frequent visits to or from parents among those living in the same place. The fact that those with such characteristics are least likely to be in the same neighborhood as the husband's parents, even when they lived in the same place, suggests that such couples may distance themselves from the husband's parents.

The frequency of giving money to the husband's parents has increased in the last two decades, probably as a result of the sharp increase in family income. While income was the principal determinant of such giving, there was considerable giving in all economic strata.

Social and economic change have eroded, but by no means eliminated, the traditional extended household in Taiwan. Patrilineal and patrilocal principles still play an important role in Taiwan kinship ties within and between households.

Thirteen

Determinants of Co-Residence in Extended Households

R. Freedman, A. Thornton, and L. S. Yang

The Co-Residence Patterns to be Explained

As indicated in chapter 12, the Chinese ideal has long been that older parents and their married sons should live together in a large joint-stem household. This is a household extended vertically to include two or more generations and horizontally to include the families of several married brothers, sons of the household head. In practice, however, the emphasis has been on vertical extension, with the older parents living with one married son—a stem family. In 1965 only 26% of young married couples lived in joint-stem units, while 36% were in stem units. By 1986 the proportion in joint-stem units had declined to 7%, while 35% were still in stem units.

Newly married couples were expected to begin married life in the household of the husband's parents. This was almost universally the case not long ago. Ninety-four percent of couples married in 1955–59 were co-resident with the husband's parents just after marriage, providing at least one of the husband's parents was alive. In successive marriage cohorts the proportion co-resident decreased steadily, reaching 68% by 1980–84. While this is a very significant decrease, nevertheless after twenty-five years of considerable social and economic change two-thirds of young married couples still began married life in extended households.

Co-residence was almost always patrilocal, whether at marriage or later. In five successive surveys between 1965 and 1986 the proportion of households in which co-residence was with the wife's parents was always a low 3–4%. Although the status of women has improved considerably in this period, co-residence with the wife's side of the family is still not an accepted family pattern.

The dominance of the patrilineal and patrilocal principles has meant that new brides almost always married into the household of the husband's parents. If the prospective wife and husband lived in different communities, the wife migrated from her community to his. The wife's tendency to migrate at marriage was increased by traditions of exogamy in communities with considerable real or fictive common ancestry. The tendency for much greater migration by women before marriage was indicated by the fact that 67% of the prospective brides, but only 37% of the prospective grooms, lived in a different place at marriage than at birth for the whole period, 1962–84. Unfortunately, the data do not indicate when the migration took place. As we shall see, the husband's migration was especially significant because he might migrate away from his parents.

Once co-resident at marriage, the young couple was likely to live with the husband's parents for a considerable time. Ninety-one percent of the marriage cohort of 1953–58 initially co-resident were still co-resident three years after marriage and 76% after nine years. While these proportions were substantially less for the cohort of 1976–80, even that recently the percentage co-resident was still 73% after three years and 48% after nine years.

Since the older parents often had more than one son and filial responsibility could be fulfilled by one son, the proportion of parents co-resident has always been greater than that of married sons. For example, in 1973, 82% of parents with a married son were co-resident with at least one married son, but only 50% of the married sons were co-resident with a parent. As we shall see, co-residence, both at marriage and at the time of the interview, was negatively related to the number of married male siblings the husband had.[1]

Plausible Determinants of Co-Residence

The purpose of this chapter is to answer two interrelated sets of questions. The first set concerns the individual determinants of the living arrangements of married couples. What determines whether a young couple begins married life living with the husband's parents, and, if they begin married life that way, what determines how long they live together? The second question concerns the determinants of the historical *changes* in living arrangements of young couples that have been documented. What have been the social and economic changes in Taiwan that account for the changes in living arrangements during the past several decades?

1. The custom of "rotating," living in the independent households of several married sons, would only have a small effect on this relationship, since there were relatively few such cases—3% of respondents at the time of the 1986 survey. Besides, this would be most likely to happen after married sons were well established in their own households.

Obviously, co-residence is not possible if neither of the husband's parents is alive or if they live outside Taiwan. Therefore, our analysis will deal only with couples with one or both of the husband's parents alive and in Taiwan both at marriage and at the time of the interview. Co-residence rates obviously would be less if the denominator included all couples irrespective of availability of parents. The effect of availability decreased over time with the decline of mortality, the principal determinant of availability of parents.

Following the theoretical thrust of the earlier chapters, our expectation is that co-residence at marriage will be less, the greater the extent to which the young couple is exposed before marriage to nonfamilial contexts and interactions. We also expect that nonfamilial experiences will lead to shorter periods of living in the parental home for those who begin married life sharing living quarters with parents.

Such nonfamilial influences include the following:

— length of exposure to schools and colleges;
— work in nonfamilial enterprises; other social interactions with young people free from parental supervision, especially independent dating;
— choice of a mate without parental intervention;
— later age at marriage, associated with greater maturity and experience, conducive to behavior less subject to parental control;
— residence in more urban places, where young people are less constantly under the eye of parents, relatives, and neighbors, with greater opportunity for exposure to new ideas and people;
— migration, which may involve moving away from parents and family but, in any case, is likely to be motivated by seeking out new opportunities and stimuli;
— the number of married brothers the husband had at marriage, a different kind of determinant. If emphasis is on the importance of co-residence of parents with a married son, then the greater the number of married sons, the less the obligation for co-residence for any one.

We have data which measure such variables, albeit imperfectly. However, there are a large number of other plausible determinants for which we have no measures. Examples are the extent of parental and other familial authority over children, whether co-resident or not; the financial situation of the couple and parents at the time of marriage and later; the influence of the mass media, which became increasingly prevalent in Taiwan during the period under study; and more generally the diffuse influence of an increasingly urban society, linked to the worldwide system of communications, trade, science, and ideas.

Of course, as we documented in chapter 3, a transformation of Taiwanese society has changed the distribution of many of the determinants of household living arrangements. Changes in both macro- and micro-determinants of family structure, measured and unmeasured, have resulted in the following historical changes in co-residence at marriage:

MARRIAGE COHORT	PERCENT CO-RESIDENT AT MARRIAGE
1955–59	94
1960–64	86
1965–69	82
1970–74	75
1975–79	70
1980–82	68

There have been similar declines in the length of time spent co-residing with parents among those who do so at marriage. Explanation of these time series is one important aim of this chapter. We specifically examine the extent to which variation in co-residence over historical time can be accounted for by the changes that have occurred in the explanatory variables we specify in our individual models of living arrangements. We will both consider the success of the variables taken together to explain changes in co-residence and ask what specific factors were most important in producing the decline in extended residence during this period.

The Data

Data on the extent and duration of co-residence beginning at marriage are available in three of our surveys. However, after preliminary work with these surveys, the analysis was restricted to data for the most recent survey (1986) because of the greater richness of the data on determinants available in that survey. This restriction was particularly important because of our concern that determinant measures be prior in time to the co-residence at marriage or, if necessary, contemporary with it.

Important examples are the two most powerful predictors of co-residence—migration status and the urbanization level of the place of residence at marriage. The 1986 survey was the only one with information on the specific place of residence of the couple when they were married. This permits classifying the couple as to urbanization level of residence at marriage. Further, if the residence at marriage is different from that at birth, the husband can be identified as a migrant some time during the period between birth and marriage. The other surveys only provide data on place of residence at birth and at the time of the interview, which would only yield urbanization level and migration status for periods often long after the marriage or the termination of co-residence.

Even for the 1986 data, we are unable to specify just when the migration took place between the time of the husband's birth and marriage or whether he migrated with his parents.[2] We have no reason to believe that many husbands migrated just at the time of marriage, so we are assuming that most moved prior to the marriage. We believe that migrants are likely to live with parents if the parents migrated to the same community. As evidence for this, there were relatively few migrants who had parents living separately in the same community at the time of the interview.[3] Further, the fact that co-residence rates were very high for nonmigrants is consistent with the expectation of co-residence where parents and sons are in the same place. Migrants from rural or urban townships, particularly those with parents who were farmers, were likely to have had more married brothers than nonmigrants. So the parents of migrants from those areas could have lived—and probably did live— with other married sons at the place of origin.

Using the data from the 1986 survey only, we can represent marriage cohorts from 1962–64 to 1980–84. We could have gone back to 1955–61 with data from earlier surveys, but that would have necessitated giving up the important data on migration status and urbanization at the time of marriage.

The concern for causal order required that we exclude from the analysis a fairly rich body of data on attitudes about such matters as intergenerational relations, religious practices, and expectations for co-residence with children, which were measured for the time of the interview. Responses at the time of interview may have been affected by the earlier facts of co-residence at marriage or by whether the couple was separated from the parental household between marriage and the interview.

The variables used in the multivariate analysis are displayed in table 13.1. The categories used for marriage cohort, wife's education, wife's age at marriage, and number of husband's married brothers at the time of marriage are self-explanatory.

The premarital familial index is a summary based on the four vari-

2. It is possible that some men migrated from their place of birth before marriage but moved back to the parental home at place of birth at the time of marriage, presumably to fulfill their filial duty and to take advantage of the subsidy of living at home and working in the original home community. Such cases would be classified as nonmigrants with the available data. We think it is unlikely that there were many such cases.

3. It would have been better, of course, to have data on where the parents were at the time of marriage.

TABLE 13.1 Logistic Regression Analysis of Effects of Selected Variables on Co-Residence with Husband's Parents at Marriage for Couples with Husband's Parents Alive at Marriage

	N	Unadj.	Model 1 Adj.	Model 2 Adj.	Model 3 Adj.	Model 4 Adj.	Model 5 Adj.
Marriage cohort							
1962–64	260	82	78	75	76	78	78
1965–69	485	79	76	74	76	80	80
1970–74	643	72	71	71	71	76	76
1975–79	883	67	69	71	72	74	74
1980–84	919	68	72	75	75	76	76
Chi square			11.18*	5.11	5.46	4.67	4.88
No. of husband's married brothers							
0	1,351	76	77	77	78	78	80
1	869	72	73	74	74	74	77
2	515	68	68	69	70	69	74
3 or more	455	61	61	61	62	59	64
Chi square			43.14†	44.33†	45.42†	38.23†	36.88†
Wife's ethnicity							
Fukienese	2,494	72	72	73	75	76	76
Hakka	433	71	73	75	72	77	78
Mainlander	143	55	64	65	68	72	71
Other	120	69	70	69	68	70	70
Chi square			5.02	5.45	4.62	3.59	4.38
Wife's education							
Illiterate	264	83	82	78	75	74	74
Primary	1,491	76	76	74	74	77	77
Jr. high	567	69	70	72	73	76	76
Sr. high	667	64	66	71	73	77	76
College	201	53	56	66	70	74	72
Chi square			44.87†	6.83	1.73	1.66	2.24
Wife's age at marriage							
15–17	278	78	—	78	77	78	79
18–19	542	77	—	77	77	78	79
20–21	851	74	—	74	74	77	78
22–24	1,003	70	—	72	73	75	75
25 and above	516	60	—	66	68	72	71
Chi square				16.12‡	9.26	5.78	8.33
Premarital familial index							
More familial 4	135	91	—	90	87	83	83
5	137	87	—	86	84	84	85
6	264	82	—	81	80	82	81
7	383	76	—	76	76	77	77
8	450	74	—	75	76	77	78
9	688	72	—	73	75	77	77
10	584	59	—	61	64	70	69
Less familial 11–12	339	58	—	60	64	70	70
N.A.	210	73	—	73	72	76	76
Chi square				77.37†	53.52†	22.32‡	23.89‡

TABLE 13.1 continued

	N	Unadj.	Model 1 Adj.	Model 2 Adj.	Model 3 Adj.	Model 4 Adj.	Model 5 Adj.
Type of residence at marriage							
Rural township	1,046	84	—	—	83	—	—
Urban township	790	77	—	—	77	—	—
Small city	447	56	—	—	60	—	—
Large city	848	60	—	—	63	—	—
N.A.	59	68	—	—	70	—	—
Chi square					111.48†		
Husband's migration/type of residence at marriage							
Nonmigrant							
Rural township	871	90	—	—	—	90	—
Urban township	584	87	—	—	—	87	—
Small city	149	84	—	—	—	85	—
Large city	365	79	—	—	—	80	—
Migrant							
Rural township	157	50	—	—	—	53	—
Urban township	184	46	—	—	—	45	—
Small city	263	41	—	—	—	45	—
Large city	416	44	—	—	—	48	—
N.A.	201	56	—	—	—	58	—
Chi square						429.84†	
Husband's migration/farm background							
Nonmigrant							
Rural/urban township	1,455	89	—	—	—	—	88
Small/large city	514	80	—	—	—	—	82
Migrant							
From rural/urban twp., HP is farmer	382	34	—	—	—	—	36
From rural/urban twp., HP not farmer	326	50	—	—	—	—	53
From small/large city	228	56	—	—	—	—	64
N.A.	285	51	—	—	—	—	54
Chi square							455.43‡
Chi square for whole model			138.12†	232.98†	348.54†	718.91†	750.71†
Degree of freedom			14	26	30	34	31

Note: The data for this and following tables are from the Taiwan KAP-VI Survey carried out in 1986. The sample is restricted to couples married only once, with at least one of the husband's parents available at marriage, and, to minimize truncation bias, only couples married between 1962 and 1984 are included. * Indicates that an individual variable chi square is statistically significant at the .05 level. ‡Indicates a significant difference at .01 level. †Indicates a significant difference at .001 level. The same symbols indicate the level at which chi-square values for the model as a whole are signficantly different from 0.

TABLE 13.2   Effects of Components of Premarital Familial Variables on Co-Residence with Husband's Parents at Marriage

	N	Percentage Co-Resident with Husband's Parents at Marriage
Wife's premarital work		
None or at home	742	81
Away from home		
Gave money to parents	1,714	71
Kept money	514	63
Husband's premarital work		
Worked for self, family, relatives	851	80
Worked for others	2,104	69
Who arranged marriage		
Parents	878	82
Parents and couple	1,448	72
Couple	681	61
Dating pattern		
None	655	83
With parental permission	1,714	71
Without parental permission	627	64

ables listed in table 13.2, which are measures of various ways in which the wife or husband might have been more or less independent of their parents before marriage:

1. Wife's premarital work pattern differentiates those who did not work or worked at home from those who worked away from home, subdivided by whether the workers gave their wages to their parents or kept them mainly for themselves.
2. Husband's premarital work distinguishes those who were self-employed or worked for family or relatives, on one hand, from those who worked for nonrelatives, on the other.
3. Who arranged the marriage: the parents alone, the parents and couple together, or the couple alone?
4. Dating pattern distinguishes those who never dated before marriage, those who dated with parental supervision, and those who dated without such supervision.

The summary familial index was calculated by assigning scores of 1 to 3 to the categories of each of the four variables, with 3 representing the least familial category. The four sets of scores were then added, producing a possible range of 4 to 12.[4]

Previous work on Taiwan has found that the two Taiwanese ethnic

4. The two categories for the husband's work variable were scored as 1 or 3.

groups (Fukienese and Hakka) do not differ in demographic terms but that Mainlanders often are different from the Taiwanese. The Mainlanders came to Taiwan only in the late 1940s and usually had a much smaller kinship network in Taiwan than the Taiwanese. The younger generation of these migrants, therefore, was socialized in a family context where there were fewer relationships beyond the conjugal family and parent-child relationships were less emphasized compared with their Taiwanese counterparts. It is thus plausible that the Mainlanders might have lower co-residence rates than the Taiwanese. While we should logically be using the ethnicity of the husband in our analysis, since it is his parents who are crucial for co-residence, we have chosen to use the wife's ethnicity, because those data were more complete, and preliminary analysis indicated similar patterns for the husband.

The levels-of-urbanization variable follows the official governmental definitions used for administrative and statistical purposes. The classifications of some specific places have changed from time to time as their character changed. Large cities have populations of 250,000 or more; there were five of these before 1982 and seven thereafter. Small cities have populations of 50,000–249,999. Urban townships generally have considerable agricultural population but no cities. The rural townships are the most agricultural.

The effects of urbanization cannot be understood without taking into account the fact that the proportion of husbands who were migrants between birth and marriage differs greatly by level of urbanization and, as we shall see, that migration is the most powerful determinant of co-residence. Consider the proportion who were migrant by type of place of residence at marriage:

Type of Place	Percent Migrant
Rural township	15
Urban township	24
Small city	64
Large city	53

In order to consider the joint effects of migration status and type of place of residence at marriage, we created a migration/residence-type variable that includes both elements. This is done by subclassifying both migrants and nonmigrants by type of residence at marriage (see table 13.1).

We have not included the migration status of the wife in the models presented, because exploratory work indicated that it was the husband's migration status that determined co-residence with his parents.

In addition, we also use a migrant/farm background variable. This is a simplified version of a much more detailed classification used in preliminary analyses. In the earlier version, nonmigrants were classified in detail by the type of place in which they lived and migrants were classified in detail by both place of origin and place of destination. Apart from the fact that the sample size could not sustain such detailed classification, it turned out that for both migrants and nonmigrants there were only small distinctions in co-residence rates between rural and urban townships and between small and large cities. In addition, only the place of origin made a difference in co-residence for migrants. It seemed plausible that if the migrants from rural/urban townships had parents who were farmers when they were growing up, the parents might be motivated by their ties to the land, which is highly valued in Taiwan, to stay in the home community. This supposition is consistent with the fact that the lowest co-residence rates by a wide margin were for such migrants. These considerations led to the variable definition shown in table 13.1.

An additional migration/residence status variable was used in the analysis of departures from the parental home after marriage. This variable was the migration/residence status at the time of the interview. It indicates the experience of the couple between marriage and the time of the interview.

Unfortunately, the causal interconnections between postmarital migration and the length of co-residence are not straightforward or simple. In many cases the geographical migration and the separation from the parental home occur simultaneously. They are also probably mutually determined by other causal factors. For these reasons, the observed relationships between this postmarital migration variable and length of time spent with parents should not be interpreted as the simple influence of migration on the termination of co-residence. Nevertheless, by including the variable, the close association between migration and residential separation can be documented.

The Models

The following chart shows the five models that were used, both in the analyses of co-residence at marriage and in the rate of separating from the parental home for those who began married life there. An additional model, including migration/residence status at interview, was used in analyses of the termination of co-residential arrangements.

	MODEL 1	MODEL 2	MODEL 3	MODEL 4	MODEL 5
Marriage cohort	X	X	X	X	X
Number of husband's married brothers at marriage	X	X	X	X	X
Wife's ethnicity	X	X	X	X	X
Wife's education	X	X	X	X	X
Wife's age at marriage		X	X	X	X
Premarital familial relations		X	X	X	X
Urban/rural type of residence at marriage			X		
Migration/residence at marriage				X	
Migration/farm background					X

Model 1, in addition to marriage cohort, includes the wife's ethnicity and education and the number of husband's married brothers. The wife's age at marriage and the premarital familial index were not included in this model, because they were hypothesized to be partially determined by the wife's education. They are, therefore, added in model 2. Thus, the effect of education can be evaluated in model 1 without dilution of its effect by controlling for some of its consequences.

We will discuss models 1 and 2 first and then turn to models 3–5, which add variables centered on migration status and type of residence at marriage. Migration is the crucial ingredient because, as we shall see, it is the most strongly related to co-residence. We have chosen to introduce these migration-affected variables in later models, because migration is probably the variable through which other personal and familial characteristics affect co-residence. If migration were introduced early in the analysis, the effects of the personal characteristics in models 1 and 2 would be improperly diluted by controlling a variable they help to determine.

The Multivariate Analysis of Co-Residence at Marriage

Co-residence at marriage is defined for this analysis as a dichotomous variable: coded 1 if the couple lived with the husband's parents at marriage and 0 if they did not. We analyzed this variable using logistic regression, with the results reported in table 13.1. The results shown in table 13.1 are the expected percentage living with the husband's parents at marriage for each category of the predictor variables. These expected values were calculated as in the earlier chapters.

The number of husband's married brothers at the time of marriage has the expected negative relationship to co-residence (table 13.1). This relationship is not reduced at all by the controls for any of the other variables in models 1–5. We have previously seen that co-residence in stem families (the older parents and one married son and his family) has become by far the major form of extended co-residence. If what is important is co-residence with one married son, then the greater the number of married sons, the less likely that any one son will be fulfilling the essential filial obligation. The fact that adjustment for other variables does not diminish this effect indicates that this principle is pertinent, irrespective of the other characteristics of the couple.

We found in a separate analysis that whether the husband had unmarried brothers or sisters at the time of marriage had no added effect on co-residence. Unmarried siblings, whether male or female, are not a substitute for the essential married son where co-residence is concerned.

Wife's education, one indicator of exposure to important nonfamilial influence, has a strong negative, monotonic relationship to co-residence. There is a 30-percentage-point differential in co-residence between the most and least educated. This is reduced but remains strong when adjusted for marriage cohort, wife's ethnicity, and number of husband's married brothers in model 1. However, addition of the wife's age at marriage and the familial index in model 2 greatly reduces the education effect and makes it statistically nonsignificant. Presumably, this is because education affects co-residence in large part through its effect on age at marriage and the familial index. While the education effect is still monotonic and negative in model 2, adding the migration-affected variables in models 3–5 largely eliminates the education effect—probably because migration is a consequence of education. It appears then that education is an important determinant of co-residence, which has its effect indirectly through its influence on when the wife marries, on the nature of the couple's premarital familial relations, and on the migration experience of the husband she marries.

It is plausible that educated wives, more exposed than the less educated to the mass media and to new ideas about family relationships and the role of women, would seek the independence of beginning married life in their own households. The education of husbands, which might be expected to have a similar effect, was not included in the model, because in preliminary analyses it was found that the negative relationship of husbands' education and co-residence disappeared with adjustment for the effect of the wife's education. This is consistent with the idea that many educated women do not want to begin married life in the household of relative strangers. The subservient role of the incoming young daughter-in-law, which was so common in the past, may be increasingly lacking in appeal to educated women. However, the effect of the wife's education should not be exaggerated. After all, 53% of college-educated women were co-resident at marriage. There are reports that the roles of young wives and their mothers-in-law now get reversed when the educated young bride who goes out of the household to work finds that the mother-in-law takes care of the household chores and helps with childcare.

Mainlander couples are distinguished by lower co-residence rates than the much more numerous Fukienese and Hakka couples, who do not differ in this respect. Perhaps this reflects the much less dense familial network of the Mainlanders. This differential is somewhat diminished by the multivariate controls and, given the relatively small number of the Mainlanders, does not have a significant effect on overall co-residence rates in any model.

The premarital familial index may be the most direct measure we have of the couple's exposure to nonfamilial contexts before marriage. Table 13.2 shows that the four components of the index all had expected relationships to co-residence. When summarized in combination in the premarital familial index (table 13.1), there is a strong zero-order negative relationship of nonfamilial scores with co-residence. This relationship is only moderately reduced by multivariate control for the other five variables of model 2. While reduced by further controls for migration-affected variables, it remains significant in all models.

Wife's age at marriage is, as expected, negatively related to co-residence. Women who marry later are more mature, better educated, with more work experience in nonfamilial labor and with weaker premarital familial ties. This could well lead to a greater desire for independent residence. Indeed, age at marriage is monotonically and negatively related to co-residence. This relationship remains monotonic and significant with controls for the five other variables in model 2. It is only with the introduction of the migration-affected variables of models 3–5 that this relationship becomes nonsignificant, although the pattern is still evident.

Model 3 adds type of residence at marriage to the variables of model 2. As expected, the level of urbanization as officially measured is negatively related to co-residence (model 3). This relationship remains significant and is only modestly reduced when controlled for the five other variables. However, the effects of urbanization cannot be understood without taking into account the fact that the proportion of the couples who are migrants differs greatly by level of urbanization and that migration is by far the most powerful determinant of co-residence. Therefore, in model 4 we add a combined residence/migration variable to the variables of model 2. This makes it very clear that migration status is much more important than urbanization level per se for co-residence.

It is clear from model 4 in table 13.1 that nonmigrants, irrespective of their place of residence, have much higher co-residence rates than migrants. Continuity in the community apparently makes for continuity in family ties even in big cities. It is often argued that secularizing forces in cities make for weaker familial ties, so we expected relatively low co-residence rates in cities for those who always had lived there before marriage, but that is not the case. While nonmigrants in cities did have lower co-residence rates than those in rural/urban townships, it is striking that, nevertheless, city rates for nonmigrants are very high both before and after adjustment for all other variables. It is possible, of course, that the financial advantages of co-residence in cities, where housing is expensive, may lead to more co-residence despite secularizing influences.

The joint migration/residence variable (model 4) has a much stronger relationship to co-residence than residence alone or any grouping of other variables (as indicated by chi square values for all variables and models). The differentials between migration/residence categories are little affected by control for the five other variables. On the other hand, addition of the migration/residence variable in model 4 reduces further the effects (compare model 2) of the education, familial relations, and age at marriage variables. However, familial relations and number of married brothers remain significantly related to co-residence even in model 4.

In model 5, migration is again the key element in a complex variable in which nonmigrants are subdivided by type of place of residence and migrants are subclassified by whether they were born in a rural/urban township or a city, with the migrants from rural/urban townships further subclassified by whether the husband's father was a farmer. The most important additional information from this new variable in model 5 is that migrants from rural/urban townships with farm fathers have by far the lowest co-residence rates for any subcategory of any variable, either before or after adjustment for the other variables. As previously indicated, we think this is because the farmer parents are likely to have strong motivations to stay at the home base even when a married son migrates. It is also possible that parents in rural/urban townships may perceive the move to a city as involving a larger adjustment than those who move between cities. That could account for the fact that even migrants from those areas without farmer fathers had low co-residence rates.

The migration variable in several versions captures and represents much of the effect of the other variables. It appears that migration may be an intervening variable between other characteristics and co-residence. The better educated, those with more nonfamilial premarital influences, and those marrying late have higher migration rates. The motivation to move may sometimes simply be to get away from the parental home and authority. This could be an integral part of wanting to be more independent. But that need not be the case. It is undoubtedly the case that many of the migrants are moving to take advantage of the expanding opportunities in Taiwan's dynamic economy. Many of these moves may be with the support and encouragement of the husband's parents. There is evidence of such a familial strategy linking households in different places (e.g., Greenhalgh 1984). But it may also be true that migration away from the parental home may be part of a nonfamilial orientation in many cases, whether or not there are continuing economic ties to the home base.

Interpretation of the correlation between migration and residential arrangements at marriage requires us to consider the possibility that both variables are jointly determined decisions. As young people mature, they, or their parents, make decisions about their social and economic futures. Many of these decisions probably involve consideration of both migration from the area of childhood residence and the establishment of an independent household. While the migration itself may have preceded marriage, the decision to move and to have an independent household at marriage may have been part of the same decision. If so, there would be no independent effect of migration on postmarital living arrangements.

It may also be true that many people migrate away from their parental home before marriage without any concrete plans about where they will live after they marry. The experience away from the parental home may, in turn, integrate them into social and economic settings in the new areas that militate against the possibility of returning home when they marry.

Our analysis has highlighted the important role of migration, but to understand its multifaceted relations to other factors affecting co-residence will require much more information on the related migration history of the parents and on the financial and other relationships of the two generations. It will also require more information on the dynamics of the decision-making process across the life courses of the individuals and families involved.

The causal models summarized in table 13.1 are very successful in explaining the cohort trends in residence at marriage. As the unadjusted column of table 13.1 indicates, there was a 14-percentage-point decline in co-residence at marriage between the marriage cohorts of the early

1960s and those of the early 1980s. With the introduction of the multivariate controls in models 2–5, this differential is virtually eliminated. This means that the trends in residence patterns can be entirely explained by shifts across time in the levels of the predictor variables in those equations.

Closer scrutiny of the models reveals which variables are most influential in explaining the trends in living arrangements. With just the introduction of the variables in model 1, the 14-percentage-point differential between the earliest and latest cohorts is reduced to just 6 percentage points—a reduction of four-sevenths of the total. Thus, shifts of the number of married brothers, ethnicity, and education can explain most of the historical trend.

An equation not reported in table 13.1 suggests that changes in ethnicity and number of husband's married brothers can explain little of the observed change. With just these two variables included in an equation with marriage cohort, the difference between the earliest and latest cohort remains at 12 percentage points. Thus, even though these two variables have their own independent effects on living arrangements, they can only account for a small proportion of the historical trend.

This conclusion, of course, leaves education as the major factor reducing the observed cohort spread of 14 percentage points to 6 percentage points in model 1. The strong upward trend in education, along with the strong negative influence of education on co-residence, thus, explains a substantial part of this important historical trend.

The introduction of the wife's age at marriage and premarital familial index further reduces the differences across the marriage cohort groups. In fact, the introduction of these two variables in model 2 entirely eliminates the difference between the earliest and latest marriage cohorts. The effect of the premarital familial index on co-residence is substantially stronger than the effect of age at marriage, which suggests that the premarital familial index is also the most important of the two in accounting for the historical trend. All of these considerations indicate that education, paid employment, and other forms of premarital independence from parents are the major changes in Taiwanese social and economic life that have produced the trends in the living arrangements of newlyweds.

Multivariate Analysis of Length of Co-Residence

What determines the length of co-residence for couples who begin marriage co-resident with the husband's parents? We will consider as possible determinants the same variables analyzed in relation to the fact of beginning co-residence at marriage. We begin by considering with data in table 13.3 the cumulative rate, computed on a life-table basis, of terminating co-residence with the husband's parents at two, four, and six years after marriage. Then, using initially the same models as for beginning co-residence, we use proportional hazard models to specify the estimated rate of terminating co-residence on a multivariate basis. Table 13.4 summarizes the results of the hazard models by listing the ratio of the estimated rate of leaving the parental home for each category of the independent variables relative to the termination rate for the reference category for that variable, which is noted with a coefficient of one.

Number of husband's married brothers at time of marriage. Having at least one married brother at the time of marriage significantly increases the rate of termination as compared to having none, but this rate does not increase with the number of married brothers. Irrespective of what set of variables is controlled in models 1–6, the rate of termination for those with at least one married brother is about 60–75% higher than that for those with no married brothers. So, as in the case of beginning co-residence, the effect of having a married brother is completely independent of other variables.

Wife's age at marriage. This variable has no significant effect on the probability of termination over time, whether on a bivariate or a multivariate basis. This, of course, is in contrast to the findings for co-residence at marriage, when there is a substantial negative effect of age at marriage.

Wife's education. The cumulative termination probability at two, four, and six years increases monotonically with wife's education (table 13.3). The unadjusted rate of termination of co-residence with parents also increases monotonically and significantly with wife's education (table 13.4). The rate for primary school graduates is 33% greater than that of the illiterate reference group, and this differential increases to 89% for those who attended college.

The education effect persists, although not completely monotonically, with controls in model 1 for marriage cohort, wife's ethnicity, and number of married brothers. However, as in the case of beginning co-residence, when we control additionally in model 2 for the premarital familial index and wife's age at marriage, the education relationship becomes statistically nonsignificant. This is presumably because education has a large part of its effect on length of co-residence through the familial relations index. Age at marriage is not relevant as a variable

TABLE 13.3 Cumulative Percentages Terminating Co-Residence at Two, Four, and Six Years after Marriage, by Characteristics of the Couple

| | N | CUMULATIVE PERCENTAGE TERMINATING CO-RESIDENCE AFTER | | |
		2 Years	4 Years	6 Years
Marriage cohort				
1962–64	157	13.4	19.7	28.7
1965–69	297	15.8	26.6	33.3
1970–74	417	18.9	28.5	38.1
1975–79	572	20.4	32.3	41.8
1980–84	619	28.3	38.1	47.5
Number of husband's married brothers at marriage				
0	967	14.0	22.8	31.3
1	567	26.5	38.3	47.6
2	296	25.9	41.0	49.4
3 or more	232	32.9	38.2	47.0
Wife's education				
Illiterate	183	13.7	20.8	29.2
Primary	986	19.8	29.6	38.6
Jr. high	374	23.3	35.4	42.4
Sr. high	416	24.4	36.7	46.1
College	103	28.5	33.5	45.5
Wife's ethnicity				
Fukienese	1,632	20.8	30.9	40.0
Hakka	279	21.8	31.2	37.3
Mainlander	75	24.1	37.5	46.6
Other	76	26.4	36.6	44.8
Wife's age at marriage				
15–17	189	19.6	32.3	40.2
18–19	372	21.6	32.2	40.5
20–21	578	18.6	26.7	35.6
22–24	639	21.4	32.7	41.1
25 and above	284	27.0	36.1	46.7
Premarital familial index				
More familial 4	98	6.1	11.2	19.4
5	100	11.0	21.2	26.5
6	186	18.3	28.7	38.6
7	262	19.9	27.2	34.3
8	309	22.1	31.9	42.4
9	457	24.1	35.2	43.8
10	331	25.2	39.2	47.9
Less familial 11–12	183	25.9	36.1	44.0
N.A.	136	19.3	28.2	40.0

TABLE 13.3 continued

| | N | Cumulative Percentage Terminating Co-Residence After | | |
		2 Years	4 Years	6 Years
Type of residence at marriage				
Rural township	794	22.2	31.4	39.6
Urban township	548	20.0	31.8	39.0
Small city	239	20.3	30.0	41.7
Large city	457	20.1	30.0	40.7
N.A.	24	50.0	58.3	58.3
Husband's migration/type of residence at marriage				
Nonmigrant				
Rural township	710	22.1	31.4	39.2
Urban township	461	19.4	31.1	37.7
Small city	116	15.7	25.6	37.1
Large city	256	19.0	30.3	41.5
Migrant				
Rural township	75	21.6	31.9	44.9
Urban township	75	24.2	39.1	49.1
Small city	106	23.9	36.9	47.2
Large city	169	22.0	31.7	41.0
N.A.	94	29.8	39.7	48.6
Migration/residence status at interview				
Nonmigrant				
Rural township	569	12.8	20.8	27.7
Urban township	399	12.6	22.3	29.3
Small city	169	14.4	24.1	37.2
Large city	344	16.8	25.9	35.7
Migrant				
Rural township	136	41.2	55.4	67.1
Urban township	125	36.1	49.0	54.1
Small city	105	50.5	66.0	75.4
Large city	140	42.9	58.8	67.8
N.A.	75	24.0	35.1	46.6
Husband's migration/farm background at marriage				
Nonmigrant				
Rural/urban township	1,171	21.0	31.1	38.4
Small/large city	372	18.0	27.4	38.9
Migrant				
From rural/urban township, HP is farmer	117	26.6	39.8	51.0
From rural/urban township, HP not farmer	153	16.5	25.8	34.0
From small/large city	124	27.8	41.2	50.6
N.A.	125	27.2	35.6	47.4

Note: Proportions terminating are calculated on a life-table basis. In tables 13.3 and 13.4 the sample is restricted to couples married only once, with at least one of husband's parents available at interview, and, to minimize truncation bias, only couples married between 1962 and 1984 are included.

TABLE 13.4 Proportional Hazards Models for Rate of Co-Residence Termination with Husband's Parents after Marriage, for Couples Co-Resident at Marriage

	Unadjusted Effects[a]	ADJUSTED EFFECTS[a]					
		Model 1	Model 2	Model 3	Model 4	Model 5	Model 6
Marriage cohort							
1962–64	1	1	1	1	1	1	1
1965–69	1.191	1.016	1.105	1.104	1.082	1.104	1.046
1970–74	1.494‡	1.407‡	1.301*	1.290	1.276	1.290	1.282
1975–79	1.589†	1.371*	1.210	1.214	1.214	1.208	1.317*
1980–84	2.178†	1.800†	1.586‡	1.579‡	1.594†	1.585‡	1.872†
Number of husband's married brothers at marriage							
0	1	1	1	1	1	1	1
1	1.657†	1.655†	1.645†	1.641†	1.647†	1.643†	1.594†
2	1.701†	1.697†	1.694†	1.693†	1.706†	1.698†	1.695†
3 or more	1.657†	1.680†	1.677†	1.688†	1.689†	1.681†	1.749†
Wife's education							
Illiterate	1	1	1	1	1	1	1
Primary	1.328*	1.224	1.120	1.120	1.128	1.131	1.022
Jr. high	1.641†	1.370*	1.167	1.189	1.180	1.189	1.057
Sr. high	1.795†	1.556‡	1.300	1.343*	1.320	1.326	1.137
College	1.885†	1.537*	1.212	1.269	1.193	1.223	0.990
Wife's ethnicity							
Fukienese	1	1	1	1	1	1	1
Hakka	0.943	0.869	0.886	0.868	0.868	0.865	0.928
Mainlander	1.216	1.045	1.025	1.022	0.996	0.992	0.949
Other	1.386*	1.290	1.272	1.264	1.250	1.253	1.146
Wife's age at marriage							
15–17	1	—	1	1	1	1	1
18–19	1.034	—	1.013	1.021	1.021	1.008	0.977
20–21	0.919	—	0.925	0.931	0.932	0.924	0.893
22–24	1.042	—	0.985	0.990	0.993	0.990	0.969
25 and above	1.276	—	1.078	1.077	1.069	1.074	1.038
Premarital familial index							
More familial 4	1	—	1	1	1	1	1
5	1.183	—	1.120	1.136	1.130	1.126	1.098
6	1.768‡	—	1.701‡	1.743‡	1.735‡	1.724‡	1.443*
7	1.620‡	—	1.432*	1.496*	1.464*	1.459*	1.285
8	2.009†	—	1.667‡	1.732‡	1.715‡	1.694‡	1.385
9	2.142†	—	1.737‡	1.799†	1.784‡	1.763‡	1.433*
10	2.479†	—	1.963†	2.039†	1.986†	1.979†	1.564*
Less familial 11–12	2.414†	—	1.897†	1.958†	1.930†	1.912†	1.615*
N.A.	1.670‡	—	1.501*	1.503*	1.510*	1.500‡	1.319
Type of residence at marriage							
Rural township	1	—	—	1	—	—	—
Urban township	0.944	—	—	0.930	—	—	—
Small city	1.074	—	—	0.864	—	—	—
Large city	1.071	—	—	0.898	—	—	—
N.A.	1.893‡	—	—	1.822‡	—	—	—

TABLE 13.4 continued

	Unadjusted Effects[a]	Adjusted Effects[a]					
		Model 1	Model 2	Model 3	Model 4	Model 5	Model 6
Husband's migration/type of residence at marriage							
Nonmigrant							
Rural township	1	—	—	—	1	—	—
Urban township	0.902	—	—	—	0.897	—	—
Small city	0.975	—	—	—	0.809	—	—
Large city	1.022	—	—	—	0.840	—	—
Migrant							
Rural township	1.046	—	—	—	0.889	—	—
Urban township	1.304	—	—	—	1.157	—	—
Small city	1.154	—	—	—	0.877	—	—
Large city	1.139	—	—	—	0.963	—	—
N.A.	1.412*	—	—	—	1.239	—	—
Husband's migration/farm background							
Nonmigrant							
Rural/urban township	1	—	—	—	—	1	—
Small/large city	1.049	—	—	—	—	0.866	—
Migrant							
From rural/urban township, HP is farmer	1.269	—	—	—	—	1.089	—
From rural/urban township, Hp not farmer	1.069	—	—	—	—	0.922	—
From small/large city	1.440‡	—	—	—	—	1.079	—
N.A.	1.316*	—	—	—	—	1.159	—
Migration/residence status at interview							
Nonmigrant							
Rural township	1	—	—	—	—	—	1
Urban township	1.079	—	—	—	—	—	1.106
Small city	1.372*	—	—	—	—	—	1.141
Large city	1.418	—	—	—	—	—	1.244
Migrant							
Rural township	3.262†	—	—	—	—	—	3.120†
Urban township	2.865†	—	—	—	—	—	2.959†
Small city	4.571†	—	—	—	—	—	4.087†
Large city	3.820†	—	—	—	—	—	3.722†
N.A.	2.072†	—	—	—	—	—	1.919†
Chi square for whole model		127.08†	152.87†	162.84†	164.81†	160.08†	446.34†
Degrees of freedom		14	26	30	34	31	34

Note: * Indicates that an individual category is significantly different from the reference category (indicated by 1) at the .05 level. ‡ Indicates a significant difference at the .01 level. † Indicates a significant difference at the .001 level. The same symbols indicate the level at which chi-square values for the model as a whole are significantly different from 0.

[a] The effects shown represent the ratio of the rate of co-residence termination for each category of the predictor variables relative to the reference group for that variable, which is indicated by a 1. The unadjusted effects represent bivariate relationships, while the adjusted effects are estimated from the multivariate equations listed.

explaining the education effect, since it has no relation to length of co-residence, either on a bivariate or a multivariate basis.

Premarital familial index. The cumulative probability of terminating co-residence by two years after marriage increases monotonically with the extent of nonfamilial behavior. At four and six years the relationship is similar but not completely monotonic.

The unadjusted co-residence termination rate increases with nonfamilial behavior contexts, although not completely monotonically. The rates for all but one of the categories are significantly different from the most familial behavior category, which is the reference point. Those with the most nonfamilial experiences have termination rates that are nearly two and one-half times those of women with the fewest nonfamilial experiences.

When adjusted for other variables in models 1–5, it remains the case that the more nonfamilial the category, the greater the relative probability of termination. However, with the introduction of the multivariate controls, the magnitude of this variable's effects is reduced substantially. Nevertheless, even with the model 2–5 controls, the most nonfamilial have termination rates that are nearly double those of the least nonfamilial.

The additional control in model 6 of migration between marriage and interview further reduces the effect of the familial index so that only four of the less familial categories are significantly different from the most familial category and then at only the .05 level. This result suggests that migration after marriage may be an important intervening variable between premarital experiences and postmarital living arrangements.

Wife's ethnicity. Mainlanders have a higher probability of termination at two, four, or six years (table 13.3). The difference between Mainlanders and others in the termination rate, though, is not statistically significant on either a zero-order or multivariate basis (table 13.4).

Type of place of residence at marriage. Urbanization level at marriage has no significant relationship to termination probability on either a bivariate or a multivariate basis. However, as we shall see below, urbanization level of place of residence at interview is related negatively to the termination rate for nonmigrants.

Migration Status at Marriage and between Marriage and Interview

Migration status at marriage, the most powerful correlate of initiating co-residence at marriage, does not significantly affect the estimated rate of termination of co-residence on either a bivariate or a multivariate basis. This is true whether we consider the migration/ residence variable in model 4 or the migration/farm background variable in model 5.

However, whether the couple migrated between marriage and the time of interview is substantially correlated with the length of co-residence. This is evident in model 6, where we consider a variable combining whether the couple migrated between marriage and the time of interview and the type of residence at the time of interview. For this period, migrants have a much higher rate of termination of co-residence than nonmigrants, irrespective of type of residence.

At six years after marriage the cumulative percentage terminating co-residence is 28 to 37% for nonmigrants in contrast to 54 to 75% for migrants (table 13.3). The rate of co-residence termination, on either an unadjusted basis or when adjusted for five other variables, is three to four times as high for all categories of migrants as it is for all groups of nonmigrants. The effects of migration on rates of termination are very little affected by adjustments for the other variables in model 6 (table 13.4).

Unfortunately, interpretation of these results is difficult because the postmarriage migration variable may be a result rather than a cause of terminating co-residence. Whether to migrate and whether to continue co-residence may also be jointly determined decisions that have little direct causal connection between them. But it is clear that termination rates are low for nonmigrants at every urbanization level. Migration after marriage is associated with higher rates of termination, as was migration before marriage for initiating co-residence. Further research will be necessary to sort out these causal interconnections.

Summary of the Length of Co-Residence Analysis

Shifting now to historical trends and their explanation, we find that the cumulative probability of terminating co-residence has increased monotonically at all marital durations across all cohorts (table 13.3). For example, whereas only one-fifth of the earliest cohorts left the parental home within four years of marriage, nearly two-fifths of the most recent marriage cohorts had done so. However, it is still true that more than three-fifths of the most recent cohort who had lived with parents at marriage continued in that arrangement for at least four years.

The rate of termination of co-residence with parents more than doubled between the marriage cohort of the early 1960s and that of the 1980s (table 13.4). Our multivariate models are successful in explaining a significant part of this historical trend. The introduction of multivariate controls in models 2–5 reduces the gap between the earliest and latest cohorts from 2.18 to 1.59 (model 2 of table 13.4). This reduction of the difference by about .59 suggests that our multivariate model can account for about 27% of the overall change. Thus, while the multivariate model can explain a significant portion of the trend, there is even a greater portion that we cannot account for.

As with the explanation for trends in co-residence at marriage, the most important variables explaining the trends in the rate of terminating co-residence are education and the premarital familial index. In model 1 the difference across marriage cohorts is reduced from 2.18 to 1.80. An analysis not shown in table 13.4 reveals that, if we exclude education from the model, there is virtually no reduction in the cohort effect. This suggests that neither ethnicity nor the availability of other married sons helps to explain the trend over time for shorter co-residence periods.[5] Thus, education is responsible for most of the explanation of the time trend associated with model 2.

The rest of the explanation of the time trends in co-residence termination is provided by the premarital familial index. The introduction of this variable (along with age at marriage, which has no effect) reduces the difference across cohort from 1.80 to 1.59. This means that trends in the components of this index—including work outside the home, independent living, and more autonomous decision making—can help to explain the historical trends observed.

This analysis has emphasized the increase in the rate of terminating co-residence in relation to variables indicating an increase in nonfamilial contexts. However, for perspective, it is important to emphasize that half or more of those initially co-resident were still co-resident six years after marriage in every subcategory of the variables considered except for migrants (compare table 13.3).

5. We also experimented with more complex family composition variables that included information about the presence of unmarried brothers and sisters. This variable also failed to help explain the historical trend in the termination of co-residence, further supporting our conclusion that family composition, while having an important effect on co-residence, cannot explain the trends that have occurred.

Fourteen

Weakening the Linkage between the Ancestors, the Living, and Future Generations

A. Thornton, L. S. Yang, and T. Fricke

Introduction

The concept of family historically held in Chinese culture is cosmological in scope, extending not only far beyond the household but also beyond this life (see chap. 2). This cosmological view of the family goes beyond the group of related living individuals to include the dead of past generations and the prospective children of the future (Freedman 1970b; Yang 1945). The family is seen as a rope or chain stretching endlessly backward to the ancestors and forever forward to generations yet unborn. Thus, the individual becomes the link between the deceased ancestors and future generations, an orientation which shapes individual values and behaviors, structures family relationships, and helps to maintain kinship ties (Ahern 1971; Freedman 1970b; Hsu 1971; Yang 1945).

Just as earthly family relationships are bound within a complex web of reciprocal obligations, support, and exchange, Chinese people have historically seen their kinship relationships as extending beyond this life. Life after death for a Chinese person is, in many respects, an extension of the experience on earth, with a continuing need for the basic necessities of life, including food, clothing, and money (Ahern 1971; Hsu 1971). The deceased rely on the living to provide many of these necessities of life so that the quality of the afterlife experience is directly tied to the diligence of the descendants in caring for those needs. Filial piety, therefore, not only is believed to be necessary while parents are alive but is just as important for deceased parents (Ahern 1971). But, as on the earth, the intergenerational flow of assistance is not limited to help from the children to the ancestors, but the deceased can also assist the living. The spirits of those who have died can protect the living from harm and bring them good fortune. The quality of intergenerational relationships with the ancestors, as in earthly relationships, is believed to have important repercussions. Ancestors who do not receive proper care from their descendants may be less diligent in caring for their descendants; in fact, relationships can deteriorate to the extent that the ancestors may bring harm and misfortune to the family. Thus, the good health and fortune of a family is believed to depend not only on the quality of relationships within the living family but also on the quality of interactions with the ancestors.[1]

To maintain the quality of relationships with the deceased and to repay the former generation for life and earthly possessions, the living provide offerings to the dead and reserve a place in the house so that the spirits of dead ancestors can return to be with the family. The living believe they should also provide a good environment for the burial of the dead to make them comfortable in the afterlife. The living, as they contemplate the future and their own deaths, try to be certain that the family chain will be perpetuated and that their children will remember them and demonstrate their filial piety. Given the patrilineal nature of Chinese kinship, the availability of a male heir to carry on the family chain has been historically imperative both for old age and for life after death.

Since the ancestors are perceived as having the ability to foresee the future, they are often asked to help their descendants make important decisions. For example, the ancestors are consulted in the choice of a marriage partner and the engagement ceremony was historically done in front of the ancestral altar of the bride's family. During the wedding ritual a ceremony is performed in the bride's home to inform the ancestors of her departure, and upon her arrival at her husband's family, an additional ceremony is performed before the husband's ancestral altar to inform his ancestors of the arrival of a new family member (Wolf 1972, 100–127). The bride also assumes her responsibility toward her husband's ancestors. Thus, the recognition and involvement of the ancestors is a key element of historical Chinese marriage.

The ancestral chain is also a key element of Taiwanese funeral ceremonies. While the funeral ceremonies differ by ethnicity in Taiwan, all are handled as familial matters, with the living conducting the necessary

---

1. The relationships between the living and the dead ancestors may be even more complicated than described here. While most Chinese people believe that their ancestors will always be benevolent if the living carry out their filial responsibilities, some believe that there are ancestors who are not easy to please and who do not properly look out for their descendants even when those descendants believe they have fulfilled their filial obligations (Ahern 1971; Li 1985).

ceremonies for the deceased ancestor (Chuang 1987). Filial piety is a central value expressed in these funeral ceremonies.

There are many good theoretical reasons to believe that the social, economic, and cultural changes during recent decades have had important implications for the multigenerational family chain. The transformation of the family mode of production has dramatically shifted the nature of intergenerational ties, providing alternative sources of economic well-being. As a result, Taiwanese men and women today are less dependent on production from the land received from their ancestors and more reliant on their schooling, which may be viewed as a more individualistic accomplishment. Schools have also shifted the nature of children's relationships with their parents and have become new sources of ideas, authority, and means of interactions with peers. Nonfamily living arrangements have also shifted relationships from families to peers. The mate selection process has been transformed from a parent-run system to one with great emphasis on the relationship between the young couple, with more importance placed on husband-wife links as opposed to the intergenerational chain. Taiwan has also experienced substantial exposure to Western ideas and values, which strongly emphasize current relationships, particularly those between spouses and between parents and children, and minimize linkages between the ancestors and future descendants. As a result of these changes, the core historical Chinese emphasis upon the family chain may have been weakened, more emphasis now being placed upon a narrower circle of close family members.

Life Values

Data

The importance of the family chain in Chinese culture can be demonstrated by data from the 1976 Value of Children Study. This study interviewed an island-wide sample of married women between the ages of 20 and 44; a subsample of their husbands was also interviewed. These respondents were asked to rate the importance of nine things that many people value: being financially secure; not being disliked by people; having fun and enjoyment in life; being close to your spouse; having companionship or not being lonely; having a sense of accomplishment or doing things well; being remembered and cherished after you die; having a happy family; and linking ancestors, the living, and descendants (which we will sometimes refer to as maintaining or continuing the family chain or line). It is important to note that the last value listed, linking ancestors, the living, and descendants, refers directly to the central concern of this chapter. The question explicitly refers to the ancestors, the idea of passing or handing something down to the descendants and of joining or connecting generations. This item is, thus, a measure of how important it is to the respondent to continue the family chain connecting the ancestors, the individual, and future generations. The item about being remembered and cherished after you die also refers to this key Chinese value of intergenerational linkages between the living and the dead.

In addition to rating each of the nine values, the study participants were asked to choose the two most important values. Table 14.1 documents the percentage of women saying that each of the items was very important while table 14.2 provides similar data for their husbands. Tables 14.3 and 14.4 summarize the rankings of the values for the women and their husbands. All of the tables provide breakdowns of the responses by birth cohort, marriage cohort, and educational attainment. As in earlier chapters, both birth and marital cohorts are used as markers of historical time to take into account differential age at marriage truncation across the various cohorts. Since the sample of women was limited to those who were married, only wives who were relatively young at marriage were included in the most recent birth cohorts. Similarly, since women over age 44 were excluded from the study, the earliest marriage cohorts are restricted to those who married relatively early. Any correlation of age at marriage with the value measures would therefore bias trends measured by birth and marriage cohorts in the opposite direction. Thus, the nature of the true trend is probably bounded by the two sets of historical measures.[2] Since the men participating in the study were limited to those who were married to women between the ages of 20 and 44, the truncation biases are even more serious for them.

Confounding Cohort and Age

One conceptual and methodological problem must be mentioned before proceeding with the discussion of the data in the tables. Since the data were collected in a single survey at one time point, there is a perfect correspondence between birth cohort and age and between marital co-

---

2. For recent marriage cohorts there is also the issue of excluding from the sample married women under the age of 20. We investigated the extent of this problem by estimating the fraction of marriages in the 1970–74 marriage cohort that would not be represented in the 1976 sample. Using 1980 census data on age and age at marriage, we estimated that less than 2% of that marriage cohort would be excluded by not including younger women in the survey.

TABLE 14.1 Percentage of Women Saying That Each Life Value Is Very Important, by Birth Cohort, Marriage Cohort, and Education, 1976

| | BIRTH COHORT | | | | | |
	1930–34	1935–39	1940–44	1945–49	1950–54	Total
Being financially secure	94	95	92	90	87	91
Not being disliked by people	78	80	77	74	76	77
Having fun and enjoyment in life	75	75	68	67	66	70
Being close to your husband	70	73	71	70	75	72
Having companionship or not being lonely	78	81	78	74	73	77
Having a sense of accomplishment . . .	79	77	77	74	78	77
Remembered and cherished after you die	72	72	67	60	60	65
Having a happy family	96	98	97	97	97	97
Linking ancestors, living, and descendants	92	94	88	83	86	88
Number of respondents	281	435	481	465	454	2,169

| | MARRIAGE COHORT | | | | | |
	1950–54	1955–59	1960–64	1965–69	1970–74	Total
Being financially secure	96	94	93	90	88	91
Not being disliked by people	82	78	79	76	74	77
Having fun and enjoyment in life	79	76	70	66	66	70
Being close to your husband	70	72	71	72	73	72
Having companionship or not being lonely	83	81	78	75	73	77
Having a sense of accomplishment . . .	78	79	76	76	76	77
Remembered and cherished after you die	75	73	67	67	56	66
Having a happy family	96	97	98	97	97	97
Linking ancestors, living, and descendants	93	93	90	89	81	88
Number of respondents	224	401	411	480	522	2,169

| | EDUCATION | | | | | |
	None	Primary	Junior High	Senior High	College/ Univ.	Total
Being financially secure	97	90	89	84	81	91
Not being disliked by people	83	75	79	70	55	77
Having fun and enjoyment in life	80	67	65	61	55	70
Being close to your husband	74	70	71	76	74	72
Having companionship or not being lonely	85	75	72	68	62	77
Having a sense of accomplishment . . .	80	76	79	70	62	77
Remembered and cherished after you die	79	65	58	38	28	65
Having a happy family	98	96	96	99	97	97
Linking ancestors, living, and descendants	97	90	81	59	50	88
Number of respondents	545	1,226	205	135	58	2,169

Note: The women were between the ages of 20 and 44 at the time of the survey. Some women outside the listed birth and marriage cohort categories are included in the totals.

TABLE 14.2 Percentage of Men Saying That Each Life Value Is Very Important, by Birth Cohort, Marriage Cohort, and Education, 1976

| | BIRTH COHORT | | | | |
	1930– 34	1935– 39	1940– 44	1945– 49	Total
Being financially secure	90	94	90	87	91
Not being disliked by people	81	77	75	70	76
Having fun and enjoyment in life	74	74	71	69	71
Being close to your wife	72	74	71	72	73
Having companionship or not being lonely	75	76	76	75	75
Having a sense of accomplishment . . .	82	81	82	77	80
Remembered and cherished after you die	72	69	68	58	67
Having a happy family	97	96	96	97	97
Linking ancestors, living, and descendants	87	92	83	79	86
Number of respondents	190	201	209	159	849

| | MARRIAGE COHORT | | | | | |
	1950– 54	1955– 59	1960– 64	1965– 69	1970– 74	Total
Being financially secure	93	95	91	89	89	91
Not being disliked by people	80	79	78	75	69	76
Having fun and enjoyment in life	78	78	70	69	67	71
Being close to your wife	71	73	81	66	73	73
Having companionship or not being lonely	77	79	76	70	76	75
Having a sense of accomplishment . . .	79	84	77	81	77	80
Remembered and cherished after you die	72	73	67	66	60	67
Having a happy family	96	97	97	95	97	97
Linking ancestors, living, and descendants	93	94	89	85	75	86
Number of respondents	82	169	181	241	203	849

| | EDUCATION | | | | | |
	None	Primary	Junior High	Senior High	College/ Univ.	Total
Being financially secure	91	94	85	88	84	91
Not being disliked by people	85	79	72	69	63	76
Having fun and enjoyment in life	80	76	63	65	62	71
Being close to your wife	73	74	69	72	71	73
Having companionship or not being lonely	85	80	70	67	63	75
Having a sense of accomplishment . . .	83	82	78	78	72	80
Remembered and cherished after you die	77	74	65	50	46	67
Having a happy family	96	97	98	96	92	97
Linking ancestors, living, and descendants	95	94	81	72	59	86
Number of respondents	75	443	116	139	76	849

Note: The men included in this table were born between 1925 and 1949. Even though the men in the birth cohort of 1925–29 are not listed separately in the table because of their small numbers, they are included in the birth cohort total and in the marriage cohort and education panels.

TABLE 14.3 Women's Rankings of the Three Most Important Life Values, by Birth Cohort, Marriage Cohort, and Education

	PERCENTAGE DISTRIBUTION BY BIRTH COHORT					
	1930–34	1935–39	1940–44	1945–49	1950–54	Total
Being financially secure						
Not first or second most important	57	52	53	58	59	56
Second most important	24	26	23	24	17	22
Most important	20	22	24	19	24	22
Total	100	100	100	100	100	100
Having a happy family						
Not first or second most important	42	41	38	34	31	37
Second most important	28	29	30	32	33	30
Most important	30	30	32	34	36	33
Total	100	100	100	100	100	100
Linking ancestors, living, and descendants						
Not first or second most important	36	40	45	51	50	45
Second most important	25	24	22	20	24	23
Most important	39	36	33	30	25	32
Total	100	100	100	100	100	100

	PERCENTAGE DISTRIBUTION BY MARRIAGE COHORT					
	1950–54	1955–59	1960–64	1965–69	1970–74	Total
Being financially secure						
Not first or second most important	53	55	50	60	58	56
Second most important	26	22	27	20	21	22
Most important	21	24	23	20	21	22
Total	100	100	100	100	100	100
Having a happy family						
Not first or second most important	46	42	40	36	28	37
Second most important	29	31	28	32	30	30
Most important	26	27	32	31	42	33
Total	100	100	100	100	100	100
Linking ancestors, living, and descendants						
Not first or second most important	32	40	43	45	55	45
Second most important	26	23	23	22	23	23
Most important	42	37	34	33	22	32
Total	100	100	100	100	100	100

	PERCENTAGE DISTRIBUTION BY EDUCATION					
	None	Primary	Junior High	Senior High	College/ Univ.	Total
Being financially secure						
Not first or second most important	54	58	49	57	60	56
Second most important	23	22	25	24	22	22
Most important	24	21	25	18	17	22
Total	100	100	100	100	100	100

TABLE 14.3 continued

| | PERCENTAGE DISTRIBUTION BY EDUCATION | | | | | |
	None	Primary	Junior High	Senior High	College/ Univ.	Total
Having a happy family						
Not first or second most important	47	36	33	18	14	37
Second most important	32	30	25	29	34	30
Most important	21	34	42	53	52	33
Total	100	100	100	100	100	100
Linking ancestors, living, and descendants						
Not first or second most important	29	44	66	81	81	45
Second most important	24	24	20	13	9	23
Most important	46	32	15	7	10	32
Total	100	100	100	100	100	100

Note: The women were between the ages of 20 and 44 at the time of the survey. The number of respondents is reported in table 14.1. Some women outside the listed birth and marriage cohort categories are included in the totals.

hort and marital duration at the time of the survey. Although the variables are labeled birth cohort and marital cohort in the tables, they could just as accurately be labeled age and marital duration. As the birth and marital cohorts advance forward across historical time, the succeeding cohorts are increasingly younger and of shorter marital duration at the time of the survey. While our analysis focuses on historical change, it is possible that as Chinese women and men age across their own life courses, they change their orientations toward the importance of the family chain, this personal transformation being totally unrelated to historical change. Thus, while it is theoretically plausible that the cohort data in tables 14.1–14.4 reflect historical change, so is a framework that interprets the differences across cohorts as simply reflecting aging processes. Unfortunately, the perfect correlation between historical and life course indicators in the 1976 data makes the choice between historical and individual change a difficult one.

Although the difficulty of untangling historical and life course influences when these measures are totally confounded is recognized, we believe that a substantial fraction of the association between family values and cohort documented below is the result of historical change rather than individual life course aging. This conclusion was reached using the approach outlined in chapter 1—introducing into the analysis theoretical variables that are believed to account for the cohort effects on the dependent variable of interest.

TABLE 14.4 Men's Rankings of the Three Most Important Life Values, By Birth Cohort, Marriage Cohort, and Education

	PERCENTAGE DISTRIBUTION BY BIRTH COHORT				
	1930–34	1935–39	1940–44	1945–49	Total
Being financially secure					
Not first or second most important	49	53	49	63	53
Second most important	27	16	24	19	22
Most important	24	31	27	18	25
Total	100	100	100	100	100
Having a happy family					
Not first or second most important	47	49	45	31	42
Second most important	25	30	32	32	30
Most important	29	21	23	36	27
Total	100	100	100	100	100
Linking ancestors, living, and descendants					
Not first or second most important	49	43	49	59	49
Second most important	19	27	21	16	21
Most important	33	31	30	25	30
Total	100	100	100	100	100
Number of respondents	190	201	209	159	849

	PERCENTAGE DISTRIBUTION BY MARRIAGE COHORT					
	1950–54	1955–59	1960–64	1965–69	1970–74	Total
Being financially secure						
Not first or second most important	40	54	52	58	56	53
Second most important	30	22	21	22	18	22
Most important	29	24	27	21	26	25
Total	100	100	100	100	100	100
Having a happy family						
Not first or second most important	50	43	47	39	36	42
Second most important	27	30	27	33	33	31
Most important	23	26	26	28	30	27
Total	100	100	100	100	100	100
Linking ancestors, living, and descendants						
Not first or second most important	44	42	47	51	58	49
Second most important	23	23	24	20	16	21
Most important	33	35	29	29	25	30
Total	100	100	100	100	100	100
Number of respondents	82	169	181	214	203	849

	PERCENTAGE DISTRIBUTION BY EDUCATION					
	None	Primary	Junior High	Senior High	College/ Univ.	Total
Being financially secure						
Not first or second most important	54	54	53	55	52	53
Second most important	23	22	22	18	21	22
Most important	23	24	25	27	27	25
Total	100	100	100	100	100	100

TABLE 14.4 continued

| | PERCENTAGE DISTRIBUTION BY EDUCATION | | | | | |
	None	Primary	Junior High	Senior High	College/ Univ.	Total
Having a happy family						
Not first or second most important	58	46	39	30	28	42
Second most important	27	29	31	34	35	31
Most important	15	24	30	36	37	27
Total	100	100	100	100	100	100
Linking ancestors, living, and descendants						
Not first or second most important	27	40	54	72	76	49
Second most important	27	25	22	11	9	21
Most important	46	35	23	17	15	30
Total	100	100	100	100	100	100
Number of respondents	75	443	116	139	76	849

Note: The men included in this table were born between 1925 and 1949. Even though the men in the birth cohort of 1925–29 are not listed separately in the table because of their small numbers, they are included in the birth cohort total and in the marriage cohort and education panels.

Linking Ancestors, the Living, and Descendants

The data from the men and women most likely to represent historical Chinese cultural values—the oldest and those without formal education—show the tremendous importance historically placed upon family matters. Although all nine items were deemed very important by at least 70% of the women born in the 1930s and by equally high numbers of women without formal schooling, the percentage attributing such great importance to having a happy family and to linking the ancestors, the living, and descendants exceeded 90% (table 14.1). The only other value receiving such high endorsement was financial security. At least 97% of the sample women without formal schooling endorsed these three values as very important. Financial security, having a happy family, and maintaining the family chain were also the highest rated values for the older and least educated men.

The priority of maintaining the family chain is even more striking in the rankings of values, where respondents were forced to choose between the life values. While the least educated and those from the earliest birth and marriage cohorts *rated* financial security, a happy family, and maintaining the family chain as about equally important, they generally *ranked* the family chain as much more important than the other two values. As table 14.3 shows, about four out of every ten women born in the early 1930s or married in the early 1950s ranked the family chain as the most important value.[3] The next most frequently endorsed value of the oldest women was having a happy family, which was the first choice of 26–30%. This was followed by financial security, which was chosen first by approximately 20% of the oldest women. Among the remaining six values, none received first-choice ranking from more than 4% of the oldest women (data not shown in tables). The predominance of the maintenance of the family chain value is even more striking among the least educated women; nearly one-half made this their first choice, approximately doubling the fraction ranking any other value first (table 14.3). Less than one-third of those without formal schooling did not rank maintaining the family line as one of the two most important values. The pattern for the older and less educated men was very similar to that for the women. However, the older men placed slightly more emphasis on financial security than did the women (table 14.4).

A cross-cultural comparison further highlights the relative importance of continuation of the family line in historical Chinese society. In 1975, a Value of Children Study was conducted of married women between the ages of 20 and 39 in the United States. In that survey only 12 women out of a sample of 1,509 said that passing on the family line was one of the two most important values for them—contrasting rather sharply with the 55% who said that the continuity of the family line was one of the two most important values in Taiwan.

There was a modest decline across marriage and birth cohorts in the percentage of Taiwanese men and women choosing continuation of the family line as a very important value (tables 14.1 and 14.2). Looking first at the trend across birth cohorts, we see that strong endorsement of this value declined from over 90% among women born in the 1930s to 86% for those born during the early 1950s. Across marriage cohorts the decline was larger—moving from 93% for the marriage cohorts of the 1950s to 81% for the marriage cohorts of the early 1970s. The pattern of change across birth cohorts was similar in both direction and magnitude for men (table 14.2).

A related value—being remembered and cherished after you die—

---

3. From 3 to 5% of the birth and marriage cohorts participating in the 1976 Value of Children Study were Christian, with no clear trends across cohorts. The Christian women are included in the analyses reported in this chapter. Additional analyses show that their exclusion would have no effect on the conclusions about the nature and determinants of the trends reported here. However, the exclusion of the Christian women results in even higher percentages endorsing the continuity of the family line as an important value.

declined more markedly. About 70% of the women and men born in the 1930s said being remembered and cherished was very important, while only about 60% of those born in the late 1940s and early 1950s gave such a positive endorsement. Again, the trend across marriage cohorts was stronger than across birth cohorts, with strong endorsement of being remembered declining from 75% for the earliest female marriage cohort to 56% for the most recent one. Several other values registering declines across cohorts were financial security, not being disliked, and having fun and enjoyment.

At the same time that the endorsement of the continuity of the family line and being remembered and cherished after you die declined across cohorts, the fraction of women and men endorsing the importance of having a happy family remained almost constant at 95–98% across all marriage and birth cohorts (tables 14.1 and 14.2). There is even an inkling of a slight increase in the importance of being close to your husband, the value endorsed least frequently among the oldest women. But there is little evidence for a trend among the men in the importance of being close to their wives.

The relative decline of the importance of continuing the family chain across cohorts is even more dramatic when explicit comparisons among the various values are made (tables 14.3 and 14.4). Whereas 39% of the women born between 1930 and 1934 chose maintaining the family line as the most important of the nine values, this fraction declined steadily across birth cohorts, with only 25% of the youngest women giving it their highest endorsement. At the same time, the fraction of women not ranking continuity of the family line as one of their first two choices increased from 36 to 50% across the same birth cohorts. Even larger trends were observed across marital cohorts. While the trends for men were in the same direction, the magnitude of change was apparently somewhat less for them (compare tables 14.3 and 14.4).

While the fraction of men and women endorsing the continuity of the family line as the most important value was declining, the number giving top priority to a happy family was increasing (tables 14.3 and 14.4). In fact, the 11 percentage point increase across birth cohorts in the number of women ranking a happy family as one of the two most important values nearly accounts for the 15 percentage point decline in the rankings of continuity of the family line. The relative endorsement of financial security remained fairly constant as did the endorsement of the other six less central values. Again, the trends were similar but less marked for men.

Shifting our attention from the cohort variables to educational attainment, we find even stronger associations with the values endorsed. Across educational categories, the percentage of women ranking continuation of the family line as very important drops from 97% for women without formal schooling to 50% for the college educated (table 14.1). An equally impressive decline with education is observed for being remembered and cherished after you die—a value endorsed as very important by 79% of the women who had not attended school as compared to 28% of the college-educated women. While the associations between education and these values are less marked for men, they are also of substantial magnitude.

It is possible that the magnitudes of these empirical relationships are inflated somewhat by a tendency of the better-educated women and men to be less emphatic in their ratings of values. This possibility is suggested by the rather substantial relationships between education and some of the other values, particularly not being disliked by people, having fun and enjoyment in life, having companionship, and having a sense of accomplishment. Nevertheless, there were two values with very small associations with education: being close to your spouse and having a happy family. The fraction of men and women rating these two family values as very important is similar across all educational experiences (tables 14.1 and 14.2).

The relative shifting of importance from family continuity to family happiness across educational categories is demonstrated even more clearly in tables 14.3 and 14.4. Whereas only 29% of the women without formal schooling did not choose continuing the family line as one of the two most important values, fully 81% of the women who had at least attended high school took this position. Similarly, while 47% of the women with no formal schooling did not rank having a happy family as one of the two most important values, only 18% of the high school women and 14% of the university women omitted a happy family from their two most important values (table 14.3). The educational effects on these rankings are equally impressive for men (table 14.4).

The observed trends in life values are consistently greater across marriage cohorts than across birth cohorts. This pattern probably reflects the age-at-marriage truncation bias working in opposite directions for the two cohort approaches, along with an important correlation of life values with age at marriage. This expectation is confirmed in table 14.5, where the woman's age at marriage is cross-tabulated with her ranking of a happy family and continuing the family line. These cross-tabulations are presented within birth cohorts.

Among the women married at ages 18 and older in the total sample,

TABLE 14.5 Women's Rankings of Having a Happy Family and Linking Ancestors, Living, and Descendants as Most Important Life Values by Birth Cohort and Age at Marriage

	BIRTH COHORT					
Age at Marriage	1930–34	1935–39	1940–44	1945–49	1950–54	Total[a]
	Percentage Saying that Having a Happy Family is Most Important					
17 or younger	30	25	26	29	36	31
18–19	29	21	26	24	34	27
20–21	30	27	30	38	40	34
22–24	29	44	35	37	31	36
25 or older[b]	*	42	47	42	—	44
	Percentage Saying that Linking Ancestors, Living, and Descendants is Most Important					
17 or younger	37	33	28	37	24	30
18–19	45	46	36	40	28	38
20–21	41	38	32	30	26	33
22–24	34	22	37	26	24	29
25 or older[b]	*	34	26	12	—	24
	Number of Respondents					
17 or younger	43	63	57	59	78	316
18–19	69	115	105	93	115	524
20–21	80	127	120	125	154	617
22–24	62	89	150	137	98	536
25 or older[b]	25	38	47	48	—	163

Note: The cell entries indicate the percentage of people in each age-at-marriage group that endorsed each of the two life values as the most important.

* Number of respondents less than 30, and no estimates made.

[a] Although the detailed data were limited to women born between 1930 and 1954, the few women born before and after that period are included in the totals.

[b] The oldest women in the 1950–54 birth cohort were only age 26 at the time of the survey in 1976. Consequently, there is no information about women marrying at later ages among this birth cohort.

the endorsement of a happy family increases with age at marriage while endorsement of continuation of the family line declines with age at marriage. Although women marrying younger than 18 do not continue the monotonic trend, they are still lower on endorsement of a happy family and higher on continuation of the family line than those married at ages 22 or older. This pattern suggests that women who postpone marriage place more emphasis on immediate family ties and give relatively less emphasis to the family line. Since the age-at-marriage truncation bias is an inherent feature of these data, this correlation between age at marriage and the life values results in the earlier marriage cohorts and the later birth cohorts being overrepresented by those who marry young and place relatively more importance on the family line. Therefore, the actual amount of historical change probably lies between those indicated by the birth and marriage cohort indicators. Although we do not present age at marriage data for other measures of family chain observance and commitment, the conclusions arrived at from table 14.5 also apply to them.

Value of Children

Additional confirmation of the relative shifting of family values and motivations is provided by information from the same survey concerning the value of children. The respondents in the study were asked whether or not they considered a number of life values as important reasons for having children. Many of the reasons listed for wanting children overlapped the general life values discussed above. Unfortunately, the study participants were not asked to choose the two most important reasons for valuing children. The percentages of women saying that each of the reasons was very important are documented in table 14.6, cross-tabulated by birth cohort, marital cohort, and education.

The value-of-children data clearly confirm the historical role of Chinese children in continuing the family chain. Among the oldest women in the study, having children to link the ancestors, the living, and descendants is clearly the most highly endorsed of all the suggested reasons for having children—surpassing other such central reasons as old age security and working and helping the family. In fact, nearly nineteen out of twenty women born in the 1930s believed that the family chain was an important reason to have children. And, among the women without any school attendance, fully 98% said this was a reason to have children. The older and less educated men also placed great importance on children as a way of continuing the family line (not shown in tables). Other values drawing high levels of endorsement as reasons for having children were to prevent loneliness, to complete the family, because it is part of being a woman, and to have someone to depend on in old age.

There has been a shift in the value of children across marriage and birth cohorts. Among women born in the 1930s, over 90% thought that continuation of the family line was an important reason to have children; among those born in the 1950s, the percentage was 86. Across marriage cohorts the decline was more substantial, reaching a low of 82% for the women married in the early 1970s. Although this reason declined in importance, it remained one of the most important values for the

TABLE 14.6 Percentage of Women Saying That Each Value of Children Is Very Important, by Birth Cohort, Marriage Cohort, and Education, 1976

	BIRTH COHORT					
	1930–34	1935–39	1940–44	1945–49	1950–54	Total
So that you will not be lonely	87	88	89	84	82	86
Because children are needed to complete the family	85	88	88	85	86	87
Because children are fun	75	76	78	73	72	75
Because children can work and help the family	66	65	57	41	43	53
Because of your religion	46	43	40	31	32	37
To watch them grow and develop	79	77	76	77	76	77
To feel that you are doing something important	66	71	70	66	66	68
Because it would be odd not to have children	71	75	74	69	68	71
Because it's part of being a woman	83	85	81	79	78	81
To have someone to depend on when you are old	87	87	82	72	70	79
So that you will be remembered and cherished after you die	69	70	65	56	55	62
Because children will look up to you	70	74	70	61	64	68
To please your parents-in-law or other relatives	71	71	70	65	70	69
To strengthen the bond between you and your husband	64	72	70	65	68	68
Because children can make you feel proud of them	66	65	62	59	58	62
Because children bring you love	70	70	74	68	68	70
To link ancestors, living, and descendants	92	95	89	84	86	89
To be seen as a better person	54	52	47	40	38	45
To have someone who needs you	56	54	46	45	47	49
Number of respondents	281	435	481	465	454	2,169

	MARRIAGE COHORT					
	1950–54	1955–59	1960–64	1965–69	1970–74	Total
So that you will not be lonely	89	86	88	88	81	86
Because children are needed to complete the family	87	88	88	85	87	86
Because children are fun	77	77	75	77	71	75
Because children can work and help the family	72	66	58	47	42	53
Because of your religion	50	42	40	36	28	37
To watch them grow and develop	82	76	77	77	74	77
To feel that you are doing something important	71	69	71	69	64	68
Because it would be odd not to have children	75	73	76	73	65	71
Because it's part of being a woman	85	84	84	83	74	81
To have someone to depend on when you are old	89	88	84	82	65	79

TABLE 14.6   continued

	Marriage Cohort					
	1950–54	1955–59	1960–64	1965–69	1970–74	Total
So that you will be remembered and cherished after you die	74	70	66	64	51	62
Because children will look up to you	71	74	72	66	60	67
To please your parents-in-law or other relatives	74	72	71	68	66	70
To strengthen the bond between you and your husband	64	70	74	67	67	68
Because children can make you feel proud of them	67	65	64	62	57	62
Because children bring you love	70	71	72	71	67	70
To link ancestors, living, and descendants	93	94	92	90	82	89
To be seen as a better person	55	53	49	46	36	45
To have someone who needs you	59	54	46	49	45	49
Number of respondents	224	401	411	480	522	2,169

	Education					
	None	Primary	Junior High	Senior High	College/ Univ.	Total
So that you will not be lonely	90	86	83	73	67	86
Because children are needed to complete the family	88	87	84	79	81	86
Because children are fun	82	74	74	62	57	75
Because children can work and help the family	80	52	28	16	10	53
Because of your religion	52	37	24	13	5	37
To watch them grow and develop	81	76	75	70	62	77
To feel that you are doing something important	75	68	59	56	47	68
Because it would be odd not to have children	81	73	61	47	45	71
Because it's part of being a woman	89	82	77	59	52	81
To have someone to depend on when you are old	96	82	60	35	19	79
So that you will be remembered and cherished after you die	80	63	48	25	16	62
Because children will look up to you	80	67	62	48	31	68
To please your parents-in-law or other relatives	79	70	55	55	38	69
To strengthen the bond between you and your husband	71	68	68	66	47	68
Because children can make you feel proud of them	73	62	54	44	26	62
Because children bring you love	76	68	71	65	53	70
To link ancestors, living, and descendants	98	91	79	66	47	89
To be seen as a better person	60	45	37	18	9	45
To have someone who needs you	60	49	42	32	17	49
Number of respondents	545	1,226	205	135	58	2,169

Note: Data are for women 20–44 at the time of the survey. Some women who are outside the listed birth and marriage cohort categories are included in the totals.

younger women. The related value, being remembered and cherished after you die, also declined in importance across cohorts. Whereas nearly 70% of the oldest women said this was a very important reason to have children, only 55% thought so among the latest birth cohorts and the figure was even lower for the most recent marriage cohorts. A number of other reasons for having children also declined in perceived importance across the cohorts, including for religious reasons, to work and help the family, for old age support, and to be a better person. Other values, however, showed almost no association with cohort. Some of the latter included watching children grow and develop and to bring a woman closer to her husband. All of these relationships are generally evident for the husbands as well (data not shown in tables).

There is a strong association between educational attainment and the value of children, with the importance of virtually all the reasons to have children declining with higher educational attainment. While this probably reflects a general impact of education on orientations toward children, the effects of education are particularly strong on some of the values, including two most relevant for the present discussion—to continue the family line and to be remembered and cherished after you die. For continuing the family line the decline is from 98% of the uneducated women, who believed it a very important reason for having children, to just 47% among women who attended college. Similarly, the decline in being remembered and cherished after death was from 80 to 16% across the full range of educational groups. Other reasons for valuing children displaying an educational differential as large as 45 percentage points across the educational spectrum include the following: they will work and help the family; there are religious reasons for having children; they will support you in old age; they will look up to you; they will make you feel proud of them; and having children will make you a better person. Motives with the least association with education include the need to complete the family and the desire to watch them grow and develop.

Ancestors and Descendants

Multiple Cross Sections of Data

Further evidence of trends in family relationships beyond this life can be drawn from relevant questions included in three island-wide surveys of women conducted in 1973, 1980, and 1986. The individual surveys can be used to examine how attitudes and behavior relative to the family chain relate to birth cohort, marriage cohort, and education, just as they were with the 1976 Value of Children Survey discussed in the preceding pages. In addition, since a small number of identical questions were asked in all three surveys, the combined data can be used to evaluate changes occurring across the thirteen-year period, while controlling for age. Since all three surveys can be defined to include women of the same ages, differences among the distributions in the three studies must be associated with historical change.

In table 14.7 we examine historical trends in the commitment to the ancestral and descendant chain during the thirteen years from 1973 through 1986 for married women between the ages of 20 and 39 at the survey dates. Those data indicate that the great majority of Taiwanese are maintaining their commitment to the family chain. In 1973, nine out of ten women believed that it was important or very important to have a boy to continue the family line, three out of four thought that the ancestors' graves had important implications for their family's well-being, and four out of five observed ceremonies for their ancestors. In 1980, two-thirds had ancestral tablets in the house and worshiped on the appropriate days in the lunar calendar. Finally, in 1986, over half expressed confidence in the importance of the ancestral ceremonies for the family's future.

Despite the persistent commitment of Chinese women to the continuity of the family chain, there is also evidence of change in these data. Between 1973 and 1980 the fraction saying that having a boy to continue the family line was not so important more than doubled from 11 to 24%, and in the next six years increased to 32%. This change supports the idea of a weakening emphasis on the chain linking the ancestors through the living to future descendants.

Between 1973 and 1986 there was a small increase in skepticism about the relevance of ancestral graves for the future of families. However, this increase was not monotonic across these years. In fact, the big change was between 1973 and 1980, with a small reversal between 1980 and 1986.

While there was a small decline in the expressed importance of ancestral graves, there was no decline in the observance of ceremonies for ancestors. In fact, there was a modest trend in the opposite direction, with the fraction not observing ceremonies declining from 19 to 10% between 1973 and 1986.

Pinning down the meaning of these opposite trends is difficult. One possible explanation is that the improving standard of living in Taiwan has facilitated the ability of people to observe ancestral ceremonies while

TABLE 14.7 The Importance of Ancestors and the Family Line, 1973, 1980, and 1986

	PERCENTAGE DISTRIBUTIONS BY YEAR		
	1973	1980	1986
Number of respondents	5,540	3,821	3,199
Importance of a boy to link ancestors, living, and descendants			
Unimportant or not so important	11	24	32
Important	41	44	35
Very important	48	32	34
Total	100	100	100
Importance of ancestors' graves			
Don't believe or doubtful	26	34	30
Believe	56	57	59
Believe very much	18	8	11
Total	100	100	100
Observance of ceremonies for ancestors			
Do not observe	19	12	10
Observe on birth and/or death dates	3	7	4
Observe important festivals	28	32	40
Observe both birth/death dates and festivals	49	48	46
Total	100	100	100
Ancestral tablets in house			
No	—	34	—
Yes	—	66	—
Total	—	100	—
Monthly family worship			
No	—	31	—
Yes	—	69	—
Total	—	100	—
Importance of ancestral ceremonies			
Not important at all	—	—	12
Not very important	—	—	33
Somewhat important	—	—	44
Very important	—	—	11
Total	—	—	100

Note: Data are for women 20–39 at the time of the respective surveys.

factors such as education and contact with Western values have reduced the importance of the ancestors. There may have also been a shift from the sacred relationship with ancestors to a more secular view of the world and family relationships.

A Cohort View

We now shift our attention from differences in the importance of the family chain looking across successive cross-sectional surveys to looking at differences across marital cohorts of women within the same survey. This will allow us to examine the extent to which the importance of ancestors and continuation of the family line varies by the timing of adulthood in Taiwan. These data are reported in table 14.8.[4]

Looking first at the three indicators measured in all three surveys, we see a pattern of relationships between the three variables and marital cohort that bears considerable similarity to the pattern observed in table 14.7 between period and the three variables. That is, in all three surveys there is a fairly strong association between cohort, the indicator of historical change, and the expressed importance of having a boy to continue the family line, a moderate association between cohort and the expressed importance of the graves of ancestors, and little association between cohort and the observance of ancestral ceremonies.

Looking more closely at the individual indicators, we see that the expressed importance of having a boy to continue the family line declines steadily across all marriage cohorts in all three surveys. For example, in the 1986 survey, which contains the widest range of marriage cohorts, the fraction of women saying that having a boy to continue the family line is very important declines steeply across marriage cohorts—from 56% for those married in the late 1950s to 28% among those married in the early 1980s. This trend is completely monotonic across all of the marriage cohorts.

A similar, although weaker, relationship holds for the importance of ancestral graves for the fortune of the family. In all surveys the fraction believing the ancestral graves to be very important declines fairly steadily across cohorts of wives. In the 1986 survey the fervent believers declined from 21% for the 1955–59 marriage cohort to 9% for the women married in the early 1980s.

The observance of ancestral ceremonies shows little relationship to marriage cohort. The lack of a strong association between cohort and the observance of ancestral ceremonies, coupled with the increasing observance noted across the 1973–86 period (table 14.7), suggests that whatever historical change occurred between 1973 and 1986 may have been specific to that time period and may not have reflected any important socialization experience during the childhood years of the women involved.

The two behavioral indicators measured only in 1980, having ances-

---

4. We also examined relationships between the same variables and birth cohort. We have not shown these in the tables because they generally show the same picture as the marriage cohort data. The most important difference between the two is the somewhat larger associations of the variables with marriage cohort than with birth cohort.

TABLE 14.8 The Importance of Ancestors and the Family Line, by Year of Survey and Marriage Cohort

	PERCENTAGE DISTRIBUTIONS BY MARRIAGE COHORT						
	1950–54	1955–59	1960–64	1965–69	1970–74	1975–79	1980–84
Number of respondents							
1973	380	1,161	1,422	1,634	930		
1980		103	563	880	1,063	1,209	
1986		236	538	647	773	964	978
Importance of a boy to link ancestors, living, and descendants, 1973							
Unimportant or not so important	6	5	10	13	19		
Important	32	37	39	44	45		
Very Important	62	58	51	44	36		
Total	100	100	100	100	100		
Importance of a boy to link ancestors, living, and descendants, 1980							
Unimportant or not so important		8	14	19	23	34	
Important		52	46	46	45	41	
Very Important		40	39	36	32	25	
Total		100	100	100	100	100	
Importance of a boy to link ancestors, living, and descendants, 1986							
Unimportant or not so important		10	17	18	26	31	40
Important		34	38	38	38	34	32
Very Important		56	45	44	36	34	28
Total		100	100	100	100	100	100
Importance of ancestors' graves, 1973							
Don't believe or doubtful	22	23	26	28	29		
Believe	54	54	56	56	57		
Believe very much	24	23	18	16	14		
Total	100	100	100	100	100		
Importance of ancestors' graves, 1980							
Don't believe or doubtful		26	32	32	34	39	
Believe		61	57	59	57	55	
Believe very much		14	11	9	9	6	
Total		100	100	100	100	100	
Importance of ancestors' graves, 1986							
Don't believe or doubtful		23	28	26	29	27	34
Believe		56	54	60	61	61	57
Believe very much		21	18	14	11	12	9
Total		100	100	100	100	100	100

TABLE 14.8 continued

	PERCENTAGE DISTRIBUTIONS BY MARRIAGE COHORT						
	1950–54	1955–59	1960–64	1965–69	1970–74	1975–79	1980–84
Observance of ceremonies for ancestors, 1973							
Do not observe	14	17	20	20	22		
Observe on birth and/or death date	5	3	3	3	3		
Observe important festivals	29	29	29	29	26		
Observe both birth/death dates & festivals	52	52	49	48	49		
Total	100	100	100	100	100		
Observance of ceremonies for ancestors, 1980							
Do not observe		9	14	12	11	14	
Observe on birth and/or death date		6	8	7	7	8	
Observe important festivals		35	31	32	32	31	
Observe both birth/death dates & festivals		50	47	49	50	47	
Total		100	100	100	100	100	
Observance of ceremonies for ancestors, 1986							
Do not observe		7	10	8	11	9	11
Observe on birth and/or death date		2	5	5	4	3	4
Observe important festivals		38	41	42	39	40	40
Observe both birth/death dates & festivals		53	44	45	46	48	46
Total		100	100	100	100	100	100
Ancestral tablets in house, 1980							
No		24	30	32	35	38	
Yes		76	70	68	65	62	
Total		100	100	100	100	100	
Monthly family worship, 1980							
No		24	29	31	30	34	
Yes		76	72	69	70	66	
Total		100	100	100	100	100	
Importance of ancestral ceremonies, 1986							
Not important at all		8	11	9	11	11	13
Not very important		20	22	28	32	33	36
Somewhat important		50	48	46	47	44	42
Very important		22	19	17	10	12	8
Total		100	100	100	100	100	100

Note: Data are for women aged 20–39 for the 1973 and 1980 surveys. For the 1986 survey, women are aged 20–49.

tral tablets in the family home and worshiping on the appropriate days in the lunar month, both have the same relationship to marriage cohort. There is an almost monotonic decline of both across time. There is, however, no simple monotonic relationship with birth cohort (data not shown). Since the marriage and birth cohort indicators are biased by age-at-marriage truncation bias in the opposite directions, this pattern suggests a modest trend toward less ancestral centrality in these two measures.

Finally, we shift our attention to another attitudinal variable, this one measuring, in 1986, the importance of ancestral ceremonies for the well-being of the family. This variable has the same general pattern of relationships to cohort as evaluations of the importance of having a boy to continue the family line and the importance of ancestral graves. The importance of ancestral ceremonies declines steadily across marriage cohorts, with 72% of the women married during the late 1950s saying that they were important as compared to just one-half of the women married during the early 1980s.

Our evaluation of the data in tables 14.7 and 14.8 suggests that any discussion of trends in family relationships beyond this life needs to make an important distinction between behavioral observance of ancestral obligations and subjective evaluations of the meaning of that behavior among the living. While there is some evidence in the marriage cohort data of a modest decline in having ancestral tablets and worshiping monthly, there is very little association of cohort with observing ancestral ceremonies (table 14.8). And when we look at the multiple cross sections, we see an actual increase in the observance of ancestral ceremonies between 1973 and 1986 (table 14.7). Yet there is fairly consistent evidence that subjective evaluations of ancestral ceremonies, ancestral graves, and the need to continue the family line into the future are declining across both historical period and cohort. This contrast suggests that there may not have been a turning away from historical Chinese behavior as it relates to ancestors and descendants, but that the family chain may now be less central and have less importance for individuals than it did in the past.

Educational Differentials

In table 14.9 the family chain variables are cross-tabulated by educational attainment for each of the three survey dates. The trends observed in table 14.7 for the total samples are, for the most part, repeated in table 14.9 for each of the educational subgroups. The steady decline over time in the importance of having a boy to continue the family

TABLE 14.9 Importance of Ancestors and the Family Line, by Education and Year, 1973, 1980, and 1986

	None	Primary	Junior High	Senior High	College/ Univ.
			AMOUNT OF EDUCATION		
Percentage saying it is important or very important to have a boy to link ancestors, living, and descendants					
1973	97	91	76	65	46
1980	92	81	71	55	47
1986	88	78	66	54	39
Percentage believing very much that ancestral graves affect the fortune of the family					
1973	83	75	58	53	39
1980	78	70	57	53	40
1986	78	76	72	60	52
Percentage observing ceremonies for ancestors					
1973	84	82	76	70	60
1980	89	89	89	83	76
1986	92	92	92	87	83
Percentage having ancestral tablets in home, 1980	79	70	64	49	43
Percentage having monthly family worship, 1980	79	74	67	51	35
Percentage saying that ancestral ceremonies are important or very important, 1986	71	64	54	42	32
Number of respondents					
1973	1,477	3,190	467	298	106
1980	548	2,128	427	490	227
1986	181	1,479	585	738	216

Note: Data are for women 20–39 at the time of the respective surveys.

line occurred within all of the educational subgroups, with one small exception. At the same time, the fraction observing ceremonies for their ancestors increased steadily across the entire thirteen-year period for each educational subgroup, just as it did for the samples as a whole.

The data in table 14.9, like the Value of Children data, demonstrate very important relationships between educational attainment and the family chain variables, a finding clearly consistent with the theoretical framework underpinning this study. For every variable, both the behavioral and attitudinal ones, and for every year, people who are more educated observe ancestral ceremonies less diligently and accord them less importance. For example, in 1973, 97% of the uneducated women said that it was important to have a boy to continue the family line, as compared to 46% among the college educated. Similarly, in 1980, 79% of the uneducated women had ancestral tablets in their homes, while only 43% of the college-educated women did. These large differentials suggest the power of educational institutions in changing attitudes and behavior concerning ancestors and descendants.

Disentangling Historical and Aging Effects

At this point we return to the complicated issue of the entanglement of historical and aging effects. As noted earlier, some of our central conclusions about social change in this chapter are based on strong empirical correlations between life values and marriage or birth cohort in one-time cross-sectional surveys. However, with family indicators measured in only one survey, birth and marriage cohort could just as easily be labeled age or marital duration. That is, with the year of the survey fixed, birth cohort and age are perfectly correlated, as are marriage cohort and marital duration. This means that the marriage and birth cohort effects that we identified earlier as representing historical trends could just as easily be interpreted as aging effects and have nothing to do with historical change.

The problems of separating the effects of perfectly confounded variables are well understood, but the solutions are not easy (Glenn 1976; Mason et al. 1973; Rodgers 1982, 1990). One approach is to estimate multivariate equations with constraints on certain parameters, but this requires strong assumptions, and any erroneous assumptions can dramatically influence the estimated effects. A second approach, advocated by many methodologists but seldom implemented because of the strong theoretical and data requirements, is to conceptualize and measure the theoretical constructs that are believed to intervene between the historical and aging effects and the dependent variable. These theoretical intervening variables then can be analyzed in a multivariate model to examine the extent to which they can account for the observed effects of the cohort/age variable. A variant of this second approach has been used in this analysis.

Our approach to the solution of this problem is based on the observation that many, but not all, of the theoretical factors identified in chapter 4 as determinants of family change operate primarily during the younger years of life—during childhood, adolescence, and the transition to adulthood. These include the characteristics of the parental family, education, marital arrangements and timing, and premarital experiences with nonfamily employment and residence. These variables are fixed early in life and are not changed by subsequent experiences across the life course. They may also have influence on the values and ideas of young people that extend far into adulthood. If such theoretical explanatory variables are changing across successive birth or marriage cohorts, as they are in Taiwan, and if they have long-lasting effects on family values and behavior, they would also cause each succeeding cohort to display different values and behavior across all their adult years. The result would be a cohort effect as classically defined in the literature. This model would also lead to the interpretation of empirical correlations between cohort measures and family values and behaviors as reflecting historical rather than aging effects.

The data sets used in this chapter contain several theoretical variables that fit this cohort model. They are fixed early in the life course, have been changing across birth and marriage cohorts, and are expected to have long-lasting effects on family attitudes and behavior. We use these variables in empirical models to determine the extent to which they can account for the relationship between cohort and the family values of interest.

The analysis proceeds by estimating two equations. The first includes birth or marriage cohort as the only predictor of family values. The relationship between cohort and family values in this equation could, as we have seen, be interpreted as either a historical or an aging effect. The second equation adds the kind of theoretical variables described above as predictor variables along with the cohort measure. By comparing the estimated effect of the cohort variable in the two equations, one can determine what part of the original correlation of cohort with family values is due to historical rather than to aging factors. The relationship of cohort to family values attributable to historical explanations is the part of the cohort variable that operates through the substantive variables. This is determined by comparing the total effect of the cohort variable in the first equation with the estimated effect of cohort in the second equation. The difference between the two estimated effects is the part operating through the theoretical variables and, therefore, is attributable to historical rather than aging processes.

If successful, this approach not only identifies what part of the cohort correlation with the dependent variable is due to historical change but also provides an explanation for that historical trend. That is, the theoretical variables that are able to account statistically for the observed effect of the cohort variable are the important dimensions of the changing childhood and young adult environment important to the changing family processes and values in question.

While labeling as "historical trends" any of the cohort correlations with family variables that operate through theoretical variables measured during the growing-up years is reasonable, interpretation of any remaining effects remains ambiguous. Any such residual or unexplained effects could be due either to aging or to changes in the young adult environment not captured by the theoretical variables used in the analysis. The question about the nature of any remaining cohort correlation requires the identification of additional variables which specifically tap either other cohort effects or the influence of aging. Also, any interpretation of residual effects should note that substantive age and cohort effects can be offsetting—that is, working in opposite directions. However, such offsetting effects are unlikely in the current analysis because both increasing age and growing up during earlier historical time would probably produce more emphasis on the importance of the family chain among older women.

We turn now to the specifics of the analysis of general life values using the 1976 Value of Children Study, which includes several factors that meet our criterion for use as theoretical variables representing early childhood or young adult experiences—namely education, age at marriage, the father's occupation, and the mother's number of children. All these variables are fixed in value by early adulthood, and all can plausibly be expected to influence commitment to the family chain.[5] In this analysis we use date of marriage rather than date of birth as our cohort indicator.[6] Multiple Classification Analysis, a form of dummy variable regression, was used to estimate the equations. Table 14.10 displays the unadjusted and adjusted means across categories of the independent variables for the ratings of continuing the family line and being remembered and the rankings of having a happy family and continuing the family line.

The introduction of the experience variables has a substantial effect on the observed influence of marriage cohort on all of the variables summarized in table 14.10. Whereas the unadjusted mean rating of the importance of being remembered and cherished after death declines by .30 (2.69 minus 2.39) between the earliest and latest marriage cohorts, that decline is only .14 (2.62 minus 2.46) in an equation containing the theoretical variables. For the continuation of the family line the unadjusted decline of mean ratings across marriage cohorts of .15 (2.93 minus 2.78) is reduced to .06 (2.90 minus 2.84), with the multivariate equation using the theoretical variables. Similarly, for the ranking of the family line value an unadjusted decline of .43 is reduced to .24 in the multivari-

5. Unfortunately, this data set contained no measures of the wife's early experience with nonfamily work and living arrangements.
6. A parallel analysis using birth cohort produced very similar results to the marriage cohort analysis. We report only the marriage cohort results because we believe that the age-at-marriage truncation effect may be less in the marriage cohort analysis.

ate equation. At the same time, the ranking of a happy family increases across marriage cohorts by .34 between the earliest and latest marriages. This difference is reduced to .18 in an equation containing the wife's childhood and young adulthood variables. These results suggest that substantial fractions, between 44 and 60%, of the observed trends of these values across marriage cohorts can be explained by the theoretical variables included in the analysis.[7]

Since the wife's values might be influenced by those of her husband, we estimated a set of equations, including the husband's education, age at marriage, and mother's number of children, in addition to the wife's variables listed in table 14.10. In all cases these equations resulted in the estimated direct effects of marriage cohort being reduced even more from those estimated in table 14.10. The original unadjusted differences across marriage cohorts decreased between 50 and 73% when both the husband's and wife's variables were included in the equations (data not included in tables).

The large portions of the observed cohort relationships which were explained by the experience variables measured in young adulthood demonstrate the importance of historical changes in family values in Taiwan. These data also suggest that the environments of childhood and early adulthood were changing, and these trends, in turn, affected cosmological family values in lasting ways.

A similar set of analyses was conducted for the four family chain variables included in the 1986 survey. Two additional variables from this survey about the family and youth experiences of the respondents were used in our analysis: the respondent's father's education; and the respondent's premarital experience with nonfamilial employment and living arrangements. The husband's mother's fertility was also added as a variable. The results of this analysis are summarized in table 14.11.

The conclusions from table 14.11 resemble those obtained from table 14.10: the observed effects of marriage cohort on the family chain variables are reduced substantially by the multivariate equations containing measures of the wife's early experience. The spread between the earliest and latest marriage cohorts is reduced by between 43 and 80% with

7. The denominator for these percentage calculations is the difference between the unadjusted means of the earliest and latest marriage cohorts. The numerator is equal to the denominator minus the difference between the adjusted means of the same two marriage cohorts. The resulting proportions were then converted to percentages. For example, for the importance of continuing the family line, the observed difference between the earliest and latest marriages was .15 (2.93 minus 2.78). This difference was reduced to .06 when the substantive variables were added to the equation (2.90 minus 2.84). This reduction of .09 in the difference across cohorts represents 60% of the original difference.

TABLE 14.10 Multiple Classification Analysis of Women's Family Chain Values in 1976

| | | Value Ratings[a] | | | | Value Rankings[b] | | | |
| | | Being Remembered and Cherished after You Die | | Linking Ancestors, the Living, and Descendants | | Having a Happy Family | | Linking Ancestors, the Living, and Descendants | |
	N[c]	Unadj. Mean[d]	Adj. Mean[e]	Unadj. Mean[d]	Adj. Mean[e]	Unadj. Mean[d]	Adj. Mean[e]	Unadj. Mean[d]	Adj. Mean[e]
Marriage cohort									
1950–54	224	2.69	2.62	2.93	2.90	1.80	1.88	2.11	2.02
1955–59	401	2.65	2.60	2.93	2.89	1.84	1.90	1.97	1.89
1960–64	411	2.56	2.54	2.88	2.86	1.92	1.94	1.91	1.87
1965–69	480	2.57	2.57	2.88	2.88	1.95	1.93	1.88	1.90
1970–74	521	2.39	2.46	2.78	2.84	2.14	2.06	1.68	1.78
$Eta^2/beta^2$	—	0.023	0.007	0.021	0.004	0.020	0.006	0.024	0.007
Significance		***	*	***	*	***	*	***	*
Education									
None	534	2.73	2.70	2.98	2.96	1.74	1.78	2.18	2.14
Primary	1,157	2.56	2.56	2.89	2.89	1.97	1.97	1.89	1.90
Junior high	183	2.45	2.46	2.79	2.80	2.08	2.06	1.46	1.48
Senior high	112	2.10	2.15	2.53	2.57	2.38	2.29	1.23	1.32
College/univ.	52	1.85	1.90	2.35	2.39	2.40	2.31	1.33	1.40
$Eta^2/beta^2$	—	0.069	0.056	0.117	0.093	0.042	0.026	0.094	0.074
Significance		***	***	***	***	***	***	***	***

Age at 1st marriage									
17 or less	300	2.64	2.56	2.89	2.84	1.93	1.99	1.85	1.75
18–19	516	2.58	2.54	2.89	2.86	1.87	1.91	1.97	1.91
20–21	584	2.58	2.57	2.90	2.89	1.95	1.95	1.90	1.89
22–24	496	2.48	2.54	2.85	2.89	2.01	1.96	1.82	1.90
25 or more	142	2.37	2.50	2.70	2.80	2.17	2.06	1.69	1.86
$Eta^2/beta^2$	—	0.010	0.001	0.016	0.005	0.008	0.002	0.008	0.004
Significance		***		***	*	**		**	
Father's occupation									
Farmer	1,041	2.59	2.55	2.93	2.90	1.88	1.92	2.00	1.93
Nonfarmer	912	2.50	2.55	2.80	2.84	2.05	1.99	1.73	1.81
N.A.	85	2.56	2.53	2.86	2.84	1.88	1.93	1.98	1.93
$Eta^2/beta^2$	—	0.005	0.000	0.027	0.005	0.010	0.002	0.024	0.005
Significance		***		***	**	***		***	**

Note: Statistical significance: * = 0.05; ** = 0.01; *** = 0.001.

[a]For the ratings, the dependent variables are coded as follows: 3, very important; 2, important; and 1, not important.

[b]For the rankings, the variables are coded as follows: 3, the most important; 2, the second most important; and 1, neither first nor second most important.

[c]Because of missing data on the dependent variables, the number of cases varies somewhat across dependent variables. The numbers listed are for the total sample, including the small number of missing data on the dependent variables.

[d]The unadjusted mean is the observed mean for each category of the predictor variables.

[e]The adjusted mean is the mean adjusted for the effects of the other variables in the equation.

TABLE 14.11 Multiple Classification Analysis of Women's Ancestors and Descendants Values and Observance in 1986

	N^d	Importance of Boy to Link Ancestors, Living, and Descendants[a]		Observance of Ceremonies for Ancestors[b]		Importance of Ancestral Ceremonies[c]		Importance of Ancestors' Graves[a]	
		Unadj. Mean[e]	Adj. Mean[f]	Unadj. Mean[e]	Adj. Mean[f]	Unadj. Mean[e]	Adj. Mean[f]	Unadj. Mean[e]	Adj. Mean[f]
Marriage cohort									
1955–59	236	2.47	2.33	2.46	2.44	2.86	2.68	1.98	1.89
1960–64	538	2.28	2.18	2.34	2.32	2.75	2.63	1.89	1.83
1965–69	647	2.26	2.19	2.37	2.35	2.70	2.61	1.88	1.83
1970–74	773	2.09	2.07	2.35	2.35	2.57	2.54	1.82	1.80
1975–79	964	2.03	2.07	2.39	2.39	2.56	2.61	1.85	1.87
1980–84	978	1.89	2.00	2.35	2.38	2.46	2.60	1.75	1.82
$Eta^2/beta^2$	—	0.044	0.012	0.002	0.002	0.019	0.002	0.009	0.002
Significance		***		*		***		***	
Education									
None	532	2.40	2.27	2.45	2.48	2.92	2.85	2.00	1.96
Primary	1,978	2.22	2.19	2.39	2.39	2.71	2.69	1.90	1.89
Junior high	652	2.05	2.09	2.40	2.39	2.53	2.54	1.79	1.80
Senior high	746	1.79	1.89	2.27	2.26	2.30	2.36	1.68	1.72
College/univ.	225	1.56	1.71	2.19	2.22	2.13	2.24	1.55	1.66
$Eta^2/beta^2$	—	0.082	0.039	0.012	0.013	0.065	0.042	0.038	0.020
Significance		***		***		***		***	
Age at 1st marriage									
17 or less	465	2.18	2.04	2.33	2.33	2.65	2.55	1.83	1.78
18–19	781	2.19	2.10	2.36	2.33	2.69	2.61	1.88	1.83
20–21	1,101	2.17	2.13	2.39	2.38	2.67	2.63	1.88	1.85
22–24	1,175	2.05	2.12	2.39	2.40	2.56	2.61	1.83	1.86
25 or more	614	1.89	2.08	2.31	2.36	2.42	2.58	1.73	1.83
$Eta^2/beta^2$	—	0.017	0.001	0.002	0.002	0.011	0.001	0.006	0.002
Significance		***		*		***		***	

	N								
Premarital work[g]									
No paid work	1,114	2.29	2.14	2.36	2.34	2.78	2.65	1.93	1.87
Paid work home	158	2.06	2.04	2.40	2.39	2.56	2.56	1.78	1.79
Work outside									
Home, give	1,187	2.03	2.08	2.42	2.43	2.54	2.58	1.81	1.83
Home, keep	367	1.84	2.07	2.37	2.45	2.36	2.56	1.70	1.82
Dorm, give	923	2.09	2.10	2.36	2.34	2.61	2.60	1.86	1.84
Dorm, keep	254	1.97	2.10	2.17	2.21	2.40	2.52	1.73	1.79
$Eta^2/beta^2$	—	0.030	0.001	0.008	0.009	0.024	0.002	0.014	0.001
Significance		***		***	***	***		***	
Father's education									
None	1,927	2.18	2.10	2.40	2.38	2.69	2.61	1.89	1.84
Primary	1,408	2.08	2.13	2.38	2.39	2.56	2.61	1.84	1.86
Junior high	239	1.76	1.96	2.23	2.28	2.33	2.54	1.67	1.79
Senior high	133	1.63	1.91	2.12	2.18	2.26	2.53	1.56	1.71
College/univ.	81	1.69	2.04	2.14	2.23	2.10	2.44	1.42	1.62
$Eta^2/beta^2$	—	0.034	0.006	0.011	0.006	0.025	0.001	0.023	0.005
Significance		***	***	***	**	***		***	**
Father's occupation									
Farmer	2,050	2.21	2.13	2.40	2.38	2.71	2.63	1.92	1.87
Nonfarmer	1,897	1.98	2.08	2.34	2.37	2.48	2.57	1.75	1.80
$Eta^2/beta^2$	—	0.019	0.001	0.002	0.000	0.017	0.001	0.017	0.003
Significance		***	***	*		***	*	***	**
Mother's number of children									
4 or fewer	950	2.05	2.11	2.35	2.37	2.56	2.61	1.80	1.84
5	825	2.03	2.08	2.36	2.37	2.55	2.58	1.79	1.81
6	800	2.09	2.10	2.35	2.34	2.55	2.55	1.82	1.82
7	643	2.12	2.07	2.42	2.40	2.65	2.61	1.90	1.88
8 or more	884	2.22	2.14	2.37	2.36	2.71	2.64	1.89	1.85
$Eta^2/beta^2$	—	0.007	0.001	0.001	0.001	0.006	0.001	0.006	0.002
Significance		***	***		***	***		***	***

TABLE 14.11 continued

	N^d	Importance of Boy to Link Ancestors, Living, and Descendants[a]		Observance of Ceremonies for Ancestors[b]		Importance of Ancestral Ceremonies[c]		Importance of Ancestors' Graves[a]	
		Unadj. Mean[e]	Adj. Mean[f]	Unadj. Mean[e]	Adj. Mean[f]	Unadj. Mean[e]	Adj. Mean[f]	Unadj. Mean[e]	Adj. Mean[f]
Husband's mother's number of children									
4 or fewer	1,166	2.06	2.09	2.32	2.33	2.54	2.57	1.77	1.79
5	714	2.09	2.13	2.37	2.37	2.61	2.63	1.87	1.88
6	714	2.10	2.11	2.41	2.42	2.62	2.63	1.84	1.84
7	591	2.12	2.09	2.42	2.41	2.64	2.61	1.87	1.85
8 or more	845	2.16	2.12	2.44	2.43	2.67	2.64	1.90	1.88
$Eta^2/beta^2$	—	0.002	0.002	0.030	0.030	0.006	0.006	0.008	0.007
Significance			***		***		***		***
Unadjusted R^2		0.103		0.061		0.080		0.060	

Note: Statistical significance: * = 0.05; ** = 0.01; *** = 0.001.

[a]This variable is coded as follows: 3, very important; 2, important; and 1, unimportant or not so important.

[b]This variable is coded as follows: 3, observe both birth/death dates and festivals; 2, observe either birth/death dates or festivals; and 1, observe neither.

[c]This variable is coded as follows: 4, very important; 3, somewhat important; 2, not very important; 1 not important.

[d]Because of missing data on the dependent variables, the number of cases varies somewhat across dependent variables. The numbers listed are for the total sample including the small number of missing data on the dependent variables.

[e]The unadjusted mean is the observed mean for each category of the predictor variables.

[f]The adjusted mean is the mean adjusted for the effects of the other variables in the equation.

[g]This is a variable composed of three dimensions of work: location of work; living arrangements while employed; and whether gave money to parents. The four categories listed under work outside home are the result of a pattern variable for those who had experienced paid employment before marriage: whether they lived in a dormitory or at home (or with other relatives) and whether they kept or gave most of the money to their parents.

the multivariate equations—a range of percentage reductions somewhat greater than that observed in table 14.10.

The historical interpretation of these data, plus the changing experiences of successive cohorts of children, suggests that changes were probably already under way when the oldest cohorts of women in our sample reached adulthood. Support for this assertion is the fairly steady shifting of values across all cohorts, including the earliest marriage cohorts. Since the oldest women were teenagers by the end of World War II, these family changes had probably begun by the late 1940s or early 1950s. While the trends could have commenced even earlier, no data exist for testing this possibility.

This research also identifies the element of historical change that is most important in modifying family values—education. As we have already seen, the effect of education on family chain values is powerful, and this effect remains strong even in the multivariate analyses. There also appears to be an additional effect of a woman's father's educational attainment net of her own school achievement. Apparently, both the educational environment of the parental home and the woman's school attainment influence her attitudes, values, and behavior concerning the family chain. The husband's mother's fertility also influences three of the four values listed in table 14.11, with women who marry into small families placing less emphasis on the ancestors than others. The influence of the other variables in the equations is not large or consistent once educational attainments are taken into account.

Earlier, we observed an important correlation between age at marriage and some of the family chain values. The age-at-marriage truncation occurring in the birth and marriage cohort analyses produced a bias in the historical time trends associated with both birth and marriage cohort. Tables 14.10 and 14.11 indicate that this age-at-marriage truncation bias probably is primarily an educational truncation effect since the age-at-marriage relationship largely disappears with education controlled.

The Ancestors and Getting Married

Previously, we noted the historical importance of ancestors in mate selection and marital ritual. Though we lack systematic survey data to document such trends in the role of the ancestors, the authors' experiences in Taiwan suggest that the roles of the ancestors in marriage may be fading away.

Mate selection in Taiwan has gone a long way from arranged marriages in the direction of love matches (see chap. 6). The locus of decision making has shifted from the parents to the couple, while the input of fortune-tellers and the ancestors has probably declined. While some families may still consult fortune-tellers about the wisdom of a particular match, the influence of such opinions has probably declined. The practice of checking a prospective match with the ancestors has, to our knowledge, largely disappeared.

We also believe that the involvement of the ancestors in engagement and marriage ceremonies may have declined. This may have occurred with the increasing emphasis upon the use of large restaurants and banquet halls, which may have led to some deemphasis of the importance of family altars and ancestral tablets. We emphasize, however, that we have no systematic data to confirm our observations of the changing role of ancestors in marriage arrangements.

Summary

The family rope linking together the dead, the living, and the unborn has been regularly described as the key symbolic feature of the historical Chinese family. This cosmological view has historically been a key principle for organizing relationships with parents and other ancestors, for defining the central features of marriage, and for orienting adults toward their offspring. The survey data discussed in this chapter confirms the centrality of these concepts in the lives of middle-aged Taiwanese women in the 1970s and 1980s.

This view of the Chinese family remains important in Taiwan today, despite the persuasive evidence that the fibers of this cosmological family rope are beginning to fray and strain under the pressures of social change. Our survey data indicate less commitment to these family linkages in the 1980s than in the 1970s and also show that younger women and those with higher educational attainments place less importance on these family values and commitments than do their older and less educated sisters. Apparently, the symbolic importance of the family rope is declining more rapidly than the observance of specific ceremonies associated with these family linkages; the family rituals may continue at the same time that their importance and centrality diminish.

Of course, it would be easy to exaggerate both the rapidity and the degree of change in these Chinese family values and ceremonial observances. Although the evidence for change appears strong, the extent and speed of that trend lags significantly behind that shown for marriage, reproduction, nonfamily employment, and living arrangements before marriage. In addition, there appears to be little outright rejection of the historical family world view.

While it is possible to exaggerate the rapidity and extent of change in fundamental values concerning the family rope, it is difficult to exaggerate the potential importance of these trends, especially if they continue well into the future. If these changes continue and if the Chinese family rope becomes greatly frayed and weakened, it may no longer bind together important kinship relationships; the effects on family relationships and processes could be profound. Such an eventuality could modify intergenerational authority structures, care for the elderly, the living arrangements of both the young and the old, the meaning of marriage, authority relationships between husbands and wives, the relative emphasis on vertical versus lateral relationships, and the values and roles of children.

Fifteen

Continuity and Change

A. Thornton and H. S. Lin

We began this book by asking questions about the influence of large-scale economic and social transformations on family structures and processes in Taiwan. How was family life in Taiwan influenced by the expansion of education, the increase in wage employment, the movement of people from the countryside to the cities, the improvements in economic productivity, the decline in mortality, and increased contact with different cultures? As the preceding chapters have demonstrated, individual Taiwanese and their kinspeople responded to the changing social and economic environment by modifying their historical family structures and relationships to fit the new milieu. The result was a complex mosaic of family change and persistence in Taiwan. Several dimensions of family life in Taiwan have remained fairly constant, while others have changed dramatically, especially during the last four decades. In this chapter we examine this mosaic of continuity and change in Taiwanese family life and consider the forces that intermixed many new colors and shapes into the historical design of Chinese family life to create the family system currently observed in Taiwan.

The Changing Mode of Social Organization

Perhaps the most important family change in Taiwan in recent decades, both in terms of magnitude and in its ramifications for other aspects of family life, is the movement of Taiwanese society from a strong familial mode toward a nonfamilial mode of organization. Despite some early important nonfamilial elements, most activities in the past were conducted within family units. Kinspeople usually provided the means of subsistence and information, and the Chinese view of both this world and the next stressed familial elements. Close associates were primarily kinsmen, and family authority was important for the lives of individuals. While familial relationships continue to be very important, social networks have become more differentiated and now include many nonfamilial activities, associates, sources of information, authority, and means of subsistence (chaps. 1 through 5).

Although the Japanese colonial government had little interest in modifying Taiwanese family structures and processes, it instituted changes which moved Taiwanese social life in nonfamilial directions (chaps. 2 through 4). Of central importance was the introduction of a state-run educational system which taught substantial numbers of young Taiwanese children by the end of the colonial period. The Japanese colonizers also fostered an agricultural extension service that brought new information and technology to Taiwanese farmers. Wage employment also increased somewhat as the colonial government invested resources in the industrial infrastructure. Linkages of Taiwanese families to the outside world were expanded by improvements in the communication and transportation network. Colonial governmental public health interventions significantly lowered the level of mortality, resulting in larger numbers of surviving children and a rapidly growing population. One direct Japanese intervention into family affairs was the elimination of the widespread practice of female footbinding that had severely restricted the mobility of many Chinese women.

The transformation of Taiwanese society toward nonfamilial modes of organization quickened in the years following World War II. Taiwan was reincorporated into China, and the Nationalist government, with its army, moved to Taiwan in 1949. The introduction of universal military service immersed every young Taiwanese male in a totally nonfamilial military setting at a very impressionable period of life (chap. 4). Another important innovation was the introduction of a government family planning program in the early 1960s that encouraged couples to have fewer children and provided effective means of contraception to make that possible (chap. 11).

During the 1950s the Nationalist government devoted considerable attention to agriculture, which at that time involved the majority of the population (chap. 3). One important intervention was the expansion of the extension service which brought new information and techniques to farmers. Another important program was land reform, which redistributed land from absentee landowners to the tillers. Unlike most other changes during this period, this program decreased one important nonfamilial relationship, that between tenants and their unrelated landlords.

The transformation of Taiwan's economy from agriculture to industry shifted the economy from a family mode of production toward a bureaucratic organization of production. Although numerous businesses continue to be owned and managed as family enterprises, increasingly large numbers of people became wage workers in companies owned and managed by unrelated people. By the middle of the 1980s over nine-tenths of all young Taiwanese wives reported that they worked for wages outside the home before marriage (chap. 5). As a result, the family economy was largely transformed from labor-pooling enterprises managed by senior family members toward wage-pooling organizations involving people in economic enterprises outside the family.

Although Taiwan's economic planners have explicitly tried to bring new economic opportunities to rural areas, the industrialization of the economy shifted employment opportunities and population to urban areas. While many in the older generation continued to maintain family farms, their children frequently migrated to wage jobs in the cities. While some young rural migrants found accommodations with relatives, many had to live in industry-run dormitories. By the middle 1980s, two-fifths of all young wives reported experience in a work-related dormitory before marriage (chap. 5).

The shift from familial socialization and education toward a nonfamilial mode of education in state-supported schools began under the Japanese and accelerated during the years following World War II. Elementary and junior high enrollment expanded rapidly, and junior high education became compulsory in 1968. By the end of the 1980s enrollment in senior high school reached three-fourths of the population, and nearly one-third were attending college (chap. 3). Taiwanese youth now spend a large fraction of their maturing years in educational institutions separated from the parental home and supervision.

Although family members continue to be important sources of information and news, the expansion of the mass media has brought most Taiwanese men and women into a worldwide network of information. Most Taiwanese are now inundated with information and messages from newspapers, magazines, television, and movies. Japanese colonization, the American military, and international tourists and businesspeople have also brought international messages to Taiwan, while numerous Taiwanese are now traveling abroad. This international expansion of information and messages has brought the Chinese in Taiwan in contact with the different family and personal life-styles of Western societies.

The state has played a substantial role in shifting the character of social organization in Taiwan. Among the nonfamilial institutions organized directly by the government or fostered by governmental policy were the agricultural extension agencies, public health organizations, educational institutions, the military, and industrial economic organizations. Together these nonfamilial institutions have markedly shifted the locus of social life in Taiwan from a familial mode of organization toward a more nonfamilial form.

While our discussion has emphasized Taiwan's movement from the familial toward the nonfamilial end of the modes of organization continuum, it is important to emphasize that this shift has been far from complete. Despite the introduction and expansion of numerous nonfamilial institutions in the Taiwanese social landscape, the family continues to be a centrally important institution. Numerous activities, including production, consumption, socialization, and education, continue to be organized by and conducted within family units. The family also continues as a crucial center of authority, resources, and information for individual Taiwanese. Families are still important sources of social interaction and connectedness. In addition, family values and relationships continue to shape the Chinese cosmos in Taiwan. Thus, despite the increasingly complex web of nonfamilial institutions now shaping the life courses of individual Taiwanese, the family continues to be a central locus of social organization. It is also difficult to imagine that Taiwanese families would disappear as important social units in the future.

Trends in Family Behavior and Experience

Taiwan's recent history is consistent with the theoretical arguments of chapter 4 suggesting that the movement from a familial toward a nonfamilial mode of organization would be accompanied by numerous other changes in family life. The shift in modes of organization along with other social changes significantly altered the social and economic milieu in which individual Taiwanese and their families conducted their lives. The introduction of many new elements and institutions into the environment substantially altered the opportunities and constraints faced by Taiwanese women, men, and children. As these individuals and their families interacted with a greatly altered world, they experienced substantial pressure and opportunity to modify the historical Chinese ways of organizing interpersonal relationships. The consequence has been significant changes in marriage formation and dissolution, childbearing, living arrangements, interrelationships between parents and children, and the linkages between the living, the ancestors, and the future generations of unborn children.

Of course, Chinese individuals and their families brought a rich supply of norms, values, and social institutions to the new environment, and this cultural heritage provided both the background and the framework for adjustments to the new circumstances. As individuals and families encountered the changing environment, they responded in terms of their historical relationships, values, and patterns of interacting. Consequently, it has not been surprising to find that many of the central historical values of Chinese culture have persisted in the new environment, even as their manifestations have been modified by the new forces. The result in Taiwan has been an intricate mixing of continuity and change in family life.

The marriage system in Taiwan has been transformed from being parent-directed to involving both parents and children, with significant numbers of young people now making this decision themselves. While we cannot date the beginning of this shift, we know that the percentage of parent-arranged marriages declined from over 60% in the late 1950s to less than 15% in the early 1980s (chap. 6). Close to one-third of all marriages are now decided entirely by the young couple. Whereas most young people in the past met their future spouses through parents or matchmakers, most now meet them on their own. Dating has also become common. Forty percent of the women married in the early 1980s experienced premarital intercourse, and increasingly large fractions are having their first sexual experience before an engagement ceremony. One-third of the women married in the early 1980s reported that they were pregnant at the time of marriage.

At the same time, however, parents continue to have an important role in the mate selection process (chap. 6). Parents had a significant say in spouse choice in a substantial majority of recent marriages, and in a significant minority the young couple were introduced by their parents or matchmakers. In addition, while most young people have dated, the great majority have dated only with parental approval and most have only dated their future spouses. Similarly, while there has been an increase in premarital sex and pregnancy, the out-of-wedlock childbearing rate has actually declined.

The timing of marriage has changed significantly (chap. 8). Early in the twentieth century marriage was both young and universal. The majority of Taiwanese women married as teenagers, and most men married by their middle 20s. Prior to World War II, marriage prevalence increased for men and declined for women. During World War II, the prevalence of marriage declined sharply and was then followed by a significant, but short-lived, marriage boom. Subsequently age at marriage for both men and women substantially increased, with the average marriage age in the late 1980s exceeding 25 for women and 28 for men.

Despite the increasing postponement of marriage in Taiwan, marriage continues to be nearly universal (chap. 8). With the exception of the cohorts containing large numbers of single migrant men from the mainland, most Taiwanese of both sexes born before 1950 have married. By the 1980s, however, a growing number of men and women in their 30s had never married. While this may only be a continuation of the shift toward later marriage, it also could represent the beginning of a trend toward lifelong singleness.

Marital dissolution has changed substantially in recent decades (chap. 10). In the early 1900s both mortality and divorce were high, together producing a very high rate of marital dissolution. Improving health caused the rate of widowhood to decline dramatically throughout the course of the twentieth century. The high mortality rates of 1915 would terminate 80% of the marriages within thirty years. By contrast, the low mortality rates at the end of the 1980s would terminate only 15% in the same period of time.

The divorce rate declined during the first half of the century and remained quite low through the early 1970s. But beginning in the early 1970s voluntary marital dissolution increased dramatically—tripling during the decades of the 1970s and 1980s. The high divorce rates of 1989 would terminate about 20% of all marriages within thirty years. However, even with the recent increase in divorce, the total rate of union dissolution from mortality and divorce together remains significantly below the levels recorded early in this century.

The crucial story concerning fertility is the substantial decline in childbearing beginning in the middle 1950s (chap. 11). During the period between 1956 and 1990 the gross reproduction rate fell from 3.2 to .86. This trend resulted from important shifts in preferences concerning childbearing and the introduction and adoption of effective fertility control measures. For example, average preferred family size declined from 4.0 in 1965 to 2.6 in 1985. In 1965 only 28% of married women 22–39 reported ever having practiced contraception, but by 1985 that number had increased to 90%. Taiwanese couples have increasingly used the most effective methods of contraception, and by 1985 sterilization had become the modal method. Taiwan, however, has not experienced a significant movement toward the endorsement of childlessness, and preferences for sons over daughters continue.

Steady declines in extended family living have occurred among both young married couples and their parents, although the decline has been most substantial for younger couples (chap. 12). The decline in lateral extension (married couples of the same generation sharing living quarters) has been greater than the decline in vertical extension (married couples of different generations living together). But the changes in extended family living have been less rapid and substantial than those in family formation and dissolution. As late as 1986, two-thirds of all recently married couples reported beginning married life living with the husband's parents. Furthermore, the great majority of elderly Taiwanese today live with one of their children. In addition, patrilocal and patrilineal principles still govern extended co-residence patterns, and there is no evidence of any increase in the proportion of couples living with the wife's parents.

The family chain or rope was a central feature of Chinese cosmology in the past. Family relationships included both the ancestors of the past and the unborn children of the future. This family chain has been weakened so that young people now place less emphasis upon the family chain than do their elders (chap. 14). Relatively more emphasis is now placed on nuclear family relationships than on the larger network of kin relationships that includes the ancestors and unborn children.

Despite the declining significance of the ancestral chain in individual lives, the vast majority of young Taiwanese continue to say that the ancestral chain is very important (chap. 14). In addition, nearly one-half of young Taiwanese rate the ancestral chain as one of the two most important values in their lives. Furthermore, there have not been large recent declines in the actual observance of ceremonies for the ancestors.

This interweaving of continuity and change in Taiwanese family life suggests that many of the old values and principles have persisted into the present. Loyalty to the family chain has continued in that individual Chinese men and women still value their linkages to their parents and children. This filial piety continues to be manifest in the existence of a nearly universal commitment to marry and bear children. It is also manifest today in the extraordinary investment parents make in the futures of their children through the provision of education. Parents today are also concerned about the continuation of the family through their children's marriages.

Extensive filial piety also continues to be exercised up the familial chain toward the ancestors. This is demonstrated in the contributions of unmarried children to the family economy even when those children are working and living outside the parental home. It is also displayed as married adults provide their parents extensive social and economic support, including the sharing of living quarters in old age. This filial piety is also expressed today, as it was in the past, by attention to the ancestors who have died.

Unfortunately, the limitations of our primary data prevent us from examining the extent to which family relationships among the living now extend beyond the immediate network of parents and children—an important weakness of our data since those extended family connections have been very important historically in Taiwan. Other research, however, indicates that extended family relations have continued as important organizational forms in Taiwan's adjustment to the emerging social and economic world (Greenhalgh 1984, 1988; Hamilton and Kao 1988; Winckler and Greenhalgh 1988).

The strong continuity in marrying, having children, nurturing one's offspring, interacting with a family web of production and support, caring for the elderly, and respecting the ancestors suggests that these family behaviors may be close to the core of the Chinese family system. That is, they may be the closest behavioral manifestations of the central Chinese value of commitment to the family system. As such, they have persisted tenaciously through the remarkable social and economic transformations of recent decades. Of course, one of the things that makes the future so interesting is that some of these persistent and central aspects of Taiwanese family life may undergo more intensive change in the future.

Other dimensions of Chinese family life have proven more malleable to the changing social and economic environment, perhaps because they were less central to the historical Chinese value of filial piety. Among these more malleable features of Chinese families have been marital arrangements, interactions of future spouses before marriage, the timing of marriage, the number of children born, living arrangements early in the life course, and the relative importance of nuclear versus more distant kin. Apparently the forces of the changing social and economic world could modify these dimensions of implementation, timing, number, and emphasis more rapidly and extensively than some of the other aspects of family life.

Determinants of Individual Family Behavior and Experience

Our argument that the changing social and economic environment has significantly modified family life in Taiwan is buttressed by extensive analyses of the determinants of individual family behavior and experience. Consistent with the theoretical arguments of chapter 4, these analyses demonstrate that many of the economic and social forces associated with historical trends in family life in Taiwan are also related to individual-level behavior and attitudes. Prominent among these determinants of individual family experience are school enrollment, industrial employment and wage labor, urban residence, nonfamily residence, and migration from the countryside to the city.

Our research demonstrates that nonfamilial educational institutions significantly influence individual family behavior and experience in Taiwan. Educational attainment is an important determinant of almost every family process and relationship investigated, and in most instances the effects of education on family structures and processes are substantially stronger than those for the other family determinants examined.

Highly educated young people both want and have more say than the less-educated about whom they will marry, have more involvement in dating, and are less likely to meet their spouse through their parents or matchmakers (chap. 7). The highly educated also prefer getting married at an older age, and those desires are reflected in their behavior (chap. 9). Fertility is also related to education; the well-educated prefer fewer children, use contraception more effectively, and have smaller families (chap. 11). Education is associated with lower levels of extended family living because the well-educated are less likely to begin married life with parents and terminate such extended household arrangements more rapidly (chap. 13). Furthermore, the familial rope linking together the ancestors, the living, and future generations is weakened by extensive educational achievements (chap. 14). While the relationships between education and the family behaviors and values just discussed are generally monotonic, there is an inverse-U association between education and premarital sex and pregnancy; the incidence of premarital sex and pregnancy is high for those in the middle of the educational distribution and low for those at both ends of the distribution.

Our data indicate that the modes of production influence family behavior and process. Both first- and second-generation involvement outside the family labor-pooling economy influence the family experiences of the second generation. Young people growing up in nonagricultural families have significantly more say in the choice of their spouse, more chance of meeting their spouse without parental or other adult introduction, and more dating experience before marriage. They also have higher preferred and actual ages at marriage. Adults who were reared in nonagricultural families place less emphasis on the ancestral line linking together the ancestors, the living, and the unborn generations. While these influences of first-generation economic organization generally operate at least partially through each person's own educational and occupational experiences, there are also independent direct effects of nonagricultural origins.

Personal participation in the nonfamilial wage economy also has important implications for several dimensions of life course experience. Women with premarital employment experience outside the home are significantly more likely than others to meet their spouse by themselves or through friends, to have a substantial choice in the marital decision, to date both their husbands and others, to experience premarital sex, and to have a premarital pregnancy (chap. 7). Premarital wage employment outside the home also reduces early entrance into marriage (chap. 9). Women who work for wages are less likely to live with the husband's parents at marriage and more quickly terminate such living arrangements (chap. 13). Nonfamilial employment, however, has little influence on the strength of the linkage to the ancestral chain (chap. 14).

Residence in nonfamilial institutions has significant implications for several dimensions of family life. Dormitory living is associated with more independence in the mate selection process. Compared with young wage-earning women who live at home, those living and working outside the home are somewhat more likely to choose their own spouse, to meet their future spouse without senior-generation involvement, to date, to have premarital sexual intercourse, and to be pregnant at marriage (chap. 7). While these effects are relatively small, they indicate an additional influence of nonfamilial employment through its effect on nonfamilial residence.

Living arrangements at marriage are closely tied to decisions about migration. Among young newlyweds living in the geographical area where the husband was born, more than 80% lived with the husband's parents after marriage, a fraction substantially higher than the approximately 50% living with the husband's parents among those who had migrated from the husband's place of birth. Among migrant couples where the husband's father was a farmer, only about a third lived with the parents at marriage (chap. 13). These data indicate that while some young migrants from agricultural areas move to the cities with their parents, numerous other city-bound migrants are separated from their parental family because the parents remain in the ancestral village caring for the family home and farm (chap. 13).

The degree of urbanization is positively related to young couples living in nuclear households. Much of this association results from more migrants living in the cities than in the countryside and the fact that many of these migrants are separated from their parents when they move. Once migration status is controlled, city residents are only somewhat more likely than others to live apart from parents. Nevertheless, even with migration controlled, there remains a rural-urban differential in postmarital residence, which suggests that there are additional forces in urban areas mitigating against extended family residence (chap. 13).

In chapter 4 we identified numerous causal mechanisms linking education, wage employment, dormitory living, urban residence, and rural-to-urban migration to family behavior. While our analyses suggest that at least some of these causal mechanisms translate differences in the modes of organization into differential family behavior, we are unable to identify the strength and sequence of intervening mechanisms, since we lack empirical measures of those mechanisms. Research with more detailed measurement of the intervening causal mechanisms is needed to estimate the relative importance of those factors.

Accounting for Aggregate Family Change

Just as education, wage employment, nonagricultural family origins, and dormitory living are important determinants of individual family behavior and experiences, historical trends in these variables are significant determinants of aggregate changes in family behavior. Numerous analyses evaluated the extent to which historical trends in the determinants of family structure and process could account for the changes in the family variables. In every analysis, trends in the explanatory variables account for at least some of the trends in family behavior and process and substantial fractions of observed family change can frequently be explained by trends in the predictor variables.

Our analyses of the trends in marital introductions, who chose the spouse, and dating show that one-half to two-thirds of the historical changes between marriage cohorts of the early years of the 1960s and 1980s could be explained by trends in the predictor variables (chap. 7). Similarly, between 40 and 80% of the changes between the 1950s and 1980s marriage cohorts in the importance of the family chain linking the ancestors, the living, and the unborn generations could be explained by trends in the explanatory variables (chap. 14). Changes in preferred marital ages during the 1970s and early 1980s show that between one-third and one-half of that trend can be explained by the predictor variables examined (chap. 9). Our multivariate models were able to explain all of the trend in the rate of marriage formation between the birth cohorts of the early 1940s and those of the early 1960s (chap. 9). We also could account for all of the historical trend (across marriage cohorts of 1962–84) in living arrangements at the time of marriage. However, our analytical model of the termination of extended living arrangements after marriage could explain only one-fourth of the historical decline from the early 1960s through the early 1980s (chap. 13). We could explain about 40% of the historical trend in premarital sex and pregnancy when measures of marital introductions, who chose the spouse, and dating were added to our standard explanatory indicators (chap. 7).

Increasing educational attainment was frequently the most important measured determinant of historical familial trends. Furthermore, in many cases trends in educational attainment alone were able to account for substantial fractions of the changes in family behavior. Perhaps the most striking example of the power of educational trends to explain changes in family behavior is the timing of marriage. Between the birth cohorts of 1941 and 1966, increases in education account for virtually all of the historical decline in the rate of marriage (chap. 9). Other family trends where educational expansion had significant effects include marital arrangements and introductions, dating, fertility, living arrangements, and the strength of the linkages with the ancestors and unborn future generations.

The strong influence of education on changes in family behavior illustrates how continuities in historical values may undergird the shift toward nonfamily modes of organization. Education has long been valued in Chinese culture as a source of social mobility and respect. The desire for education has been enhanced by recent social changes, and the current demand for education in Taiwan appears to be nearly insatiable. Both the increased amount of time spent in school and the transformation of the school system from village- and lineage-based to a state institution have made education an important mechanism for transforming historical Chinese family behavior and values into those emerging at the end of the twentieth century.

While the measured empirical variables can account for large proportions of several major trends in family behavior and experience in Taiwan, we recognize that important parts of other family trends remain unexplained. Measurement weakness may be one reason for our inability to explain all the trends in family behavior and experience. Our indicators of such key constructs as education, nonfamilial employment, agricultural experience, urban exposure, and dormitory residence may contain substantial measurement error, which reduces both the observed correlations between variables and their ability to explain family change.

Our multivariate models may also be unable to account for all the trends in family behavior because measures of some relevant explanatory variables are not available. Particularly important is the lack of measures of individual contact with the mass media which our theoretical discussion posited to be important. Also missing is information about contact with people outside Taiwan and about beliefs concerning the importance of adopting Western family patterns in order to follow the Western model of economic and social development.

Our research also lacks adequate comprehensive measures of the influence of the state. For example, the actions of governmental and other nonfamilial organizations to improve health and reduce mortality have had significant effects on family life in Taiwan. They have played a major role in reducing the rate of marital dissolution and the importance of remarriage. The decline in mortality also has reduced the number of children orphaned by parental deaths and has increased the longevity and availability of parents.

The marriage market during the first half of the twentieth century was influenced by changing patterns of mortality. Mortality was higher among girls than boys in the early 1900s, and this differential, along with the higher prevalence of boys to girls at birth, produced a significant surplus of males during the prime marrying years. As a result of this imbalanced sex ratio, women had an advantage in the marriage market, which increased marriage rates for women and decreased them for men. The greater declines in female mortality during the first few decades of the twentieth century reduced the surplus of men and improved their position in the marriage market. Consequently, over the first few decades of the twentieth century the prevalence of marriage increased for men and declined for women (chap. 8). The improved marriage market for men relative to women may also have played a role in the reduction of both minor and matrilocal marriage (Barclay 1954; Wolf and Huang 1980).

Other state-based influences on family life in Taiwan, already mentioned, include the elimination of footbinding early in the Japanese era, the family planning program of more recent decades, and the introduction of compulsory military service in the 1950s. Such changes, with wide-ranging potential effects on family life, cannot be evaluated quantitatively with the data and methodology currently available.

While our research has been organized as a case study of Taiwan, we believe that our conclusions have considerable relevance for other settings. As we have argued elsewhere (Thornton and Fricke 1987), many societies have been shifted from the familial toward the nonfamilial modes of organization by industrialization, urbanization, rural-urban migration, education expansion, and the growth of the mass media. We believe that shifts in organizational modes in other societies will have implications for family change in these societies as well. While many of the causal forces and results documented for Taiwan are probably evident elsewhere, the Taiwanese experience cannot be applied mechanically to other settings because the idiosyncrasies of each society's family system in the past and the nature of each society's specific economic and social transformation will shape the exact trajectory of family change occurring in that society. Even within the same cultural setting, differences in political and economic change can have important implications for family adjustments (Whyte 1992). Thus, the theoretical framework and ideas successfully applied to the case of Taiwan will have to be tailored to the specific realities of other societies. Nevertheless, the Chinese family system and the trajectory of Taiwan's social and economic change are similar enough to historical family life and social change in other societies that we believe many of the theoretical ideas and empirical findings of this research have relevance elsewhere. However, application of these ideas and findings to other societies is beyond the scope of this volume.

The Future

In this book we have shown that Taiwan has been transformed in the twentieth century, particularly in the years following World War II, by the impact of industrialization, urbanization, increased education, rural-to-urban migration, the expanding state, increased income, and extended contacts with other societies. These forces have moved Taiwan from the familial toward the nonfamilial end of the modes of organization continuum. They also introduced numerous new ideas, values, and technologies. The result was a substantially modified social and economic environment that created extensive opportunities and pressures for innovations in family structures and relationships.

The distinctive Chinese family system in the past meant that Taiwan's adjustment to these social and economic changes would incorporate a uniquely Chinese character. Historical patterns of Chinese family relationships were modified by individuals and their kinspeople to accommodate to the new environment. As a result, the trajectory of family change in Taiwan has reflected both historical Chinese social structure and the island's specific patterns of economic and social change.

Adjustments to Taiwan's social and economic history have included dramatic changes in family structures and processes intermixed with adherence to old ways. Among the most dramatic changes have been the increased autonomy of young people, the shift from arranged marriages toward love matches, the postponement of marriage, the decline and subsequent rise in divorce, the fall in fertility, the decline of extended family living, and the weakening of the chain linking the ancestors, the living, and the unborn generations. Yet these significant changes have been balanced by equally dramatic persistence in other aspects of family life: marriage continues to be nearly universal; parenthood is desired by nearly all; children receive extensive care from their parents; the elderly obtain support from their children; and the ancestral chain remains a central, even though weakened, value.

We anticipate that many of the social and economic trends of the past will extend well into the future. Taiwan's vibrant economy is likely to support continued expansion of education, wage employment, urban living, higher living standards, and greater contact with the outside world. Given the clear linkage of these economic and social forces with family structure and process, we expect that many of Taiwan's current family trends will also continue. We anticipate that there will be further movement towards a nonfamilial mode of organization, additional weakening of the family chain, more autonomy of young people, fewer arranged marriages, later ages at marriage, more divorce, lower fertility, and more nuclear family living.

Unfortunately, our prediction of the continuation of recent trends into the immediate future provides few glimpses of the duration and ultimate levels of these trends. Our current theoretical and empirical knowledge do not allow us to anticipate when these trends will finally end and at what levels they will flatten out. Our current information also provides few clues about the emergence of any new causal forces that might counteract or accentuate recent trends. As a result, it is extremely difficult to predict how independent Chinese children will eventually become, how much of a dating culture will emerge, how high the premarital pregnancy rate will rise, where the increase in age at marriage will stop, how low fertility will drop, the extensiveness of nuclear family living, and the fraction of marriages that will eventually terminate in divorce.

It is equally difficult to make predictions about future changes in the dimensions of family life that have been most persistent in the past: commitment to the family chain, universal marriage and parenthood, and the care of children and elderly parents. On the one hand, we might expect that the continued weakening of the family chain will ultimately cause it to break, that increasing age at marriage will result in many remaining single throughout life, that the postponement of marriage and childbearing will eventually end in many people never experiencing parenthood, and that the trend toward nuclear residence will eventually result in even the elderly living independently. On the other hand, however, we might anticipate that core Chinese family values will continue to assert themselves and maintain people's commitment to the family chain, cause those postponing marriage to eventually enter the relationship, persuade everyone of the necessity of parenthood, and continue the co-residence of elderly parents with their children. While these questions about the future are of great interest to scholars, policymakers, and individual citizens, their answers, unfortunately, must await the future itself.

Although it is extremely difficult to predict where current and emerging family trends will eventually take Taiwanese family life, we are confident of the long-term continuation of one important principle. Central Chinese cultural values from the past have provided the guiding principles for Taiwan's recent familial adjustments to economic and social change, and we anticipate that these same core values will guide future family changes. Just as the family adaptations in Taiwan's past have been uniquely Chinese, so will be the changes of the future. We believe that the continuity of basic past elements of Chinese family structures and processes into the present augurs well for the persistence of distinctive Chinese family ways well into the future.

Appendix A

Sources of Data

A. Thornton and J. S. Chang

The data for the analyses reported in this book were drawn from several sources. Of central importance is a series of island-wide surveys conducted between 1965 and 1986 by the Taiwan Population Studies Center and by the Taiwan Provincial Institute of Family Planning. These surveys were conducted under the direction of Te-Hsiung Sun, Ming-Cheng Chang, and Hui-Sheng Lin. We have also drawn data from a series of censuses conducted in Taiwan across the twentieth century and from Taiwan's household registration system.

In this appendix we document the general outlines of the data sources used in the book. We focus first on several island-wide surveys, including a series of surveys of married women and a set of surveys of young women. Then we briefly discuss the available census and household registration data.

Survey Data

I. Surveys of Married Women

A series of six island-wide surveys of married women were conducted between 1965 and 1986, and these surveys constitute a primary source of data for this book. These surveys were designed to sample married women in the central childbearing ages and addressed questions concerning family relations, fertility, and family planning. They contain a wide range of family, social, economic, and demographic data, including rich material concerning the family and demographic histories of both the woman and her husband. Some of the surveys included older women and women who were not currently married but had been previously married. The specific sample for each survey is provided in table A.1.

The 1970 study was designed so that it could be used as a cross-sectional sample and as a panel study. The 1970 study reinterviewed women who were initially interviewed in the 1967 study. In order to make the 1970 study also cross-sectionally representative, women who

TABLE A.1 Summary of Island-Wide Married Women Survey Samples

Survey	Date	Age	N	Marital Status
I	Oct.–Nov. 1965	20–44	3,717	Currently married women
II	Oct.–Nov. 1967	20–44	4,986	Currently married women
III	Jan.–Mar. 1970	22–41	2,689	Currently married women
IV	July–Aug. 1973	20–39	5,540	Currently married women
V	Jan.–Feb. 1980	20–39	3,821	Currently married women
VI	Jan.–Mar. 1986	20–49	4,290	Ever-married women

had married since the 1967 interview were sampled and interviewed. In mid-1969, the husbands of approximately one-half of the 1967 sample were interviewed with a questionnaire that focused on the economic activities and statuses of the family, with particular attention to the sources and nature of income.

The 1980 survey included interviews with a subsample of the husbands and mothers-in-law of the women in the main sample. In addition, a second interview was obtained with the wife in the subsample of families chosen for additional study. The families chosen for more intensive study were selected to emphasize contrasts between rural and urban families. Consequently, that study interviewed husbands and mothers-in-law in about 260 families. In the supplemental surveys extensive information was obtained about the experiences and attitudes of the additional respondents (as well as the wife), permitting a broader analysis of Taiwanese family and household relationships than would be possible from just the interviews with the wives.

Each successive survey has collected increasingly extensive data on many aspects of the respondents' lives. The 1973 survey was particularly important in that many questions about family structure and history were first added to the series in that year. The material about family relationships and experiences was further expanded with the 1986 study. Thus, for some variables, the time series does not extend all the way back to 1965. However, more complete histories of personal and family experiences were collected in the more recent surveys, which helps to compensate for the smaller amounts of family information available from the earlier surveys. In most cases the questions asked in the earlier studies were retained in subsequent surveys. Great care was taken to ensure that exact question wording was maintained across surveys to enable trend analysis.

All the surveys collected information on the dates and sex of live births, and the number and dates of all pregnancies have been collected since the third round. Information on ever and current use of contraception and parity at the time of first use of contraception has been collected at each survey date. In addition, the fourth survey collected an extended history of contraceptive use which tracked methods used in each birth interval and the time of use for each method.

Increasingly detailed information for couples' residence histories has been collected since the first survey. In addition to the actual residence situation, data concerning visits and monetary exchange among family members have been collected. The most recent (sixth) survey collected not only current residence and residence history with the husband's family but the residence with the wife's family as well. Finally, the fifth and sixth surveys collected data on whether the respondent's parents lived with the husband's married brothers or sisters.

The 1973, 1980, and 1986 data collections focused attention on the premarital family and nonfamily experiences of the wives and their husbands. Of particular importance was information concerning schooling, employment, and living arrangements before marriage. The marriage process itself was studied, with questions concerning how the marriage was arranged, whether there was premarital sex with the husband, and what were the living arrangements at marriage. The 1986 study supplemented this information with more detailed questions about the timing and nature of employment in the work force and nonfamily residence before marriage. The 1986 study also expanded information about the courtship process with questions about the circumstances under which the husband was met, dating, engagement, and the timing of premarital sexual experience. The 1973, 1980, and 1986 surveys also collected information about attitudes and behavior on family relationships beyond this life, particularly regarding the importance of ancestors and the family line.

The same sampling design was used across all of the surveys of married women. The sample was selected in three stages. The first stage of the sampling was selected from four different types of administrative units grouped under the generic name of "township." These primary sampling units consisted of precincts of the five major cities (*chu*), entire small cities (*shih*), and urbanized and rural townships (*chen* and *hsiang*). The geographical universe, which consisted of the 331 nonaboriginal townships, was divided into twenty-seven strata based on three variables measuring levels of urbanization, education, and fertility.

Within strata, townships were geographically ordered, and fifty-six primary sampling units (townships) were selected systematically for the 1965 study. The primary sampling units (townships) were selected across the strata with probabilities proportional to the number of people in the

TABLE A.2   Summary of Island-Wide Young Women Surveys

Survey	Date	Age	N	Marital Status
I	1971	18–29	1,555	Unmarried women
			2,035	Married women
II	1978	18–29	701	Unmarried women
III	1984	15–29	1,791	Unmarried women
			1,351	Married women

universe within each township. Subsequent samples have been designed to maximize the probability of retaining these fifty-six original sample townships.

The basic administrative unit for sampling at the second stage was the block (*lin*). To ensure an adequate geographic distribution of the sample, blocks were listed according to their neighborhoods (*li*'s) and the neighborhoods were stratified geographically. The blocks within the selected townships were selected with probabilities proportional to the number of women in the study universe, and the actual selection was made by systematic sampling.

The sampling unit at the third stage of the design was the individual woman. The household register of each geographical unit selected was used as the frame for the list of eligible respondents. Three respondents were selected systematically from each sampled block. Women who had moved from the sampling area where they were selected were located and interviewed at their new locations.

II. Young Women Surveys

Three island-wide surveys of younger women, including both unmarried and married samples, were conducted between 1971 and 1984. The data collected included attitudes toward mate selection, age at marriage, family planning, and living arrangements after marriage. Marriage and fertility histories were also collected in the surveys. These studies also obtained information about knowledge and use of contraceptives. In addition, questions regarding social and economic issues were included. These surveys of young women followed the same basic sampling design used for the married women surveys as described before. That basic sampling design was adjusted to be appropriate for the surveys of young women. A summary of these three Young Women Surveys is presented in table A.2.

For the 1971 survey, the sample included both unmarried and married women aged 18 to 29. These women were selected with equal probability to represent unmarried and married women aged 18–29 who maintained their household registration in the 331 nonaboriginal townships in Taiwan as of August 1971.

The 1978 survey consisted of two samples. The first was a new sample of unmarried women aged 18–29. The second part of the 1978 study consisted of a follow-up of the 1971 sample. All of the unmarried women in the 1971 survey had their marital history updated through either a household register check or a home visit. This information permitted the use of the 1971 data to explain subsequent marital experiences. In addition, a subsample of people who had ever married by 1978 were interviewed again that year. These women were subsampled both from those who were married and from those who were still single in 1971. Totally, 1,666 married women aged 25–36 were in the 1978 survey (Lin 1988).

For the 1984 survey, the lower age limit was reduced to include younger women. This study drew a random stratified sample of both unmarried and married women aged 15 to 29. The single women aged 15–17 was a special subsample for policy concern regarding adolescent sexuality. The module on sexually related awareness, knowledge, attitudes, and behavior was developed particularly for this survey.

III. The 1984 Survey of Secondary School Students

In January 1984 the Taiwan Provincial Institute of Family Planning conducted an island-wide sample survey of adolescent sexual awareness, attitudes, and behavior. The sample for this study was drawn to represent students (both male and female primarily aged 15–19) in Taiwan's public and private senior and vocational high schools, as well as in five-year junior colleges. A two-stage stratified probability sample was drawn. At the first stage fifty-seven sample schools were drawn within strata defined by geographic area and school type with probability of selection proportional to the number of students. Second, 7,831 students were drawn from classes in all grade levels of the sample schools. These students represent 1% of all secondary students in Taiwan. To increase response validity, the questionnaires were completed anonymously, were largely multiple choice, and were administered with no teachers present (Cernada et al. 1986). The questionnaires included questions about social, economic, and demographic issues, as well as questions about dating and sexual behavior.

IV. The 1976 Value of Children Survey

The Value of Children Survey was conducted in 1976 by the Taiwan Provincial Institute of Family Planning. This island-wide survey interviewed a three-stage probability sample of 2,217 currently married women under age 45. In addition, 1,023 of their husbands and about 500 of their mothers-in-law were interviewed (Bulatao 1978). This survey utilized the basic sampling design used in the surveys of married women and young women. Data contained extensive social, economic, psychological, family, and demographic information. Extensive information regarding life values and the importance of the family chain was also collected.

V. Estimation of Sampling Errors and Statistical Significance

While the multistage sampling design used in these surveys enhances interviewing efficiency and cost effectiveness, it makes the precise estimation of sampling variability more complex and difficult than in simple random samples. This occurs because the multistage design produces sampling points that are geographically clustered, which adds an additional element to the sampling variability in the study. This usually results in the sampling errors in multistage samples exceeding those that would be produced by a simple random sample of the same size. Consequently, the estimation of sampling errors and statistical significance in multistage samples using the standard formulas of simple random sampling generally overestimates the true level of statistical significance. The influence of this design effect on sampling variability itself varies across different measures and subgroups of the population. Unfortunately, the estimation of sampling errors in multistage clustered designs across multiple surveys is difficult and time consuming. Further information about sampling variability in these surveys is provided by Kish et al. (1976) and Coombs and Freedman (1979).

Our approach to this problem was to estimate sampling errors and statistical significance using the standard formulas of simple random sampling but with multiple levels of statistical significance. By showing statistical significance from .05 to .001 (with simple random sample assumptions), the results can be interpreted at more conservative levels.

Household Registration Data

There has been a household registration system in Taiwan since 1905. This population register is widely recognized as producing vital statistics and demographic data of very high quality. In establishing the initial set of household registers during the colonial period, the Japanese not only recorded the composition of families but also determined the birthdates of all family members, as well as the date and means of their entry into the family (Wolf and Huang 1980). After the retrocession of Taiwan to the Republic of China, a series of Household Registration Statistics of Taiwan based on the household registration data have been published. Also, the *Taiwan Demographic Fact Books* have been available since 1961, which include age-specific data on fertility, mortality, migration, marriage, and employment-related statistics. In 1973 the procedures and statistical tables for the *Fact Books* were revised to enrich the contents of the statistics produced from the household registration data (1990 *Taiwan-Fukien Demographic Fact Book*).

Census Data

Seven censuses were conducted during the Japanese colonial period (1905, 1915, 1920, 1925, 1930, 1935, 1940) (Barclay 1954). Four population and housing censuses have been taken since the retrocession of Taiwan to the Republic of China (1956, 1966, 1980, 1990). The censuses include information about nationality, mobility, natality, education, economic characteristics, and housing conditions (Extract Report on the 1980 Census of Population and Housing). The censuses were designed so that the census data can be interfiled with the data obtained from the annual compilations of the household registration data.

Appendix B

Truncation Bias

A. Thornton

As we discussed in chapter 1, historical family change can be studied using one-time cross-sectional surveys that ask individuals to report retrospectively their experiences, relationships, or events at one age or position in the life course such as childhood, adolescence, young adulthood, or marriage. The experiences of the individuals are cross-classified by their birth or marriage cohort and the cohort differences interpreted as reflecting changes across historical time.

Many of our analyses of social change implementing this procedure utilize samples that are restricted to married women of childbearing years. Unfortunately, these sample limitations introduce a methodological problem: the differential truncation of marriage ages across the respective cohorts represented in the study. This means that the range of marriage ages is necessarily different for each cohort. This differential truncation of marriage ages occurs for both birth and marriage cohorts.

An example of the ways in which marriage ages are artificially and differentially truncated across birth and marriage cohorts in restricted samples is provided in table B.1. The data set used for this illustration is our 1986 study of ever-married women aged 20 to 49. The truncation bias problem using a birth cohort approach is demonstrated in columns 1 and 2 while columns 3 and 4 indicate the problem using marriage cohorts. Columns 2 and 4 list the ranges of ages at marriage that the study design permits for each of the birth and marriage cohorts in columns 1 and 3.

As columns 1 and 2 demonstrate, the range of marriage ages represented within each birth cohort shrinks monotonically from the earliest to the latest birth cohorts. While the data collection included all members of the birth cohort of 1937 who had married by age 49, the 1957 cohort included only those married by age 29 and the 1966 cohort was limited to those married by age 20. As a result of this reduction in the maximum ages at marriage included within the successive birth cohorts, each successive cohort is less representative of that cohort's total population.

As columns 3 and 4 of table B.1 show, the use of marriage rather

TABLE B.1 Ages at Marriage That Can Be Represented within Different Birth and Marriage Cohorts in a Sample of Ever-Married Women Aged 20–49 in 1986

Birth Cohort	Possible Ages at Marriage	Marriage Cohort	Possible Ages at Marriage
1937	0–49	1952	0–15
1942	0–44	1957	0–20
1947	0–39	1962	0–25
1952	0–34	1967	1–30
1957	0–29	1972	6–35
1962	0–24	1977	11–40
1966	0–20	1982	16–45
		1986	20–49

than birth cohort as the indicator of historical time provides a different, but still difficult, twist to the age-at-marriage truncation problem. With the marriage cohort approach, it is the most recent marriage cohorts that include women married at a wide range of ages, while earlier marriage cohorts are increasingly limited to women married at younger ages. While the marriage cohort of 1986 includes women married up through age 49, the marriage cohort of 1967 excludes women married over age 30 and women married older than 20 are excluded from the 1957 marriage cohort. Thus, the marital cohort approach makes the truncation effect work in the opposite direction from the way it operates with birth cohorts. Whereas the birth cohort approach truncates later cohorts toward younger marriages, marriage cohort analyses truncate earlier cohorts toward younger marriages.

The marital cohort approach also adds an additional complication to the truncation problem: the marriage cohorts differ not only in their upper bounds of marriage ages but in their lower bounds as well. There is no lower bound on possible ages at marriage for the earliest marital cohorts, but such a bound emerges with the marriage cohort of 1967 and becomes increasingly larger with each successive marriage cohort. This lower bound is substantially below the earliest ages at marriage for the marriage cohorts of the 1960s and 1970s, but by the marriage cohorts of the 1980s it is high enough to eliminate some marriages.

Of course, the seriousness of these age-at-marriage truncations depends upon the distributions of marital ages. In populations with very young marital ages, the imposition of an upper bound on age at marriage would have an inconsequential effect, whereas in populations with very old ages at marriage, an upper bound on age at marriage could seriously restrict the ability of a sample to represent the experience of the full birth or marriage cohort. Similarly, in a population with young ages at marriage, a lower bound on age at marriage could eliminate many of those in a cohort, while a lower bound on age at marriage for a cohort would have very little effect in a population with old ages at marriage.

Table 8.1 provides data useful to evaluate the importance of age at marriage truncation for our 1986 study of ever-married women. In 1956, the percentages of women ever married at ages 15–19, 20–24, and 25–29 were 11, 71, and 95%, respectively. At least 98% of all women older than 30 in 1956 had been married. These data suggest that the limitation of a marriage cohort in the 1950s to women married as teenagers would produce a major truncation of the cohort. However, enough of the women had married by their middle 20s that the exclusion of those married at older ages would produce only a moderate age at marriage truncation.

Age-at-marriage truncations are more serious for the birth cohorts of the 1960s, which reached adulthood in the 1980s, than they are for the marital cohorts of the 1950s. This is because of the substantial increases in age at marriage which have occurred in recent decades. The fraction of women ever married at ages 20–24 and 25–29 had fallen to 34 and 76%, respectively, in 1985 (table 8.1). In 1985, 91% of those aged 30–34 had ever been married, and at ages over 35 at least 94% had been married. These data suggest that the limitation of a birth cohort to those who had married before age 25 would produce a substantial truncation of the cohort. However, the limitation of a birth cohort reaching adulthood in the 1980s to those who had married before age 30 would not produce a substantial truncation of the birth cohort.

The increases in age at marriage during recent decades also reduce the importance of the lower bound on age at marriage for the marriage cohorts of the 1980s. Less than 2% of the first marriages in 1985 were to teenagers, and their exclusion from a marriage cohort would result in very little truncation.

The differential truncation of marriage ages across birth and marriage cohorts is a problem *only* if there is a correlation between age at marriage and the substantive behavior being studied. If women marrying as teenagers, in their 20s, and in their 30s all had the same characteristics—such as the same education and mate selection experience—the truncation of a birth or marriage cohort to those marrying as teenagers would produce no bias for the cohort as a whole. With no correlation between age at marriage and other characteristics, women drawn from any age-at-marriage group could adequately represent their whole marriage or birth cohort.

TABLE B.2 Educational Attainment and Premarital Sex by Marriage and Birth Cohort

	Percentage Reporting More than Junior High Education	Percentage Reporting Premarital Sex with Husband
Birth cohort		
1935–39	6	9
1940–44	10	13
1945–49	16	14
1950–54	25	23
1955–59	40	37
1960–64	34	53
Marriage cohort		
1955–59	2	11
1960–64	6	11
1965–69	8	16
1970–74	17	22
1975–79	31	35
1980–84	45	40

Note: Data abstracted from chapters 5 and 6.

However, if there is a correlation between age at marriage and the subject being studied, as there often is, the truncation of birth and marriage cohorts by age at marriage could bias several important results. First, the levels of the substantive variable—such as education and mate selection experience—would be biased for all cohorts. This would occur because the people excluded by the age-at-marriage truncation would be different from those who were included as representatives of a particular marriage or birth cohort. Second, there would be differential bias across cohorts because, as we have seen in table B.1, the amount of age-at-marriage truncation varies across cohorts. This differential bias across cohorts is important for studies of social change because any age-at-marriage truncation bias would be confounded with true historical change. Third, the confounding of age-at-marriage truncation bias effects with cohort effects operates in opposite directions for marriage and birth cohorts. This is true because age-at-marriage truncation increases from the past to the present for birth cohorts while decreasing over time for marriage cohorts.

Two illustrations of these potential age-at-marriage truncation biases are provided in table B.2. One considers educational trends while the other focuses on changes in premarital sex. Table B.2 lists by both birth and marriage cohort the percentage of women who received more than a junior high school education and who had premarital sex with their husbands.

Looking first at educational attainment, we see that both the birth and marriage cohort data demonstrate the same central story: dramatic increases in high school attendance across time. However, upon closer examination, we see important differences between the birth and marital cohort series which can be attributed to age-at-marriage truncation bias. First, the percentage attending high school appears to be greater for the earliest birth cohorts than for the earliest marital cohorts. Second, the percentage attending high school is lower for the latest birth cohorts than for the latest marital cohorts. In fact, the birth cohort series suggests that educational attainment declined between the birth cohort of 1955–59 and that of 1960–64, a decline that does not exist in the marriage cohort series. Finally, we note that the increase in educational attainment between the earliest and latest cohorts is greater for the marital cohort series than for the birth cohort series. Whereas the percentage going beyond junior high school increased by 28 percentage points (from 6 to 34%) across birth cohorts, the increase across marriage cohorts was 43 percentage points (from 2 to 45%).

We attribute these differences, at least in part, to age-at-marriage truncation bias. We know that there is a positive association between age at marriage and educational attainment (see chap. 9). Because of the strong age-at-marriage truncation among the earlier marital cohorts, the observed educational attainments of these marriage cohorts are depressed below their actual levels. Similarly, the strong age-at-marriage truncation among the later birth cohorts artificially depresses the observed educational attainments of these cohorts. This truncation bias for the latest birth cohort is so large that it makes it appear that education decreased for this cohort when we know from other sources that education was increasing across these cohorts (see chap. 3). The negative truncation biases on education for the early marriage cohorts and late birth cohorts result in the observed trends being greater across marital than across birth cohorts.

Turning now to the premarital sex data in table B.2, we find again that both the marriage and birth cohort series reveal the same big picture—increasing incidence of premarital sex—but demonstrate important differences in details. In this case, however, the estimates of the prevalence of premarital sex are higher for the earliest marital cohorts than for the earliest birth cohorts, while premarital sexual prevalence is lower in the latest marital cohorts than in the latest birth cohorts. As a result, the increase in premarital sex appears to be smaller across marriage cohorts than across birth cohorts.

Again, we interpret these differences between the birth and marriage cohort data primarily in terms of age-at-marriage truncation bias. However, whereas the relationship between age at marriage and education is positive, the relationship between age at marriage and premarital sex is negative (see chap. 6). Consequently, the limitation of the earliest marital cohorts to those marrying young artificially inflates the percentage of the earliest marital cohorts having premarital sex. Similarly, the artificial limitation of the latest birth cohorts to those marrying young inflates the estimate of those experiencing premarital sex. Since, as chapter 6 documents, the negative relationship between age at marriage and premarital sex increased over time, the artificial inflation of the estimates for the latest birth cohorts was greater than the inflation of the estimates for the earliest marriage cohorts.

Our experience with the age-at-marriage truncation problem has led to several decisions concerning the conduct and presentation of our analyses. First, we have accorded this problem sufficient importance that we have conducted a substantial proportion of our analyses of historical trends using both marriage and birth cohorts. In a number of cases we have found the differences sufficiently important to present results for both marriage and birth cohorts.

Second, since the marriage and cohort time series are generally biased in opposite directions by the age-at-marriage truncation bias, we believe that the two time series provide an upper and lower bound on the amount of change that has actually occurred. That is, the "true" amount of change probably lies somewhere between the trends estimated by the two series. However, we also believe that in most cases the actual magnitude of historical change is probably closer to the marriage cohort series than to the birth cohort series. This is based on the observation that age-at-marriage truncation is greater for the later birth cohorts than for the earlier marital cohorts.

Finally, the marriage cohort data are probably more useful than the birth cohort data for characterizing behavior and experience in Taiwan's very recent past. This conclusion is based on the fact that the most recent marriage cohorts contain a broad range of ages at marriage while the most recent birth cohorts are limited to those who married relatively young.

REFERENCES

Ahern, Emily Martin. 1971. *The Cult of the Dead in Ch'inan, Taiwan: A Study of Ancestor Worship in a Four-Lineage Community.* Ann Arbor, MI: University Microfilms.

———. 1973. *The Cult of the Dead in a Chinese Village.* Stanford: Stanford University Press.

Alison, Archibald. 1840. *The Principles of Population.* Vol. 1. Edinburgh: William Blackwood and Sons.

Alwin, Duane F. 1988. "Religion in Detroit, 1958 to 1988." Unpublished paper, Institute for Social Research, University of Michigan, Ann Arbor.

Anderson, Michael. 1971. *Family Structure in Nineteenth Century Lancashire.* London: Cambridge University Press.

———. 1972. "Household Structure and the Industrial Revolution; Mid-Nineteenth Century Preston in Comparative Perspective." In *Household and Family in Past Time,* ed. Peter Laslett, pp. 215–35. Cambridge: Cambridge University Press.

———. 1986. *Approaches to the History of the Western Family, 1500–1914.* London: Macmillan.

Arrigo, Linda G. 1980. "The Industrial Work Force of Young Women in Taiwan." *Bulletin of Concerned Asian Scholars* 12 (2) (April/June): 25–38.

Atoh, Makoto. 1988. "Changes in Family Patterns in Japan." Seminar on Theories of Family Change, IUSSP Committee on Family Demography and Life Cycle, 29 November–2 December, Tokyo, Japan.

———. 1990. "Attitudes toward Marriage among the Youth: Causes for the Recent Rise in the Proportion Single among the Twenties in Japan." In *Summary of Twentieth National Survey on Family Planning,* Population Problems Research Council. Tokyo: The Mainichi Shinmbun.

Bachman, Jerald G. 1983. "Premature Affluence: Do High School Students Earn too Much?" *Economic Outlook USA* 10 (3) (Summer): 64–67.

Baker, Hugh D. R. 1968. *A Chinese Lineage Village: Sheung Shi.* Stanford: Stanford University Press.

———. 1979. *Chinese Family and Kinship.* New York: Columbia University Press.

Barclay, George W. 1954. *Colonial Development and Population in Taiwan.* Princeton: Princeton University Press.

Barclay, George W., Ansley J. Coale, Michael A. Stoto, and James T. Trussell.

1976. "A Reassessment of the Demography of Traditional Rural China." *Population Index* 42 (4) (October): 606–35.

Barnes, John A. 1951. *Marriage in a Changing Society: A Study in Structural Change among the Fort Jameson Ngoni.* Published for the Rhodes-Livingstone Institute by Oxford University Press, New York.

Barrett, Richard E. 1980. "Short Term Trends in Bastardy in Taiwan." *Journal of Family History* 5 (3): 293–312.

———. 1985. "Demographic Processes in China since the Nineteenth Century." Unpublished book manuscript.

———. 1989. "The Changing Status of Women in Taiwan." In *Taiwan: A Newly Industrialized State,* ed. Hsin-Huang Michael Hsiao, Wei-Yuan Cheng, and Hou-Sheng Chan, pp. 463–92. Taipei, Taiwan: Department of Sociology, National Taiwan University.

Bongaarts, John, Thomas K. Burch, and Kenneth W. Wachter, eds. 1987. *Family Demography: Methods and Their Applications.* Oxford: Oxford University Press.

Brandon, Anastasia J. 1990. "Marriage Dissolution, Remarriage, and Childbearing in West Africa." Ph.D. diss., University of Pennsylvania, Philadelphia.

Bulatao, Rodolfo A. 1978. "On the Nature of the Value of Children in Taiwan." *Current Studies on the Value of Children,* no. 60-A. Honolulu: East-West Population Institute.

Burgess, Ernest W., and Harvey J. Locke. [1945] 1953. *The Family: From Institution to Companionship.* New York: American Book Company.

Caldwell, John C. 1976. "Toward A Restatement of Demographic Transition Theory." *Population and Development Review* 2 (3 and 4) (September and December): 321–66.

———. 1982. *Theory of Fertility Decline.* New York: Academic Press.

Caldwell, John C., P. H. Reddy, and Pat Caldwell. 1983. "The Causes of Marriage Change in South India." *Population Studies* 37 (3) (November): 343–61.

Casterline, John B. 1980. "The Determinants of Rising Female Age at Marriage: Taiwan, 1905–1976." Ph.D. diss., University of Michigan, Ann Arbor.

Cernada, George P., Ming-Cheng Chang, Hui-Sheng Lin, Te-Hsiung Sun, and Ching-Ching Chen Cernada. 1986. "Implications for Adolescent Sex Education in Taiwan." *Studies in Family Planning* 17 (4) (July/August): 181–87.

Chang, Chi-Yun, ed. 1981. *Chung-Hua Encyclopedia.* Vol. 3. Taipei, Taiwan: Chinese Cultural University and Chung-Hua Scholarly Association. (In Chinese.)

Chang, Jui-Shan. 1990. "The Transition to Sexual Experience for Women in Taiwan." Ph.D. diss., University of Michigan, Ann Arbor.

———. 1991. "Change and Persistence: Autonomy of Dating, Engagement, and Premarital Sex for Women in Taiwan." Unpublished manuscript.

Chang, Ming-Cheng. 1989. "Fertility Transition and Shifting Attitudes toward Intergeneration Support—The Case of Taiwan." Paper presented at the Conference of Institutional Transition in Changing Societies, Taipei, Taiwan.

———. 1990. "Fertility Transition and the Change in Aging Population Structure in Taiwan Area." Paper presented at the Demographic Transition and Socio-Economic Development Seminar, Institute of Economics, Academia Sinica, Taipei, Taiwan.

Chang, Ming-Cheng, Ronald Freedman and Te-Hsiung Sun. 1981. "Trends in Fertility, Family Size Preferences, and Family Planning Practice: Taiwan, 1961–80." *Studies in Family Planning* 12 (5) (May): 211–28.

Chang, Ming-Cheng, Ronald Freedman, and Te-Hsiung Sun. 1987. "Trends in Fertility, Family Size Preferences, and Family Planning Practice: Taiwan, 1961–85." *Studies in Family Planning* 18 (6) (November/December): 320–37.

Chao, Paul. 1983. *Chinese Kinship*. London: Kegan Paul.

Chekki, Danesh A. 1974. *Modernization and Kin Network*. Leiden, The Netherlands: E. J. Brill.

Chen, Chung-Min. 1985. "Dowry and Inheritance." In *The Chinese Family and Its Ritual Behavior,* ed. Jih-Chang Hsieh and Ying-Chang Chuang, pp. 117–27. Monograph series B, no. 15. Taipei, Taiwan: Institute of Ethnology, Academia Sinica.

Chen, Kuanjeng. 1986. "On the Change of Household Composition in Taiwan." Paper presented at the annual meeting of the American Sociological Association, New York.

Cherlin, Andrew. J. 1981. *Marriage, Divorce, and Remarriage*. Cambridge, MA: Harvard University Press.

Chester, Robert, ed. 1977. *Divorce in Europe*. Leiden, The Netherlands: Martinus Nijhoff, Social Sciences Division.

Cheung, Paul P. L. 1988. "Marriage Market, Timing, and Policy in Singapore." Paper presented at the annual meeting of the Population Association of America, New Orleans.

———. 1990. "Consequences of Low Fertility in Singapore." Paper presented at the annual meeting of the Population Association of America, Toronto.

Chuang, Ying-Chang. 1973. "The Adaptation of Family to Modernization in Rural Taiwan: A Case Study." *Bulletin of the Institute of Ethnology* 34:88. Taiwan, R.O.C.: Academica Sinica.

———. 1987. "A Comparison of Hakkien and Hakka Ancestor Worship." Paper presented at the annual meeting of the American Anthropological Association, Chicago.

Coale, Ansley J. 1971. "Age Patterns of Marriage." *Population Studies* 5 (2): 193–214.

———. 1977. "The Development of New Models of Nuptiality and Fertility." *Population, numero special,* pp. 131–54.

Coale, Ansley J., and Chen Sheng Li. 1987. "Basic Data on Fertility in the Provinces of China, 1940–82," no. 104. Honolulu: East-West Population Institute.

Coale, Ansley J., and James T. Trussell. 1974. "Model Fertility Schedules: Variations in the Age Structure of Childbearing in Human Populations." *Population Index* 40 (2): 185–258.

Coale, Ansley J., and Susan Cotts Watkins, eds. 1986. *The Decline of Fertility in Europe*. Princeton: Princeton University Press.

Cohen, Myron L. 1970. "Development Process in the Chinese Domestic Group." In *Family and Kinship in Chinese Society*, ed. Maurice Freedman, pp. 21–36. Stanford: Stanford University Press.

———. 1976. *House United, House Divided: The Chinese Family in Taiwan*. New York: Columbia University Press.

———. 1985. "Lineage Development and the Family in China." In *The Chinese Family and Its Ritual Behavior*, ed. Jih-Chang Hsieh and Ying-Chang Chuang, pp. 210–18. Monograph series B, no. 15. Taipei Taiwan: Institute of Ethnology, Academia Sinica.

Coombs, Clyde H., Lolagene C. Coombs, and Gary H. McClelland. 1975. "Preference Scales for Number and Sex of Children." *Population Studies* 29 (2): 273–98.

Coombs, Lolagene C. 1974. "The Measurement of Family Size Preferences and Subsequent Fertility." *Demography* 11 (4): 587–611.

Coombs, Lolagene C., and Ronald Freedman. 1979. "Some Roots of Preference: Roles, Activities and Familial Values." *Demography* 16:339–76.

Council for Economic Planning and Development, Manpower Planning Department. 1986. *Social Welfare Indicators of Republic of China, 1986*. Taipei, Taiwan: Executive Yuan.

———. 1988. *Social Welfare Indicators of Republic of China, 1988*. Taipei, Taiwan: Executive Yuan.

———. 1989. *Social Welfare Indicators of Republic of China, 1989*. Taipei, Taiwan: Executive Yuan.

Council for International Economic Cooperation and Development. 1981. *Taiwan Statistical Data Book*. Taipei, Taiwan: Council for International Economic Cooperation and Development.

———. 1987. *Taiwan Statistical Data Book*. Taipei, Taiwan: Council for International Economic Cooperation and Development.

———. 1988. *Taiwan Statistical Data Book*. Taipei, Taiwan: Council for International Economic Cooperation and Development.

———. 1989. *Taiwan Statistical Data Book*. Taipei, Taiwan: Council for International Economic Cooperation and Development.

Cox, D. R. 1972. "Regression Models and Life Tables." *Journal of the Royal Statistical Society* B34:187–202.

Davis, Kingsley. 1955. "Institutional Patterns Favoring High Fertility in Underdeveloped Areas." *Eugenics Quarterly* 2:33–9.

———. 1984. "Wives and Work: The Sex Role Revolution and Its Consequences." *Population and Development Review* 10 (3) (September): 397–417.

Demographic Reference: Taiwan, Republic of China. Vol. 2. 1965. Taichung, Taiwan: Taiwan Population Studies Center.

Demos, John. 1970. *A Little Commonwealth: Family Life in Plymouth Colony*. New York: Oxford University Press.

de Tocqueville, Alexis. [1863] 1955. *Democracy in America*. Cambridge: Sever and Francis.

Diamond, Norma. 1969. *K'un Shen: A Taiwan Village*. New York: Holt, Rinehart, and Winston.

———. 1979. "Women and Industry in Taiwan." *Modern China* 5:317–40.

Directorate-General of Budgets, Accounts and Statistics. 1961. *Statistical Abstract of the Republic of China, 1961.* Taipei, Taiwan: Executive Yuan.*

———. 1964. *Statistical Abstract of the Republic of China, 1964.* Taipei, Taiwan: Executive Yuan.

———. 1966. *Statistical Abstract of the Republic of China, 1966.* Taipei, Taiwan: Executive Yuan.

———. 1968. *Statistical Abstract of the Republic of China, 1968.* Taipei, Taiwan: Executive Yuan.

———. 1971. *Statistical Abstract of the Republic of China, 1971.* Taipei, Taiwan: Executive Yuan.

———. 1975. *Statistical Yearbook of Republic of China, 1975.* Taipei, Taiwan: Executive Yuan.

———. 1978. *Statistical Yearbook of Republic of China, 1976.* Taipei, Taiwan: Executive Yuan.

———. 1984. *Report on Results of Readjustment Estimates of Labor for 1984.* Taipei, Taiwan: Executive Yuan.

———. 1988a. *Statistical Yearbook of Republic of China, 1988.* Taipei, Taiwan: Executive Yuan.

———. 1988b. *National Income in Taiwan Area of the Republic of China, 1988.* Taipei, Taiwan, Executive Yuan.

———. 1988c. *Report on the Survey of Personal Income Distribution in Taiwan Area of the Republic of China, 1987.* Taipei, Taiwan: Executive Yuan.

———. 1989a. *Abstract of Employment and Earnings Statistics in Taiwan Area of R.O.C., 1988.* Taipei, Taiwan: Executive Yuan.

———. 1989b. *Statistical Yearbook of the Republic of China, 1989.* Taipei, Taiwan: Executive Yuan.

———. 1989c. *Report on the Survey of Personal Income Distribution in Taiwan Area of the R.O.C., 1988.* Taipei, Taiwan: Executive Yuan.

———. 1989d. *Yearbook of Manpower Statistics, Taiwan Area, Republic of China, 1988.* Taipei, Taiwan: Executive Yuan.

———. 1990. *National Income in Taiwan Area of the Republic of China, 1990.* Taipei, Taiwan: Executive Yuan.

Dublin, T. 1979. *Women at Work.* New York: Columbia University Press.

Dull, Jack L. 1978. "Marriage and Divorce in Han China: A Glimpse at 'Pre-Confucian' Society." In *Chinese Family Law and Social Change,* ed. David C. Buxbaum, pp. 23–74. Seattle: University of Washington Press.

Durch, Jane S. 1980. *Nuptiality Patterns in Developing Countries: Implications for Fertility.* Washington, D.C.: Population Reference Bureau.

Durkheim, Emile. 1978. *On Institutional Analysis.* Edited, translated, and with an introduction by Mark Traugott. Chicago: University of Chicago Press.

---

*Starting in 1975 publications from this office cited here appear as the Directorate-General of Budget, Accounting, and Statistics.

―――. 1984. *The Division of Labor in Society*. New York: Free Press.

Early, Frances H. 1982. "The French-Canadian Family Economy and Standard-of-Living in Lowell, Massachusetts, 1870." *Journal of Family History* 7 (2): 180–99.

Easterlin, Richard A. 1980. *Birth and Fortune*. New York: Basic Books.

Elder, Glen H., Jr. 1977. "Family History and the Life Course." *Journal of Family History* 2 (4): 279–304.

―――. 1987. "Family and Lives: Some Development in Life-Course Studies." *Journal of Family History* 12 (1–3): 179–99.

Featherman, David L., and Richard M. Lerner. 1985. "Ontogenesis and Socio-genesis: Problematics for Theory and Research about Development and Socialization across the Lifespan." *American Sociological Review* 50 (5) (October): 659–76.

Feeney, Griffith. 1985. "Progression to First Marriage in Japan: 1870–1980," no. 24. Tokyo: Nihon University Population Research Institute.

―――. 1990. "The Demography of Aging in Japan: 1950–2025," no. 55. Tokyo: Nihon University Population Research Institute.

―――. 1991. "Fertility Decline in Taiwan: A Study Using Parity Progression Ratios." *Demography* 28 (3) (August): 467–79.

Fei, Hsiao-Tung. 1939. *Peasant Life in China: A Field Study of Country Life in the Yangtze Valley*. London: Kegan Paul.

Fei, John C. H., Gustav Ranis, and Shirley W. Y. Kuo. 1979. *Growth with Equity, the Taiwan Case*. New York: Oxford University Press.

Fischer, Claude S. 1976. *The Urban Experience*. New York: Harcourt Brace Jovanovich.

Free China Journal, 1/23/89, Kwang Hwa Publishing Co., Taipei, Taiwan, Republic of China.

Freedman, Deborah S. 1967. "The Role of Consumption of Modern Durables in a Developing Economy: The Case of Taiwan." Ph.D. diss., University of Michigan, Ann Arbor.

Freedman, Maurice. 1958. *Lineage Organization in Southeastern China*. London: University of Athlone Press.

―――. 1964. "The Family in China, Past and Present." In *Modern China*, ed. Albert Feuerwerker, pp. 27–40. Englewood Cliffs, NJ: Prentice-Hall.

―――. 1966. *Chinese Lineage and Society: Fukien and Kwangtung*. New York: Humanities Press.

―――. 1970b. "Ritual Aspects of Chinese Kinship and Marriage." In *Family and Kinship in Chinese Society*, ed. Maurice Freedman, pp. 163–87. Stanford: Stanford University Press.

―――. 1979. *The Study of Chinese Society*. Stanford: Stanford University Press.

Freedman, Maurice, ed. 1970a. *Family and Kinship in Chinese Society*. Stanford: Stanford University Press.

Freedman, Ronald, and Arjun L. Adlakha. 1968. "Recent Fertility Declines in Hong Kong: The Role of the Changing Age Structure." *Population Studies* 22 (2): 181–98.

Freedman, Ronald, and John Casterline. 1979. "Nuptiality and Fertility in Taiwan." In *Nuptiality and Fertility,* ed. Lado T. Ruzicka, pp. 61–9. Liege, Belgium: Ordina.

Freedman, Ronald, Ming-Cheng Chang, and Te-Hsiung Sun. 1982. "Household Composition, Extended Kinship, and Reproduction in Taiwan: 1973–1980." *Population Studies* 36:395–411.

Freedman, Ronald, and John Y. Takeshita. 1969. *Family Planning in Taiwan.* Princeton: Princeton University Press.

Fricke, Thomas E., Sabiha H. Syed, and Peter C. Smith. 1986. "Rural Punjabi Social Organization and Marriage Timing Strategies in Pakistan." *Demography* 23 (4): 489–508.

Fricke, Thomas E., Arland Thornton, and Dilli R. Dahal. 1990. "Family Organization and the Wage Labor Transition in a Tamang Community of Nepal." *Human Ecology* 18:283–313.

Fried, Morton H. 1953. *Fabric of Chinese Society: A Study of the Social Life of a Chinese County Seat.* New York: Praeger.

Gallin, Bernard. 1966. *Hsin Hsing, Taiwan: A Chinese Village in Change.* Berkeley: University of California Press.

———. 1978. "Rural to Urban Migration in Taiwan: Its Impact on Chinese Family and Kinship." In *Chinese Family Law and Social Change in Historical and Comparative Perspective,* ed. David C. Buxbaum, pp. 261–82. Seattle: University of Washington Press.

Gallin, Bernard, and Rita S. Gallin. 1980. "Recent Socio-Economic Changes and Development in Rural Taiwan." Paper presented at the International Conference on Sinology, Academia Sinica, 15–17 August, Taipei, Taiwan.

———. 1985. "Matrilateral and Affinal Relationships in Changing Chinese Society." In *The Chinese Family and Its Ritual Behavior,* ed. Jih-Chang Hsieh and Ying-Chang Chuang, pp. 101–16. Monograph series B, no. 15. Taipei, Taiwan: Institute of Ethnology, Academia Sinica.

Gates, Hill. 1987. *Chinese Working Class Lives: Getting By in Taiwan.* Ithaca, NY: Cornell University Press.

Geertz, Hildred. 1961. *The Javanese Family.* New York: Free Press.

Gernet, Jacques. 1982. *A History of Chinese Civilization.* Translated from the French by J. R. Foster. Cambridge: Cambridge University Press.

Glenn, Norval D. 1976. "Cohort Analysts' Futile Quest: Statistical Attempts to Separate Age, Period, and Cohort Effects." *American Sociological Review* 41:900–904.

———. 1987. "Social Trends in the United States: Evidence from Sample Surveys." *Public Opinion Quarterly* 51:S109–26.

Goldstein, Sidney. 1985. "Forms of Mobility and Policy Implications: A Comparison of Thailand and China." Eighth Annual Amos H. Hawley Lecture, Population Studies Center, University of Michigan, Ann Arbor.

Goode, William J. 1963. *World Revolution and Family Patterns.* New York: Free Press.

———. 1970. *World Revolution and Family Patterns,* 2d ed. New York: Free Press.

———. 1982. *The Family.* Englewood Cliffs, NJ: Prentice-Hall.

Goody, Esther N. 1962. "Conjugal Separation and Divorce among the Gonja of Northern Ghana." In *Marriage in Tribal Societies,* ed. Meyer Fortes, pp. 14–54. Cambridge: Cambridge University Press.

Greenhalgh, Susan. 1982a. "Demographic Differentiation and the Distribution of Income: The Taiwan Case." Ph.D. diss., Department of Anthropology, Columbia University.

———. 1982b. "Income Units: The Ethnographic Alternative to Standardization." *Population and Development Review* 8 (suppl.): 70–91.

———. 1984. "Networks and Their Nodes: Urban Society on Taiwan." *China Quarterly* 99 (9): 529–52.

———. 1985. "Sexual Stratification: The Other Side of 'Growth with Equity' in East Asia." *Population and Development Review* 11 (2): 265–314.

———. 1988. "Families and Networks in Taiwan's Economic Development." In *Contending Approaches to the Political Economy of Taiwan,* ed. Edwin A. Winckler and Susan Greenhalgh, pp. 224–45. Armonk, NY: M. E. Sharpe.

———. 1990. "Land Reform and Family Entrepreneurship in East Asia." In *Rural Development and Population: Institutions and Policy,* ed. Geoffrey McNicoll and Mead Cain, pp. 77–118. New York: Oxford University Press.

Groves, Ernest R., and William F. Ogburn. 1928. *American Marriage and Family Relationships.* New York: Henry Holt and Co.

Guttentag, Marcia, and Paul F. Secord. 1983. *Too Many Women?* Beverly Hills, CA: Sage Publications.

Hagestad, Gunhild O., and Bernice L. Neugarten. 1985. "Age and the Life Course." In *Handbook of Aging and the Social Sciences,* 2d ed., ed. Robert H. Binstock and Ethel Shanas. New York: Van Nostrand Reinhold.

Hajnal, John. 1965. "European Marriage Patterns in Perspective." In *Population in History,* ed. David V. Glass and David E. C. Eversley. Chicago: Aldine Publishing Co.

———. 1982. "Two Kinds of Preindustrial Household Formation System." *Population and Development Review* 8:449–94.

Hamilton, Gary G., and Cheng-Shu Kao. 1988. "The Institutional Foundations of Chinese Business in the Family Firm in Taiwan." Program in East Asian Culture and Development Research, Working Paper no. 8. Institute for Governmental Affairs, University of California, Davis.

Hanada, Kyo, Tatsuya Itoh, and Shigemi Kono. 1988. "The Future of Japanese Families: A Micro Simulation Study." Seminar on Theories of Family Change, IUSSP Committee on Family Demography and Life Cycle, 29 November–2 December, Tokyo.

Hanlan, James P. 1981. "The Working Population of Manchester, New Hampshire: 1840–1886." *Studies in American History and Culture* (29). Ann Arbor: UMI Research Press.

Hareven, Tamara K. 1982. *Family Time and Industrial Time.* New York: Cambridge University Press.

Harrell, Stevan. 1982. *Ploughshare Village: Culture and Context in Taiwan.* Seattle: University of Seattle Press.

Hawley, Amos H. 1971. *Urban Society.* New York: Ronald Press.

Hermalin, Albert I. 1978. "Spatial Analysis of Family Planning Program Effects in Taiwan, 1966–72," no. 48. Honolulu: East-West Population Institute.

Hermalin, Albert I., and William Lavely. 1979. "Agricultural Development and Fertility Change in Taiwan." Paper presented at annual meeting of the Population Association of America, Philadelphia, Pennsylvania.

Hermalin, Albert I., Mary Beth Ofstedal, and Chi Li. 1991. "The Kin Availability of the Elderly in Taiwan: Who's Available and Where Are They?" Paper prepared for the 44th Annual Scientific Meeting of the Gerontological Society of America, San Francisco.

Hirosima, Kiyosi. 1988. "Does Very Low Fertility Accelerate Nuclearization? Seminar on Theories of Family Change." IUSSP Committee on Family Demography and Life Cycle, 29 November–2 December, Tokyo.

Ho, Ping-Ti. 1962. *The Ladder of Success in Imperial China: Aspects of Social Mobility, 1368–1911.* New York: Columbia University Press.

Ho, Samuel P. S. 1968. "Agricultural Transformation under Colonialism: The Case of Taiwan." *Journal of Economic History* 28 (3): 329–32.

———. 1978. *Economic Development of Taiwan, 1860–1970.* New Haven: Yale University Press.

Ho, Yhi-Min. 1966. *Agricultural Development of Taiwan, 1903–1960.* Nashville: Vanderbilt University Press.

Hofferth, Sandra L., Joan R. Kahn, and Wendy Baldwin. 1987. "Premarital Sexual Activity among U.S. Teenage Women over the Past Three Decades." *Family Planning Perspectives* 19 (2) (March/April): 46–53.

Hsing, Mo-Huan. 1971. *Taiwan: Industrialization and Trade Policies.* London: Oxford University Press.

Hsu, Francis L. K. 1971. *Under the Ancestors' Shadow: Kinship, Personality and Social Mobility in China.* Stanford: Stanford University Press.

Hsueh, Li-Min. 1989. "Judging Standards of Living." *Free China Review* 39 (10): 10–15.

Hu, Tai-Li. 1984. *My Mother-in-Law's Village: Rural Industrialization and Change in Taiwan.* Taipei, Taiwan: Institute of Ethnology, Academia Sinica.

Huang, Nora Chiang. 1984. "The Migration of Rural Women to Taipei." In *Women in the Cities of Asia: Migration and Urban Adaptation,* ed. James T. Fawcett, Siew-Ean Khoo, and Peter C. Smith, pp. 247–69. Boulder, CO: Westview Press.

Hull, Terrence H., and Valerie J. Hull. 1977. "Indonesia." In *The Persistence of High Fertility,* ed. John C. Caldwell, pp. 827–96. Canberra: Australian National University.

Inkeles, Alex, and David H. Smith. 1974. *Becoming Modern: Individual Change in Six Developing Countries.* Cambridge, MA: Harvard University Press.

Jacoby, Neil. 1966. *U.S. Aid to Taiwan.* New York: Praeger.

Jiang, Ping-Lun, and Vincent Shen. 1989. "Compound-Complex Growing Pains. Interview translated into English by Amy Lo." *Free China Review* 39 (10) (October): 16–21.

Johnson, Kay Ann. 1983. *Women, the Family, and Peasant Revolution in China.* Chicago: University of Chicago Press.

Joint Commission on Rural Reconstruction, Rural Economics Division. 1966. *Agricultural Statistics, 1901–1965.* In *Economic Digest Series,* no. 18. Taipei, Taiwan: Joint Commission on Rural Reconstruction.

———. 1977. *Taiwan Agricultural Statistics, 1961–1975.* In *Economic Digest Series,* no. 22. Taipei, Taiwan: Joint Commission on Rural Reconstruction.

Jordan, David K. 1972. *Gods, Ghosts, and Ancestors.* Berkeley: University of California Press.

———. 1985. "Sworn Brothers: A Study in Chinese Ritual Kinship." In *The Chinese Family and Its Ritual Behavior,* ed. Jih-Chang Hsieh and Ying-Chang Chuang, pp. 232–62. Monograph Series B, no. 15. Taipei, Taiwan: Institute of Ethnology, Academia Sinica.

Kahn, Robert L., and Toni C. Antonucci. 1981. "Convoys of Social Support: A Life-Course Approach." In *Aging: Social Change,* ed. James G. March (ed. in chief), Sara B. Kiesler, James N. Morgan, and Valerie Kincade Oppenheimer, pp. 383–405. New York: Academic Press.

Kessinger, Tom G. 1974. *Vilayatpur 1848–1968: Social and Economic Change in a North Indian Village.* Berkeley: University of California Press.

Kirby, Stuart. 1960. *Rural Progress in Taiwan.* Taipei, Taiwan: Chinese-American Joint Commission on Rural Reconstruction.

Kish, Leslie, Robert M. Groves, and Karol P. Krotki. 1976. *Sampling Errors for Fertility Surveys.* Occasional Paper of the World Fertility Survey, no. 17. Voorburg, The Netherlands: International Statistical Institute.

Klass, Morton. 1978. *From Field to Factory: Community Structure and Industrialization in West Bengal.* Philadelphia: Institute for the Study of Human Issues.

Kobrin, Francis E. 1976. "The Fall of Household Size and the Rise of the Primary Individual in the United States." *Demography* 13 (1) (February): 127–38.

Kojima, Hiroshi. 1989. "Intergenerational Household Extension in Japan." In *Ethnicity and the New Family Economy,* ed. Frances K. Goldscheider and Calvin Goldscheider, pp. 163–84. Boulder, CO: Westview Press.

Kumagai, Fumie. 1983. "Changing Divorce in Japan." *Journal of Family History* 8 (1): 85–107.

———. N.d. "Families in Japan: Beliefs and Realities." *Journal of Comparative Family Studies,* forthcoming.

Kung, Lydia. 1983. "Factory Women in Taiwan." *Studies in Cultural Anthropology* (5). Ann Arbor, MI: UMI Research Press.

Kussmaul, Ann. 1981. *Servants in Husbandry in Early Modern England.* Cambridge: Cambridge University Press.

Lamley, Harry J. 1970. "The 1895 Taiwan War of Resistance: Local Chinese Efforts against a Foreign Power." In *Taiwan: Studies in Chinese Local History,* ed. Leonard H. D. Gordon, pp. 23–77. New York: Columbia University Press.

———. 1981. "Subethnic Rivalry in the Ch'ing Period." In *The Anthropology of Taiwanese Society,* ed. Emily Ahern Martin and Hill Gates, pp. 282–318. Stanford: Stanford University Press.

Lang, Olga. [1946] 1968. *Chinese Family and Society*. Hamden, CT: Archon Books.

Laslett, Peter, ed. 1974. *Household and Family in Past Time*. London: Cambridge University Press.

———. 1978. *Family Life and Illicit Love in Earlier Generations*. Cambridge: Cambridge University Press.

———. 1984. *The World We Have Lost: England before the Industrial Age*, 3d ed. New York: Charles Scribner's Sons.

———. 1987. "The Character of Familial History, Its Limitations and the Conditions for Its Proper Pursuit." *Journal of Family History* 12 (1–2): 263–84.

Lavely, William. 1982. "Industrialization and Household Structure in Rural Taiwan." Ph.D. diss., University of Michigan, Ann Arbor.

Lavely, William, and Li Bohua. 1985. "A Tentative Survey on Family Structure in Liaoning, Hebei, and Fujian Provinces." Paper presented at the Symposium on China's One-per-Thousand National Fertility Survey, 14–18 October, Beijing, China.

Lee, Hung-Tak, and Nam-Hoon Cho. 1991. "Consequences of Fertility Decline: Social, Economic and Cultural Implications in Korea." Unpublished paper for United Nations Economic and Social Commission for Asia and the Pacific, Seminar on Impact of Fertility Decline on Population Policies and Program Strategies: Emerging Trends for the 21st Century, Seoul, Korea, 6–19 December 1991.

Lee, Mei-Lin. 1984. "Social Correlates of Divorce in Taiwan." *Chinese Sociological Review* (8) (December).

Lee, Teng-Hui, Ching-Yung Liu, and Hung-Chin Tsai. 1972. "Comparative Study of Population and Agricultural Change in Taiwan." In *Agriculture and Economic Development in Taiwan*, vol. 2., ed. Teng-Hui Lee, pp. 1474–1795. Taichung, Taiwan: Ta-Kung Printing Co.

Le Play, Frederic. [1855] 1982. "Les ouvriers européens" (Paris: Imprimerie Imperiale, 1855.), pp. 9–12, 16–18, 286–287, 281–282. In *Frederic Le Play on Family, Work and Social Change*, ed. Catherine Bodard Silver. Chicago: University of Chicago Press.

Lesthaeghe, Ron J. 1980. "On the Social Control of Human Reproduction." *Population and Development Review* 6 (4) (December): 527–48.

Lesthaeghe, Ron J., and Johann Surkyn. 1988. "Cultural Dynamics and Economic Theories of Fertility Change." *Population and Development Review* 14:1–45.

Lesthaeghe, Ron J., and Chris Wilson. 1986. "Modes of Production, Secularization and the Pace of the Fertility Decline in Western Europe, 1870–1930." In *The Decline of Fertility in Europe*, ed. Ansley J. Coale and Susan Cotts Watkins, pp. 261–92. Princeton: Princeton University Press.

Li, Kuo-Ting. 1988. *The Evolution of Policy behind Taiwan's Development Success*. New Haven: Yale University Press.

Li, Yih-Yuan. 1985. "On Conflicting Interpretations of Chinese Family Rituals." In *The Chinese Family and Its Ritual Behavior*, ed. Jih-Chang Hsieh and

Ying-Chang Chuang, pp. 263–81. Monograph Series B, no. 15. Taipei, Taiwan: Institute of Ethnology, Academia Sinica.

Lin, Hui-Sheng. 1987. "Premarital Sex, Premarital Pregnancy and Nonmarital Fertility in Taiwan." Paper presented at annual meeting of the Population Association of America, 30 April–2 May, Chicago.

———. 1988. "The Determinants of the Timing of First Marriage for Women in Taiwan." Ph.D. diss., University of Michigan, Ann Arbor.

Liu, Hi-Chen Wang. 1959. *The Traditional Chinese Clan Rules.* Locust Valley, NY: J. J. Augustin.

Liu, Paul K.C. 1983. "The Role of Education in Fertility Transition in Taiwan." Discussion Paper 8302. Taipei, Taiwan: Institute of Economics, Academia Sinica.

———. 1988. "Employment, Earnings, and Export-Led Industrialization in Taiwan." *Industry of Free China,* 70 (4) (October): 1–14 and 70 (4) (November): 7–32.

Liu, Paul K. C., and Ching-Lung Tsay. 1982. "Health, Population, and Socioeconomic Development in Taiwan." In *Conference on Experiences and Lessons of Economic Development in Taiwan, 18–20 December 1981,* ed. Kwoh-Ting Li and Tzong-Shian Yu, pp. 533–86. Taipei, Taiwan: Institute of Economics, Academia Sinica.

Liu, Shao-T'ang, ed. 1979. *Daily Records of Major Events in the Republic of China.* Vol. 2. Taipei, Taiwan: Chuang-Chi Literature Press. (In Chinese.)

Lu, Gary L. T. 1978. "Expectations of Life in Taiwan, R.O.C, 1948–1977." *JCRR Rural Health Series* (1): 13–41.

Macfarlane, Alan. 1976. *Resources and Population: A Study of the Gurungs of Nepal.* Cambridge: Cambridge University Press.

———. 1979. *The Origins of English Individualism: The Family, Property, and Social Transition.* Cambridge: Cambridge University Press.

———. 1986. *Marriage and Love in England: Modes of Reproduction, 1300–1840.* Oxford: Basil Blackwell.

Malthus, Thomas Robert. [1803] 1986. "An Essay on the Principle of Population." In *The Works of Thomas Robert Malthus,* ed. Edward A. Wrigley and David Souden. London: William Pickering.

Mason, Karen O., William H. Mason, Halliman H. Winsborough, and W. Kenneth Poole. 1973. "Some Methodological Issues in Cohort Analysis of Archival Data." *American Sociological Review* 38 (2): 242–58.

McDonald, Peter F. 1975. *Marriage in Australia: Age at First Marriage and Proportions Marrying, 1860–1971.* Australian Family Formation Project, Monograph no. 2. Canberra: Australian National University Press.

Meskill, Johanna Menzel. 1979. *A Chinese Pioneer Family: The Lins of Wu-Feng, Taiwan, 1729–1895.* Princeton: Princeton University Press.

Michael, Robert T., Victor R. Fuchs, and Sharon R. Scott. 1980. "Changes in the Propensity to Live Alone, 1950–1976." *Demography* 17 (February): 39–56.

Millar, John. [1771] 1979. "The Origin of the Distinction of Ranks." In *John

Millar of Glasgow. 1735-1801, ed. William C. Lehmann, [1960] 1979. New York: Arno Press.

Millman, Sara. 1986. "Trends in Breastfeeding in a Dozen Developing Countries." *International Family Planning Perspectives* 12 (3): 91–5.

Ministry of Education. 1968. *Educational Statistics of the Republic of China, 1968*. Taipei, Taiwan: Ministry of Education.

———. 1988. *Educational Statistics of the Republic of China, 1988*. Taipei, Taiwan: Ministry of Education.

Ministry of the Interior. 1956. *1956 Household Census Report*. Vol. 2. Book 2. Taipei, Taiwan: Ministry of the Interior.

———. 1960–73. *Taiwan Demographic Fact Book*. Taipei, Taiwan: Ministry of the Interior.

———. 1974–91. *Taiwan-Fukien Demographic Fact Book*. Taipei, Taiwan: Ministry of the Interior.

———. 1974a. *Taiwan Demography Monthly*. Vol. 8, no. 12 (December 1973). Taipei, Taiwan: Ministry of the Interior.

———. 1980a. *Extract Report on the 1980 Census of Population and Housing*. Taipei, Taiwan: Ministry of the Interior.

———. 1988a. *Taiwan Demographic Quarterly*. Vol. 14, no. 4, table 2. Taipei, Taiwan: Ministry of the Interior.

Modell, John, and Tamara K. Hareven. 1973. "Urbanization and the Malleable Household: An Examination of Boarding and Lodging in American Families." *Journal of Marriage and the Family* 35 (3) (August): 467–79.

Morgan, S. Philip, and Kiyosi Hirosima. 1983. "The Persistence of Extended Family Residence in Japan: Anachronism or Alternative Strategy." *American Sociological Review* 48:269–81.

Mount, Ferdinand. 1982. *The Subversive Family*. London: Jonathan Cape.

Namboodiri, Narayanan K., and Chirayath M. Suchindran. 1987. *Life Table Techniques and Their Applications*. Orlando, FL: Academic Press.

Nation. 1868. "Why Is Single Life Becoming More General?" 6 (March): 190–91.

Notestein, Frank W. 1953. "Economic Problems of Population Change." In *The Economics of Population and Food Supplies*, pp. 13–31. Proceedings of the Eighth International Conference of Agricultural Economics, London: Oxford University Press.

Ogburn, William F., and Meyer F. Nimkoff. [1955] 1976. *Technology and the Changing Family*. Westport, CT: Greenwood Press.

Ogburn, William F., and Clark Tibbitts. 1933. "The Family and Its Functions." In *Recent Social Trends in the United States*, the President's Research Committee of Social Trends, report 1. Vol. 1:661–708. New York: Mcgraw Hill Book Company.

Omohundro, John T. 1981. "Social Networks and Business Success for the Philippine Chinese." In *The Chinese in Southeast Asia*, ed. Linda Lim and Peter Gosling, pp. 66–85. Singapore: Maruzen Asia.

O'Rand, Angela M., and Margaret L. Krecker. 1990. "Concepts of the Life

Cycle: Their History, Meanings, and Uses in the Social Sciences." *Annual Review in Sociology* 16:241–62.

Palmore, James A., Robert E. Klein, and Arrifin bin Marzuki. 1970. "Class and Family in a Modernizing Society." *American Journal of Sociology* 76:375–98.

Parish, William L., and Martin King Whyte. 1978. *Village and Family in Contemporary China.* Chicago: University of Chicago Press.

Parsons, Talcott, and Robert F. Bales. 1955. *Family, Socialization and Interaction Process.* Glencoe, IL: Free Press.

Pasternak, Burton. 1972. *Kinship and Community in Two Chinese Villages.* Stanford: Stanford University Press.

———. 1983. *Guests in the Dragon: Social Demography of a Chinese District, 1895–1946.* New York: Columbia University Press.

———. 1985. "The Disquieting Chinese Lineage and Its Anthropological Relevance." In *The Chinese Family and Its Ritual Behavior,* ed. Jih- Chang Hsieh and Ying-Chang Chuang, pp. 165–91. Monograph Series B, no. 15. Taipei, Taiwan: Institute of Ethnology, Academia Sinica.

———. 1989. "Age at First Marriage in a Taiwanese Locality, 1916–1945." *Journal of Family History* 14 (2): 91–117.

Pollock, Linda A. 1985. *Forgotten Children: Parent-Child Relations from 1500 to 1900.* Cambridge: Cambridge University Press.

Potter, Jack M. 1968. *Capitalism and the Chinese Peasant.* Berkeley: University of California Press.

———. 1970. "Land and Lineage in Traditional China." In *Family and Kinship in Chinese Society,* ed. Maurice Freedman, pp. 121–138. Stanford: Stanford University Press.

Provincial Government of Taiwan, Bureau of Accounting and Statistics. 1946. *Taiwan Province: Statistical Summary of the Past 51 Years.* Taipei, Taiwan: Taiwan Provincial Government. (In Chinese.)

———. 1965. *Taiwan Statistical Abstract, No. 24.* Taipei, Taiwan: Provincial Government of Taiwan.

Provincial Government of Taiwan, Department of Agriculture and Forestry. 1978. *Taiwan Agricultural Yearbook, 1978 Edition.* Taipei, Taiwan: Provincial Government of Taiwan.

Ranis, Gustav. 1979. "Industrial Development." In *Economic Growth and Structural Change in Taiwan, the Postwar Experience of the Republic of China,* ed. Walter Galenson, pp. 207–62. Ithaca, NY: Cornell University Press.

Rindfuss, Ronald. R., and S. Philip Morgan. 1983. "Marriage, Sex, and the First Birth Interval: The Quiet Revolution in Asia." *Population and Development Review* 9 (2) (June): 259–78.

Rodgers, Willard L. 1982. "Estimable Functions of Age, Period, and Cohort Effects." *American Sociological Review* 47 (6) (December): 774–87.

———. 1990. "Interpreting the Components of Time Trends." In *Sociological Methodology,* ed. Clifford C. Clogg, pp. 421–28. Oxford: Basil Blackwell.

Roof, Wade C., and William McKinney. 1987. *American Mainline Religion.* New Brunswick, NJ: Rutgers University Press.

Ruggles, Steven. 1987. *Prolonged Connections: The Rise of the Extended Family in Nineteenth-Century England and America*. Madison: University of Wisconsin Press.

Sahlins, Marshall. 1972. *Stone Age Economics*. New York: Aldine.

Salaff, Janet W. 1981. *Working Daughters of Hong Kong: Filial Piety or Power in the Family?* Cambridge: Cambridge University Press.

———. 1988. "The Chinese Connection: Management Control Structures and the Search for Labor in Taiwan." Unpublished manuscript.

Sangren, P. Steven. 1984. "Traditional Chinese Corporations: Beyond Kinship." *Journal of Asian Studies* 43 (3): 391–415.

Schak, David C. 1975. *Dating and Mate-Selection in Modern Taiwan*. Taipei, Taiwan: Chinese Association for Folklore.

Schuman, Howard, and Jacqueline Scott. 1989. "Generations and Collective Memories." *American Sociological Review* 54:359–81.

Shu, Leung-Hay, and Chung-Cheng Lin. 1989. "Family Structure and Social Change: A Follow-up Study." In *Social Phenomena in Taiwan—An Analysis of Family, Population, Policy, and Social Stratification,* ed. Chin-Ch'un Yi and Jui-Lin Chu, pp. 25–36. Taipei, Taiwan: Sun-Yat-Sen Institute for Social Sciences and Philosophy, Academia Sinica. (In Chinese.)

Smith, Daniel S. 1981. "Historical Change in the Household Structure of the Elderly in Economically Developed Societies." In *Aging: Stability and Change in the Family,* ed. James G. March (ed. in chief), Robert W. Fogel, Elaine Hatfield, Sara B. Kiesler, and Ethel Shanas, pp. 91–114. New York: Academic Press.

Smith, Peter C. 1980. "Asian Marriage Patterns in Transition." *Journal of Family History* 5 (1) (Spring): 58–96.

Speare, Alden, Paul K. C. Liu, and Ching-Lung Tsay. 1988. *Urbanization and Development: The Rural-Urban Transition in Taiwan*. Boulder, CO: Westview Press.

Spence, Jonathan D. 1978. *The Death of Woman Wang*. New York: Viking Press.

———. 1984. *The Memory Palace of Matteo Ricci*. New York: Viking Press.

Srikantan, Kodaganallur S. 1967. "Effects of Neighborhood and Individual Factors on Family Planning in Taichung." Ph.D. diss., University of Michigan, Ann Arbor.

Stacey, Judith. 1983. *Patriarchy and Socialist Revolution in China*. Berkeley: University of California Press.

Stone, Lawrence. 1982. "Family History in the 1980's, Past Achievements and Future Trends." In *The New History: The 1980's and Beyond,* ed. Theodore K. Rabb and Robert I. Rolberg, pp. 51–87. Princeton, NJ: Princeton University Press.

Sun, Te-Hsiung. 1987. "An Overall Review of Fertility Control Policies in Taiwan, R.O.C." Research Report no. 21, March. Taipei, Taiwan: Taiwan Provincial Institute for Family Planning.

Taeuber, Irene B. 1958. *The Population of Japan*. Princeton, NJ: Princeton University Press.

Tai, Yen-Hui. 1978. "Divorce in Traditional Chinese Law." In *Chinese Family*

Law and Social Change, ed. David C. Buxbaum, pp. 75–106. Seattle: University of Washington Press.

Taiwan Population Studies Center. 1965. *Demographic Reference: Taiwan, Republic of China, 1965.* Vol. 1. Taipei, Taiwan: Taiwan Population Studies Center.

Taiwan Provincial Government, Department of Civil Affairs, Republic of China. 1959. *Taiwan Provincial Household Statistics Summary, 1946–1958.* Taipei, Taiwan: Taiwan Provincial Government. (In Chinese.)

———. 1968. *The Monthly Bulletin of Population Registration Statistics of Taiwan, Republic of China.* Vol. 2, no. 12 (December 1967). Taipei, Taiwan: Taiwan Provincial Government.

———. 1971. *Taiwan Demography Monthly, Republic of China.* Vol. 5, no. 12 (December 1970), Nantou, Taiwan: Taiwan Provincial Government.

Teachman, Jay D. 1982. "Analyzing Social Processes: Life Tables and Proportional Hazard Models." *Social Science Research* 12:263–301.

Thornton, Arland. 1985. "Reciprocal Influences of Family and Religion in a Changing World." *Journal of Marriage and the Family,* 47:381–94.

———. 1989. "Changing Attitudes toward Family Issues in the United States." *Journal of Marriage and the Family* 51 (November): 873–93.

———. 1991. "Reading History Sideways: A Critical Evaluation of Western Family History and Theory." Unpublished book manuscript.

Thornton, Arland, Ming-Cheng Chang, and Te-Hsiung Sun. 1984. "Social and Economic Change, Intergenerational Relationships, and Family Formation in Taiwan." *Demography* 21 (4) (November): 475–99.

Thornton, Arland, and Deborah Freedman. 1983. "The Changing American Family." *Population Bulletin* 38 (4) (October): 1–44.

Thornton, Arland, Ronald Freedman, Te-Hsiung Sun, and Ming-Cheng Chang. 1986. "Intergenerational Relations and Reproductive Behavior in Taiwan." *Demography* 23:185–97.

Thornton, Arland, and Thomas E. Fricke. 1987. "Social Change and the Family: Comparative Perspectives from the West, China and South Asia." *Sociological Forum* 2 (4): 746–72.

Thornton, Arland, and Willard L. Rodgers. 1987. "The Influence of Individual and Historical Time on Marital Dissolution." *Demography* 24:1–22.

Tilly, Louise A., and Joan W. Scott. 1978. *Women, Work, and Family.* New York: Holt, Rinehart, and Winston.

Tsui, Elaine Yi-Lan. 1987. *Are Married Daughters "Spilled Water?"—A Study of Working Women in Urban Taiwan.* Taipei, Taiwan: Women's Research Program, Population Studies Center, National Taiwan University.

Tsui, Young-Chi. 1959. "A Summary Report on Farm Income of Taiwan in 1957 in Comparison with 1952." In *Economic Digest Series* (13). Taipei, Taiwan: Joint Commission on Rural Reconstruction.

Tsurumi, E. Patricia. 1977. *Japanese Colonial Education in Taiwan, 1895–1945.* Cambridge, MA: Harvard University Press.

Tsuya, Noriko O. 1990. "Changing Attitudes toward Marriage and the Family in Japan." Paper presented at the Nihon University International Symposium on the Family and the Contemporary Japanese Culture: An International Perspective, 20–24 October, Tokyo, Japan.

Tu, Edward Jow-Ching, Jersey Liang, and Shaomin Li. 1987. "Mortality Decline and Chinese Family Structure." Paper presented at the annual meeting of the Population Association of America, 30 April–2 May, Chicago.

United Nations. Various years. *Demographic Year Book*. New York: United Nations.

———. 1989. *1987 Demographic Year Book*. New York: United Nations.

———. 1991. *1989 Demographic Year Book*. New York: United Nations.

United Nations, Department of International Economic and Social Affairs. 1989. *World Population Prospects, 1988*. Population Studies no. 106. New York: United Nations.

U.S. Department of Health, Education, and Welfare. 1954. *Summary of Marriage and Divorce Statistics: United States, 1952*. Vital Statistics–Special Reports 40 (3). Washington, D.C.: National Office of Vital Statistics.

van der Valk, Marc. 1939. *An Outline of Modern Chinese Family Law*. Peking, China: Henri Vetch.

Ward, Barbara. 1972. "A Small Factory in Hong Kong: Some Aspects of Its Internal Organization." In *Economic Organization in Chinese Society*, ed. W. E. Willmott, pp. 353–86. Stanford: Stanford University Press.

Watkins, Susan Cotts. 1986a. "Regional Patterns of Nuptiality in Western Europe, 1870–1960." In *The Decline of Fertility in Europe*, ed. Ansley J. Coale and Susan Cotts Watkins, pp. 314–36. Princeton: Princeton University Press.

———. 1986b. "Conclusions." In *The Decline of Fertility in Europe*, ed. Ansley J. Coale and Susan Cotts Watkins, pp. 420–49. Princeton: Princeton University Press.

Watson, Rubie S. 1985. *Inequality among Brothers: Class and Kinship in South China*. Cambridge: Cambridge University Press.

Westermarck, Edward Alexander. [1891] 1894. *The History of Human Marriage*. London: Macmillan and Co.

Westoff, Charles F. 1978. "Marriage and Fertility in the Developed Countries." *Scientific American* 239 (6): 51–57.

Whyte, Martin King. 1988. "Changes in Mate Choice in Chengdu." Center for Research on Social Organization, Working Paper Series, September, no. 361, University of Michigan, Ann Arbor.

———. 1992. "From Arranged Marriages to Love Matches." Paper presented at the International Conference on Family Formation and Dissolution: Perspectives from the East and West, 21–23 May, Academia Sinica, Taipei, Taiwan.

Whyte, Martin King, and William L. Parish. 1984. *Urban Life in Contemporary China*. Chicago: University of Chicago Press.

Wickberg, Edgar B. 1981. "Continuities in Land Tenure, 1900–1940." In *The Anthropology of Taiwanese Society*, ed. Emily Ahern Martin and Hill Gates, pp. 212–38. Stanford: Stanford University Press.

Wilson, Chris, and Tim Dyson. 1987. "Family Systems and Cultural Change: Perspectives from Past and Present." Paper prepared for IUSSP Seminar on

Changing Family Structures and Life Courses in LDCS, East-West Population Institute, 5–7 January, Honolulu.

Winckler, Edwin A., and Susan Greenhalgh, eds. 1988. *Contending Approaches to the Political Economy of Taiwan.* Armonk, NY: M. E. Sharpe.

Wirth, Louis. 1938. "Urbanism as a Way of Life." *American Journal of Sociology* 44 (July): 3–24.

Wolf, Arthur P. 1966. "Childhood Association, Sexual Attraction, and the Incest Taboo: A Chinese Case." *American Anthropologist* 72 (3): 503–15.

———. 1970. "Chinese Kinship and Mourning Dress." In *Family and Kinship in Chinese Society,* ed. Maurice Freedman, pp. 189–208. Stanford: Stanford University Press.

———. 1975. "The Women of Hai-Shan: A Demographic Portrait." In *Women in Chinese Society,* ed. Margery Wolf and Roxanne Witke, pp. 89–110. Stanford: Stanford University Press.

———. 1981a. "Women, Widowhood, and Fertility in Premodern China." In *Marriage and Remarriage in Populations of the Past,* ed. Jacques Dupaquier, pp. 139–47. London: Academic Press.

———. 1981b. "Domestic Organization." In *The Anthropology of Taiwanese Society,* ed. Emily Martin Ahern and Hill Gates, pp. 341–60. Stanford: Stanford University Press.

———. 1985a. "Introduction: The Study of Chinese Society on Taiwan." In *The Chinese Family and Its Ritual Behavior,* ed. Jih-Chang Hsieh and Ying-Chang Chuang, pp. 3–18. Monograph Series B, no. 15. Taipei, Taiwan: Institute of Ethnology, Academia Sinica.

———. 1985b. "Chinese Family Size: A Myth Revitalized." In *The Chinese Family and Its Ritual Behavior,* ed. Jih-Chang Hsieh and Ying-Chang Chuang, pp. 30–49. Monograph Series B, no. 15. Taipei, Taiwan: Institute of Ethnology, Academia Sinica.

Wolf, Arthur P., and Chieh-Shan Huang. 1980. *Marriage and Adoption in China, 1845–1945.* Stanford: Stanford University Press.

Wolf, Eric. 1982. *Europe and the People without History.* Berkeley: University of California Press.

Wolf, Margery. 1972. *Women and the Family in Rural Taiwan.* Stanford: Stanford University Press.

Yang, Ching-chu. 1978. *Under the Factory Smoke.* Taipei, Taiwan: Duen-li Press. (In Chinese.)

———. 1982a. *The Same Root.* Taipei, Taiwan: Yuan-chin Press. (In Chinese.)

———. 1982b. *The Factory Daughters.* Taipei, Taiwan: Yuan-chin Press. (In Chinese.)

———. 1987. *Factory People.* Kao-Hsiung: Wen-huan Press. (In Chinese.)

Yang, Martin C. 1945. *A Chinese Village: Taitou, Shantung Province.* New York: Columbia University Press.

Yao, Souchou. 1987. "The Fetish of Relationships: Chinese Business Transactions in Singapore." *Soujourn* 2:89–111.

Yi, Zeng. 1986. "Changes in Family Structure in China: A Simulation Study." *Population and Development Review* 12:675–703.

LIST OF CONTRIBUTORS

JUI-SHAN CHANG
Department of Sociology
University of Tasmania
GPO Box 252C
Hobart, Tasmania
Australia 7001

MING-CHENG CHANG
Director
Taiwan Provincial Institute of Family Planning
#503, Section 2 (5th floor), Li-Ming Road
Post Office Box 47-40
Taichung, Taiwan 408
Republic of China

DEBORAH FREEDMAN
University of Michigan
Population Studies Center
1225 S. University
Ann Arbor, MI 48109-2590

RONALD FREEDMAN
University of Michigan
Population Studies Center
1225 S. University
Ann Arbor, MI 48109-2590

THOMAS E. FRICKE
University of Michigan
Institute for Social Research
P.O. Box 1248
Ann Arbor, MI 48106-1248

ALBERT HERMALIN
University of Michigan
Population Studies Center
1225 S. University
Ann Arbor, MI 48109-2590

MEI-LIN LEE
Institute of Social Welfare
National Chung-cheng University
160 San-hsing, Ming-Hsiung
Chia-yi, Taiwan

HUI-SHENG LIN
Chief
Research & Planning Division
Taiwan Provincial Institute of Family Planning
#503, Section 2 (5th floor), Li-Ming Road
Post Office Box 47-40
Taichung, Taiwan 408
Republic of China

PAUL K. C. LIU
Institute of Economics
Academia Sinica
Nankang
Taipei, Taiwan
Republic of China

TE-HSIUNG SUN
Research, Development and Evaluation Commission
Executive Yuan
#4, Section 1 (12th Floor)
Chung-Hsiao West Road
Taipei, Taiwan 10023
Republic of China

ARLAND THORNTON
University of Michigan
Institute for Social Research
P.O. Box 1248
Ann Arbor, MI 48106-1248

MAXINE WEINSTEIN
Department of Demography
Poulton Hall
1437 37th Street NW, Room 238
Georgetown University
Washington, D.C. 20057

LI-SHOU YANG
University of Michigan
Population Studies Center
1225 S. University
Ann Arbor, MI 48109-2590